Living Language

Blackwell Primers in Anthropology

Each volume in this series is a lively first look at a traditional area of anthropological study. These concise books provide theoretically sophisticated yet accessible and engaging introductions for nonspecialists. They will be invaluable for undergraduate instruction as well as offering pithy overviews to those unfamiliar with the primary issues in the chosen subdiscipline.

Published

1. *People and Nature: An Introduction to Human Ecological Relations* by Emilio F. Moran
2. *Living Language: An Introduction to Linguistic Anthropology* by Laura M. Ahearn

Living Language

An Introduction to Linguistic Anthropology

Laura M. Ahearn

WILEY-BLACKWELL
A John Wiley & Sons, Ltd., Publication

This edition first published 2012

Blackwell Publishing was acquired by John Wiley & Sons in February 2007. Blackwell's publishing program has been merged with Wiley's global Scientific, Technical, and Medical business to form Wiley-Blackwell.

Registered Office
John Wiley & Sons Ltd, The Atrium, Southern Gate, Chichester, West Sussex, PO19 8SQ, United Kingdom

Editorial Offices
350 Main Street, Malden, MA 02148-5020, USA
9600 Garsington Road, Oxford, OX4 2DQ, UK
The Atrium, Southern Gate, Chichester, West Sussex, PO19 8SQ, UK

For details of our global editorial offices, for customer services, and for information about how to apply for permission to reuse the copyright material in this book please see our website at www.wiley.com/wiley-blackwell.

Library of Congress Cataloging-in-Publication Data

Ahearn, Laura M., 1962–
Living language : an introduction to linguistic anthropology / by Laura M. Ahearn.
p. cm. – (Blackwell primers in anthropology)
Includes bibliographical references and index.
ISBN 978-1-4051-2440-9 (hardback) – ISBN 978-1-4051-2441-6 (paperback)
1. Anthropological linguistics. 2. Language and culture. I. Title. II. Series.
P35.A38 2011
306.44–dc22

2010049292

A catalogue record for this book is available from the British Library.

This book is published in the following electronic formats: ePDFs 9781444340532; Wiley Online Library 9781444340563; ePub 9781444340549

Set in 11.5/13.5 Bembo by SPi Publisher Services, Pondicherry, India
Printed in Singapore by C.O.S. Printers Pte Ltd

8 2015

For Mellie,

whose words and smiles
have brought me indescribable joy

Contents

Figures

Tables

Preface

Language as used in real-life social contexts is fascinating but extremely challenging to study. Linguistic anthropology as a discipline offers a set of concepts and tools for undertaking this challenge. My goal in this book is to provide an accessible introduction to the main principles and approaches of linguistic anthropology without overly simplifying the complex contributions of scholars in the field. To the degree that this book succeeds in accomplishing this goal, it will be useful not just to graduate and undergraduate students studying linguistic anthropology for the first time (to whom I very much hope to communicate my enthusiasm for the field) but also to all sorts of other readers who might for various reasons be interested in "living language." These readers might include, for example, cultural anthropologists, sociologists, or political scientists who have never looked closely at language in their research but could benefit from doing so. I also hope the book will be of value to linguists whose work thus far has been more technical and abstract in nature but who would like to turn their attention to the study of actual instances of linguistic practice. And finally, I hope the book will appeal to anyone who has a natural curiosity about the central role language plays in shaping and reflecting cultural norms and social interactions.

Within the United States, linguistic anthropology is one of the four traditional fields of anthropology: archaeology, biological (also called physical) anthropology, cultural anthropology, and linguistic anthropology. When Franz Boas helped to establish the discipline of anthropology in the United States more than one hundred years ago, most anthropologists were trained in all four of these fields and often conducted research in more than one of them. As scholarship became more specialized over the past century, however, such breadth became much rarer. One of my main purposes in writing this book is to convince anthropologists in other subfields, especially cultural anthropology, of the advantages of becoming well-trained in linguistic anthropology as well as their "home" subdiscipline. After all, much of the data collected by cultural anthropologists (and by many researchers in other fields) is linguistic in nature. Linguistic anthropologists (e.g., Briggs 1986:22) have argued that such data should not be treated as a transparent window through which the researcher can reach to obtain facts or information. Rather, interviews and other sources of data for social scientists should be considered as communicative events in which meanings are co-constructed and interwoven with various forms of context. This book will, I hope, provide useful tools and examples of analyses that help researchers produce nuanced analyses of many different kinds of social and linguistic practices.

I should say a few words about nomenclature and the sometimes arbitrary nature of disciplinary boundaries. Anthropology as a discipline is not found in every university in the United States and certainly not in every country around the world. Sometimes it is subsumed under sociology; other times individual anthropologists work in academic departments ranging from political science to educational psychology. Linguistic anthropology as a subdiscipline is even more specific to the United States and is rarely identified as such in other countries. And yet, the core themes and approaches of linguistic anthropology as set forth in this book are ever more commonly at the forefront of cutting-edge research in many different fields, even when "linguistic anthropology" as such is not the label under which the research takes place. In the United Kingdom, for example, "linguistic ethnography" has become increasingly popular as a term describing the work of scholars who study language ethnographically, as linguistic anthropologists generally do (cf. Creese 2008). Some sociolinguists, who usually hold PhDs in the discipline of linguistics rather than anthropology or sociology (though there are exceptions), also produce scholarship very much in keeping with the approaches I describe in this book. In addition, linguistic anthropologists themselves have sometimes used other terms to label what they do, such as anthropological linguistics, ethnolinguistics, or "anthropolitical" linguistics, and many researchers produce important and relevant work in other related fields such as pragmatics, sociopolitical linguistics, discourse analysis, rhetoric, applied linguistics, or communication (Duranti 1997, 2003, forthcoming; Zentella 1996). I draw upon the work of many of these scholars in this book, along with researchers in other fields. While I consider myself firmly rooted in linguistic anthropology, I share with Mary Bucholtz and Kira Hall (2008) a desire to take an "all of the above" approach to the study of linguistic practices in real-life social contexts. There is nothing to be lost and everything to be gained, in my opinion, from engaging in a cross-disciplinary dialogue.

As valuable as I find much of the research on language from all these different fields, I do attempt to differentiate the approach I advocate from an approach that considers language solely as an abstract set of grammatical rules, detached from any actual linguistic interaction. Linguistic structure and the insights surrounding it that have emerged from the discipline of linguistics since first Ferdinand de Saussure and then Noam Chomsky began to dominate the field so many decades ago are extremely important to most linguistic anthropologists, but as Chomsky's hegemonic grip on linguistics as a discipline has begun to weaken, there is even more reason to offer the approach presented in this book – that of treating language use as a form of social action – as an alternative that can either complement or cause a reconceptualization of Chomsky's perspective on language. Ideally, scholars who consider linguistic practices to be a form of social action will be able to make use of the most valuable findings on linguistic structure conducted in a Chomskyan manner while also paying close attention to the ways in which such practices are embedded in webs of social hierarchies and identities. This is a challenging task. As Michael Silverstein has noted, it can lead to "the same feeling one has in that sitcom situation of standing with one foot on the dock and another in the boat as the tide rushes away from shore" (2006:275). Silverstein goes on to state the following:

> The serious metaphorical point here is that it takes a great deal of bodily force to keep standing upright, with one foot firmly planted in language as a structured code and the other in language as a medium of the various sociocultural lifeways of human groups and their emergently precipitated sociohistorical macrostructures at several orders of magnitude. (2006:275)

The goal of this book is to provide some concrete assistance in the form of theoretical insights, methodological tools, and ethnographic examples for those who would like to remain standing upright – those who wish to look closely at language both in terms of its grammatical patterning and in terms of its role in the shaping of social life.

Living Language is divided into three parts, each of which is comprised of four chapters. In the first part, "Language: Some Basic Questions," I explain how language use can be conceived of, and productively studied as, a form of social action. The introductory chapter, "The Socially Charged Life of Language," presents four key terms that will act as anchors for readers as they proceed through the ensuing chapters. These four key terms – *multifunctionality*, *language ideologies*, *practice*, and *indexicality* – can be applied in many different social contexts to obtain a deeper understanding of how language works. Chapter 2, "The Research Process in Linguistic Anthropology," describes the many different methods linguistic anthropologists use to conduct their research and discusses some of the practical and ethical dilemmas many researchers face when studying language in real-life situations. Chapter 3, "Language Acquisition and Socialization," focuses on the way that linguistic anthropologists study how young children learn their first language(s) at the same time that they are being socialized into appropriate cultural practices. This way of understanding linguistic and cultural practices as being thoroughly intertwined can also apply to adolescents and adults who engage in language socialization whenever they enter new social or professional contexts. Chapter 4, the final chapter in the first part of the book, "Language, Thought, and Culture," looks at some of the controversies and foundational principles underlying the so-called "Sapir–Whorf Hypothesis" and the ways in which language relates to thought and culture.

The second part of the book, "Communities of Speakers, Hearers, Readers, and Writers," moves on from these basic questions to consider the constitution of various forms of linguistic and social communities. Chapter 5, "Communities of Language Users," explores the concept of "speech community" and surveys some of the scholarship on this topic, concluding with a discussion of the valuable alternative concept of "community of practice." Chapter 6, "Multilingualism and Globalization," places these communities in a global context to demonstrate how important it is to consider multilingualism in individuals and communities when conducting research on linguistic or social practices anywhere in the world. Chapter 7, "Literacy Practices," makes a case for the importance of looking at the interwoven nature of literacy and orality. Many linguistic anthropologists focus solely on spoken language, but studying literacy practices in conjunction with verbal interactions can be quite illuminating. Chapter 8, "Performance, Performativity, and the Constitution of Communities," the final chapter in the second part of the book, disentangles the various theoretical and ethnographic approaches to performance and performativity and discusses the importance of these themes for understanding how linguistic and social communities come to be formed.

The final part of the book, "Language, Power, and Social Differentiation," moves more deeply into the constitution of actual communities by examining various dimensions of social and linguistic differentiation and inequality within particular communities. Chapter 9, "Language and Gender," explores some common language ideologies concerning the ways in which women and men speak and reviews the research on the complex nature of gendered linguistic practices. Chapter 10, "Language, Race, and Ethnicity," engages with two other common forms of social and linguistic differentiation, that of racialization and ethnicization. This chapter describes the rule-governed nature of African American English, the Ebonics controversy of 1996–1997, and the racializing aspects of Mock Spanish. Chapter 11, "Language Death and Revitalization," looks at the reasons why so many of the world's languages are endangered and asks what social inequalities and language ideologies underpin these discourses of endangerment. The concluding chapter, "Language, Power, and Agency," pulls together the threads of the previous chapters to present a view of linguistic practices as embedded within power dynamics and subject to various forms of agency. This chapter provides an overview of the social theorists, including Raymond Williams, Michel Foucault, Sherry Ortner, and Pierre Bourdieu, who are in my view the most useful for developing a deeper understanding of language, power, agency, and social action.

In sum, this book is meant to be an invitation to all readers to explore more fully the notion that to use language is always to engage in a form of social action. Embarking on this exploration will lead to a better appreciation for what "living language" can mean.

Acknowledgments

This book has been many years in the making, and I could never adequately thank everyone to whom I am indebted in various ways for helping me write this book. I owe so much to the scholars who most deeply influenced me during my graduate training: Tom Fricke, Bruce Mannheim, and Sherry Ortner. During and after my years in graduate school, I have continued to be inspired by the work of Alessandro Duranti, Susan Gal, Marjorie Harness Goodwin, Jane Hill, Judy Irvine, Paul Kroskrity, Elinor Ochs, Bambi Schieffelin and Jim Wilce. I am also fortunate to be situated within a cultural anthropology program at Rutgers, Critical Interventions in Theory and Ethnography, that takes seriously the need to integrate a close analysis of language into any study of social or cultural practices. My colleagues at Rutgers, especially Parvis Ghassem-Fachandi, Daniel Goldstein, Angelique Haugerud, Dorothy Hodgson, and David Hughes, as well as the members of the NEWT (No Excuses Writing Team) have all been extremely supportive of this project. Other colleagues, including Janina Fenigsen, Bridget Hayden (who also caught my initial misspelling of "purl" in the knitting analogy), Kathy Hunt, Dillon Mahoney, Ryne Palombit, Gary Rendsburg, Heidi Swank, Suzanne Wertheim, Jim Wilce, and John Zimmerman, have also read and commented on some or all of these chapters, or have even "test driven" them in their own linguistic anthropology classes, and for all their feedback I am enormously grateful. Jim Wilce, in particular, has been a most consistently encouraging and patient supporter throughout this long process, and his belief in this book helped me move forward at several critical periods when I was unsure of how to proceed.

My students have also provided me with inspiration and concrete advice on how to improve the book. Students in my undergraduate linguistic anthropology classes, including Liane Alves, Chris Correa, Tingting Gao, Mickey Hennessey, Christina Le, Eugene Leytin, Erika Varga, and Alysis Vasquez, were amazingly patient with me as I turned them into guinea pigs in this process; they offered extremely perceptive comments on how to make the book more accessible to college students. My brilliant graduate students were equally generous with their advice. I am particularly grateful to all the students who took my Language as Social Action seminar over the past few years, especially Chelsea Booth, Assaf Harel, Noelle Molé, and Kartikeya Saboo, for pushing me to think in new ways about the material presented in this book.

I am also thankful to Jane Huber, the editor at Wiley-Blackwell who got me interested in this project, and to Rosalie Robertson and Julia Kirk, the editor and editorial assistant, respectively, who guided it successfully through to completion. Eric Richardson wisely urged a more user-friendly title, and Ayala Fader and Liliana Sanchez offered helpful feedback. Peter Laipson, my loyal critic, read the first four chapters of this book and dictated copious comments for me using Dragon Naturally Speaking, thereby providing an excellent demonstration of the limitations of speech recognition software (but also of course improving my eloquence quotient enormously for those chapters). The anonymous readers of the prospectus buoyed me with their wonderful comments and feedback, and the five anonymous reviewers of the entire manuscript humbled me with their close readings and wise advice. I only wish I had had the time and intellectual capacity to implement more of their suggestions.

Finally, I am indebted beyond words to my family. My parents, Eileen and Fred Ahearn, have always encouraged me with loving support and intellectual stimulation. My sisters, Peggy Schroeder and Kerry Ahearn-Brown, remain my dearest friends. My husband (also known as my in-house editor and favorite correspondent), Rick Black, has offered me more guidance, inspiration, and constant encouragement than I could ever enumerate or reciprocate. I am so, so lucky to have him as my "life friend."

And to my daughter, Melanie Anne Ahearn Black, I dedicate this book, which has been in the making in one form or another for the entire six years of her life. So much of what has come to fascinate me about language and what I have come to value in life can be traced to Mellie.

Laura M. Ahearn
Rutgers University

Part I Language: Some Basic Questions

1

The Socially Charged Life of Language

> All words have the 'taste' of a profession, a genre, a tendency, a party, a particular work, a particular person, a generation, an age group, the day and hour. Each word tastes of the context and contexts in which it has lived its socially charged life...
>
> Bakhtin 1981:293

Words *do* live socially charged lives, as Bakhtin observes in the epigraph that opens this chapter. Language is not a neutral medium for communication but rather a set of socially embedded practices. The reverse of Bakhtin's statement is also true: social interactions live linguistically charged lives. That is, every social interaction is mediated by language – whether spoken or written, verbal or nonverbal. Consider the following three examples.

Example 1: Getting Stoned in San Francisco

During the 1995–1996 school year, a special anti-drug class was run as an elective in a large high school in the San Francisco Bay Area.[1] Students were trained as peer educators in preparation for visiting other classes to perform skits about the danger of drugs and tobacco. The class was unusually diverse, with boys as well as girls and with students from many different class ranks, ethnicities, and racial groups. On the day that the students were preparing to perform their skits in front of an audience for the first time, they asked the teacher, Priscilla,

Living Language: An Introduction to Linguistic Anthropology, First Edition. Laura M. Ahearn.

Figure 1.1 Cartoon demonstrating how certain styles of speech can both reflect and shape social identities.
Source: Jump Start © 1999 United Feature Syndicate, Inc.

what they should say if someone in the audience asked whether they themselves smoked marijuana. Priscilla recommended that they say they did not. Then the following exchange took place between Priscilla and the students:

Priscilla:	Remember, you're role models.
Al Capone:	You want us to lie?
Priscilla:	Since you're not coming to school stoned – (*students laugh*)
Calvin:	(*mockingly*) Stoned?
Priscilla:	What do you say?
Calvin:	I say high. Bombed. Blitzed.
Brand One:	Weeded.
Kerry:	Justified.
Brand One:	That's kinda tight.

Example 2: Losing a Language in Papua New Guinea

In 1987, the residents of the tiny village of Gapun in Papua New Guinea (a country north of Australia) were some of the last speakers of a language called Taiap, which at the time had at most 89 remaining speakers.[2] Adult villagers were almost all bilingual in Taiap and in Tok Pisin, one of the three national languages of Papua New Guinea, and all children were exposed to rich amounts of both Taiap and Tok Pisin in their early years. By 1987, however, no child under the age of ten actively spoke Taiap, and many under the age of eight did not even possess a good passive knowledge of the language. The usual theories about how and why so many of the world's languages are becoming extinct did not seem to apply to Taiap. Material and economic factors such as industrialization and urbanization were not sufficiently important in the remote village of Gapun to explain the language shift away from Taiap. Why, then, was Taiap becoming extinct? According to linguistic anthropologist Don Kulick, the adults in Gapun claimed that the shift was occurring because of the actions of their (often preverbal) children. Kulick writes: "'We haven't done anything,' one village man explained when I asked him why village children don't speak the vernacular, 'We try to get them to speak it, we want them to. But they won't … They're *bikhed* [big-headed, strong-willed]'" (Kulick 1992:16).

Example 3: The Pounded Rice Ritual in Nepal

On a warm February afternoon in 1993, a wedding procession made its way down a steep hill in Junigau, Nepal. Several men carefully maneuvered the bride's sedan chair around the hairpin turns. At the foot of the hill, under a large banyan tree, the wedding party settled down to rest and to conduct the Pounded Rice Ritual.[3] The bride, Indrani Kumari, remained in her palanquin, while some members of the wedding party, including the groom, Khim Prasad, approached her. Taking out a leafplate full of pounded rice, a popular snack in Nepal, Indrani Kumari's bridal attendant placed it in her lap. Khim Prasad, coached by his senior male kin, tentatively began the ritual, holding out a handkerchief and asking his new wife to give him the pounded rice snack. He used the most polite, honorific form of "you" in Nepali (*tapāī*), and so his remark translated roughly as a polite request to someone of higher social status: "Please bring the pounded rice, Wife; our wedding party has gotten hungry."

But this first request was not very effective. Indrani Kumari and her bridal attendant poured just a few kernels of the pounded rice into the handkerchief Khim Prasad was holding. Upon further coaching from his elders, Khim Prasad asked a second time for the rice, this time in a more informal manner using "*timi*," a form of "you" in Nepali that is considered appropriate for close relatives and/or familiar equals. This time, Khim Prasad's request could be translated roughly as a matter-of-fact statement to someone of equal social status: "Bring the pounded rice, Wife; our wedding party has gotten hungry." But

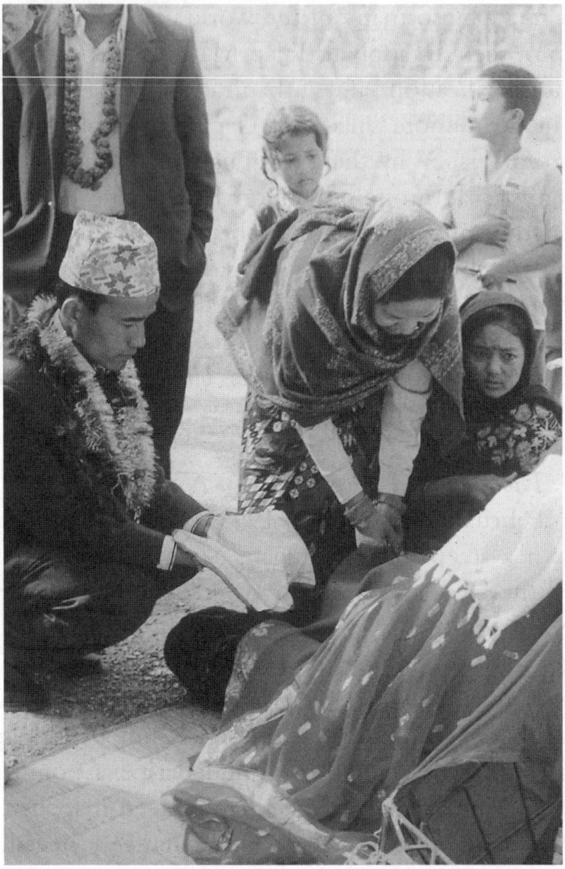

Figure 1.2 Khim Prasad (left) during the Pounded Rice Ritual, with the bride, Indrani Kumari (seated at the right, completely covered by a shawl), and the bridal attendant (standing in the center).
Source: Laura M. Ahearn, *Invitations to Love: Literacy, Love Letters, and Social Change in Nepal.* Ann Arbor: University of Michigan Press, 2001.

again, the bridal attendant and Indrani Kumari poured only a few kernels of pounded rice into Khim Prasad's waiting handkerchief. One last time Khim Prasad's senior male kin instructed him to ask for the rice, but this time he was told to use "*tã*," the lowest form of "you" in Nepali – a form most commonly used in Junigau to address young children, animals, and wives. Khim Prasad complied, but his words were halting and barely audible, indicating his deeply mixed feelings about using such a disrespectful term to address his new wife. This third request translated roughly as a peremptory command to someone of greatly inferior social status: "Bring the pounded rice, Wife! Our wedding party has gotten hungry!" Hearing this, Indrani Kumari and her attendant finally proceeded obediently to dump all the remaining rice into the groom's handkerchief, after which he handed out portions of the snack to all members of the wedding party.

As different as these three examples are, they all describe situations in which neither a linguistic analysis alone nor a sociocultural analysis alone would come close to providing a satisfying explanation of the significance of the events. The purpose of this book is to show how the perspectives and tools of linguistic anthropology, when applied to events as wide-ranging as an anti-drug class in a San Francisco high school, language shift in Papua New Guinea, or a ritual in Nepal, can shed light on broader social and cultural issues as well as deepen our understanding of language – and ourselves. As we move through the chapters that follow, we will be addressing a number of questions, including:

- What can such situations tell us about the ways in which language is enmeshed with cultural values and social power?
- How do dimensions of difference or inequality along lines such as gender, ethnicity, race, age, or wealth get created, reproduced, or challenged through language?
- How can language illuminate the ways in which we are all the same by virtue of being human as well as the ways in which we are incredibly diverse linguistically and culturally?
- How, if at all, do linguistic forms, such as the three different words in Nepali for "you" or the various slang words for "stoned," influence people's thought patterns or worldviews?
- How might people's ideas about language (for example, what "good" language is and who can speak it – in other words, their "language ideologies") affect their perceptions of others as well as themselves?
- How does the language used in public rituals and performances both differ from and resemble everyday, mundane conversations?
- What methods of data collection and analysis can we use to determine the significance of events such as those described above?

The starting point in the search for answers to all of these questions within linguistic anthropology is this fundamental principle: language is inherently social. It is not just a means through which we act upon the social world; speaking *is itself* a form of social action, and language is a cultural resource available for people to use (Duranti 1997:2). We *do* things with words, as the philosopher J.L. Austin (1962) reminded us decades ago. Even when we speak or write to ourselves, our very choices of words, as well as our underlying intentions and desires, are influenced by the social contexts in which we have seen, heard, or experienced those words, intentions, and desires before. Linguistic anthropologists therefore maintain that the essence of language cannot be understood without reference to the particular social contexts in which it is used. But those contexts do not stand apart from linguistic practices or somehow "contain" them, as a soup bowl would contain soup.[4] Rather, social contexts and linguistic practices mutually constitute each other. For this reason, language should be studied, Alessandro Duranti writes, "not only as a mode of thinking but, above all, as a cultural practice, that is, as a form of action that both presupposes and at the same time brings about ways of being in the world" (1997:1).

This approach to language differs from the popular view of language as an empty vehicle that conveys pre-existing meanings about the world. Language, according to this view, which is held by many members of the general public as well as many linguists and other scholars, is largely a set of labels that can be placed on pre-existing concepts, objects, or relationships. In this mistaken way of thinking, language is defined as a conduit that merely conveys information without adding or changing anything of substance (Reddy 1979).

Within the field of linguistics, a similar approach to language is dominant: one in which language is reduced to a set of formal rules. Such reductionism extends back hundreds of years but was made the dominant approach of the field of linguistics by Ferdinand de Saussure, a famous Swiss linguist who lived a century ago. De Saussure maintained that it was not only possible but *necessary* to decontextualize the study of language: "A science which studies linguistic structure is not only able to dispense with other elements of language, but is possible only if those other elements are kept separate" (Saussure 1986[1916]:14).[5] This perspective was reinforced by Noam Chomsky, an American linguist who revolutionized the field and has dominated it for the past 50 years. Chomsky and his followers are interested in discovering Universal Grammar (UG), which they define as: "The basic design underlying the grammars of all human languages; [it] also refers to the circuitry in children's brains that allows them to learn the grammar of their parents' language" (Pinker 1994:483).

This is not to say that linguistic anthropologists are uninterested in grammar or believe that linguistic forms cannot be studied systematically – on the contrary, many build upon the "considerable progress in the understanding of formal properties of languages" made by scholars in the field of linguistics (Duranti 1997:7), but they ask very different kinds of questions that explore the intersections between grammar and social relations, politics, or emotion. Even linguistic anthropologists who value the work done by linguists believe that in order to acquire a comprehensive understanding of language, it must be studied in real-life contexts (cf. Hanks 1996). Grammar, according to linguistic anthropologists, is just one part of language's "socially charged life" (Bakhtin 1981:293).[6]

So, What Do You Need to Know in Order to "Know" a Language?

In order to understand what it means to study language as a linguistic anthropologist would, it is helpful to ask what it means to "know" a language (Cipollone et al. 1998). Linguists generally use the Chomskyan distinction between "competence," the abstract and usually unconscious knowledge that one has about the rules of a language, and "performance," the putting into practice – sometimes imperfectly – of those rules. De Saussure made a similar distinction between *langue* (the language system in the abstract) and *parole* (everyday speech). This distinction is partly analogous to the way a person might have abstract knowledge about how to knit a sweater but in the actual knitting of it might drop a stitch here or there or perhaps make the arms a bit shorter than necessary. In both the Chomskyan and Saussurean approaches, it is the abstract knowledge of a language system (competence or *langue*) that is of primary, or even sole, interest for a science of language; performance or *parole* is irrelevant.

To take the knitting analogy further, if Chomsky were a knittist instead of a linguist, he would be interested only in the abstract rules of Knitting (capitalizing the word, as he does with Language) such as the following: *Row 20: P 1, (k 1, p 1) 11(13-15) times, k 5, T R 2, k 4, T R 2, k 1, p 12, k 1, T L 2, k 4, T L 2, k 5, p 1, (k 1, p 1) 11(13-15) times.*[7] Chomsky the knittist would posit the existence of a Knitting Acquisition Device (KAD, rather than LAD, a Language Acquisition Device), a specialized module of the brain that allows people to acquire knitting skills. While he would acknowledge that people require exposure to knitting in their social environments in order to learn how to knit, he would be completely uninterested in the following:

- How or why people learn to knit in various cultures and communities.
- How knitting practices have changed over time.
- The gendered nature of knitting and other handicrafts in many societies (although knitting is often associated with girls and women in this society, for example, handicrafts such as weaving were until recently conventionally produced by lower-caste men in Nepal).
- The role of Madame Defarge in *A Tale of Two Cities*, by Charles Dickens, as she secretly encodes the names of counterrevolutionaries into her knitting.[8]
- The global economics involved in the many different yarns people use to knit – anything from yak wool from Nepal to Icelandic wool to synthetic mohair.
- The many different kinds of products of economic, social, or emotional value that are made by knitters to be worn by themselves, given to loved ones, donated to charity, or sold to tourists.
- The ways in which knitting is viewed by different groups in the society – as a hip, in-group practice by some, as an old, fuddy-duddy practice by others, as a useful, money-making skill by yet others.
- How one's individual and social identities can be reflected in and shaped by whether, how, what, and with whom one knits.

While this analogy with knitting is not by any means a perfect one, it does nevertheless demonstrate how narrowly Chomsky and most other linguists view language. Other practices such as playing music, dancing, or painting would work equally well in the analogy I set up above because knitting and all these other practices are – like language – socially embedded and culturally influenced. Of course there are abstract cognitive and biological dimensions to anything that we as humans do, including language, but to reduce language solely to these dimensions, as Chomsky and others do when they claim they are interested only in competence and not in performance, is to miss the richness and complexity of one of the most fundamental aspects of human existence.

Linguistic anthropologists therefore reject the Chomskyan/Saussurean distinction between competence (*langue*) and performance (*parole*), though they do so in various ways. Some deny the existence of any distinction at all between competence and performance (*langue* and *parole*), while others give primacy to performance (*parole*). Still others either expand the definition of competence to include the ability to use language skillfully and appropriately in particular social contexts (cf. Hymes 2001[1972]), and many view competence and performance (*langue* and *parole*) as equally important. What all linguistic anthropologists agree upon, however, is that to know a language, one must know far more than an abstract set of grammatical rules.

What else must one know in order to know a language, then, aside from grammatical rules? According to Cipollone et al. (1998:8-11), there are five basic components of a language that can be studied, and one must master all five of these areas in order to know a language:

- *Phonology*. The study of sound in language. In order to know a language, one must be able to recognize and produce the sounds that are meaningful in that language. In the case of sign languages, instead of sounds, one must be able to recognize and produce the appropriate gestures.
- *Morphology*. The study of the internal structure of words. In order to know a language, one must be able to use suffixes, prefixes, or infixes (depending on the language). In English, for example, one must know how to create plurals by placing an "-s" on the end of most (but not all) words, and must know what adding "un-" to the beginning of a word does to its meaning. In many Native American languages, these sorts of affixes are placed inside a word to create infixes,

while in Chinese languages, each morpheme, or unit of meaning, is a separate word, including morphemes indicating tense or plurality.
- *Syntax*. The study of the structure of sentences, including the construction of phrases, clauses, and the order of words. In order to know a language, one must be able to combine subjects, verbs, and objects in a grammatically correct way.
- *Semantics*. The study of meaning in language, including analysis of the meanings of words and sentences. In order to know a language, one must know how to construct and interpret meanings.
- *Pragmatics*. The study of language use, of actual utterances, of how meanings emerge in actual social contexts. This includes culturally and linguistically specific ways of structuring narratives, performances, or everyday conversations. In order to know a language, one must be able to use language in socially and culturally appropriate ways.

Most linguists focus primarily or solely on one or more of the first three components (phonology, morphology, or syntax), with syntax being accorded primacy ever since Chomsky became dominant in the field. In contrast, most linguistic anthropologists (as well as some scholars in related fields such as sociolinguistics or discourse analysis) study the final two components (semantics and pragmatics) in ways that integrate these two components with the first three. Indeed, linguistic anthropologists consider phonology, morphology, and syntax to be so fundamentally affected by the social contexts in which these aspects of language are acquired and used that to consider them in isolation from these contexts is at best artificial and at worst inaccurate. For the linguistic anthropologist, every aspect of language is socially influenced and culturally meaningful. To use language, therefore, is to engage in a form of social action laden with cultural values.

So, How Do Linguistic Anthropologists Study Language as Social Action?

While linguistic anthropologists hold in common the view that language is a form of social action, there is nevertheless great diversity in topic choice and research methods within the field. Chapter 2 will

Figure 1.3 "Zits" cartoon about the varying cultural meanings associated with language use.
Source: Reproduced with kind permission of Dan Piraro and Bizarro.com. Distributed by King Features Syndicate.

examine the various research methods used by linguistic anthropologists, so what I present here are some examples of the topics scholars have chosen and an explanation of how these topics contribute to our understanding of language as a form of social action. These studies illustrate but by no means exhaust the wide-ranging diversity of contemporary linguistic anthropology.

Keith Basso

Keith Basso's (1996) ethnography, *Wisdom Sits in Places: Landscape and Language Among the Western Apache*, explores "place-making" as a linguistic and cultural activity. This book was written after Ronnie Lupe, chairman of the White Mountain Apache tribe, asked Basso to help make some maps: "Not whitemen's maps, we've got plenty of them, but Apache maps with Apache places and names. We could use them. Find out something about how we know our country. You should have done this before" (Basso 1996:xv). When Basso took up this suggestion and traveled with Apache horsemen to hundreds of locations in the region, he began to notice how place names were used in everyday Apache conversations in ways that were very new to him. He also spoke with consultants, asking about the stories associated with various places. Through entertaining vignettes and engrossing storytelling, Basso explains how the richly descriptive Western Apache uses of language and place names (such as "Whiteness Spreads Out Descending to Water," "She Carries Her Brother on her Back," and

"Shades of Shit") help reinforce important Apache cultural values. For example, Western Apache speakers invoke these place names in conversations to allude indirectly to cautionary tales from recent or ancient history that may be relevant to the current speakers' dilemmas. This practice, called "speaking with names," is a verbal routine that "allows those who engage in it to register claims about their own moral worth, about aspects of their social relationships with other people on hand, and about a particular way of attending to the local landscape that is avowed to produce a beneficial form of heightened self-awareness" (Basso 1996:81). In this book, then, Basso shows how the physical environment is filtered through language to solidify social relations and strengthen Western Apache notions of wisdom and morality.

Marjorie Harness Goodwin

In her book, *He-Said-She-Said: Talk As Social Organization Among Black Children*, Marjorie Harness Goodwin (1990) chooses a very different focus: that of a mixed-age and mixed-gender neighborhood group of peers in a Philadelphia neighborhood. By analyzing "situated activities" such as arguments, storytelling, and gossip, Goodwin shows how the children's relationships and values are reflected in and shaped by their conversations. Her meticulously transcribed conversations (over 200 hours of tape recordings) provide evidence for the complexity of children's social worlds. They also demonstrate the necessity of situating any analysis of language and gender (or any other social dimension of difference) in actual contexts, for when this sort of study is undertaken, Goodwin notes, stereotypes about so-called "female" speech patterns fall apart (Goodwin 1990:9). Boys and girls do not use language in two completely different ways, Goodwin discovered, but rather interact in same-sex and mixed-sex groups using complex, overlapping sets of linguistic practices. In studying phenomena such as gender differences, therefore, Goodwin argues, it is essential to look closely at actual conversations, for "talk itself is a form of social action, so that any rigorous account of human interaction must pay close attention to the detailed structure of talk that occurs within it" (Goodwin 1990:2).

Bonnie Urciuoli

The focus of Bonnie Urciuoli's (1996) ethnography, *Exposing Prejudice: Puerto Rican Experiences of Language, Race, and Class*, is "language prejudice" – the ways in which Puerto Ricans in New York City's Lower East Side experience, accept, or resist the judgments that they and others make about what constitutes "good" and "bad" language, whether Spanish, English, or a mixture. There is a "political economy" of language, Urciuoli argues, the workings of which she explains as follows: "[T]he ways in which people formulate, value, and use words, sounds, phrases, and codes are constituted through power relations: bureaucratic, economic, racial, and any combination thereof" (1996:4). The boundaries between Spanish and English can be clearly demarcated or fuzzy, depending on the context. When the socioeconomic class of the speakers is similar, as when Lower East Side Puerto Rican men are playing basketball with their English-speaking African American neighbors, shifting between Spanish and English ("code-switching") occurs more fluidly and comfortably, for example, though the ways in which this happens differs according to gender, Urciuoli finds. In contrast, when there is a stark difference in socioeconomic class, race, or ethnicity between speakers, Urciuoli notes, the boundaries between Spanish and English are strictly enforced, so little if any code-switching occurs, for example, in interactions between Puerto Ricans and white social workers, even when those social workers may speak some Spanish. Language use is therefore an important part of unequal social relations, Urciuoli maintains, as it both reflects and sometimes reinforces differences in status.

Alessandro Duranti

Alessandro Duranti (1994) explores language use in a very different part of the world. His ethnography, *From Grammar to Politics: Linguistic Anthropology in a Western Samoan Village*, analyzes political rhetoric in the local village council (*fono*) and shows how speechmakers' seemingly apolitical, technical choices of grammatical markers can have important political ramifications. Duranti argues persuasively that a close look at the micro level of grammar – at one tiny Samoan grammatical particle in particular – offers important insights into how "the choice of specific linguistic framings for people's actions, beliefs, and feelings does not simply reflect existing power relations, it also constitutes them" (1994:139). In other words, how people describe their actions, beliefs, and feelings – how they frame them linguistically – both influences and is influenced by the power dynamics of the community. Just as the title of Duranti's book indicates, a grammatical analysis, when situated in actual social contexts, can lead to a better understanding of both grammar and politics.

Alexandra Jaffe

Alexandra Jaffe's (1999) ethnography, *Ideologies in Action: Language Politics on Corsica*, also investigates the intersections between language and politics, though she takes a more macro-level focus than Duranti in her research on the activities and attitudes of language activists and ordinary residents on the Mediterranean island of Corsica. Jaffe looks at the different statuses of the two main languages spoken on the island, French and Corsican, and shows how attitudes toward them are intertwined with issues of cultural identity and economic and political power. She argues that "language planning/revitalization is an immensely complex process ... there are no neutral or purely linguistic choices or policies. Language choices and language form are heavily invested, in Corsica, with social and political significance" (Jaffe 1999:7).

James M. Wilce

James M. Wilce's (1998) ethnography, *Eloquence in Trouble: The Poetics and Politics of Complaint in Rural Bangladesh*, looks closely at "troubles talk," or complaints, including the special genre of laments (improvised crying songs) in Bangladesh. The "eloquence in trouble" of Wilce's title has two meanings: Bangladeshis who resort to laments to describe their suffering are often quite eloquent; and these sorts of laments are becoming less and less common, and therefore represent a genre in trouble – that is, in danger of disappearing. Wilce's interest in medical and psychological anthropology leads him to pay special attention to the laments of people others label "crazy." In so doing, Wilce demonstrates how laments are more than just lengthy, monologic complaints; instead, they are aesthetic performances and social interactions during which labels can be both attached and resisted by the performer and the audience members, and realities can be "officialized" (1998:201). A focus on linguistic practices such as laments sheds light not only on the experiences of particular individuals' sufferings, Wilce argues, but also on broader cultural ideas about appropriate and inappropriate ways to speak and act, especially for Bangladeshi women.

What these six very different ethnographies have in common is their insistence that (1) language must not be studied in isolation from social practices or cultural meanings, and (2) questions about social relations and cultural meanings can best be answered by paying close attention to language. The remainder of this book presents a detailed case for each of these assertions.

Key Terms in Linguistic Anthropology

In order to provide readers with some tools they can use to approach linguistic anthropology, I have chosen four key terms that provide insight into the socially embedded nature of language and the linguistically mediated nature of social life: *multifunctionality*, *language ideologies*, *practice*, and *indexicality*. These terms draw upon an array of theoretical approaches from within the field of linguistic anthropology and beyond. As a rule in this book I try to avoid jargon, but linguistic anthropology is no different from other fields such as chemistry or art in having developed a set of specialized terms in order to refer efficiently and accurately to important concepts. The terms that I have chosen here are "key" in two ways: first, they are central to the main areas of research in the discipline, and second, they can provide readers with important keys to understanding the social nature of language because they come from the social and linguistic theories that have had the greatest influence on current scholarship in the field. Like the terms that are defined in Duranti's (2001) edited volume, *Key Terms in Linguistic Anthropology*, the four terms defined below illustrate some of the features that unify the discipline and will therefore provide common points of reference as we consider specific topics and areas of study within the field.

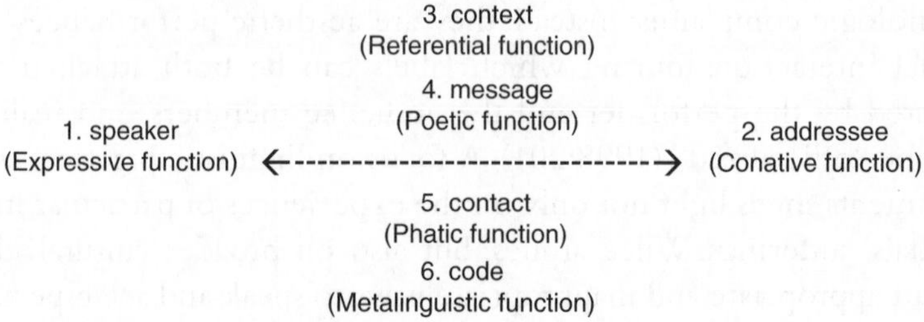

Figure 1.4 Jakobson's model of the multifunctionality of language.
Source: Thomas A. Sebeok, *Style in Language*, pp. 150, 154, 350–377, © 1960 Massachusetts Institute of Technology, by permission of The MIT Press.

Multifunctionality

In the mainstream view of language that is very common in the United States, language is thought to be a way to describe events or to label objects or concepts. Language is much more than this, however – people accomplish many things with words. Linguistic anthropologists use the term "multifunctional" to refer to all the different kinds of work that language does. One of the first scholars to analyze the various functions of language was Roman Jakobson, a Russian linguist who helped form what became known as the "Prague School" of linguistic theory. Jakobson (1960) identifies six "constitutive factors" in any speech event, and then attaches a corresponding function to each of these constitutive factors. All functions are always present in each speech event, Jakobson argues, but in certain cases, one function may predominate over the others. Figure 1.4 is a slightly modified version of Jakobson's own model (1960:150, 154).

Jakobson's multifunctional model can be understood in the following way:

1 If an utterance (or what Jakobson calls the "message") is primarily oriented toward the speaker, the predominant function is *expressive*. Examples include "Ouch!" when someone stubs a toe, or "I feel so embarrassed!" Of course, these kinds of speech events also function in other ways, but to the degree that they mainly express the speaker's feelings or opinions, Jakobson considers the predominant function to be expressive.

2 If an utterance is primarily oriented toward the addressee, Jakobson states that the predominant function is *conative*, an uncommon word Jakobson used to denote "addressee-oriented." Examples in which this function is the principal one would be questions or commands, as they are focused mainly on the addressee, or vocatives ("Hey, Susie!").

3 When the utterance is oriented largely toward a third person, toward the context, or toward events, Jakobson states that the primary function is *referential*. Examples include, "The Dow Jones plummeted 500 points today," or, "Nepal is sandwiched between India and China." These types of utterances form the core of the folk model of language mentioned at the outset of this section; for many people, the referential function is the assumed main or even sole function of language. Jakobson argues, however, that referentiality is but one of six functions of language, and other scholars (e.g., Rosaldo 1982) have shown that it is not even considered to be the default mode of communication in some cultures.

4 When the utterance is oriented primarily toward itself – when it somehow calls attention to the very sounds and patterns that are used in its articulation – this makes the *poetic* function predominate, Jakobson asserts. By "poetic," Jakobson does not mean poetry per se; instead, he is referring to occurrences in everyday speech that involve rhyme, alliteration, repetition, parallelism, or other sorts of playing around with the sound or structure of words. Examples of the poetic function being evident outside of poetry include political slogans such as, "I like Ike" (i.e., Eisenhower), and grammatical parallelism such as that which occurs in a statement such as, "I don't want to hear you, I don't want to see you, and I don't want to know you!" Jakobson has a great deal more to say about the poetic function, but this will have to suffice for our purposes.

5 If the utterance is oriented primarily toward the channel that carries it, whether the channel is social or physical, the associated function is *phatic*, according to Jakobson.[9] An example of this type of utterance would be, "Testing, 1, 2, 3…," as it focuses mainly on the physical channel or mode of contact (a microphone) between the

speaker and the addressee(s). When the channel is a more abstractly conceived social connection rather than a physical one – a relationship of friendship or kinship, for example – an utterance that orients itself primarily to this connection would also be considered mainly phatic in function. An example of this would be the common exchange, "Hi – how are you?" and the reply, "Fine, thanks." In most instances, the main function of this question and its answer is to draw attention to (and thereby reinforce) the social connection between the two speakers. Sometimes the predominant function of entire conversations can be said to be phatic – that is, mainly serving the function of maintaining or solidifying a social connection.

6 If the utterance is oriented primarily toward language itself, the predominant function is *metalinguistic*. Examples include, "Do you understand what I just said?", "How do you spell 'relief'?", or, "'Metalinguistic' means 'language that is about language.'" Some metalinguistic comments can be about language use (what Silverstein [1993] calls "metapragmatic" discourse) rather than language structure, as in "It's never appropriate to tell a joke on the first date." Many of these kinds of utterances are also examples of language ideologies, which will be discussed further below. For some linguistic anthropologists, the metalinguistic function of language represents the quintessentially human ability to be reflexive about one's own language use – in other words, the ability to use language in reported speech or to reflect upon linguistic practice, structures, and contexts of use (cf. Agha 2007; Lucy 1993).

So, language is multifunctional; it accomplishes much more than simply referring to or labeling items or events. Through language, people convey nuanced emotions, display or hide judgmental attitudes about others, reinforce or sever social bonds, and talk about language itself. It is to this latter function of language that we now turn.

Language ideologies

Language ideologies[10] are the attitudes, opinions, beliefs, or theories that we all have about language. We may or may not be conscious of them, and they may or may not square with scholars' views about

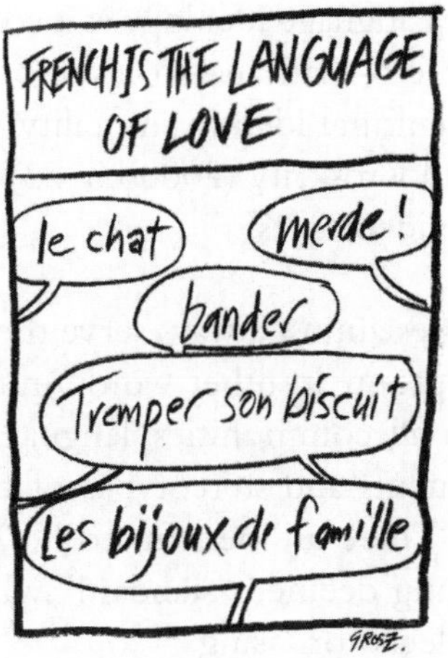

Figure 1.5 Cartoon playing off the language ideology that considers French a romantic language.
Source: www.CartoonStock.com

language (which are also, of course, language ideologies). Language ideologies can be about language as a whole (e.g., "Language is what separates humans from other species"), particular languages (e.g., "French is such a romantic language!"), particular linguistic structures (e.g., "Spanish is complicated as it has two forms of the verb 'to be'"), language use (e.g., "Never end a sentence with a preposition") – or about the people who employ specific languages or usages (e.g., "People who say 'ain't' are ignorant," or, "People who live in the United States should speak English," or, "Women are more talkative than men"). Scholars working within this fast-growing, exciting area of language ideology study, for example, how socially and politically influenced attitudes toward an endangered language can affect the likelihood of its survival (e.g., Jaffe 1999; Kulick 1998), or how teenagers and adults embrace or reject ways of speaking that link them with various racial, ethnic, or gendered identities (e.g., Briggs 1998; Bucholtz 2001; Cameron 1997; Cutler 2003; Gaudio 2001; Kroskrity 2000a).

In almost all cases, language ideologies turn out to be about much more than just language. As Judith Irvine notes, language ideologies are "the cultural (or subcultural) system of ideas about social and linguistic relationships, together with their loading of moral and political interests" (1989:255). Language ideology as a concept therefore allows scholars to connect micro- with macro-level social interactions and to analyze questions of cultural identity, morality, power, inequality, and social stereotypes. Paul Kroskrity (2000b:8–23) lists four features that characterize language ideologies.

1 Language ideologies almost always serve the interests of a specific social or cultural group. In other words, in the uneven social terrain that exists in all communities, language ideologies come to express the judgments and stereotypes of particular segments of each community. There are benefits to be had from certain language variants being deemed "standard" while others are labeled "sub-standard dialects" or "slang."
2 Language ideologies in any given society are best conceived of as multiple because all societies consist of many different divisions and subgroupings. There will therefore be many different ideas about language in any single community. Moreover, people can belong to many different social groups simultaneously and may therefore hold multiple (sometimes contradictory) language ideologies.
3 People may be more or less aware of their own or others' language ideologies. Certain types of ideas about language use or linguistic structures tend to be more accessible to people, while others are less so (Silverstein 1979, 2001). At times, language ideologies become the subject of public debate, as happened during the 1996–1997 Ebonics controversy, and these occurrences can be very illuminating to study. Just as interesting and potentially even more powerfully influential, however, are the language ideologies that people do not realize that they hold.
4 People's language ideologies mediate between social structures and forms of talk. This bridging of micro-level speech and macro-level social structures is one of the most important contributions a study of language ideologies can make.

In many respects, therefore, attention to language ideologies can help scholars in linguistic and cultural anthropology (and beyond) understand how both language and culture shape and are shaped by human actions. To understand this recursive relationship further, we turn now to the concept of practice.[11]

Practice

Consider Marx's famous words in "The Eighteenth Brumaire of Louis Bonaparte": "Men make their own history, but they do not make it just as they please; they do not make it under circumstances chosen by themselves, but under circumstances directly found, given and transmitted from the past" (Marx 1978[1852]:595). In place of the word "history" in this remark, one could easily substitute "language," "society," or "culture," and the statement would remain equally insightful. At the core of what is known as "practice theory" is this seeming paradox: that language, culture, and society all apparently have a preexisting reality but at the same time are very much the products of individual humans' words and actions.[12] Many linguistic anthropologists explicitly or implicitly draw upon practice theory in their work.

The basic idea underlying practice theory is that structures (both linguistic and social) at the same time constrain *and* give rise to human actions, which in turn create, recreate, or reconfigure those same structures – and so on, with structures and actions successively giving rise to one another. This kind of human action – that which is embedded within social and linguistic structures, that which both reflects and shapes such structures – is known as "practice" or "agency." Many practice theorists define practice further as being imbued with dimensions of inequality. Sherry Ortner, for example, considers any form of human action or interaction to be practice "insofar as the analyst recognized it as reverberating with features of inequality, domination, and the like in its particular historical and cultural setting" (1989:11–12; see also Ortner 1984). "Practice," Ortner goes on to assert, "emerges from structure, it reproduces structure, and it has the capacity to transform structure" (Ortner 1989:12).

Practice theorists are interested in questions of social reproduction and social transformation – why, in other words, things sometimes change and sometimes remain the same. One concept practice theorists have used to explain this process is Bourdieu's notion of *habitus*, which he uses to refer to a set of predispositions that produce practices and representations conditioned by the structures from which they emerge. These practices and their outcomes – whether people intend them to do so or not – then reproduce or transform the *habitus* (Bourdieu 1977:78). *Habitus* is a difficult concept but one that is potentially very illuminating, for it can be used to describe how people socialized in a certain way will often share many perspectives and values, as well as styles of eating, talking, or behaving. To simplify, *habitus* refers to how we are predisposed (though *not* required) to think and act in certain ways because of how we have been socialized. And usually, once we act upon these predispositions, we end up reproducing the very conditions and social structures that shaped our thoughts and actions to start with. Not always, however. Because of the tensions and contradictions inherent in the *habitus*, actors are neither free agents nor completely socially determined products. Instead, Ortner (1989:198) suggests that they are "loosely structured." The central question for practice theorists, then, is determining how such loosely structured actors manage at times to transform the systems that produce them.

Such loose structuring can occur linguistically as well as socioculturally. Speakers of a given language are constrained to some degree by the grammatical structures of their particular language, but they are still capable of producing an infinite number of grammatically well-formed utterances within those constraints. Moreover, languages, like cultures, change over time through drift and contact despite their supposedly self-reproducing structures. It is therefore helpful to look closely at language (both its grammatical structures and its patterns of use) in order to gain a more thorough understanding of how people reproduce and transform both language and culture.

Social systems – languages, *habitus*, structures, cultures, etc. – are created and recreated, reinforced, reshaped, and reconfigured by the actions and words of particular individuals, groups, and institutions acting in socioculturally conditioned ways. In other words, languages and cultures emerge dialogically in a continuous manner through the social and linguistic interactions of individuals "always already situated in a social, political, and historical moment" (Mannheim and Tedlock 1995:9). Neither structure nor practice, therefore, should be seen as analytically prior to the other. Instead, each should be seen as being embedded in the other. Social and linguistic structures emerge from the everyday actions of real people, and vice versa.

The concept of emergence as it is used here originated in biology, and it goes beyond the simple everyday sense in which one thing gives rise to another. In addition to this sense, emergence as it is used in linguistic anthropology (as well as other fields) also refers to instances when the whole is more than the sum of the parts. Ernst Mayr, the famous biologist, writes of inorganic as well as organic systems that they "almost always have the peculiarity that the characteristics of the whole cannot (not even in theory) be deduced from the most complete knowledge of the components, taken separately or in other partial combinations. This appearance of new characteristics in wholes has been designated as *emergence*" (1982:63, emphasis in the original). Mayr is quick to point out that there is nothing mystical about such a view of emergence; in fact, the characteristics (for example, its liquidity) of a system as "simple" as water cannot, according to Mayr, be deduced from a study of its hydrogen and oxygen atoms. Similarly, language, culture, and social structures emerge from social practice on the part of individuals but cannot be understood with reference only to those individuals.

Nevertheless, emergence does not imply absolute, unconstrained unpredictability. On the contrary, Mannheim and Tedlock (1995:18) emphasize that cultures have their own organizing principles that emerge through the linguistic and social interactions of individuals who themselves embody and enact social structures and cultural patterns, just as practice theorists maintain. Take, for example, the actions of individuals who are protesting something in their society by engaging in street demonstrations. Their underlying assumptions, methods, and principles are very likely to have been deeply influenced by the very norms that they are protesting, even if the individuals work extremely hard to counter such influences. What emerges from such formal protests, as well as from informal, everyday activities, is shaped and constrained by these influences – but not totally determined. Understanding the constrained yet at least partially indeterminate outcomes of human actions can help explain how social and linguistic structures that usually reproduce themselves nevertheless always change over time. Whether reproduction or transformation results, all languages and cultures can be said to be emergent from social and linguistic practice.

Indexicality

Identifying the precise ways in which language and social relations intersect is one of the most pressing issues in linguistic anthropology. A key concept that assists scholars in pinpointing these intersections is

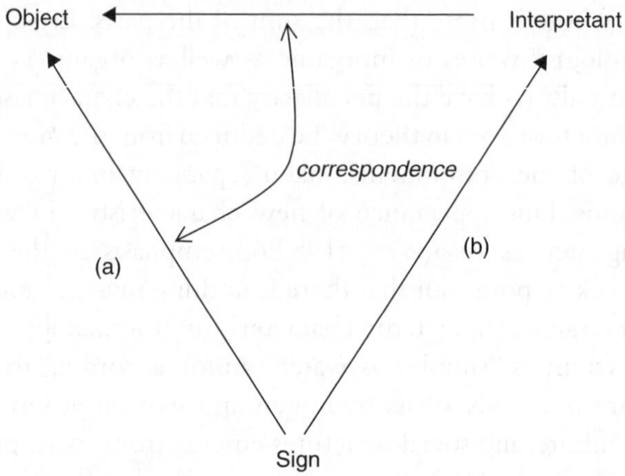

Figure 1.6 Semiosis as a relation between relations.
Source: From Kockelman (2007:377). Reproduced by permission of Paul Kockelman. *Current Anthropology*, a journal published by University of Chicago Press.

"indexicality" (Hanks 1999), which, as it is used here, stems from Charles Sanders Peirce's semiotics (Peirce 1955; cf. Mertz 2007b). Semiotics, the study of signs, can be prohibitively difficult to grasp but it is well worth going over some of the essentials in order to obtain a fuller understanding of the term "indexicality." Semiotics starts with the definition of the linguistic sign. Perhaps the best-known definition is de Saussure's: a sign is the link between a concept (the "signified") and a sound pattern (the "signifier") (Saussure 1986:66). Thus, in de Saussure's famous example, the word "tree" is a sign because it links the mental concept of a tree with the pattern of sounds that comprises the word. For Peirce, however, semiosis, or meaning-making through signs, involves a concept of the linguistic sign that is quite different from de Saussure's, for it is a process that "involves three components: *signs* (whatever stands for something else), *objects* (whatever a sign stands for), and *interpretants* (whatever a sign creates insofar as it stands for an object)" (Kockelman 2007:376; see Figure 1.6). In other words, meaning-making involves a *sign* such as the word "tree," the *object* that is represented, such as the actual tree – so far, these two aspects could be said to be fairly similar to de Saussure's "signifier" and "signified" – but then there is in Peirce's model the extremely important *interpretant* – the effect or outcome of the semiotic relationship between the *sign* and the *object*, such as a feeling of appreciation for the beauty of a tree or the act of running away from smoke for fear of a fire. Peirce's tripartite signs do not reside solely in one person's head, therefore, as de Saussure's signs do, but extend out into the physical and social world.

There are three ways in which a sign can be related to its object, according to Peirce, and it is the second of these ways that leads us to the important concept of indexicality. These three types of signs – icon, index, and symbol – are defined as follows (Peirce 1955:102–115):[13]

- *Icon*. A sign that refers to its object by means of similarity. Examples include photographs, diagrams, or sketches. Onomatopoeic words (e.g., "choo choo train," "meow") have an iconic dimension because of the similarity in sound to that which they represent.
- *Index*. A sign that refers to its object "because it is in dynamical (including spatial) connection both with the individual object, on the one hand, and with the senses or memory of the person for whom it serves as a sign, on the other hand" (Peirce 1955:107). In other words, just as an index finger points to an object, an indexical sign "points to" its object through some connection or contiguity, that is, a co-occurrence in the same context. Examples of indexical signs include the classic one of smoke, which indexes fire; a rolling gait, which indexes the profession of sailor; and a clock, which indexes the time of day. Other indexical signs include pronouns and words such as "here" or "now" because they are connected to (indeed, cannot be understood without knowledge of) particular elements of the context. More will be said about this property of indexicality below.
- *Symbol*. A sign that refers to its object by virtue of convention or habit. Most words fall primarily into this category (though words can have iconic, indexical, and/or symbolic aspects simultaneously). The word "bird," for example, does not represent its object by virtue of similarity or any sort of "dynamical connection"; it is simply conventional in English to call most flying animals with wings "birds." Some signs combine iconic or indexical features with conventional ones. For example, it is conventional in English to use the word "chickadee" to label a small black, white, and grey

bird – but this symbol also has an iconic aspect to it because the name of the bird resembles the bird's call, which sounds like "chick-a-dee-dee-dee."

While all three of these types of linguistic signs have been employed by linguistic anthropologists in their analyses, Peirce's concept of the indexical sign has drawn a great deal of attention in recent decades because of its potential for showing how and where linguistic forms "point to" aspects of social or cultural contexts. Certain categories of words have been closely studied because they are completely context-dependent in that they inherently refer to particular moments in time or places in space ("here," "then," "now," "there") or social actors ("you," "I," "that person," "such individuals"). In order to understand to whom "you" refers, for example, one must know the specific context of the conversation or text in question. And these sorts of references can shift; the person referred to as "you" can easily become "I" (or vice versa), and in reported speech a statement such as, "I'm already here," can be reported using different words and verb tenses – for example, "You said that you were already there."[14]

In addition to indexicals that refer to specific times, places, individuals, objects, or concepts, there are also more general ways in which language can be indexical. In other words, as Jakobson has already informed us, language can "point to" something social or contextual without functioning in a referential way. Aspects of language use such as regional or ethnic "accents" or "dialects," for instance, "point to" the speaker's origins and are therefore examples of nonreferential or "pure" indexicality (Silverstein 1976:29).

Other indexicals have both referential and nonreferential functions. The Nepali pronouns and verb forms used in the Pounded Rice Ritual described at the outset of this chapter, for example, index not just the particular addressee (the bride) but also her social position as it plummets from the relatively high status of daughter to the lowly status of daughter-in-law. Silverstein maintains that such indexes can call into being the very social relations that they are indexing (1976:34). Similarly, the various words the San Francisco high school students used for "stoned" index their youth status and most likely membership in various social groups as well. Indexicality is also an important concept for understanding the disappearance of the language of Taiap in Papua New Guinea, as it indexed certain social identities the villagers had come to devalue. Much more will be said about these sorts of situations, as well as many others, throughout the rest of the book. For our purposes here, it is important to realize the centrality of the concept of indexicality. Duranti writes,

> To say that words are indexically related to some "object" or aspect of the world out there means to recognize that words carry with them a power that goes beyond the description and identification of people, objects, properties, and events. It means to work at identifying how language becomes a tool through which our social and cultural world is constantly described, evaluated, and reproduced. (1997:19)

The concept of indexicality is powerful but also extremely complex, culturally and linguistically specific, and, therefore, quite challenging to study (Hanks 1999:125). Nevertheless, acknowledging the socioculturally embedded nature of language is the first step toward being able to shed further light on how indexicality works. Here are just a few examples of the subtle ways in which language can index social relations, identities, or values, "pointing to" such important aspects of the sociocultural world and even creating, reinforcing, or challenging those very relations, identities, or values:

- A college student mimics the voice of a character on a television comedy show, thereby indirectly referencing not only that character and that show but also indicating that she is the sort of cool, hip, in-group sort of person who watches such a show.
- Labeling someone as an "enemy combatant," a "freedom fighter," a "terrorist," or an "insurgent" can index the speaker's political views about the conflict in question and can also sometimes establish, strengthen, or transform legal, military, or political understandings, thereby having real effects in the social world.
- Code-switching between two languages, dialects, or social registers can index different processes involved in a person's ethnic, racial, gender, and/or socioeconomic identity formation and can have different social or even moral connotations, depending on the situation.

As Silverstein notes: "Some of us have long since concluded that such phenomena are indexical all the way down" (2006:276).

The Inseparability of Language, Culture, and Social Relations

The rest of this book will provide concrete examples of how these four concepts – multifunctionality, language ideologies, practice, and indexicality – are being applied in the field of linguistic anthropology. In the process, the following chapters will also attempt to reach two specific kinds of readers of this book: those who believe that language should be studied in a technical way, isolated from any actual instance of its use, and those who believe that social relations and cultural values should be studied without a close analysis of linguistic practices. To these readers, and indeed to all other readers as well, I hope to demonstrate in the following pages that language, culture, and social relations are so thoroughly intertwined that they must be studied in connection with one another. The field of linguistic anthropology provides some of the necessary tools for arriving at a deeper understanding of such linguistic, cultural, and social phenomena.

2

The Research Process in Linguistic Anthropology

How do linguistic anthropologists actually go about conducting research? This question can be broken down into the following sub-questions, which are best addressed sequentially:

- What kinds of research questions do linguistic anthropologists formulate?
- What kinds of data do linguistic anthropologists collect, and with what methods?
- How do linguistic anthropologists analyze their data in order to find answers to their research questions?
- What sorts of ethical issues do linguistic anthropologists face?

Since methodological approaches vary greatly within linguistic anthropology, none of these questions will have a simple answer. Often, scholars in the field will make use of several different kinds of methods in order to obtain varying perspectives on the issues at hand. Many of these methods are also used by researchers in other fields, especially cultural anthropology. While linguistic anthropologists frequently borrow from methods closely associated with cultural anthropology, however, the reverse is not often the case – though maybe it should be. With greater familiarity with the tools and perspectives of linguistic anthropology, perhaps more cultural

Living Language: An Introduction to Linguistic Anthropology, First Edition. Laura M. Ahearn.

anthropologists and scholars in other fields will see the value of drawing upon the methods described below.

What Kinds of Research Questions Do Linguistic Anthropologists Formulate?

All research starts with one or more questions. Sometimes these questions are rather inchoate in the mind of the researcher; other times, they are clearly articulated in grant proposals. At the outset of research, however, a scholar must be curious about something – and in linguistic anthropology this "something" usually concerns how language reflects and/or shapes some aspect of social life. Indeed, as noted in chapter 1, this focus on language in real-life settings distinguishes linguistic anthropologists from many other scholars in fields such as linguistics or psychology who might be interested in language. As a result, the types of research questions linguistic anthropologists ask differ from those of most linguists, sociolinguists, cultural anthropologists, and other researchers.

The specific formulation of any scholar's research question may change as the research gets underway. This is also true for linguistic anthropologists because, as will be described below, many linguistic anthropologists conduct long-term fieldwork, often in very different cultural and linguistic settings than the researcher's own, and such fieldwork ends up challenging the researcher's initial assumptions. Like researchers from other fields such as cultural anthropology, linguistic anthropologists incorporate insights from their fieldwork into their research questions so that they more accurately reflect the way that the research subjects themselves talk or think about a certain topic. The research question can therefore often be a work in progress.

In chapter 1, I summarized six ethnographies written by linguistic anthropologists. What follows is a list of some research questions these books and several others address:

- How do place names and their use in conversations both illustrate and reinforce important Apache social relations and cultural values (Basso 1996)?

- What do the arguments, storytelling episodes, and gossip of African American girls and boys tell us about the gendered nature of conversations and the ability of children to create rich, complex social worlds (Goodwin 1990)?
- How does the use of Spanish and English among Puerto Ricans shed light on unequal racial, ethnic, political, and economic relations in New York City (Urciuoli 1996)?
- In what ways does the presence or absence of a particular grammatical marker in Samoan political speeches and everyday conversations strengthen existing power relations (Duranti 1994)?
- How do language ideologies regarding French and Corsican on the island of Corsica both reproduce and reshape cultural identities, influence the outcomes of Corsican revitalization efforts, and reinforce economic and political power (Jaffe 1999)?
- What are the multiple meanings of "troubles talk" and complaints, including the special genre of laments, in Bangladesh, and how do they shed light on people's conceptions of illness (especially mental illness), emotion, and gender (Wilce 1998)?
- How does the use of "Mock Spanish" (such as "hasta la vista, baby," or, "mañana") by native English speakers both directly and indirectly index the speakers' attitudes about Spanish speakers (Hill 1998, 2005, 2008)?
- How do African American hair care professionals establish authority and reinforce their professional identities through the use of particular linguistic forms (Jacobs-Huey 2006)?
- What are the causes and implications of the almost complete eradication of a form of Irish Sign Language that used to be used solely by women (LeMaster 2006)?
- How does a new literacy practice such as love-letter writing contribute to changing marriage practices, shifting gender relations, and other social transformations taking place in Nepal (Ahearn 2001a)?

Of course, these might not have been the questions these researchers entered the field to study, since in many cases, the insights that linguistic anthropologists gain from their initial fieldwork redirect their inquiries in unanticipated ways – a process that some sociologists call "grounded theory."[1] Nevertheless, the list demonstrates the extent of the diversity in topics researched by linguistic anthropologists. Such a wide range of foci requires a correspondingly broad array of research methods in order to collect the appropriate kind of information for answering particular research questions.

What Kinds of Data Do Linguistic Anthropologists Collect, and with What Methods?

Linguistic anthropologists draw upon an eclectic mixture of research methods. In order to answer one type of research question, it might be necessary to videotape or tape-record hundreds of hours of conversation, while another might require sorting through all of a government's language policy documents over a period of decades, and yet another might require nothing more (or less) than a Google search of the word "mañana" – though in the latter case, there is almost always a deep background of ethnographic and linguistic fieldwork preceding the collection of data in the form of a Google search (cf. Hill 2005). Most linguistic anthropologists end up collecting many different kinds of data through many different research methods.

The type of information collected by linguistic anthropologists might be quantitative or qualitative – or often both. Quantitative data can be counted; the researcher is investigating the quantities of something.[2] A researcher might, for example, conduct a survey about people's opinions and count how many feel strongly about a particular subject. Qualitative methods, on the other hand, do not involve counting anything. Instead, a researcher who uses qualitative methods is interested in looking in-depth at some aspect of human behavior without quantifying it in any way. For instance, linguistic and cultural anthropologists often live for long periods of time in the communities they are studying in order to observe and participate in daily life, thereby learning and absorbing as many of the details of cultural norms and social practices as possible.

Many linguistic anthropologists advocate using multiple methods in order to gather different kinds of data in an attempt to obtain a fuller picture of the phenomenon under study. Some of the most commonly employed research methods in linguistic anthropology are described below. This is just a partial list of the many different research methods used by linguistic anthropologists. Whatever methods linguistic anthropologists draw upon, however, their main goal is to gather information about language use in actual social contexts.

Participant observation

One of the most widely used research methods in linguistic anthropology is known as "participant observation" and is shared with cultural anthropology as well as other fields that engage in ethnographic research.[3] In fact, most linguistic anthropologists consider participant observation to be an essential method for their research. (The reasons why this is so should be evident after reading in chapter 1 that linguistic anthropologists consider language to be inextricably interwoven with social practices.) Participant observation requires linguistic anthropologists to spend months or years residing in a particular community (or set of communities, in the case of multi-sited ethnographic research), during which time they become fluent in the local language(s), if they are not already, and become extremely familiar with local social norms, cultural meanings, and linguistic practices. Scholars who conduct participant observation take copious notes, called fieldnotes, while participating in an event or taking part in an interaction, or as soon as possible afterwards. This sort of intensive, in-depth immersion in the group or groups being studied can provide essential insights and build important rapport with research subjects.[4]

Interviews

Linguistic anthropologists, like many other social scientists, not to mention journalists, public opinion pollsters, market researchers, social workers, and others, often make use of interviews to gather information. The types of information requested vary widely, as does the format of the interview, which can be structured (with a list of questions asked of all research subjects in the same order), semi-structured (with a list of general areas the researcher would like to discuss, but no strict order or wording), or open-ended (informal conversations designed to elicit topics of importance to the research subjects themselves). Sometimes all of these types of interviews are used at some point during a research project.

Linguistic anthropologists may use interviews to gather general background information about cultural norms and social practices in their research communities, and/or they may conduct interviews to ask people's opinions about various linguistic usages. Linguistic anthropologists might also seek out individuals to help them understand the meanings of particularly important and complex words and concepts. Those scholars working on endangered languages that have never before been studied or perhaps even written down must work closely with speakers of these languages to document as much of the grammar, vocabulary, verbal art, and social contexts of language use as possible before the languages become extinct.[5]

No matter what the content or format of the interviews conducted, however, most linguistic anthropologists do not treat interviews as transparent – as linguistic data they can reach "through" to get to the "facts." Instead, they recognize the importance of analyzing the interview context itself. Linguistic anthropologists strongly maintain that meanings emerge in specific social interactions, and interviews are no exception. As Charles Briggs (1986, 2007) has repeatedly reminded us, the interviewer is a co-participant in the interaction, and this can have an enormous effect on what is said, how it is said, and why it is said. For a scholar to gloss over or omit entirely this aspect of the interview when writing about it is at best to miss an opportunity to enrich the analysis and at worst to fail to understand the significance of what the interviewee was (or was not) saying.

Thinking back to Jakobson's model of the multiple functions of language, the "referential" function – that which communicates information about the world – is just one of six functions of language. Interviews should not, therefore, be reduced to this function alone. Briggs also warns that in many societies, the interview is not the preferred way of communicating information – if it is a speech genre familiar to the interviewees at all. A researcher who attempts to use interviews in such a society will either obtain mistaken information or no information at all. For this reason, Briggs (1986:93) strongly encourages researchers in all fields (not just linguistic anthropology) to "learn how to ask" in culturally appropriate ways by paying close attention to how people in the community use language in all sorts of situations. Briggs (2007) also urges us all to become more aware of how the ideas people express in interviews circulate in many different venues – in scholarly articles and books, informal conversations, and the mass media, for example.

In sum, as important as the interview is as a research method, it is often mistakenly assumed to provide a simple, straightforward path toward "the facts" or "the truth." Interviews can indeed provide rich insights, but they must be appreciated as the complex, culturally mediated social interactions that they are.

Surveys and questionnaires

Closely related to interviews are surveys and questionnaires, which are often employed to collect demographic data such as age, education level, languages spoken, income, and so on. Sometimes respondents fill out the survey or questionnaire themselves; other times, the researcher or a research assistant goes through it with the respondent item by item. These research instruments can be used to collect information about opinions, experiences, or beliefs. Respondents might be asked, for example, "On a scale of 1 to 5, how much do you agree with the following statements?" Or, "How many hours per day on average do you watch television?" Or, "List the first five adjectives that come into your mind when you think of your wedding." Many of the same caveats that apply to interviews also apply to surveys and questionnaires, but they can provide valuable perspectives on some topics.

Naturally occurring conversations

Linguistic anthropologists often record hours and hours of "naturally occurring" conversations in order to study actual utterances produced by speakers in their everyday interactions. Researchers also often record folk tales, political speeches, rituals, songfests, performances, and other speech events. Of course, introducing a tape recorder or video recorder frequently makes the context something other than "naturally occurring," but linguistic anthropologists are well aware of this and have responded in several ways. First, they have noted that every context is "natural," and as long as the various aspects of the context are noted and brought into the analysis, some very interesting insights can be obtained. Second, they note that people often lose whatever self-consciousness they might at first feel as they get used to being recorded. Third, some researchers have removed themselves from the immediate conversational context by giving tape recorders to the participants themselves to control, or by setting up video or tape recorders that run for long periods of time without the researcher's needing to be present. Finally, some researchers have recorded interactions surreptitiously – though this raises ethical issues that will be discussed at greater length below. One way some linguistic anthropologists have attempted to abide by the standards of ethical research is to obtain informed consent ahead of time to record people surreptitiously at some point in the future. Then, once the recording has been made, these researchers play it back for the participants to make sure that they still consent to the recording.

As important as recording naturally occurring conversations can be for many linguistic anthropologists, there are nevertheless several drawbacks to this method. Transcribing such conversations takes an average of six hours of transcription for every hour of conversation – often more. Recorded words can become detached from their social contexts, thereby making the meanings even more indeterminate than usual. And finally, the amount of data that can be analyzed in a single short conversation is enormous, so hundreds of hours of recorded conversations can quickly become overwhelming to analyze. Despite these disadvantages, however, there is an important benefit to recording as many interactions as possible: it allows the researcher to study linguistic practices in greater detail, thereby avoiding the tendency to draw conclusions based on faulty memories, received notions, or one's own language ideologies.

It is important to remember, however, that transcriptions are never neutral written records of what was said but instead are always selective, theory-laden, and inevitably partial in both senses of the word (cf. Bucholtz 2000; Duranti 1997:122ff.; Duranti 2006a; Ochs 1979). There is no perfect or final transcription of any linguistic interaction. Instead, researchers must choose which features to include, omit, or highlight in their transcripts depending on the focus of their analyses. Should they time pauses in tenths of a second, for example? How, if at all, should they indicate overlapping speech or nonverbal gestures – with brackets of some sort, or by using a format similar to a musical score in which an utterance spoken at the same time as another appears right above or below it? What sorts of emphasis or intonation should be included in the transcript, and with what symbols or fonts? How should nonstandard variants be represented – exactly as pronounced using the International Phonetic Alphabet, through standardized spellings of the words that misrepresent the exact spellings but might be easier to read, or some other alternative? How should speech translated from another language be represented in writing? These issues are difficult intellectually, logistically, ethically, and politically, but all linguistic anthropologists who transcribe naturally occurring discourse must grapple with them, and the more explicit they are in their texts about the decisions they made while transcribing, the more illuminating their analyses are likely to be.

Experimental methods

Some linguistic anthropologists, especially those interested in cognition and/or child language acquisition/socialization, conduct various experiments in order to be able to hold constant many of the variables in any given situation. For example, a researcher interested in whether different ways of expressing spatial relations in two languages correlate with different ways of perceiving space might set up an experiment that asks subjects to remember the ordering of a line of objects on a table, then to reproduce that ordering after being rotated 180 degrees (Levinson 2003b). Similarly, researchers interested in children's language acquisition and socialization might conduct an experiment using a skit with dolls in order to ascertain the children's language abilities and their understandings of others' intentions (e.g., Villiers and Villiers 2003). We will explore some of the research involving experimental methods in chapter 4.

Matched guise tests

A researcher interested in language ideologies might conduct a matched guise test, a process that involves recording individuals as they read a short passage in two or more languages or dialects ("guises"). In other words, if four people are recorded, eight (or more) readings of the same passage might be produced. For example, a researcher interested in whether listeners judge people who speak African American English differently from those who speak standard

American English might choose four individuals who can code-switch fluently between these two ways of speaking. Each of these four individuals would record two readings of the same passage, one in African American English, the other in standard American English. These eight readings would then be shuffled up and played back to other people who do not know that there were only four readers instead of eight. The listeners would be asked to rank each of the eight readings, rating each according to how honest, intelligent, sophisticated, likable, and so on, they thought the reader was. By comparing the scores listeners give to the same speaker reading in African American English vs. standard American English, it is possible to hold a person's other voice qualities constant and thereby determine how much influence simply speaking one or the other of these language variants has on listeners' attitudes toward the speaker. In other words, matched guise tests can provide a measure of people's unconscious language ideologies – which can be related to racial prejudices.[6]

One research project that used a matched guise test was Matthew Ciscel's study of linguistic practices in Moldova (part of the former Soviet Union). Ciscel used four readers, each of whom spoke some variation of at least two of the following as either first or second languages: Moldovan, Romanian, Russian, or English. Ciscel found that while the listeners' attitudes toward these languages were complex, the one clear tendency that came through in the results was that of all the variants the listeners ranked, they considered the accented, rural dialect of mixed Romanian/Moldovan to be lowest in status (2007:100; cf. Bilaniuk 2005; Booth 2009b; Urciuoli 1996). One of Ciscel's speakers (whom Ciscel numbers "Voice 2") recorded the same passage in standard Romanian, Russian, and English and was ranked by the listeners as more honest, intelligent, and so on, when she was speaking in these languages than when she was speaking the rural dialect of mixed Romanian/Moldovan. It must be remembered that the listeners thought that they were hearing four separate speakers, not the same speaker speaking in four different languages or dialects. In this way, matched guise tests can help reveal unconscious language ideologies – often a direct or indirect indicator of social hierarchies. While matched guise tests, like all methods, have their limitations, they can be quite useful, especially when combined with participant observation, interviews, and other ethnographic methods.

Written texts

Many linguistic anthropologists look closely at various written texts: historical documents copied from archives, personal letters (such as the love letters I studied – see Ahearn 2001a), newspaper articles, e-mails, or official documents. Researchers who are interested in studying literacy practices – the ways in which people produce, consume, or refer to written texts in their everyday lives – often analyze written texts as mundane as shopping lists or sign boards, drawing insightful conclusions about important cultural values and social relations. Even linguistic anthropologists who are not primarily concerned with literacy practices often find that paying close attention to the intersections between texts and contexts is not only beneficial but unavoidable in societies that are saturated by the written word.

How Do Linguistic Anthropologists Analyze their Data?

The logistics involved in conducting research in linguistic anthropology can be very challenging. Many scholars in the field employ a research assistant to help them collect data, whether by conducting a survey, distributing written questionnaires, or translating or transcribing interviews or conversations. Even when a translator is used, however, most linguistic anthropologists emphasize the importance of not relying solely on such an intermediary but instead being fluent enough in the local language(s) to carry out many parts of the research project themselves. Some linguistic anthropologists prefer to conduct every aspect of their research themselves without any help from a translator or research assistant, but this is not possible when the scope of the project is too broad for one person to handle, or when it is not considered culturally acceptable for the researcher to speak alone (or even at all) with a member of the opposite sex or of a different caste or other social group.

No matter which methods are used, it is important to remember that all research, even the most "objective," number-crunching sort, involves interpretation. From the formulation of a research question through the data collection stage, all the way through the data analysis process, all scholars, including linguistic anthropologists, knowingly or unknowingly engage in interpretation. If they are not careful, this interpretation process can involve the imposition of the researcher's own culturally specific categories, which can prevent the researcher from gaining a deep understanding of the topic being studied. The research process therefore requires constant reassessment by the scholar.

A painful but extremely instructive example of the unwitting and inappropriate imposition of a researcher's own categories comes directly out of my own fieldwork. At the outset of my dissertation research, which was about the shift away from arranged marriage toward self-initiated, or "love marriage" in Junigau, Nepal, I decided to conduct a quick survey of all the adults in the village. I asked each person whether his or her marriage was either self-initiated or arranged by parents – assuming that these were the only two types of marriage. As I went along, I would occasionally receive a response that confused me, as it sounded to my ears as though the person were saying the equivalent of, "My marriage was just like *jabar*." Now, *jabar* by itself is not a word in Nepali, so when people mentioned the actual word *jabarjasti* (violently, by force), I heard *jabar* (which I did not understand) and *jastai* ("just like"). I had spent years in Nepal by that point and was fairly fluent in Nepali after spending three years in the country as a Peace Corps volunteer, but I had never heard the word *jabarjasti*. This was partly because my fieldwork occurred before the violent Maoist insurgency that began in 1996 and partly because forced capture marriage (*jabarjasti chhopeko*) was a stigmatized practice in the village, spoken of openly by very few people. So, whenever I heard what I thought was "just like *jabar*" as an answer to what kind of marriage a person had had, I asked, "Just like what – self-initiated or arranged?" The person would then usually choose either the self-initiated or the arranged category. One day, however, in discussing the village's marriage practices with my Nepali sister-in-law, I mentioned the problem I had been having understanding *jabarjasti*, and she explained to me that there was a third category of marriage in Junigau: capture marriage, a forceful kidnapping of the bride and sometimes of the groom as well that was common in the village decades before. Since all of the responses to my initial question about whether people's marriages had been self-initiated or arranged were potentially tainted by my incorrect assumption that there were only these two types of marriage in the village, I had to start all over again with the survey. As a result of this eye-opening mishap, I eventually came to reformulate my research as a study of marriage narratives in which Nepalis talked about their involvement (or lack thereof) in the decision-making processes surrounding various types of marriage.

Once linguistic anthropologists have all of their data, interpretation becomes a process of searching for patterns in order to find answers to the research questions that inspired the project – or to answer questions that emerge during analysis of the data. For many linguistic anthropologists, this involves reading and rereading fieldnotes and other documents, transcribing interviews and naturally occurring conversations, and statistically analyzing survey responses. Some scholars then go on to conduct a micro-level analysis of conversational data, while others focus on data concerning language policies or ideologies at a broader scale.

One approach to the micro-level analysis of linguistic data is known as Conversation Analysis (CA). Developed in the 1960s and 1970s partly as an outgrowth of ethnomethodology, a school within sociology that seeks to uncover the ways in which people work to establish and maintain taken-for-granted social structures in their everyday activities (Garfinkel 1967), Conversation Analysis is both a tool within disciplines such as linguistic anthropology and a discipline in its own right. Practitioners of CA in this latter sense include the founders of the approach, Harvey Sacks, Emanuel Schegloff, and Gail Jefferson, who analyze talk-in-interaction without resorting to contextualization, interviews, or any ethnographic methods (Sacks et al. 1974; Schegloff 2007). Instead, they look closely at ordinary conversations for the patterning inherent within them. One of the most important and widespread patterns, they suggest, is turn-taking. Each utterance provides a context (and for some CA practitioners, the only relevant context) for the utterance that follows. Utterances, CA scholars have shown, often appear in what are known as "adjacency pairs" – questions and answers, for example, or greetings and responses ("Hi, how are you?" "Fine, thanks, and you?"), compliments and disavowals ("You look great today!" "Oh, no, I'm just slogging along as usual..."), and so on. Certain responses are socially preferred, while others are dispreferred, and much can be understood about cultural norms and social relationships by paying close attention to these clues.

As valuable as the insights that have emerged from work in CA have been, however, most linguistic anthropologists view CA much more as a methodological tool to be used in conjunction with other methods, especially ethnographic ones (Moerman 2007). Alessandro Duranti (1977:266) identifies three main criticisms leveled at researchers who use only CA: (1) they are uninterested in the "larger contexts" of the conversations they analyze, even such basic aspects as the relationship between the people who are talking, or where or when the conversation took place; (2) their transcripts indicate a very narrow view of "speech," omitting nonverbal interactions, changes in intonation, and the like; and (3) they are completely uninterested in what the speakers themselves might say to explain or interpret their own utterances. For these reasons, when linguistic anthropologists do use CA (and many do consider it an extremely valuable approach), they combine it with other methods and contextualize the conversations they analyze far more comprehensively than strict CA practitioners do.

Some linguistic anthropologists who analyze conversations draw on the theories of Erving Goffman, a sociologist who rejected many of the most common language ideologies regarding the ways in which conversations allegedly take place between speakers and hearers. Goffman suggested a much more complex participation framework and production format for even the simplest of conversations, arguing, for example, that the seemingly unified role of speaker in any interaction could actually be separated into three different roles (Goffman 1981:144):

- *Animator.* The person who serves as the voice box; the person who animates the words being spoken, whether they are the speaker's own words or not.
- *Author.* The person who composed the words.
- *Principal.* The person who stands behind what is said; the person whose opinions are expressed.

Goffman also helped to disambiguate the hearer role, distinguishing among ratified and unratified hearers. Some hearers are addressees (those to whom the speaker addresses an utterance), but some are bystanders, overhearers, or even eavesdroppers.

Sometimes all three speaker roles are inhabited by one person, but sometimes they can be distributed across several people. So, to give a hypothetical example, President Obama might give a speech written by a speech writer who totally disagrees with the President's policies but writes eloquently and convincingly enough to keep the job. As President Obama delivers the speech, he would be considered the animator (the voice box) and, presumably, the principal (the person whose opinions are being expressed), but the speech writer would be the author. Even in ordinary conversations, these roles frequently shift, especially when reported speech is used. Goffman called these instances *shifts in footing*:

> A change in footing implies a change in the alignment we take up to ourselves and the others present as expressed in the way we manage the production or reception of an utterance. A change in our footing is another way of talking about a change in our frame for events. … [P]articipants over the course of their speaking constantly change their footing, these changes being a persistent feature of natural talk. (1981:128)

Such shifts in footing are important to study closely, as they offer scholars clues about the multifunctionality of even the most mundane of utterances. Changes in footing also often index various social identities, cultural values, attitudes, stances, or relationships. Conversation analysis, in conjunction with other ethnographic methods, can therefore provide valuable insights into many different kinds of linguistic and social practices.

Whether the information a linguistic anthropologist collects consists of recorded or transcribed conversations, written fieldnotes, survey results, or other types of information, once it has been collected the next step facing the researcher is to analyze what usually amounts to mountains of data. Some scholars use index cards or sketch out flow charts to organize their thoughts and their data, while others turn to computer software to help them do this. There are many computer programs available to help researchers sort through their data, whatever form the information takes. Some programs allow the user to identify themes or codes in text files, graphics files, sound files, or even video files, then organize those themes in whatever ways make most sense to the researcher. Other programs help the investigator conduct a statistical analysis of quantitative data or analyze aspects of speech such as pitch or pronunciation. Even with the help of the most sophisticated computer programs, however, researchers ultimately have to discover patterns, make connections, and draw conclusions themselves.

What Sorts of Ethical Issues Do Linguistic Anthropologists Face?

The ethical issues facing any social scientist can be daunting. Ever since the reflexive turn in anthropology two or more decades ago, however, linguistic anthropologists have given a great deal of thought to the micro-politics of personal relations in the field and the ethical dimensions of representing in scholarly or popular articles, books, and presentations the people and communities they study. There is often unequal power between the researcher and the people s/he studies – though this relationship can be extremely complex, so all the power may not reside in the researcher alone. Still, researchers frequently have more money than research subjects, and they often create an entire career out of the information gathered from the people who live in their fieldsites. When genuinely close relationships of trust, friendship, or fictive kinship develop, complicated questions can emerge regarding mutual obligations, betrayal, and confidentiality. Many anthropologists have written about the theoretical, ethical, and personal implications of these issues.

Much of the research conducted by academics on human subjects must be reviewed by the Institutional Review Board (IRB) of their university or research institute. The IRB review process grew out of some horrific abuses of research, mostly in the biomedical field. As a result, many anthropologists and other social scientists consider IRB oversight of their research to be unnecessary and/or focused on irrelevant matters (such as providing access to experimental medicines in an ethical manner).[7] The American Anthropological Association has developed its own ethical code,[8] and many anthropologists consider these guidelines to be more appropriate for their research – and sometimes even stricter – than the policies enforced by IRBs.

Even the AAA's Code of Ethics, however, is intentionally vague in some places and controversial in others. For example, it makes the following seemingly straightforward statement: "Anthropological researchers have primary ethical obligations to the people, species, and materials they study and to the people with whom they work."[9] But if anthropologists are studying, say, child abusers or corrupt politicians (and some do study such groups), should these anthropologists' primary ethical obligation be to their research subjects or to the victims of their research subjects? What does it mean to be "ethically obligated" to someone?

Both the AAA's Code of Ethics and all IRBs across the United States advocate "informed consent." That is, the researcher is expected to inform each research subject fully about the nature of the study and obtain consent from each participant. This process is fairly straightforward in studies that involve something like filling out a single questionnaire, provided that the study takes place in a society such as the United States, where most people are familiar with the concept of a research study. Research subjects merely read the informed consent statement at the beginning of the questionnaire, and if they want to participate, they sign the paper or otherwise indicate their consent. When the research takes place in a different society, however, one in which people are less familiar with research projects, and when the research involves long-term participant observation, resulting in the researcher's living in a particular community for a year or longer, such a one-time informed consent process is usually inappropriate. When deep personal bonds are formed, it is often tricky for the researcher to determine which information is appropriate to use in the research and which is not. The informed consent process in such instances therefore needs to be ongoing and adapted to the particular setting in which the research takes place.

Other difficult ethical questions linguistic anthropologists (and other researchers) sometimes face include the following:[10]

- Should research assistants be paid the going rate (if there is such a thing) of the country in which the research takes place, or a fair wage according to US standards?
- What constitutes appropriate reciprocity for all of the information, advice, and assistance researchers receive from people in their

fieldsites? If a researcher is treated as a son or daughter, for example, does that mean that s/he should take on all the obligations of that role in that society, including, perhaps, keeping in touch regularly after leaving the field and taking on the care of parents in their old age?

- What are the ethical obligations of a researcher who is "studying up" (Nader 1972) in a community of individuals who are far wealthier and more powerful than the researcher herself/himself?
- Must a researcher provide medical or financial assistance to everyone who asks for such help? Only some people? No one at all? Why or why not?
- How should researchers behave when confronted by behavior they find morally repugnant? Should they respect different cultural norms or apply universal standards of human rights?
- Is "applied" or "engaged" research[11] more ethical than so-called "pure" research? Does it avoid any of the ethical dilemmas facing non-applied researchers? What ethical issues are unique to applied research? Does all applied research involve the same kinds of ethical considerations? In other words, does a linguistic anthropologist working on preserving an endangered language face the same ethical quandaries as a linguistic anthropologist working as a speech writer for a politician?

Linguistic anthropologists interpret and answer these types of questions differently, and of course answering them in the abstract does not necessarily make it easy to decide what one should do in an actual situation, for the specific details of actual cases are usually extremely complex. Nevertheless, acknowledging the presence of thorny ethical issues in any research is often the first step toward resolving such issues satisfactorily.

The research process for linguistic anthropologists differs relatively little from that of other social scientists. They must formulate compelling research questions, and yet remain open to the revision of those questions as data collection and analysis move forward. They must also decide which methods will gather the right kind of information to enable the answering of their research questions. Along the way, they must resolve the ethical dilemmas that will inevitably emerge. Finally, linguistic anthropologists must sort through the data that they have collected in order to detect patterns, interpret meanings, and write up results.

It is often said that research is partial in both senses of the word – partial as in only part of the full story, and partial as in biased. This absolutely applies to research in linguistic anthropology. What is less often appreciated, however, is that this is true of all experiences that we have in life. Nevertheless, for all its complexities, research in linguistic anthropology can be exhilarating.

3
Language Acquisition and Socialization

> Language is a great force of socialization, probably the greatest that exists.
>
> Edward Sapir (1949[1933]:15)

Katie, a three-month-old infant from a white, middle-class family in the United States, sits perched on her mother's knees. Katie and her mother face each other and have a "conversation." "Glrgg," Katie gurgles. "Hello to you, too," her mother replies in a high-pitched, sing-song voice sometimes called baby talk, motherese, or parentese. Katie turns her head to the side. Her mother follows her gaze. "Is Katie looking at the doggie? What's the doggie's name?" Katie remains silent, but her mother continues the conversation: "That's right – Spot!" In this way, Katie's mother interprets, replies to, or comments upon each sound or gesture Katie makes. Katie's mother willingly "converses" with Katie and thereby attributes intentionality and some semblance of intelligibility to Katie's prelinguistic utterances. This type of interaction is often taken for granted by people raised in homes similar to Katie's. Indeed, to such people it may seem like the only "appropriate" or "natural" way to talk to a baby, and some even think it is necessary to speak this way in order for children to learn a language – but linguistic anthropologists have shown that this way of using language with infants is "characteristic neither of all societies nor of all social groups (e.g., all social classes within one society)" (Ochs and Schieffelin

2001[1984]:268). Such research demonstrates that there are multiple ways of becoming fluent in one's native language(s) and becoming socialized into one's culture.

Consider the case of Bage, a three-month-old Kaluli boy, for example, whose language socialization process is described by Bambi Schieffelin (1990) in her ethnography about the Kaluli people of Papua New Guinea. Unlike Katie, who sat perched on her mother's knee for a face-to-face "conversation," Bage is held facing outward on his mother's lap so as to see and be seen by a larger group of household members. Bage's mother does not address him directly, as the Kaluli do not consider infants to be appropriate conversation partners, and she does not use baby talk. Instead, she involves Bage's almost-three-year-old older brother, Abi, in an exchange in which she takes Bage's role. In this triadic exchange, which is typical among the Kaluli, Bage's mother speaks "for" the infant, addressing Abi using the appropriate kinship term for brother and asking Abi to pick him up. "When speaking as the infant to older children," Schieffelin writes, "mothers speak assertively; that is, they never whine or beg on behalf of infants. Thus, in taking this role, mothers do for infants what they cannot do for themselves: act in a controlled and competent manner using language" (1990:72). In refusing to address their infants directly or to simplify the grammar of their utterances at all, Kaluli mothers show that they think very differently about infants as language learners and as social actors than mothers such as Katie's do.

In these two examples, as well as in many others (e.g., Crago et al. 1997; Demuth 1986; Heath 1983; and Ochs 1988), we can see caregivers socializing their children into becoming very different kinds of social beings *through culturally specific uses of language*. In the case of Katie, her mother was promoting a certain sense of self by interacting with her as if she were already a competent communicative partner. Such one-on-one interactions are part of a wider set of cultural practices and language ideologies in the United States surrounding child-rearing, most of which involve accommodating the situation to the child rather than adapting the child to the situation. Middle-class caregivers in the United States engage in two related practices, according to Elinor Ochs and Bambi Schieffelin: "self-lowering" on the part of caregivers, exemplified by simplifying their utterances and asking questions to which they already know the answers; and "child-raising," that is, treating the child as more competent linguistically than she really is (Ochs and

Schieffelin 2001:272, 287). In Papua New Guinea, in contrast, Bage's attention was directed outwards toward a more sizable family group as he was being socialized into a network of kin. His mother did not employ "self-lowering" or "child-raising" in interacting with Bage; indeed, his mother did not converse with Bage directly at all. Instead, Bage was expected to accommodate to the wider social group as he learned appropriate ways of interacting linguistically and culturally.

These two examples raise many fascinating questions about the process of language acquisition and socialization, several of which are addressed in this chapter: (1) How does the innate human capacity to learn a language intersect with the culturally and linguistically specific factors in each child's upbringing? (2) In bilingual or multilingual environments, do socialization practices have an impact on which languages children learn and to what levels of proficiency? (3) Does language socialization end when childhood ends, or does it continue into adulthood? In each of these areas, linguistic anthropology has a unique perspective to offer that sheds valuable light on the complex process of acquiring a language. Sometimes, this perspective complements the scholarship being done in other disciplines; other times, it challenges it.

Language Acquisition and the Socialization Process

The fact that children who are raised as differently as Katie and Bage nevertheless all become competent speakers of their native languages by about age three points to an undeniable innate component in the language acquisition process. The nature of this innate component, however, is hotly debated. Many linguists follow Noam Chomsky, who considers social or other environmental influences on language acquisition to be extremely limited. Chomsky also views language acquisition as a process over which children and their caregivers have very little control:

> Language learning is not really something that the child does; it is something that happens to the child placed in an appropriate environment, much as the child's body grows and matures in a predetermined way when provided with appropriate nutrition and environmental stimulation. (1999:41)

Not only do Chomsky and his supporters accord the environment a very minor role in the language acquisition process; they also believe that language arises out of a separate domain-specific faculty or module of the brain. Without such a special "language-acquisition device" (LAD) (Chomsky 1999:43) or "language instinct" (Pinker 1994), these scholars argue, children would not be able to acquire language so quickly, given the "poverty of the stimulus" – in other words, given the supposedly impoverished nature of the input that a child receives linguistically during the first few years of life. Hard-wired into the brain, Chomsky and others maintain, is a "universal grammar" (UG) that provides an overarching template for the range of possible human languages. All a child needs to do, in this view, is to hear a few examples of any particular grammatical feature in order to be able to set the appropriate parameter, or switch, correctly in UG. For example, some languages place prepositions at the beginning of phrases (as in English – e.g., "*in* the house"), whereas in other languages, words such as "in" are called postpositions because they occur at the end of a phrase (as in Nepali – e.g., "ghar*mā*" – literally, "house *in*," more appropriately translated as "*in* the house"). Once a child is exposed to enough examples of such phrases in a given language, the parameter is thought to be switched to the correct setting in the child's brain.

Some linguists, cognitive scientists, and child development specialists disagree, however, with the Chomskyan view that there is a domain-specific language acquisition device or module in the brain. Instead, these scholars maintain that generalized cognitive and developmental processes or learning mechanisms enable children to acquire one or more languages in the same way that they learn other advanced cognitive tasks. Elizabeth Bates and Brian MacWhinney, for example, argue the following: "[T]he human capacity for language could be both innate and species-specific, and yet involve no mechanisms that evolved specifically and uniquely for language itself. Language could be viewed as a new machine constructed entirely out of old parts" (Bates and MacWhinney 1989:10, cited in Tomasello and Slobin 2005:xxvii).

In addition, some scholars (e.g., Givón 1985; Plunkett 1995; Snow 1995) dispute the characterization of the linguistic input received by children as impoverished – "very restricted and degenerate," according to Chomsky (1968:23) – and claim instead that most children are exposed to more than enough linguistic input to acquire a language without needing to postulate the hard-wiring of specific linguistic features in Universal Grammar. Questions remain, however, as to how much and what kind of input is enough, and what effects early language exposure and different social environments have on children's language acquisition processes.

Whether the human capacity for language is the result of a language-specific module in the brain or a more generalized set of cognitive mechanisms, linguistic anthropologists maintain that social interactions play a crucial role in language acquisition, and it is here that the discipline of linguistic anthropology has a great deal to contribute to a deeper understanding of how children learn their native languages. "Language socialization" is the name of the subfield that delves into these issues. Established and still led by Elinor Ochs and Bambi Schieffelin, who have published independently and jointly on the topic of language socialization since the 1980s, the field takes the following as its two main propositions (Ochs and Schieffelin 2001:264):[1]

1 The process of acquiring language is deeply affected by the process of becoming a competent member of society.
2 The process of becoming a competent member of society is realized to a large extent through language.

The message to scholars interested in language acquisition, therefore, is that they should consider cultural values and social practices to be inseparable from language and its acquisition (Slobin 1992:6). And the message to cultural anthropologists and other social scientists interested in processes of childhood social practices, education, apprenticeship, or other ways of learning or entering into new social groups is that they should look closely at linguistic practices. In other words, learning a first language and becoming a culturally competent member of a society are two facets of a *single process*. It is virtually impossible for a child to learn a language without also becoming socialized into a particular cultural group, and, conversely, a child cannot become a competent member of such a group without mastering the appropriate linguistic practices.

Elinor Ochs's (1988) research on language acquisition and socialization in Western Samoa is a case in point. The conclusions Ochs draws after rigorous, long-term fieldwork call into question some of the standard assumptions of child development specialists in other disciplines. For example, she challenges the claim that all children learn grammatical features in the same order and at roughly the same ages. Western Samoan children, Ochs discovered, acquire the particular grammatical feature known as an ergative marker[2] later than do children who speak other ergative languages such as Kaluli or Quiché Mayan (Ochs 1988:102; cf. Schieffelin 1990, Pye 1990). This is not because the ergative marker is more difficult to learn in Samoan than in other languages where it is used but because, Ochs argues, use of the ergative case in adult Samoan varies according to the degree of social intimacy or distance of the speakers – the more intimately related the speakers are, the less likely they are to use ergative markers (cf. Duranti 1994). Ochs also found that women used ergative markers less frequently than men. Thus, young Samoan children, who spent most of their first few years in the company of close, usually female, family members, heard relatively few ergative markers and therefore learned to use such markers themselves later than children learning other ergative languages.

But Ochs's research should not be interpreted to mean that language acquisition always proceeds according to a basic input–output model in which the grammatical features children learn earliest are those that they most frequently hear. Indeed, Ochs and Schieffelin (1995) present two telling examples of grammatical features that are not acquired by Samoan children according to such a simplistic process. In the first case, Samoan children frequently hear a term meaning "come" but rarely use it themselves because it is socially inappropriate for them to do so, given their lowly status in the household hierarchy. In the second example, Samoan children rarely hear but frequently use the imperative form of the compound verb meaning "having chewed, give." Such instances, Ochs and Schieffelin argue, "should sensitize us to the fact that children's linguistic repertoire is not a simple reflection of what they do or do not hear in their surroundings, but rather that children are taking an active role in constructing language that is most useful to their needs and appropriate to their social status" (Ochs and Schieffelin 1995:87–88).

Additional evidence that standard assumptions and methods for studying child language acquisition might need to be rethought comes from other scholars. The tendency, for example, for researchers to study mainly adult–child interactions ignores the possibility that child–child speech patterns might differ substantially from those found in traditional middle-class, white, English-speaking mother–child contexts. Indeed, in her study of Sesotho-speaking children's language acquisition and socialization processes in southern Africa, Katherine Demuth found that around the age of two and a half, usually about the age when a new sibling would be born, adults would turn their attention to the newborn, and toddlers were "thrust into the peer group to fend verbally, and otherwise, for themselves" (Demuth 1992:588). One concrete linguistic result of this shift in social context, Demuth maintains, is that Sesotho-speaking children use relative clauses ("the day when we went to the river" or "my box that I was given") quite a bit earlier than English-speaking children do. The Sesotho-speaking toddlers also use such complex clauses more often with their peers than with adults. The reason for this, Demuth suggests, is because peer groups are more confrontational and less accommodating to young children than adults often are, forcing them to make use of more complex linguistic features in order to hold their own socially (Demuth 1992:617). Adequate attention to naturally occurring peer interactions among English-speaking toddlers might reveal, Demuth suggests, that such youngsters can actually produce relative clauses earlier than was previously thought.

More research such as Demuth's across many different languages would certainly help to contextualize what is known about language acquisition, and might even lead scholars to reassess what were previously held to be universals in the order in which children learn various grammatical structures.

Language Acquisition in Bilingual or Multilingual Contexts

Additional insights can be gleaned from studying children learning to speak in bilingual or multilingual contexts. When children are exposed regularly to two or more languages (there does not seem to be an upper limit) during the developmental window period of early to middle childhood, they usually becoming fluent in all the languages available to them in their social environment. Contrary to language ideologies that hold that children are somehow disadvantaged by being exposed to more than one language in early childhood, many studies show on the contrary that there are significant cognitive advantages to such exposure (e.g., Bialystok 2010; Bialystok and Viswanathan 2009). There is also evidence, however, that social factors and language ideologies can prevent children from becoming fluent in a given language despite frequent exposure to it.

Don Kulick's (1992, 1998) study of the acquisition and retention of two languages, the indigenous language of Taiap and the lingua franca Tok Pisin, in the village of Gapun, Papua New Guinea, reveals the influence of positive and negative attitudes on the acquisition (or lack thereof) of these two languages by children. As we read in one of the examples at the very beginning of this book, adult residents of Gapun, almost all of whom were bilingual in Taiap and Tok Pisin at the time of Kulick's fieldwork, told him that they were not responsible for their children learning to speak Tok Pisin instead of Taiap, the indigenous vernacular language. Kulick elaborates:

> In Gapun, parents explicitly see themselves not as acting, but as *re*-acting to language shift ... Without exception, everyone agrees that Taiap is a good language and desirable to know. No conscious decision has been made by anyone to stop transmitting the vernacular to their children, and some villagers, especially old men, occasionally express great annoyance at the fact that children only speak Tok Pisin. So what, then, is causing the shift? The children, say the adults. "It's them, these little kids," explained one woman, echoing the conclusion of others and indicating her suckling 14-month-old baby with a sharp jab of her chin, "They're all *bikhed* [big-headed, strong-willed]. They don't want to know our village language. They just want to speak Tok Pisin all the time." (1992:12–13)

Kulick's ethnography seeks to explain the shift from Taiap to Tok Pisin in Gapun by drawing upon Marshall Sahlins's (1981) influential contribution to practice theory. Sahlins argues that people may be attempting to reproduce their cultural norms and social relations, but instead they often end up unwittingly transforming them because conditions have changed. As an example of this process, Sahlins examines Captain Cook's arrival in Hawaii in the eighteenth century. The Hawaiians mistook Cook for their god, Lono, and the actions that they subsequently took to try to worship him and reproduce their social system resulted in the colonization of their society and the complete overhaul of their belief system. Similarly, Kulick maintains, the residents of Gapun believed in the 1980s that they were reproducing their traditional values, but because of the arrival of new ideas and practices brought in by Christian missionaries, villagers ended up creating conditions that led to the shift in their children away from Taiap toward Tok Pisin.

Two long-standing Gapun cultural concepts, *hed* and *save*, are central to understanding why children in the village stopped learning Taiap. *Hed*, Kulick explains, is a trait that Gapun residents believe all people have to a greater or lesser extent. It is the dimension of the self that is "individualistic, irascible, selfish, unbending, haughty, and proud" (1992:19). *Save*, literally meaning knowledge, is a much more positive quality. It is the social, cooperative part of one's personality. "All people, but especially men," Kulick asserts, "are expected to use their *save*, their 'knowledge,' to 'suppress' (*daunim*) their antisocial *heds* and cooperate with their fellow villagers" (1992:19). Women and children are thought to be less capable of controlling their selfish, argumentative *heds*.

How can these two concepts of *hed* and *save* explain the language shift that occurred in Gapun? In the past, when only Taiap was spoken in the village, the negative associations of *hed* and the positive associations of *save* had no implications for language use. With the advent of Christianity and a new language, Tok Pisin, in the village, however, these connotations were supplemented by new ones. *Hed* retained all its negative qualities but also came to be associated with Taiap and with what villagers thought of as being "backward." *Save*, on the other hand, retained its positive associations, and these were then supplemented by new linkages to Christianity, modernity, and Tok Pisin (see Figure 3.1).

Without realizing it, Gapun villagers began changing their linguistic practices as a result of the new associations that their long-standing cultural values of *hed* and *save* had begun to acquire. In a close study of children's language acquisition and socialization practices in the village, Kulick found that adults assumed that infants only a few months old spoke a few "words" in Taiap – short phrases that translate as "I'm getting out of here," "I'm sick of this," and "Stop it" – but after these initial utterances, children were not thought to be able to speak at all until about 18 months of age (Kulick 1992:202). Villagers considered these initial vocalizations to be indicative of young children's bad temper and selfishness – in other words, their *hed*.

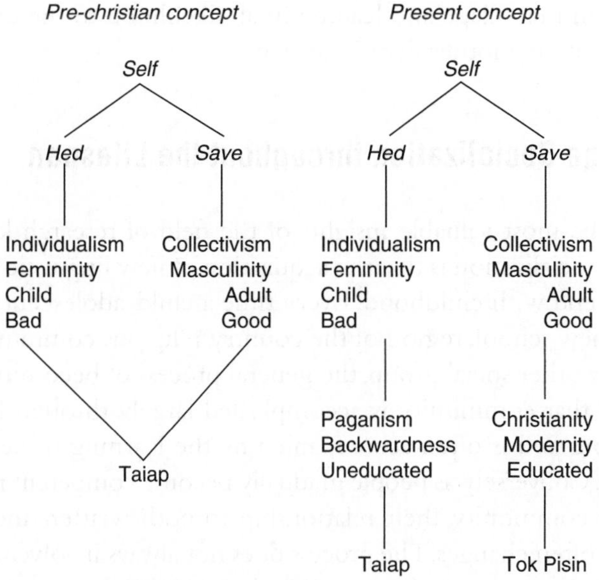

Figure 3.1 The cultural concepts of *hed* and *save* in Gapun, Papua New Guinea. *Source:* From Kulick (1992:20). Reprinted with the permission of Cambridge University Press.

Much as we saw above for the Kaluli that Schieffelin studied, the residents of Gapun spoke directly to their young children very rarely. When they did, they often mixed Taiap and Tok Pisin, just as they did in adult-adult talk. Kulick found one major difference, however: Gapun parents assumed that their children would find Tok Pisin both easier and preferable to speak as their *save* developed, so whenever parents really wanted their children to pay attention, they would switch into Tok Pisin. And other than the first few "words" that their children spoke in Taiap, parents assumed that all the rest of their attempts at speech were in Tok Pisin. They therefore reinforced these attempts to speak the language associated in the village with modernity, education, and other high-status qualities. The net result was that parents attributed the younger generation's shift in the village away from Taiap toward Tok Pisin to be caused not by the parents' own actions but by their children's preferences. The villagers' continued emphasis on the positive values of *save* and the negative values of *hed* under new social conditions ended up transforming linguistic practices in the village and leading in all likelihood to the extinction of Taiap within another decade or two.[3]

Language Socialization throughout the Lifespan

One of the most valuable insights of the field of research known as language socialization is that the acquisition of new linguistic practices does not end with childhood. Every time a child, adolescent, or adult enters a new school, region of the country, religious community, profession, or other social group, the general process of becoming socialized into that community is accomplished largely through linguistic interactions and is often accompanied by the learning of new words or usages. Conversely, as people gradually become competent members of a new community, their relationship to both written and spoken language often changes. The process does not always involve successful adaptation, however, as Stanton Wortham (2005) has shown in the case of a ninth grader who starts the school year being seen as a student who can use academic discourse skillfully to one who disrupts class and fails to participate in suitable ways by the end of the year. Such "trajectories of socialization" can reveal the complex processes involved in learning to speak and behave appropriately in new settings and demonstrate the need to look at multiple linguistic and social interactions across various timescales (Wortham 2005:110).

In her research on the socialization of Hasidic Jewish girls and women, Ayala Fader (2007, 2009) demonstrates the thoroughly interwoven nature of linguistic, cultural, and religious practices in the Brooklyn neighborhood of Boro Park. In this community, during the time of Fader's research in the 1990s, men and women had complementary roles and responsibilities for reproducing Hasidic life. While men were supposed to focus on prayer and the study of Jewish texts, women were supposed to protect men from the "polluting effects" of Gentile society (Fader 2007:2). Women therefore often had more interactions with Gentiles and non-Hasidic Jews, and as a result they came to speak better English than the men. Over the course of a marriage, however, once several children had been born, the men would often go out to work while their wives stayed home – a shift that resulted in changing linguistic competencies over a lifetime. Even though boys and girls were equally bilingual in Hasidic varieties of English and Yiddish in their early years, therefore – and even though their parents would have preferred them to stay that way – much as the Gapun parents were unable to dictate the outcome of their children's levels of fluency, so, too, were the Hasidic parents unsuccessful at ensuring that all their children remained equally bilingual. For the many social, educational, and religious reasons that Fader details, by the first grade Hasidic girls and boys started to have different levels of proficiency in English and Yiddish, with girls speaking Hasidic English and boys speaking Hasidic Yiddish (Fader 2009:21).

Paying close attention to embodied forms of identity-making, such as hairstyles, clothing, and deportment, and integrating the language socialization approach with the theories of Foucault regarding morality, ethics, and the "techniques of the self," Fader shows how Hasidic girls learn to become modest Hasidic women. Explicit verbal and nonverbal instructions on the part of parents or teachers in the form of praising or shaming play a part in this socialization, but children and adolescents themselves are active agents in the process as well. Just before they get married, young women are explicitly taught new linguistic and bodily practices in "bride class," but even before then they learn about and usually internalize community norms regarding appropriately modest dress and behavior for Hasidic women. "Everyday talk about matchmaking, engagement, and marriage is an important way that girls on the brink of adulthood (ages eighteen to twenty-one) learn to become modest Hasidic wives, ultimately responsible for bringing up the next generation of believers" (Fader 2009:179).

In a very different context, Elizabeth Mertz (2007a) argues that law schools teach students to "think like lawyers" largely by socializing them into new ways of relating to written texts and new ways of using argumentative speech. Mertz tape-recorded the first-year Contracts course at eight different law schools around the United States to identify the similarities and differences across these institutions in their approaches to legal education. Despite the many differences, Mertz found that the eight schools shared a distinctive approach to teaching students how to decipher the conflicts at the heart of legal texts. In all eight schools, students learned to put aside all "irrelevant" details in the case, such as the social or historical setting, emotional issues, and even morality or justice, and focus instead on what gives the texts legal authority – that is, the previous cases and other legal texts that a court can cite as authorities in deciding the case at hand, and the procedural lineage of the case through various lower courts (Mertz 2007a:94). Thus, law school students learn to relate in a very different way to written texts.

This new relationship to written texts is accomplished largely through classroom interactions that to a greater or lesser extent follow the Socratic method, often considered "the signal approach to law school pedagogy" in which professors impart information not through lectures or explanations but through "an ongoing stream of questions designed to challenge unquestioned assumptions and reveal underlying legal principles" (Mertz 2007a:26). Through this form of argumentative exchange, professors model for students the assumption underlying the legal system in the United States: that legal truth emerges through argumentative dialogue (Mertz 2007a:108). Just as in many societies young children are socialized through linguistic routines that engage them in formulaic responses with or without explicit instruction, so, too does the discourse in law school classrooms involve formulaic exchanges involving authoritative socializing such as the following (Mertz 2007a:125):[4]

Prof.:	Let's put it slightly differently. Is the party making the promise, "if I buy the land, I'll sell it to you," surrendering any legal right?
Student:	No.
Prof.:	What do you mean, "no"? Try "yes."
Class:	[[laughter]] (.02)
Prof.:	Say (.) "yes."
Student:	Yes.
Prof.:	Why?
Class:	[[laughter]]

In addition to these sorts of authoritative exchanges, interactions between professors and students in law schools also often involve reported speech (as can be seen in the example just given) and shifts in positions and roles. In Goffman's (1981) terms, students are frequently required to be the animators (the voice boxes) of stances or opinions for which they are not the authors (the composers) or the principals (the ones whose opinions are expressed). This sort of variable position-taking within argumentative classroom debates, Mertz claims, privileges language structure over content, and inculcates in students an ability to shift discursive positions rather than maintain fixed moral or emotional anchors. "Competence in this dialogic discourse form becomes a measure of one's ability to be and think like a lawyer" (Mertz 2007a:127).

The end result of immersion in law school linguistic interactions, Mertz maintains, is a profound transformation in students' senses of justice, morality, and themselves:

> If students entering the medical profession must endure a breaking down of everyday beliefs about the body, physicality, and death, students entering the legal profession undergo a linguistic rupture, a change in how they view and use language. This transition is, of course, itself signaled and performed through language, the language of the law school classroom. As in other forms of language socialization, new conceptions of morality and personhood are subtly intertwined with this shift to new uses of language. (2007a:22)

Thus, through the lens of language socialization, the transformation of a student into a professional like a lawyer can be illuminated in interesting and helpful ways.

Another example of the usefulness of a language socialization approach for understanding complex sociocultural transitions that occur in adulthood is Lanita Jacobs-Huey's (2006) research on the professionalization processes that African American hair stylists undergo. By attending many workshops and seminars, conducting participant observation at hair salons, and capturing many of the interactions in these settings on tape, Jacobs-Huey was able to identify several important ways in which cosmetologists were encouraged to demonstrate their expertise through language.

For example, in many of the seminars for African American hair care specialists that Jacobs-Huey attended, leaders urged participants to consider themselves "hair doctors" and to use specialized discourse that sounded scientific. In order to set themselves apart from their customers, many of whom had a great deal of experience styling their own or others' hair, the stylists were told to employ professional-sounding terms such as "silken" instead of "press" (Jacobs-Huey 2006:40). These seminars thus instructed stylists not only in specific hair care techniques but also in how to think of themselves as professionals and how to convey their professional expertise to their customers through their language use. Participants therefore became socialized into a particular professional identity as they learned specialized terminology. The same process can be seen in many other educational and professional arenas; doctors, lawyers, police officers, teachers, and college students (among many others) all learn how to enact their professional or social roles at the same time that they are learning specialized linguistic practices associated with those roles.

Conclusion

In this chapter, we learned about the diversity across cultures in the ways that parents interact with their young children as they are learning to speak. Studies by researchers such as Ochs (1988), Schieffelin (1990), and Kulick (1992) demonstrate that baby talk is not at all universal. What *is* universal is the ability of all children to become fluent in their native language(s). The cultural values, language ideologies, and social practices of a particular community cannot (barring severe abuse, of course) prevent children from learning to speak, but those values, ideologies, and practices can indeed influence important aspects of the language acquisition process, such as the order in which certain grammatical structures are learned, or even whether a particular language is acquired at all (as we saw with Taiap).

We also learned in this chapter that the language socialization process does not end with childhood. Even adults who never learn a second language nevertheless continue to learn new ways of using language in different social contexts as they go through life. Taking on new social roles, as happens after joining a sorority or fraternity, becoming a parent, or acquiring a new profession, will almost always be accompanied by – and at least partially accomplished through – the learning of new ways of speaking.

In sum, the field of language acquisition and socialization research sheds helpful light on how children learn their first languages as well as on how adults navigate their way among various social groups throughout their lives.

4
Language, Thought, and Culture

> Which was first: the language patterns or the cultural norms? In main they have grown up together, constantly influencing each other. But in this partnership the nature of the language is the factor that limits free plasticity and rigidifies channels of development in the more autocratic way.
>
> Whorf 1956[1941]:156

Imagine that you were raised speaking a different language. Would you perceive the world differently? Would your thought patterns be different? Would you categorize objects, experiences, or ideas differently?

Now imagine that you were raised without any language at all. Would your lack of language prevent you from thinking at all? Would you be able to reason in complex ways or participate meaningfully in cultural activities?

These questions have been debated across many disciplines and societies for hundreds, if not thousands, of years. The current consensus among linguistic anthropologists is that a mutually influential relationship exists among language, thought, and culture, but many linguistic anthropologists echo Whorf's assessment above that language shapes culture and thought more significantly than people realize. Although the exact nature of that relationship has yet to be established, most linguistic anthropologists working in this area maintain that the influence of language on culture and thought is more likely to be *predispositional* rather than *determinative* – in other words, the particular language you speak might predispose you to view the world a certain way, but it will not prevent you from challenging that view. Many linguistic anthropologists also prefer to speak of linguistic or semiotic "mediation" of the social order, positing that sociocultural practices, norms, and relationships are all mediated by signs of one sort or another – not just by language (written or spoken), but also by images, gestures, or actions, and by messages conveyed by certain material goods such as an expensive watch, the "right" pair of shoes, or an office full of books (Lee 1997; Mertz 2007b).[1] This view builds upon the work of Charles Sanders Peirce, introduced in chapter 1, and presents a theory of meaning-making that integrates all forms of language, thought, and culture. In addition to, or instead of, Peirce many contemporary linguistic anthropologists trace the history of research in this area back to the early twentieth century to what has come to be called "linguistic relativity" or "the Sapir–Whorf Hypothesis."[2] While the intellectual roots of this debate go back much further to European thinkers such as Johann Gottfried von Herder and Alexander von Humboldt, and even further back to Greek and Roman scholars, for our purposes, the most relevant background to contemporary debates on the ways in which language, thought, and culture all influence one another begins with Franz Boas, his student Edward Sapir, and, in turn, his student Benjamin Whorf.

A Hundred Years of Linguistic Relativity

Franz Boas (1858–1942) is often considered the father of anthropology in the United States. An important part of Boas's research agenda involved disproving racist assertions about the existence of so-called "primitive" languages, races, and cultures. At the turn of the twentieth century, when Boas was writing, some scholars were arguing that people in certain societies were incapable of complex, abstract, "scientific" thought because of the seeming lack of "logical" grammatical categories in their languages. Boas, who was keen on demonstrating the essential equality and humanity of all people despite their tremendous linguistic and cultural diversity, disputed this interpretation, proposing instead that all linguistic and cultural practices were equally complex and logical. The particular language spoken by a group of people merely tended to reflect their habitual cultural practices, Boas maintained. Language might facilitate certain types of thinking and could provide a valuable way of understanding unconscious patterns of culture and thought, Boas declared, but it would not prevent people from thinking in a way that differed from the categories presented most conveniently in their language.

Boas's student Edward Sapir (1884–1939) built upon Boas's research in this area but also departed from the views of his professor in several crucial respects. Unlike Boas, who, for the most part, considered the influence of language on thought to be "of minor importance only," Sapir believed that grammatical categories, while derived initially from experience, subsequently become part of intricate linguistic systems, resulting in the "tyrannical hold that linguistic form has upon our orientation in the world" (Sapir 1964[1931]:128, cited in Lucy 1992:20). In Sapir's best-known writings, he posited a strong influence of language on thought: "We see and hear and otherwise experience very largely as we do because the language habits of our community predispose certain choices of interpretation" (Sapir 1949[1929]:162). At the same time, however, Sapir emphasized that all forms of linguistic expression could be reduced to a common underlying human psychology, and in many of his writings he emphasized that every language is so constructed "that no matter what any speaker of it may desire to communicate … the language is prepared to do his work" (1949[1924]:153).

Benjamin Lee Whorf (1897–1941), a student of Sapir's, developed the insights of his two predecessors further, elaborating on "the relation of habitual thought and behavior to language" (as his most famous paper is entitled) and using Sapir's term "linguistic relativity" to link his work to Einstein's recently developed theory of relativity in the field of physics. So well known (though often terribly misunderstood) are Whorf's ideas on this topic that contemporary scholars in many different fields often label influences of language on thought as "Whorfian effects." Like his professor Sapir, Whorf viewed language as a system of interrelated categories, some of which were less obvious to speakers (and therefore more likely to influence their thought) than others. The sum total of a language's categories produces an overall worldview in people who speak that language, Whorf suggested.

Whorf's most famous case study involved a comparison between the Native American language of Hopi and "Standard Average

European" (SAE) languages such as English in the ways that time and matter are categorized. In this study, Whorf pointed out that grammatical categories such as plurals and verb tenses differ dramatically in Hopi and SAE. SAE languages tend to objectify and spatialize non-spatial qualities. For example, in English it is common to talk about units of time as if they could be isolated and counted ("seven days in a week," "three months ago"). In Hopi, Whorf maintained, there is a non-objectifying, cyclical way of talking about time as an undifferentiated entity. Instead of talking about discrete units of time, the Hopi language uses more process-oriented ways of talking – what Whorf said might be better termed "eventing" (1956[1941]:147). The overall patterns of these linguistic differences lead, Whorf argued, to dramatic differences in the habitual cultural behavior of speakers of these two types of languages. Among the Hopi, according to Whorf, the linguistic categories emphasizing process and continuity have led to cultural values that stress preparation, endurance, and intensity, among other things. Conversely, among speakers of SAE languages, Whorf maintained, the linguistic tendency to split time into quantifiable substances has led to a culture that values record-keeping, accounting, schedules, and historical sequencing.

Although many of Whorf's broad claims about Hopi language and culture have been challenged,[3] linguistic anthropologists have generally accepted his assertion that the grammatical categories of a particular language have the potential to affect thought processes and cultural practices. Contemporary research investigating specific Whorfian effects will be reviewed below.

As focused on linguistic effects as Whorf was, he was by no means hostile to the existence of certain linguistic, cognitive, and cultural universals. As an anthropologist who was against the evolutionary ranking of societies and races, Whorf, like Boas and Sapir, was adamantly opposed to researchers who considered Western linguistic, cognitive, or cultural categories to be superior to all others. At a fundamental level, all three of these early scholars believed that all human beings share certain commonalities – but they cautioned that these commonalities should not be assumed to be discernible from the study of Western practices alone because of the remarkable diversity across languages and cultures (Lucy 1992:35–36). All too often, they warned, the imposition of Western linguistic and cultural categories lead researchers to "find" cross-linguistic and cross-cultural universals when a closer look might reveal differences. This is the position of most linguistic anthropologists today – most fully accept the existence of both diversity and universality across languages and cultures, with the caveat that any proposed universals must be shown to be truly universal and not just the result of inappropriate generalizations stemming from Western cultural or linguistic categories (cf. Evans and Levinson 2009).

As accepted as the ideas of Boas, Sapir, and Whorf have become within linguistic anthropology, many misconceptions about their work remain among scholars who are outside of the discipline. Foremost among these are misunderstandings about the so-called "Sapir–Whorf Hypothesis," to which we now turn.

The Sapir–Whorf Hypothesis

Many researchers, especially those outside of anthropology in fields such as cognitive science, psychology, or linguistics, have used the term "Sapir–Whorf Hypothesis" as shorthand for a simplistic and easily dismissible "strong" version of Sapir and Whorf's beliefs, which purportedly (and mistakenly) states that language *determines* thought. In this view, the particular language you speak rigidly structures your thought in an inescapable manner. The causal arrow for this obviously wrong "strong" version of the so-called Sapir–Whorf Hypothesis runs in just one direction between language and thought, and culture is nowhere in the picture (see Figure 4.1).

While Boas, Sapir, and Whorf all wrote about language's relationship to thought and culture, and while they were clearly influenced by one another, what has come to be called the "Sapir–Whorf Hypothesis" is a misnomer in several respects. First, Sapir and Whorf never co-authored anything – and certainly nothing labeled a "hypothesis." Whorf was deeply influenced by his professor Sapir, but the two scholars' views on

Figure 4.1 Relationship between language and thought according to the (mistaken) "strong" version of the Sapir–Whorf Hypothesis.

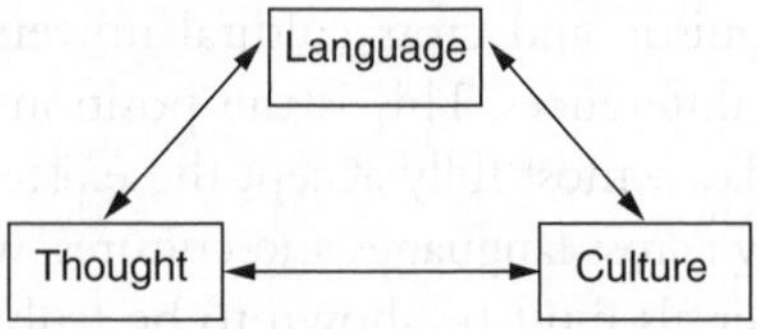

Figure 4.2 Relationship among language, thought, and culture according to contemporary understandings of the Sapir–Whorf Hypothesis within linguistic anthropology.

language, thought, and culture diverged significantly. Second, although some highly respected scholars such as John Lucy have taken on the task of formulating specific, empirically testable hypotheses stemming from the insights of Boas, Sapir, and Whorf, these scholars themselves never framed their research using these terms from the realm of science. All three had conducted fieldwork and had committed themselves to learning many Native American languages, but none ever couched what he was doing in terms of hypothesis testing.

A more accurate depiction of the view of many linguistic anthropologists can be seen in Figure 4.2, in which language, thought, and culture all influence one another.

In this model, the particular language you speak may predispose you to think a certain way or to engage in certain cultural practices or beliefs, but this relationship is by no means a rigidly deterministic one, nor is it unidirectional. Instead, language, thought, and culture are all viewed as influencing one another in a flexible, mutually constitutive way. The relative strengths of the relationships – the thickness of the arrows in Figure 4.2, if the level of influence were depicted that way on the diagram – remain unspecified and perhaps unknowable. It is possible that the relative strength of the influence of language on thought and culture is more in some cases than in others, making it an empirical question to investigate, but it is also possible that the relative strength of the influence of these three overlapping entities could never be specified with any precision.

Some linguistic anthropologists (e.g., Hill and Mannheim 1992) maintain that this sort of multidirectional relationship is best conceived of as an axiom – an assumption that informs all research on language in social contexts – rather than as an empirically testable hypothesis with dependent and independent variables. Supporters of the axiom view argue that there is no clear-cut way to distinguish that which is linguistic from that which is nonlinguistic. Everything is linguistically mediated, they contend, so it is impossible to separate something called "language" from the two allegedly nonlinguistic entities called "thought" and "culture." As with other working assumptions, Hill and Mannheim assert, treating this relationship as axiomatic means that it is not falsifiable but instead is to be judged only "on the basis of the extent to which it leads to productive questions about talk and social action" (1992:386). Researchers who endorse this approach to the relationship of language to thought and culture strongly maintain that the social world is largely constituted by, and knowable through, language, much as Sapir famously argued more than 80 years ago:

> The fact of the matter is that the 'real world' is to a large extent unconsciously built up on the language habits of the group. No two languages are ever sufficiently similar to be considered as representing the same social reality. The worlds in which different societies live are distinct worlds, not merely the same world with different labels attached. (1949[1929]:162)

While this axiomatic view is quite common within the discipline, leading many linguistic anthropologists to maintain that the exact nature of the influence that language, thought, and culture have on one another can never be known, other linguistic anthropologists support more narrowly focused research on the effects of specific, more easily identified aspects or categories of language on precise areas, categories, or modes of thought or culture. Scholars who take this approach do formulate hypotheses. Such research has enjoyed a renaissance over the past two decades as investigators in fields such as linguistic anthropology, psychology, linguistics, and cognitive science have abandoned their prejudices against work that examines how language, thought, and culture are interrelated. The next section describes some of this fascinating research.

Investigating the Effects of Language on Thought

Scholars who have sought to operationalize the Sapir–Whorf Hypothesis have done so by focusing on the effects of language on particular aspects of thought (cognition). For most of these researchers, especially those in fields such as psychology or cognitive science, culture tends to drop out of the equation. Some scholars criticize this limitation and also object to the experimental methods preferred by these researchers because they assume the ability to distinguish linguistic and nonlinguistic forms of cognition. In addition, experimental contexts always differ by definition from "naturally occurring" contexts – though of course both experimental and non-experimental contexts are social and cultural in nature. Nevertheless, despite these criticisms, the research emerging from many different fields over the past two decades points to unmistakable evidence that language can indeed influence thought.

Now, where might we start in searching for such Whorfian effects? Noted linguistic relativity expert John Lucy (1996) suggests three broad areas, each of which he believes should be investigated carefully:

- *Language-in-general.* Research of this type explores at the broadest level how having any language at all might influence thinking. Such studies ask how the cognitive processes of humans who know at least one language might differ from animals or from humans who have never learned a language.
- *Linguistic structures.* Research at this more specific level considers how some specific structures within a particular language, such as grammatical categories, might influence thinking or behavior.
- *Language use.* Investigations of this sort look at the ways that particular habits of speaking (also called discursive practices) can influence thought and interpretation. In other words, the question is whether patterns of language *use* rather than language *structure* can have an impact on cognition – either directly, or by virtue of indirectly reinforcing or reconfiguring any effects caused by linguistic structures (Lucy 1996:52).

The following sections summarize some of the research in each of these areas, reviewing in turn how language-in-general, linguistic structure, and language use might influence thought or behavior.

Language-in-General

Many researchers inside and outside of linguistic anthropology maintain that knowing any one of the world's 7,000 or so languages will lead to identifiable cognitive effects because all human languages make use of conventional symbols (in the Peircean sense described in chapter 1) and complex grammatical structures. While animals such as birds, chimpanzees, whales, and vervet monkeys have highly developed signaling mechanisms, to our knowledge no nonhuman animal communicates by means of a system anywhere near as complex as any human language. Animals that have a signaling system of some sort appear to focus for the most part on the here-and-now; they are unable, it seems, to express abstract concepts or complex relationships of the sort that human toddlers regularly understand and express.

But how can the specific effects of language-in-general on thought be studied? Some clues can be gleaned from two types of research on animals: studies of animal signals in the wild, and studies of attempts to teach animals some form of symbolic communication in captivity. In the wild, for example, vervet monkeys have different alarm calls, depending on whether the potential predator is an eagle, a leopard, or a snake (Seyfarth and Cheney 1997). Vervets who hear these specific calls take appropriate evasive action according to the type of predator warning they hear, so clearly they have the ability to interpret conventional symbols such as these alarm calls. There is also some evidence that they use calls at times to deceive other monkeys in order to obtain food or some other resource. Nevertheless, vervets do not appear to understand cause-and-effect relationships fully, as demonstrated by the fact that they do not interpret the presence of a gazelle carcass in a tree as evidence of the presence of a leopard, or the presence of python tracks as evidence that a python might be nearby (Cheney and Seyfarth 1990; Kuczaj and Hendry 2003). Other types of nonhuman primates, such as lemurs, diana monkeys, and baboons, also seem to have semantic calls and/or other forms of complex social cognition (Zuberbühler 2000; Cheney and Seyfarth 2007).

In captivity, several different kinds of animals (such as dolphins, gorillas, chimpanzees, and gray parrots) have been introduced to symbol systems, usually gestures or labels representing simple objects and actions. Learning such a system, especially when the learning is accomplished in a socially enmeshed, enculturated way rather than as a rote process of one-on-one training, appears to enhance some animals' abilities to categorize, produce analogies, process information, anticipate events, and understand complex situations (Kuczaj and Hendry 2003:260–264). In other words, even though the kinds of symbol systems learned by now-famous animals such as Koko the gorilla are extremely basic and quite far from human languages, animals' cognitive processes do seem to be enhanced by their mastery of some simple linguistic forms. Nevertheless, the linguistic accomplishments of even the most thoroughly trained animals do not begin to approach those of humans. "The admittedly scanty evidence assembled to date suggests that the communication of nonhuman animals lacks three features that are abundantly present in the earliest words of young children: a rudimentary theory of mind, the ability to generate new words, and syntax," primatologists Dorothy Cheney and Robert Seyfarth (1998:198) conclude.

Another possible way of researching the influence of language-in-general on thought is studying children who have not yet learned a language. Clearly, it would be highly unethical to deprive a child of access to a language; furthermore, studies of abused children who have not been exposed to any language involve so many complicating factors that the causes of cognitive differences are impossible to ascertain. Researchers interested in the effects of language-in-general on human thought have therefore turned to subjects such as very young, prelinguistic infants, or deaf children who are raised in normal circumstances but who have been deprived of early exposure to language because they have hearing parents who do not use sign language. In the case of infants, as noted in chapter 3, the language socialization process begins from day one (if not before), so it is impossible to study a truly "prelinguistic" infant. Nevertheless, some insights can be gleaned from observing extremely young children. It is well known, for instance, that all human babies are born equally capable of recognizing and eventually producing all the sounds used in all human languages – and yet by six months of age they begin to lose this flexible ability as they start to learn the specific sounds of their native language(s). Eventually, as adults, they will be incapable of hearing or producing many contrasts between sounds used in other languages besides their own without prolonged training (and perhaps not even then). Native English speakers will have great difficulty distinguishing among the four different "t" sounds in Nepali, for example, and native Nepali speakers will have similar difficulty distinguishing between "s" and "sh" sounds in English. It is evident, therefore, that exposure to any human language begins to change children's mental representations of the acoustic material they hear at a very early age. Some researchers, however, argue that these changes in a person's ability to hear such phonemic contrasts only occurs when the brain is operating in a "linguistic mode" (decoding speech) rather than in a more general sound-analysis mode because in experiments testing adults' abilities to distinguish between such sounds, they were able to do so if the sounds were presented very close together, or if the sounds were from languages very different from their own (Munnich and Landau 2003:123–124). Still, even if this is the case, the particular language you speak clearly has an effect on your ability to hear and produce sounds in natural speech contexts, and most researchers would therefore consider this a case of language's influence on cognition.

Deaf children of hearing parents comprise another group of people whom researchers have studied to obtain a clearer understanding of the possible effects of language-in-general on human thought (Villiers and Villiers 2000, 2003; Figueras-Costa and Harris 2001; Peterson and Siegal 2000). These deaf children's parents choose not to expose their children to sign language but instead encourage their children to read lips. Because of this, these children generally have significant language delays but have normal intelligence and are socially active. There is one area of cognitive development, however, known as "theory of mind," that is delayed up to several years in these children, possibly as a result of their much later acquisition of complex grammatical structures. Theory of mind is the "everyday ability to attribute mental states to other people and thereby to interpret, explain, and predict their behavior" (Leslie 2001:15652–15653) – the ability, in other words, to ascertain others' intentions, beliefs, and desires. According to child psychologists, normal children generally develop this ability somewhere around the age of four, depending on which aspect of theory of mind is tested, and how the test is conducted. Deaf children who learn sign language from birth develop theory of mind at the same age as their non-deaf peers. Deaf children whose parents do not sign to them, however, are significantly delayed in developing theory of mind.

One of the most commonly conducted experiments in theory-of-mind research involves a false-belief task of the following sort: a child is shown two dolls or puppets, who are labeled "Sally" and "Anne." The experimenter acts out a skit for the child, in which

Sally places a marble in a basket, then leaves the room. While Sally is gone, Anne moves the marble from the basket to a box. Then Sally returns to the room, and the child is asked (using varying verbal phrases or even a nonverbal prompt) where Sally will look for the marble. Sally did not see Anne move the marble, so the child should state that Sally will look for it in its original location, the basket. Most children under four years of age, however, will say that Sally will look for the marble in the box, even though the skit makes it clear that Sally did not see Anne move the marble from the basket to the box. The conclusion child psychologists draw from this set of experiments is that children who have not yet developed theory of mind abilities cannot yet fully separate their own beliefs and intentions from those of others.

The central question for our purposes here is whether the development of language (presumably any language, although the cross-linguistic research on this topic is extremely thin) facilitates or perhaps is even a prerequisite for the development of a mature theory of mind. Is it necessary, in other words, for a child to be able to talk about others' false beliefs using phrases such as, "Sally thought that the marble was still in the basket because she didn't see Anne move it to the box," in order to succeed in false-belief experiments? Since a great deal of research shows that the development of complex syntax in phrases such as "Sally thought that ..." occurs at roughly the same age in normal children as a mature theory of mind, it is quite challenging to tease out the cause-and-effect relationship here (if there is one) between language and thought. In a fascinating set of experiments, however, Jill and Peter de Villiers present compelling evidence showing that deaf children of hearing parents who do not use any form of sign language are delayed up to several *years* in being able to pass even the simplest nonverbal versions of false-belief tasks (Villiers and Villiers 2003:344–345). Villiers and Villiers compare this group of deaf children with two other groups of deaf children: those who have hearing parents who use some form of sign language, and those who have deaf parents who have introduced sign language to their children from birth (and who therefore have no language delay at all). In each case, the children's language ability, especially the ability to form complements ("Sally thought that ...), correlates with their ability to succeed in false-belief tasks.

Correlation does not entail causation, however. Language development might be causing the emergence of theory of mind in children, but the reverse could also be the case – cognitive development in the form of theory of mind might be enhancing linguistic abilities. Or, alternatively, both linguistic and cognitive development might be the result of some third factor, such as the general overall development of the brain. The jury is still out on these issues, but some preliminary research has shown that three-year-olds' levels of language development were predictive of their later performance on false-belief tasks at age four, but the reverse was not the case; their early performance on false-belief tasks did not predict their later levels of language development (Astington and Jenkins 1999:1318). While alternative interpretations are still possible, these researchers argue that their data can best be understood as demonstrating that theory of mind depends on language: "In our view, it is not just that children need language skills to display their theory of mind in false-belief tasks. Language plays a fundamental role in theory-of-mind development" (Astington and Jenkins 1999:1319; cf. Schick et al. 2007).

Much research remains to be conducted before a definitive understanding of the potential effects of language-in-general on various dimensions of thought can be obtained. It may even turn out to be the case that there is no such general effect, since no one actually learns "language-in-general" but instead learns one (or more) particular language. In this regard, additional research is needed to explore the timing of theory of mind development in children who speak languages other than English. There are some studies of Baka- and Japanese-speaking children, among others, indicating that they are able to pass the standard false-belief tasks at the same age as English-speaking children, but other children, such as those who speak Junin Quechua, seem not to be able to pass the classic false-belief tasks until much later, perhaps because of the specific grammatical structures of Junin Quechua or a very different cultural context (Villiers and Villiers 2003:372–373). Many linguistic anthropologists question whether standard experiments devised in the United States can be exported, either in their original form or in "culturally appropriate" versions, to be used with children (or even adults) from very different linguistic and cultural backgrounds. At the very least, what little research there is of this sort must be closely scrutinized for cultural and linguistic bias.

Discussion of the effects of the grammar on various aspects of thought brings us to the second area: how specific linguistic structures might affect cognitive processes.

Linguistic Structures

This area of inquiry looks at some classic Whorfian questions regarding the influence of the particular language you speak on how you think about or perceive the world. Researchers in this field investigate the effects of specific linguistic forms in a given language on the thought processes of speakers of that language. What parts of a language might have the greatest potential to influence thought? Before searching for these, it is important to rule out one area that researchers believe *does not* have much influence on thought – the existence, or lack thereof, of a particular word in a given language. No linguistic anthropologist believes that the lack of a single word for a concept in a particular language prevents someone from being able to think of that concept. This sort of idea is far too simplistic and too easily disproved. Look at the following three words in Nepali, for example:

dhān – unhusked rice that is still in the fields
chāmal – harvested but still uncooked rice
bhāt – cooked rice.

English does not have a single word for any of these concepts, instead collapsing them all within the general concept of "rice," modified by various phrases. Does this mean that English speakers cannot conceptualize *dhān*, for example? Of course not. There will always be culturally specific connotations and challenges to any translation of words from one language to another, but the crudely deterministic belief that one cannot conceptualize that for which there is no specific word in one's language is clearly without merit.

A related, equally mistaken view concerns the allegedly numerous "Eskimo words for snow." As Laura Martin (1986) has persuasively demonstrated in her debunking of this myth, imprecise citations by scholars, combined with offhand references in the popular press, have led to wide-ranging estimates of the number of snow terms (from 4 to 400+) in "Eskimo" languages. "Eskimo," which is considered a

We have 90 words for snow. And 943 words for sex.

Figure 4.3 Another of the many representations in popular culture of the "Eskimo words for snow" myth.
Source: www.CartoonStock.com

derogatory label by many Arctic people, is also an inexact term, as it comprises a number of different languages and dialects,[4] including Yupik and Inuit-Inupiak. Martin notes that in all of these languages and dialects there are at most two different roots for "snow," one referring to snow that is on the ground and the other referring to snow that is in the air. (Note that it is fairly simple to make this distinction in English.) All of the other allegedly different words for snow in "Eskimo" are modifications of these roots, much as we might do in English with words and phrases such as "snow shower" or "snowman." Even if the fascination with "Eskimo" words for snow is interpreted in the most favorable light, the elaboration of words in a certain part of a language's vocabulary demonstrates nothing about the thought processes of speakers of that language. At best, it points to an area of cultural practice that is important enough to people that specialized vocabulary has been developed, much as is the case for golfers, doctors, or chefs in our society.[5]

If the existence (or lack thereof) of individual words in a given language is not a fruitful area for research on the effects of language on thought, where else might we look? Researchers have generally focused on one of the following two areas:

- *Semantic domains*. These are groupings of words that have some core meaning in common, with differences in particular details (Bonvillain 2000:53). Examples of semantic domains include kinship terms (mother, father, sister, brother, cousin, etc.), color terms (red, orange, yellow, etc.), or body-part words (head, shoulders, knees, toes, etc.). These words are often learned in reference to one another by children, and as such they tend to delineate specific domains of experience, perception, or meaning. Some researchers believe that these semantic domains can shape categories of thought in measurable ways. The risk, however, is that the identification of a semantic domain by a researcher might (ironically enough) be influenced by the researcher's own linguistic categories, resulting in the study of something that might constitute a semantic domain in the researcher's own language but not in the language of the people being studied. Lucy and Gaskins (2003:467) argue that this is what has happened with the cross-linguistic study of color terms, a research topic that will be discussed further below.
- *Grammatical categories*. These are the grammatical structures of a given language that must be used in order for sentences in that language to be well formed. Examples include pronouns, verb tenses, and plurals. Ever since Whorf, scholars have looked closely at grammatical categories for potential influences on thought because they are *habitual* (i.e., they must be used frequently), *obligatory* (i.e., speakers cannot opt out of using them if they want to speak the language correctly), and for the most part *unconscious* (i.e., speakers are rarely aware of the grammatical structures of their own language).

Table 4.1 English pronouns in the nominative case.

	Singular		Plural
1st Person	I		we
2nd Person	you		you
3rd Person	Animate masculine:	he	they
	Animate feminine:	she	
	Inanimate:	it	

In both of these areas (semantic domains and grammatical categories) there is far more linguistic diversity across the roughly 7,000 languages of the world than is generally appreciated (Evans and Levinson 2009). A tiny taste of this diversity will enable readers to appreciate more fully the many different ways that speakers of various languages express particular contrasts in their physical or social worlds in their grammar, while leaving other contrasts unspecified grammatically. Consider the case of pronouns in English, as presented in Table 4.1.

Notice that contemporary standard English pronouns do not have different forms for single and plural "you" (though many Southern US dialects use "y'all" for the plural form), and there is no longer any way of marking status through formal honorific forms, as there used to be when there was a choice between "ye/you" (formal) and "thou/thee" (informal).[6] In contrast, pronouns in many European languages do provide these contrasts, as is evident, for example, in Spanish with "Usted" ("you" formal) and "tu" ("you" informal), in French with "vous" ("you" formal) and "tu" ("you" informal), and in German with "Sie" ("you" formal) and "du" ("you" informal). The dialect of Nepali spoken in the village of Junigau has three (and in some variants, four) status levels in both second- and third-person pronouns, as can be seen in Table 4.2.

In Junigau, people whom you address and people to whom you refer are obligatorily divided into those of higher status than you, those of roughly equal status, and those (like children, animals, and wives) who are of lower status. Unlike in English or in the dialect of Nepali spoken in Kathmandu (the capital of Nepal), in the Nepali that is spoken in the village of Junigau there is no gender differentiation in pronoun use. In Nepali as in English, however,

Table 4.2 Nepali pronouns in the Junigau dialect.

	Singular		Plural	
1st Person	ma		hāmi(haru)	
2nd Person	high honorific:	tapāī	high honorific:	tapāiharu
	middle level:	timī	middle level:	timiharu
	lowest level:	tã	lowest level:	timiharu
3rd Person	high honorific:	wahā	high honorific:	wahāharu
	middle level:	u	middle level:	uniharu
	lowest level:	tyo	lowest level:	tiniharu

there is only one form for the first-person singular and plural pronouns ("I" and "we" in English). In contrast, some languages, such as Tamil, Quechua, and Vietnamese, differentiate between two different forms of "we," depending on whether the addressee is included (as in "you and I, and perhaps others") or excluded (as in "s/he and I, but not you"). Other languages, such as Sanskrit, have different plural forms for just two people (called "dual") and for more than two people (called "plural"). Hebrew has two different pronouns for "you" – one for female addressees and one for male addressees. Comanche, a Native American language, distinguishes between visible/not visible and near/far when referring to an object with a third-person pronoun. This means that there are four different forms of "it" in Comanche (Cipollone et al. 1998:150–151). All of these forms constitute obligatory grammatical categories in these languages; one cannot opt out of them. It is absolutely necessary, for example, to designate the relative social status of an addressee when speaking Nepali, and to indicate whether an object is visible or not when speaking Comanche. Pronouns across the world's languages therefore require speakers to take note of very different aspects of the physical and social world around them.

Noun classes are also extremely variable across different languages. Most readers will probably be familiar with gender classifications among nouns in European languages, such as masculine and feminine nouns in Spanish or French, and masculine, feminine, or neuter nouns in German. Less familiar to many English speakers, but nevertheless found in many of the world's languages, are categorizations of nouns that are more numerous, such as the four noun classes of Dyirbal, an endangered indigenous language of Australia, in which it is obligatory to choose the correct classifier from among the following before each noun (Lakoff 1987:93; Dixon 1982):

1 *Bayi*: (human) males; animals
2 *Balan*: (human) females; water; fire; fighting
3 *Balam*: nonflesh food
4 *Bala*: everything not in the other classes.

The Bantu languages of Africa have up to 22 different noun classes. Again, speakers are obliged to use the correct classifier as a prefix before each noun that they use. Consider the many noun classes in Swahili, as represented in Table 4.3.

Table 4.3 Noun classes in Swahili.[1]

Classes (with prefixes)	Typical meaning (though there are many exceptions)
m-, mw-, mu-	singular: persons
wa-, w-	plural: persons
m-, mw-, mu-	singular: plants
mi-, my-	plural: plants
ki-, ch-	singular: things
vi-, vy-	plural: things
n-, ny-, m-, 0-	singular: animals, things
n-, ny-, m-, 0-	plural: animals, things (can also be the plural of class 6)
ji-, j-, 0-	singular: fruits
ma-, m-	plural: fruits (can also be the plural of some other classes)
u-, w-, uw-	singular: no clear semantics
ku-	indefinite locative or directive meaning
mu-, m-	locative meaning: inside something
pa-	definite locative meaning: close to something
ku-, kw-	verbal nouns (gerunds)

[1] Adapted from Wilson (1970:240) and from http://on.wikipedia.org/wiki/Noun_class, accessed 2 August 2007. 0-means no prefixes.

Other categories across different languages also differ dramatically from those of English. Verb tenses and aspects vary enormously, as do the number and type of case markings. In some languages it is obligatory to indicate whether an assertion is made as a result of direct or indirect knowledge. This form of grammatical marking is known as evidentiality. In Eastern Pomo, a Native American language spoken in California, for example, there are four suffixes from which speakers must choose when reporting an event, depending on whether the person (1) has direct (probably visual) knowledge; (2) has direct non-visual sensory knowledge (such as feeling or hearing something); (3) is reporting what others say; or (4) is inferring from circumstantial evidence what must have happened. While it is certainly possible to indicate the source and reliability of the information one reports in English, in languages in which evidentiality is expressed obligatorily through grammatical categories speakers do not have a choice about doing so (Aikhenvald 2004).

Languages, in other words, are extremely variable and "force quite different sets of conceptual distinctions in almost every sentence: some languages express aspect, others don't; some have seven tenses, some have none; some force marking of visibility or honorific status of each noun phrase in a sentence, others don't; and so on and so forth" (Levinson 2003a:29). And yet, as Roman Jakobson noted, "Languages differ essentially in what they *must* convey and not in what they *may* convey" (cited in Deutscher 2010:151). Keeping in mind this flexibility and avoiding any presumptions of determinism, let us turn now to a review of some of the relevant research on which of the dramatically different sorts of things to which languages require their speakers to pay attention have been found to have an influence on thought.

Color

The semantic domain of color terms has been investigated for over 50 years, with researchers drawing conflicting conclusions regarding the universality vs. variability of color perception and terminology. In a famous study, Brent Berlin and Paul Kay studied the color terms in 20 languages and compared them to an additional 78 languages from the literature (Berlin and Kay 1969). They argued that their findings demonstrated cross-cultural and cross-linguistic universals in the realm of color, with the major color terms of all the languages clustering around 11 primary foci: black, white, red, green, yellow, blue, brown, purple, pink, orange, gray. They also posited an evolutionary sequence for the development of color terms in any language. If a language had only two color terms, Berlin and Kay argued, they would be the equivalent of black and white. A language with only three terms would have black, white, and red. Further semantic differentiation would proceed in the following order: green and yellow, then blue, then brown, and finally purple, pink, orange, and gray (Kay 1999:33).

In the ensuing decades, Berlin and Kay (as well as others) revised this theory significantly. In recent publications, Kay and his collaborators have constructed an alternative model that still involves the assumption of a universal set of primary color terms (black, white, red, yellow, green, and blue), and a predictable, step-wise process by which languages add color terms (Kay 2005; Kay and Maffi 1999). Nevertheless, Kay's most recent universalist theory acknowledges that not all languages even *have* a semantic domain for color – they do not "partition the perceptual color space" linguistically.[7] In recent years, Kay and other scholars who argue for semantic universals in color terminology have also acknowledged that linguistic variation can in fact influence the way colors are perceived (Kay and Kempton 1984; Regier et al. 2005).[8] In other words, the cross-linguistically varying boundaries of linguistic color categories can indeed affect color cognition.

Here is how this type of Whorfian effect can be demonstrated. An experiment is designed with one group of subjects speaking a language such as English that differentiates between "green" and "blue," and another group of subjects speaking a language such as Tarahumara (an Uto-Aztecan language spoken in northern Mexico) that has a single term (*siyo'name*) that covers all shades of both green and blue (Kay and Kempton 1984). The subjects are shown groups of three bluish-green/greenish-blue color chips at a time and are asked which of the three chips is "most different" from the other two. The results show that the existence in a person's language of specific color terms differentiating the blue-green area of the color spectrum will cause that person to perceive the boundary between the two colors in a starker way than does the person who does not have two different color terms for that area of the spectrum. Other experiments that test color labeling, sorting, differentiating, or memory also show that the presence or absence of specific color terms in one's language can have a measurable effect on various thought processes. For example, Winawer et al. (2007) found that the existence in Russian of two different commonly used terms for blue (*goluboy* for light blue, and *siniy* for dark blue) gave Russians an advantage over English speakers when they were given the task of discriminating between two closely related shades of blue.

While more research remains to be conducted to decipher the precise effects of color terminology in particular languages, it seems safe to say that the specific language you speak can indeed affect, at least for borderline cases, your perception of color – or at least your performance on experimental tasks designed to test your perception of color.

Space

Another domain of human experience that has been tested for Whorfian effects is space. One might expect that the physical environment would quite severely limit the range of linguistic variation in how languages express things like frame of reference or containment, but there are in fact considerable differences cross-linguistically in this regard. We will examine the research that has been conducted on two topics related to language and spatial cognition: (1) the work by Stephen Levinson on spatial frames of reference; and (2) the work of Melissa Bowerman, Soonja Choi, and colleagues on spatial categories in Korean and English.

Spatial frames of reference

The research of Steven Levinson[9] on absolute and relative spatial coordinate systems challenges some of the most taken-for-granted presuppositions that English speakers (especially those who are cognitive scientists) have about how people map out space in their minds and languages. Languages such as English that utilize a relative frame of reference for spatial mapping allow for phrases such as "to the left of the chair," "behind me," or "to Sita's right" when describing the location of objects. In contrast, languages that use an absolute frame of reference for spatial mapping do not allow for these kinds of phrases, instead requiring speakers to describe the location of objects in absolute terms according to compass directions (north, south, etc.) or another system of fixed bearings (uphill or downstream, for example, with reference to a specific hill or river). A language incorporating this sort of absolute frame of reference requires its speakers to maintain a constant awareness of their position, "to run a mental compass in the unconscious background, as it were" (Levinson 2003b:152), so that they are able to use absolute cardinal points to describe location or directionality whenever they need to. Levinson provides the following anecdotes, along with several others, in order to illustrate the implications of absolute spatial reckoning (2003b:4–5):

- Old Tulo, a poet and painter who speaks the indigenous Australian Aboriginal language of Guugu Yimithirr, interrupts Levinson at one point to warn him that there is a big army ant "just north of" Levinson's foot.
- Levinson hikes with Dan, another Guugu Yimithirr speaker, all day long to reach a set of caves with ancient paintings in them: "We are sitting in the cave entrance, and disoriented myself, I ask him to point back to base. He does so without hesitation, right through the hillside we are sitting on. I check with an accurate prismatic compass, and ask him for other locations. Checking later on maps, it turns out that he is spot on – absolutely dead accurate, as far as my compass can discriminate" (Levinson 2003b:5).
- Slus, a Mayan speaker of the language Tzeltal, has just arrived at a hotel in a distant, unfamiliar city. She approaches the sink and asks her husband, "Is the hot water in the uphill tap?" What does she mean by this? Levinson explains that she is asking whether the hot water is in the tap that would lie in the uphill (southerly) direction if she were at home.

Lest readers think that these sorts of languages are rare, only to be found, perhaps, in certain kinds of "exotic" environments, Levinson claims that in fact approximately a third of the world's 7,000 or so languages reckon directionality primarily in a fixed, absolute way (2003b:48). Some languages provide both types of systems for speakers, but the kinds of languages Levinson studied were those that required (rather than merely allowed for) the use of an absolute spatial framework.

What did Levinson find when he investigated the effects of having an absolute vs. relative system in one's language? He and his research

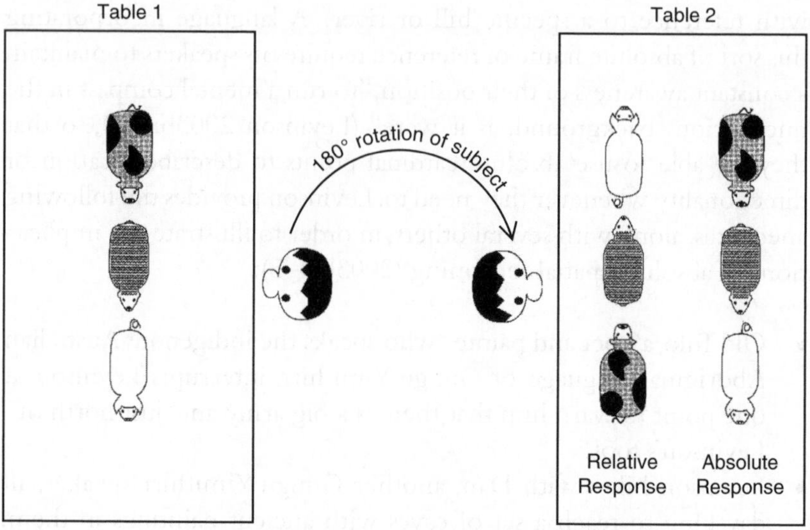

Figure 4.4 Set-up for experiment involving coordinate systems.
Source: From Levinson (2003b:156). Reprinted with the permission of Cambridge University Press.

associates conducted various experiments testing the spatial memory and reasoning abilities of speakers of Tzeltal, Guugu Yimithirr, and other languages. For example, subjects were presented with a line of model animals placed in a row on a table. After the animals were removed, the subjects were asked to replace the row of animals "exactly as it was," first on the original table, then on a different table that the subjects were facing from the opposite direction. The order in which each speaker placed the animals after rotation of the table depended on whether the speaker's language used an absolute or relative coordinate system (see Figure 4.4).

The findings of this experiment and others all indicate that an absolute or relative frame of reference in a given language influences speakers to perceive and act upon the spatial world in different ways.[10] Research with speakers of other languages with absolute frames of reference, such as Arrente from Australia, Hai//om[11] from Namibia, and Longgu from the Solomon Islands, confirm these findings (Evans 2010:167). In short, the specific language one speaks can indeed influence one's thought, at least in the conceptualization of space.

Spatial categories in Korean and English

Melissa Bowerman, Soonja Choi, and colleagues have conducted a series of experiments with Korean- and English-speaking infants, toddlers, and adults to determine whether the existence of very different ways of categorizing space linguistically in Korean and English affects how people perceive space.[12] The linguistic difference is as follows: in English, speakers differentiate between putting (or placing, stuffing, throwing, etc.) something *in* a container or enclosure of some kind and putting (or setting, spreading, etc.) something *on* a flat surface of some kind. In Korean, in contrast, the same semantic terrain is partitioned differently. The main opposition in Korean is not between the equivalent of *in* and *on* in English but between two verbs indicating tight fit (*kkita*) and loose fit (*nehta*). Three other Korean verbs further partition the semantic space of *in/on* in other ways: *nohta* is used to denote the placement of something on a horizontal surface; *ssuta* is used to describe the placement of a piece of clothing on one's head; and *pwuchita* is used when juxtaposing two surfaces, as when a magnet is placed on a refrigerator door (Bowerman and Choi 2003:394). All of these Korean words cross-cut the English *in/on* distinction and also extend to situations not covered by *in/on*. For example, English speakers would use *in* to describe putting an apple *in* a bowl and a cassette *in* its case, but Korean would use *nehta* for the former and *kkita* for the latter. Situations described by *in* in English may involve loose fit or tight fit as long as they also involve placing something inside an interior space. Situations described by *kkita* in Korean, in contrast, may involve insertion, covering, encirclement, or surface attachment, as long as they also involve a tight fit.

Through their experiments with infants and toddlers, Bowerman, Choi, and colleagues have discovered that language-related differences such as those listed in Table 4.4 were in place as early as 17–20 months (Bowerman and Choi 2003:395). Interestingly, much as all babies are born with the ability to hear all of the sound contrasts present in all of the world's languages, only to lose this flexibility later in life, young infants (9, 11, and 14 months) from both English- and Korean-speaking environments demonstrated through carefully tracked eye gazes an ability to distinguish between tight and loose fit as well as between *on*

Table 4.4 Spatial categorizing in English and Korean (Bowerman and Choi 2003:393–394).

Spatial situation	English	Korean
Put cup on table	on	nohta
Put hat on head	on	pwuchita
Put magnet on refrigerator	on	ssuta
Put ring on finger	on	kkita
Put top on pen	on	kkita
Put Lego on Lego stack	on	kkita
Button a button	–	kkita
Close a tightly latching drawer	–	kkita
Put cassette in case	in	kkita
Put book in case	in	kkita
Put piece in puzzle	in	kkita
Put apple in bowl	in	nehta
Put book in bag	in	nehta

and *in* relationships, regardless of their language environment. It appears that the ability to perceive these spatial contrasts is lost only later in life, as these researchers demonstrated in another experiment, in which Korean- and English-speaking adults were shown four figures depicting tight- and loose-fitting spatial relationships and were asked which figure differed from the other three. Korean-speaking adults were easily able to differentiate between tight and loose fit relationships most of the time, but the majority of English-speaking adults focused primarily on other properties of the objects in the figure (McDonough et al. 2003:249). The researchers therefore conclude that at some point in the language-learning process, English speakers lose the ability to easily perceive the tight- vs. loose-fit relationship because the distinction is not encoded in their linguistic categories. It is still possible, of course, for English speakers to make this distinction (as I have been making it here in this section), but the researchers' point is that nonlinguistic perception and categorization of spatial relationships, while probably universal to some degree in all human beings, are also probably deeply affected from an early age by language-specific categories (McDonough et al. 2003:251).

Shape vs. material composition

Aside from space, two other aspects of the physical world, an object's shape and its material composition, provide additional evidence that how we perceive and categorize things around us can be influenced by the particular language we speak. John Lucy's long-term, in-depth research begins with an observation that the two languages of English and Yucatec Maya (an indigenous language spoken in Mexico) differ in how they mark the plural in certain kinds of nouns.[13] In English, speakers must use the plural form for count nouns (e.g., cars, chairs, books), but using a plural form is optional for mass nouns (e.g., sugar, mud) – that is, it is possible to say "two pounds of sugar" or "seven mounds of mud," but often the noun is treated as an uncountable, malleable, non-discrete mass (e.g., "Sugar is sweet" or "Don't get stuck in the mud"). In Yucatec, all nouns are of this latter type, and plural marking is never obligatory, though speakers may opt to signal the plural if they wish to do so, much as with similar kinds of uncountable mass nouns in English.

How might this linguistic difference affect the thought of English and Yucatec speakers? Through numerous experiments with English and Yucatec speakers, Lucy and his collaborator, Suzanne Gaskins, have looked at whether treating nouns linguistically as uncountable masses leads speakers to focus more on the material composition of the item in question rather than its shape, since its boundaries are often malleable and indistinct. In one experiment, Lucy and Gaskins showed children and adults many groups of three objects familiar to all the speakers. All the objects were count nouns in English and mass nouns in Yucatec. Each triad of objects consisted of an original "pivot" object (such as a plastic comb with a handle) and then two "alternate" objects (such as a wooden comb with a handle and a plastic comb without a handle). Research subjects were then asked which of the two alternate objects was more like the pivot object – the one that was similar in shape, or the one that was similar in material composition. As expected, English speakers favored the shape alternate (the wooden comb with a handle) most of the time, while Yucatec speakers favored the material alternate most of the time (the plastic comb without a handle) (Lucy and Gaskins 2003:475).

When Lucy and Gaskins repeated this test with seven- and nine-year-old English- and Yucatec-speaking children, the results were quite interesting. Seven-year-olds across the two languages strongly favored shape, but by the age of nine, a difference had begun to appear, with Yucatec-speaking children beginning to favor the material alternates more often, though not as often as Yucatec adults. This developmental process that continues through later childhood points to the ongoing role of linguistic and cultural habituation in influencing thought patterns over a person's lifetime.

Language Use

The third way in which language might influence thought is through habitual patterns of use. That is, our thought processes might be affected not just by virtue of speaking language-in-general or because of the particular semantic or grammatical structures of our own language but because of the social patterns of everyday language use. There has been very little experimental research conducted on the specific cognitive effects of using language in a certain way because such research does not lend itself well to experimental methods, but there is every reason to believe that habitual social and linguistic practices influence thought patterns – though of course not in any kind of deterministic way.

One arena in which some scholars have claimed to identify cognitive effects of everyday language use has been literacy practices. Decades ago, Jack Goody and Ian Watt (1963) argued that there is a "cognitive divide" between "literate" and "nonliterate" groups of people, with the "literate" groups being more capable of logic, abstraction, and advancement. This view of literacy practices has been challenged by many scholars, as will be discussed in chapter 7; for our purposes here, it is important to note that an assertion of the alleged cognitive effects of "literacy" fails to distinguish among different kinds of literacy, some of which are related to schooling practices and some not. The immense cross-cultural variability of literacy practices has been well documented – to the point that "literacy" can no longer be viewed as a single, neutral technology that brings about identical cognitive or social effects wherever it arises (cf. Street 1984; Barton et al. 2000; Collins and Blot 2003). Many researchers therefore prefer to pluralize the term, using *literacies* instead *literacy*.

One extensive study has attempted to identify potential cognitive effects of specific kinds of literacies among the Vai of Liberia (Scribner and Cole 1981). At the time of Scribner and Cole's large-scale, team-led research, there were three forms of literacy among the Vai: an indigenous Vai script that was passed on informally from person to person; English, acquired in formal school settings; and Arabic, acquired in early morning sessions with Qu'ranic scholars. Scribner and Cole expected to find differences on various cognitive tests between people who were totally nonliterate in comparison with people who were literate in at least one of the three scripts – confirmation of the alleged "cognitive divide" between literate and nonliterate people. Scribner and Cole found no such divide: "Instead of generalized changes in cognitive ability, we found localized changes in cognitive skills manifested in relatively esoteric experimental settings" (1981:234). What they did discover was that each of the specific literacies of the Vai was associated with particular sets of cognitive skills, though attributing these differences to the use of a particular script alone was impossible, as each type of literacy was embedded in a set of very different social practices.

Another thought-provoking study of the effects of patterns of language use on thought processes is that of Carol Cohn (1987). In her article, "Sex and Death in the Rational World of Defense Intellectuals," Cohn describes how, during her year of residence in a think tank of nuclear strategists, she was required to learn a new way of speaking – lots of acronyms for types of missiles, for example, and many euphemisms and abstractions for describing nuclear war. In all of the discussions among the defense intellectuals, Cohn noticed, the nuclear weapons themselves were most often the subjects of sentences. Human beings, in other words, were not the active agents in what Cohn called "technostrategic" discourse; the weapons were the ones that had the power to act upon the world in this community of practice (1987:711). Cohn reports that in order to be taken seriously in this social and intellectual environment, she had to learn how to speak this "technostrategic" discourse – but as soon as she did, she found herself at first unable to articulate her anti-nuclear sentiments, and then, frighteningly, unable even to *think* about her anti-nuclear opinions:

> I had not only learned to speak a language: I had started to think in it. Its questions became my questions, its concepts shaped my responses to new ideas. Its definitions of the parameters of reality became mine … My grasp on what I knew as reality seemed to slip. (1987:713; emphasis in the original)

Of course, eventually Cohn was able to extract herself from the influence of "technostrategic" discourse in order to write her analysis. Cohn herself is not a linguist or a linguistic anthropologist, so she does not present her work as any kind of definitive statement on the effects of certain patterns of language use on thought. Nevertheless, her experiences point to the ways in which language use in certain communities of practice can predispose people to think and act in particular ways. In addition, however, it is also important to note that social and cultural factors almost certainly influenced the development of "technostrategic" language to begin with, so disentangling language, thought, and culture from one another in such instances turns out to be nearly impossible.

Susan Harding, a cultural anthropologist, also experienced the feeling that her own way of thinking had been influenced by the language use in the community she was studying (Harding 1987). Harding was studying a fundamental Baptist community, paying particular attention to the rhetorical strategies members explicitly used to try to convert nonbelievers. One day, after a long and intense interview with a preacher, during which he tried through the practice of "witnessing" to convert Harding, she was driving home and almost got into an accident. Completely unbidden (Harding was not a fundamental Baptist), the following question came into her head: "What is God trying to tell me?" "It was my voice, but not my language. I had been invaded by the fundamental Baptist tongue I had been investigating," Harding wrote (1987:169). She continued: "It was quite specifically Reverend Cantrell's language and mode of interpretation that unfurled itself in my mind as I contemplated my near accident" (1987:170). By listening to Reverend Cantrell intensively and uncritically, as ethnographers often do in an attempt to understand unfamiliar ways of viewing the world, Harding inadvertently became susceptible to influence from the rhetorical devices the preacher used. Again, like Cohn, Harding makes it clear that these influences were not deterministic in nature, but her experiences exemplify the many ways in which everyday language use can have a powerful effect on someone's thought processes.

Conclusion

In many respects, the question of the relationship among language, thought, and culture is a chicken-and-egg sort of question. Almost all linguistic anthropologists consider these three entities to be overlapping and mutually influencing, but while some linguistic anthropologists are content to accept this sort of mutual influence as a given – as a presupposition or axiom, in other words, that informs the rest of their work – other linguistic anthropologists and an increasing number of cognitive scientists prefer to investigate the exact nature of the relationship by conducting experiments. On the whole, there is general acceptance in linguistic anthropology for the existence of some underlying universals that constrain variation in language and thought, but most linguistic anthropologists believe that linguists, psychologists, and cognitive scientists tend to overestimate the type and scope of universals in this area. The dominant view in these other fields is that humans are born with a large set of pre-existing universal concepts, and that "humans invent words that label their concepts" (Li and Gleitman 2002:266). Scholars such as Levinson reject this view as "simply false" (2003a:32) and maintain that the actual relationship is much more complex. As we have seen in this chapter, even in domains such as space, where there are substantial physical, environmental, and cognitive universals that constrain linguistic variability in many ways, there are still enormous differences in how languages semantically and grammatically encode relationships. As the research in this chapter demonstrates, many of these differences influence the thought processes of those who speak particular languages.

What we have explored very little so far in this chapter is the possible effect that habitual cultural practices and norms might have on language and thought. In the mutually constitutive model of language, thought, and culture that most linguistic anthropologists support, the specific ways in which culture influences language *use* have been studied extensively and will be discussed in later chapters of this book. The possible ways in which culture might influence linguistic *structure*, however, have been much less comprehensively studied. Boas leaned toward believing more in a culture's possible influence over language rather than the reverse, though he believed that language and culture could covary freely (Lucy 1992:16). More recently, Dan Everett, a linguist, has made some fascinating but extremely controversial claims about Pirahã, a language spoken by a tiny group of indigenous people in the Brazilian Amazon. Everett argues that "Pirahã culture severely constrains Pirahã grammar in several ways, producing an array of otherwise inexplicable 'gaps' in Pirahã morphosyntax" (Everett 2005:622). Pirahã culture restricts communication to "nonabstract subjects which fall within the immediate experience" of speakers, and this explains, according to Everett, the lack in Pirahã language of numbers, color terms, and embedding (the ability to construct phrases such as "the hat that I wore"), among other things. Everett's claims have been challenged by many scholars,[14] so it remains to be seen whether the type of strong cultural influences on language that he posits are operative, either among the Pirahã or elsewhere. Unfortunately, Everett seems unaware that most contemporary linguistic anthropologists consider the relationship among language, thought, and culture to be mutually constitutive. Indeed, he says he rejects "the unidirectionality inherent in linguistic relativity" (Everett 2005:623) without realizing that the views of Whorf and his successors are considerably more sophisticated than the simplistic and mistaken linguistic determinism he attributes to them. Although the naive cultural determinism he proposes would be rejected by virtually all contemporary linguistic anthropologists, Everett's provocative research does raise some interesting questions regarding the possible effects of cultural norms and practices on linguistic and cognitive processes.

In this chapter, we explored three ways in which language might influence thought: through language-in-general, through specific linguistic structures, and through habitual language use. In each of these areas scholars have detected clear Whorfian effects. Despite this accumulation of recent research on the topic, many linguists and cognitive scientists remain not just opposed to the idea that language might influence thought but actively hostile to it. Why? Deborah Cameron, a linguist, suggests some reasons for this hostility in a short essay entitled, "Linguistic Relativity: Benjamin Lee Whorf and the

Return of the Repressed" (Cameron 1999). According to Cameron, it is often illuminating to ask who a discipline's "hate figures" might be, as they will shed light on what scholars in that discipline want most to repress. In linguistics, she argues, Whorf's suggestion that language might influence thought touches upon three of the great issues of our time: (1) the nature of power, "which is no longer believed to grow out of the barrel of a gun, but seems complex, diffuse and often hidden in its workings, with a significant symbolic (which includes linguistic) component"; (2) the nature of human agency, for linguistic determinism, like genetic determinism, seems to challenge common ideas about freedom and responsibility; and (3) the opposition between universality and diversity: "Which matters more, what unites us or what divides us?" (Cameron 1999:154–155).

It may never be possible to disentangle all of the complex ways in which language, thought, and culture are interrelated, but this should not prevent us from continuing to explore the topic. As Cameron notes,

> The point of posing problems of this kind is not to find a solution so you can move onto something else; on the contrary, it is to enable conversation to continue on subjects we think important for our understanding of our condition. We deepen that understanding by reflecting on the questions themselves, and the last thing we need is for our reflections to be cut short by a scientist saying, 'but we *know* the answer to that one.' (1999:156; emphasis in the original)

In recent decades, as the semantic and grammatical diversity of the world's languages has become more evident, as different approaches to the understanding of language and cognition have become popular, and as domains aside from color have been investigated, no longer is it the case for scholars in linguistics, psychology, or cognitive science that to admit any sympathy for, or even curiosity about, linguistic diversity is "tantamount to declaring oneself to be either a simpleton or a lunatic" (Gentner and Goldin-Meadow 2003:3). Within linguistic anthropology, the discipline's long history of research on this topic, extending back to Boas, Sapir, and Whorf, has stimulated ever more compelling and thought-provoking studies in recent years. Not only should this research be of value to scholars outside of anthropology but also, as Sapir long ago noted, such studies will benefit cultural anthropologists as well, for language can be seen as "the *symbolic guide to culture*" (Sapir 1949[1929]:162; emphasis in the original). Indeed, language, thought, and culture are so intimately interwoven that to study any one of these is to study the other two as well.

Part II Communities of Speakers, Hearers, Readers, and Writers

5 Communities of Language Users

Many linguistic anthropologists would agree with the statement that a group of people who are set apart socially from others somehow will probably be set apart linguistically as well – and vice versa: a group of people set apart linguistically from others will probably be set apart socially as well. Yet, the specifics of how, why, and even whether this generalization actually holds true in particular cases must be explored through empirical research, and this sort of research requires a clear notion of what constitutes a meaningful social or linguistic community. Can such communities be identified along the lines of age or hobby, as the cartoon that appeared at the start of chapter 1 (Figure 1.1) suggests is the case with young people and golfers? Scholars have debated this question for decades, centering initially on the term made popular by many sociolinguists, "speech community." In recent years, however, many linguistic anthropologists have shifted to some alternative terms, such as linguistic community, speech area, speech network, and, especially, *communities of practice*. These concepts, some scholars believe, allow for research that treats communities not as static, pre-existing entities but as emergent groups that are fluid and overlapping, and that have greater or lesser relevance for individuals depending on the circumstances.

This chapter provides an overview of the challenges involved in identifying communities of language users as objects of linguistic and social analysis. The chapter seeks to (1) encourage readers to question

Living Language: An Introduction to Linguistic Anthropology, First Edition. Laura M. Ahearn.

some of their taken-for-granted notions about the nature of such communities; (2) uncover some of the assumptions and unstated social theories that often underpin such concepts as "speech community"; and, (3) introduce readers to some of the most interesting research that furthers our understanding of the relationship between linguistic practices and social groups.

Defining "Speech Community"

You might think it would be fairly easy to define the term "speech community." After all, what could be so difficult about making sense of a term that pretty clearly refers to a group of speakers, right? Complications set in, however, once we start trying to specify exactly what we mean by "speech" and by "community." It turns out to be quite tricky to identify the boundaries of a speech community and to specify what the members of that community have in common. Consider the questions that can be raised regarding just these three aspects of the term: (1) the size and location of the community; (2) what is shared by members of the community; and (3) the type of interactions the community members might or must have.

Size and location of the community

- How large or small can (or must) a speech community be? Is one person too small to constitute a speech community? Is the entire population of a country, or even the earth, too large to constitute a single speech community?
- Can the concept be used to describe entities that are not defined by static physical location, where, for example, "membership can be experienced as part of a nation-state, neighborhood, village, club, compound, on-line chat room, religious institution, and so on" (Morgan 2004:4)?
- Should speech communities be conceptualized as nested within or overlapping one another, with individuals belonging to multiple speech communities simultaneously?

What is shared by the members of a speech community?

- Must everyone in a speech community speak the same language or dialect at the same level of fluency?
- Do speakers of the same language or dialect automatically constitute a speech community?
- Do people who use American Sign Language (ASL), or one of the many other sign languages in the world, constitute one or more "speech" communities?
- How important are shared attitudes toward language and evaluations of linguistic practices (i.e., language ideologies) for determining speech community membership?
- Must members of a speech community be aware that they are members of such a community?

The type of interactions that speech community members have

- Must speech community members have face-to-face interaction? If so, how frequently?
- Might people involved in online or other electronically mediated interactions constitute a virtual or literacy-based speech community?
- Might there be different kinds of membership in a speech community – central vs. peripheral, for example? In other words, might speech communities be more accurately portrayed as networks with varying density (Milroy 2002b)?

Linguists, sociolinguists, and linguistic anthropologists have answered these questions in different ways. Within the field of linguistics (as opposed to sociolinguistics or linguistic anthropology), the concept of speech community has been, some scholars have argued, "the unspoken basis of most linguistics research" (Holmes and Meyerhoff 1999:178). Even de Saussure, the famous linguist whose work at the beginning of the last century is well known for its treatment of language as an abstract system of signs and grammatical structures, and who had no interest in studying language in actual social contexts, acknowledged that "in order to have a language, there must be a

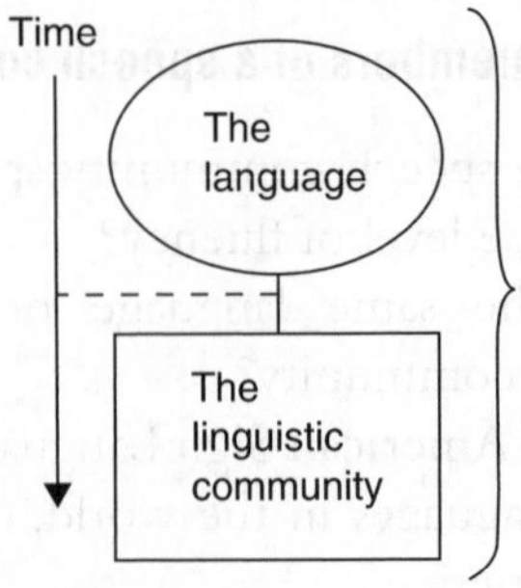

Figure 5.1 De Saussure's "linguistic community" (Saussure 1986:78).
Source: From *Course in General Linguistics* by Ferdinand de Saussure, translated by Roy Harris. Reprinted by permission of Open Court Publishing, a division of Carus Publishing Company, Chicago, IL, 1986. (Originally published 1916).

community of speakers" (Saussure 1986[1916]:77). In Figure 5.1, de Saussure demonstrates that the changes that languages inevitably undergo through time are the product of social forces. Notice, however, how "the language" is set apart as an entity unto itself, and "the linguistic community" (or "community of speakers," as he called it on an earlier page) and "social forces" are left unspecified. The implication here is that the speakers of "a language" presumably constitute a homogeneous group.

Very closely related to de Saussure's approach is Chomsky's description of an ideal individual in a hypothetical "speech-community," which even Chomsky himself later acknowledged (1975) does not exist in the real world:

> Linguistic theory is concerned primarily with an ideal speaker-listener, in a completely homogeneous speech-community, who knows its language perfectly and is unaffected by such grammatically irrelevant conditions as memory limitations, distractions, shifts of attention and interest, and errors (random or characteristic) in applying his knowledge of the language in actual performance. (1965:3)

In both de Saussure's and Chomsky's work the main focus is on linguistic structures (either of a specific language or of "Language" in general), so while both refer in passing to groups of language users, neither provides any details on the nature of those communities.

The concept of speech community, while initially defined by linguists such as de Saussure (1916) and Leonard Bloomfield (1933) in the first part of the twentieth century, began to be more widely used and more carefully defined in the 1960s and 1970s when sociolinguists and linguistic anthropologists such as Dell Hymes, John Gumperz, and William Labov were looking for ways to link linguistic practices and social groups more systematically for the purposes of their research. Decades earlier, as was discussed in chapter 4, anthropologists such as Franz Boas, Edward Sapir, and Benjamin Whorf had posited an integral relationship between language and society; Hymes, Gumperz, and Labov, each in his own way, attempted to use the concept of speech community to clarify the specific nature of this relationship and to reject the approach of de Saussure, Chomsky, and other linguists. In an influential passage from his textbook *Foundations in Sociolinguistics*, for example, Hymes stated emphatically that "the natural unit for sociolinguistic taxonomy (and description), however, is not the language but the speech community" (Hymes 1974:35). Hymes's focus on beliefs, values, attitudes, and ways of speaking within a community draws explicitly on Sapir's work (1974:46) and departs from the approach of linguists because the unit of analysis for Hymes is "a social, rather than linguistic, entity" (1974:47).

Gumperz, too, explicitly noted the ways in which his approach departed from that of formal linguists such as de Saussure and Chomsky. Whereas in formal linguistics, Gumperz noted, the object of analysis is "a particular body of linguistic data abstracted from the settings in which it occurs" (2001[1968]:43), scholars such as sociolinguists and linguistic anthropologists who are interested in studying language use in actual social contexts must choose a very different object of analysis, Gumperz argued, and must situate their study in a very different "universe":

> This universe is the speech community: any human aggregate characterized by regular and frequent interaction by means of a shared body of verbal signs and set off from similar aggregates by significant differences in language usage. Most groups of any permanence, be they small bands bounded by face-to-face contact, modern nations divisible into smaller subregions, or even occupational

> associations or neighborhood gangs, may be treated as speech communities, provided they show linguistic peculiarities that warrant special study. (2001[1968]:43)

Gumperz did not assume that members of speech communities all speak the same way – or even the same language. In fact, Gumperz has always been centrally concerned with multilingual and multidialectal communities in his research. Although members of such communities might not all share a style, a dialect, or even a language, they nevertheless share a "verbal repertoire" (2001:50). "Regardless of the linguistic differences among them," he notes, "the speech varieties employed within a speech community form a system because they are related to a shared set of social norms" (2001:44).[1]

Thus, in Gumperz's famous formulation, we see several requirements that many other scholars have also adopted in their definitions of the term "speech community":

1 Frequent interaction among the members must occur.
2 The members of the speech community must share a "verbal repertoire," even though they may not all speak the same style, dialect, or even language.
3 The members of the speech community must also share a set of social norms regarding appropriate language use – what linguistic anthropologists now call "language ideologies."

This third criterion – that of shared language ideologies – is also a central component of the definition of speech community made famous by William Labov, a well-known sociolinguist. Labov conducted a study in the 1960s of linguistic variation on the Lower East Side of New York City and concluded that the heterogeneous nature of that community was not at all unusual or problematic. "The speech community is not defined by any marked agreement in the use of language elements, so much as by participation in a set of shared norms," Labov noted in an oft-quoted passage (Labov 1972b:120–121, cited in Patrick 2002:586). So, while New Yorkers in Labov's study did not pronounce "ing" or "r" the same way, for example, Labov nevertheless contended that they evaluated speech in the same ways, as stigmatized or high status, for example. This shared evaluation of linguistic practices therefore created a single speech community in New York's Lower East Side during the 1960s, according to Labov.

Recent Research Drawing on the Concept of Speech Community

In recent years, some scholars have continued to use the concept of "speech community," while others have either redefined it or discarded it as too vague or problematic. Among those who have continued to use the concept while adapting it to fit the particularities of their fieldsites are the sociolinguists Otto Santa Ana and Claudia Parodí (1998), who propose for the population they studied in Mexico a nested, multi-level reworking of Labov's model of the speech community. Of note here are the methods Santa Ana and Parodí employed in their research because they are standard methods for the discipline of sociolinguistics but not for linguistic anthropology. Santa Ana and Parodí recorded 50 hours of data from 35 Spanish speakers using multiple methods such as sociolinguistic interviews (which are initiated by the researchers rather than by the participants), fill-in-the-blank tests, and role plays in which subjects were asked to teach a non-native speaker the appropriate way to "talk to social superiors and subordinates in specific situations – for example, how an adolescent should discuss a delicate and formal interpersonal concern with his teacher, and how a non-native-speaking adult should speak appropriately to a domestic worker about recurrent housekeeping problems" (Santa Ana and Parodí 1998:25). Santa Ana and Parodí also asked their research subjects to compare formal and informal love letters in order to elicit their judgments on matters of style.[2] They did not employ any ethnographic methods, as linguistic anthropologists almost always do.

In their analysis of the data from these methods, Santa Ana and Parodí looked for the sorts of variation Labov had found in actual linguistic usage (for example, differences in pronunciation or word choice), along with a shared set of norms that governed their evaluations of those differences. While they did discover the expected variation in actual usage, they were surprised to find that a small subset of their research subjects only used nonstandard forms of Spanish and

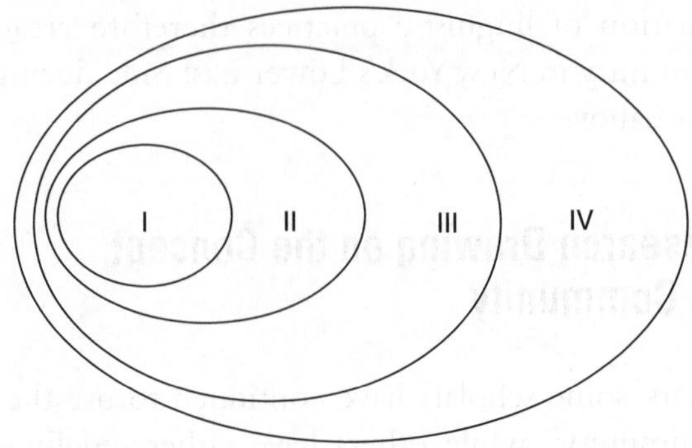

Figure 5.2 Santa Ana and Parodí's model of nested speech-community configurations.
Source: From Santa Ana and Parodí (1998:34).

did not appear to be aware at all either of the existence of standard forms or of the stigma associated with the nonstandard forms they themselves used (Santa Ana and Parodí 1998:26). The researchers acknowledge that it is difficult to prove the absence of something and imply that an ethnographic study might uncover either an alternative explanation or awareness of the stigma associated with some of the linguistic forms, but they argue that in this particular subset of the speech community they could find no evidence for the "set of shared norms" that Labov said characterized the Lower East Side of New York City.

Instead, what Santa Ana and Parodí propose for this area of Mexico is a "model of nested speech-community configurations" (1998:34, see Figure 5.2). They maintain that individuals in each of the four "Fields" of the typology – Locale (I), Vicinity (II), District (III), and National (IV) – have increasingly large fields of action that bring them into contact with more and more people whose linguistic practices and norms might differ from their own. Individuals occupying different fields often live in the same neighborhood or even in the same family, Santa Ana and Parodí claim, so the groupings are based not on geography but on the types of social relationships participants have. Their different spheres of economic and social activity lead to different levels of awareness of various sociolinguistic norms or stigmas and are related to linguistic and social hierarchies (see Table 5.1.). In the Locale Field (I), individuals are unaware of the existence of stigmatized,

Table 5.1 Santa Ana and Parodí's typology of speech-community configurations.

	Stigma	Regional	Standard
I. Locale	–	–	–
II. Vicinity	+	–	–
III. District	+	+	–
IV. National	+	+	+

Source: From Santa Ana and Parodí (1998:35).

regional, or standardized national variants. In the Vicinity Field (II), speakers are aware of the existence of stigmatized forms but not of regional or standardized national forms. In the District Field (III), individuals are aware of stigmatized and regional variants but not standardized national forms. And in the National Field (IV), speakers are aware of the existence of all of these forms (Santa Ana and Parodí 1998:35–37).

Many linguistic anthropologists would take issue with Santa Ana and Parodí's approach because it incorporates elements such as the exclusion from their study of interviewees who "spoke Spanish with a recognizable Phurhépecha accent" (1998:24), or the reliance on elicitation rather than ethnographic study of naturally occurring language use. Nevertheless, their creative reworking of Labov's model of a speech community into a typology of nested speech-community configurations is an example of how the concept of speech community continues to be relevant to researchers.

Another scholar who has argued for the usefulness of the concept of speech community while also attempting to redefine it is linguistic anthropologist Debra Spitulnik. In her ethnographic study of radio discourse in Zambia, a multilingual society in which dozens of languages are spoken, Spitulnik wonders, "[D]oes it even make sense to speak of a speech community across the nation-state when there is no one common language?" (2001:96). Spitulnik's research investigates whether the concept of speech community can be applied to a situation in which there are millions of people who never interact with or even know one another, and in which the linguistic knowledge they share is at best limited. In such a situation, the relevance of the speech community concept is clearly questionable – and yet Spitulnik argues that it can indeed be a useful concept when studying the effects of mass-mediated communication such as radio. The same conclusion might be drawn regarding other mass media, such as television, movies, or the internet, because all of these forms of communication can be characterized by a high frequency of interaction in the "vertical" sense, meaning a great deal of exposure to mass media. Thus, Spitulnik argues, radio programs in Zambia – an extremely popular type of mass-mediated communication in that country – provide common reference points for people in their everyday conversations. Zambian radio programs are also a source for linguistic innovations such as new idiomatic expressions or styles of speaking. Small snippets of talk are taken out of their original radio contexts and reinserted into ordinary social interactions, thereby indexing speakers as "modern" or conversant with various types of acronyms associated with national and international organizations. This type of decontextualization and recontextualization is extremely common with all forms of mass-mediated communication – and in fact with all forms of communication in general.

With regard to the "shared linguistic knowledge" component of many definitions of speech community, therefore, Spitulnik argues that Zambian radio programs are an important source for common reference points and subtle but important linguistic connections that can be forged across linguistic, ethnic, regional, and even national boundaries (2001:113; cf. Morgan 2004:5–6). The concept of speech community can, Spitulnik maintains, be productively refined by incorporating a consideration of factors such as frequency of media consumption and large-scale exposure to a common media source.

Alternatives to the Concept of Speech Community

Some researchers have attempted to substitute alternative terms for "speech community" because of the difficulties in defining exactly what members of a given speech community allegedly share and in determining exactly how they interact. In addition, since the concept emerged from the field of sociolinguistics without any particular connection to broader social theory, some scholars have found it to be at best insufficient and at worst misleading. Mary Bucholtz (1999:207), for example, lists six ways in which the concept of speech community is inadequate:

1 Its tendency to take language as central.
2 Its emphasis on consensus as the organizing principle of community.
3 Its preference for studying central members of the community over those at the margins.
4 Its focus on the group at the expense of individuals.
5 Its view of identity as a set of static categories.
6 Its valorization of researchers' interpretations over participants' own understandings of their practices.

For all of these reasons, Bucholtz and others have turned to alternative concepts to help them shed light on the linguistic and social practices they study.

Speech areas

Jean Jackson's (1974, 1983) oft-cited work on the Vaupés territory, a tropical rainforest that falls partly in Colombia and partly in Brazil, challenges the notion of speech community in some profound ways.[3] Among the indigenous groups who lived in this area during the time of Jackson's research in the 1960s and 1970s, all people were multilingual, speaking languages that cut across the Tukanoan, Arawak, and Carib language families. Everyone spoke at least three languages fluently, many spoke four or five, and some understood as many as ten (1974:55). The groups lived in multilingual communities comprised of longhouses. An important component of each individual's identity was membership in a particular "language aggregate" – in other words, the patrilineal descent group based on the language of his or her father. And the main rule for marriage, according to Jackson, was "linguistic exogamy" – the requirement that a person not marry someone from his or her own language aggregate.

As Jackson notes, this complex linguistic situation calls into question the utility of the concept of speech community. On the one hand, she argues, the entire central Northwest Amazon, including the both the Colombian and the Brazilian territory, can be thought of as a singly multilingual speech community (1974:55) because the people in this area share cultural and religious practices, and even though they do not all speak the same language, they share an understanding of how language should be used in daily social life. But Jackson suggests that might be more appropriate to consider the Vaupés area to be a "speech area," a term she relates to the German concept of *Sprechbund*.[4] In this speech area, Jackson claims, "All Indians share rules for speech, even though some Indians' verbal repertoires do not overlap" (1974:55). Then, she continues, if the entire Vaupés area is a speech area, the individual longhouses or villages could be considered its actual speech communities. Still, these much smaller groups of people will always be multilingual because of the rule to marry outside of one's language aggregate, so Jackson notes that ethnographic study of these kinds of communities will almost certainly deepen and possibly challenge existing notions of speech community and multilingualism.

Speech networks

Some scholars assert that it is not sufficient merely to identify the boundaries of a community of language users; it is also important, they argue, to characterize the nature of the connections and interactions that members of speech communities have with one another. Sociolinguist Lesley Milroy, for example, draws on social network analysis to understand the influence of social ties of various strengths and types on language use and language change over time (Milroy 1987, 2002a, 2002b). According to this approach, individuals might be members of numerous speech networks simultaneously and/or sequentially over the course of their lives. The memberships of the various networks to which they belong might or might not overlap or be nested within one another in some way. Individuals' ties with others in these networks will also vary in the following ways (Milroy 2002b:550–551):

- *Strong or weak ties*. In networks with strong ties, individuals have strong personal relationships, perhaps involving kinship or close friendship. In networks with weak ties, individuals are connected merely by acquaintanceship or some other relatively distant relationship.

- *Multiplex or uniplex networks.* In networks with a "multiplex" structure, individuals are connected to one another in multiple ways. For example, a woman might work in the same office as her cousin to whom she is very close socially, making that woman a co-worker, a relative, and a friend. In networks with a "uniplex" structure, individuals are connected to one another in only one way.
- *High density or low density.* In high-density networks, many of the people any one person knows will also know one another. In low-density networks, the opposite will be true.

For a particular person ("X" in Figures 5.3 and 5.4), the experience of being in a strong, multiplex, high-density network (such as the one pictured in Figure 5.3) will be very different from being in a weak, uniplex, low-density network (such as the one pictured in Figure 5.4). The implications for linguistic practices are also significant. Speech networks of the former sort that feature close-knit social ties appear to facilitate the retention of dialects or languages, whereas speech networks of the second sort can lead to the loss of nonstandard or regional dialects or languages (Milroy 1987, 2002a, 2002b; Trudgill 1996). Milroy has also suggested that differences in network structure are correlated with socioeconomic class: "Different types of network structure seem to be broadly associated with different social classes; loose-knit networks with the socially and geographically mobile mainly middle classes, and close-knit ties with very low status and very high status speakers" (2002b:566–567).

Despite these sorts of claims, the relationship of speech networks to one another and to a broader conceptualization of society as a whole remain unspecified or underspecified in this sort of network analysis because scholars who employ it wish to focus instead on less abstract, more micro-level social interactions. Some researchers consider the micro-level focus of network analysis to be a strength because it means that the approach is theoretically compatible with any number of macro-level social theories, but others fault network analysis for lacking a more explicit theorization of power and social difference at the macro level (cf. Milroy 2002b:550; Patrick 2002:583).

| ||

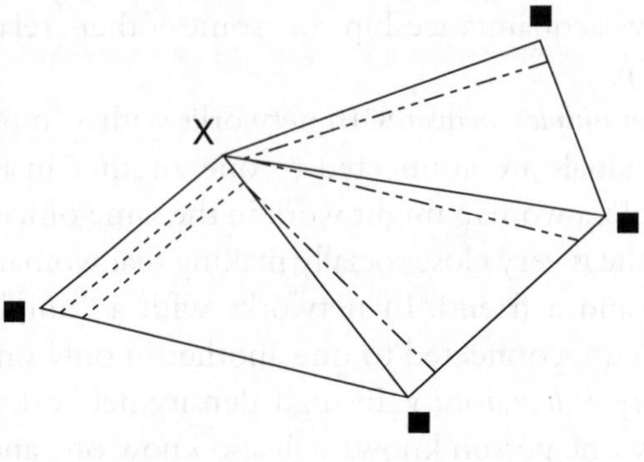

Figure 5.3 Strong, multiplex, high-density network with individual "X" at center.
Source: Adapted from Milroy (2002b:551).

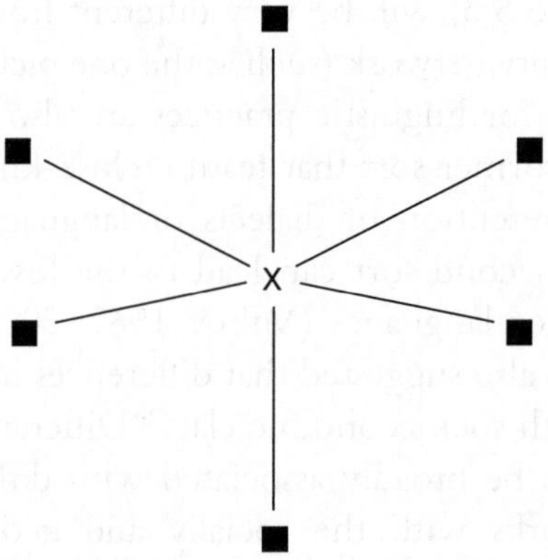

Figure 5.4 Weak, uniplex, low-density network with individual "X" at center.
Source: Adapted from Milroy (2002b:551).

Communities of practice

Within linguistic anthropology, the most influential alternative to "speech community" is the notion of "community of practice." Originally proposed by Jean Lave and Etienne Wenger (1991) in their co-authored book, *Situated Learning: Legitimate Peripheral Participation*, the concept of "community of practice" has been ground-breaking and paradigm-shifting not just in linguistic anthropology but in fields as disparate as education, government, and business (Hughes et al. 2007:2–4). *Situated Learning* makes use of the concept of community of practice in order to describe the socially embedded nature of learning. William F. Hanks, a linguistic anthropologist, describes the significance of Lave and Wenger's approach to learning in the foreword to their book: "Rather than asking what kinds of cognitive processes and conceptual structures are involved, they ask what kinds of social engagements provide the proper context for learning to take place" (Hanks 1991:14). And just as learning takes place not just in an individual's head but in the social interactions in which that individual takes part, so too does language reside not just in an individual's head but in real-life social interactions, making the concept of community of practice equally applicable to the study of language use as a form of social practice (Hanks 1991:13).

As a practice-based approach to the process of language socialization, the concept of community of practice was formally introduced to linguistic anthropology by Penelope Eckert and Sally McConnell-Ginet in their widely cited 1992 article in the *Annual Review of Anthropology*.[5] In that piece, they define the concept of community of practice as follows:

> A community of practice is an aggregate of people who come together around mutual engagement in an endeavor. Ways of doing things, ways of talking, beliefs, values, power relations – in short, practices – emerge in the course of this mutual endeavor. As a social construct, a community of practice is different from the traditional community, primarily because it is defined simultaneously by its membership and by the practice in which that membership engages. (This does not mean that communities of practice are necessarily egalitarian or consensual – simply that their membership and practices grow out of mutual engagement.) (1992:464)

The three main criteria for identifying a community of practice, according to Wenger (1998:73ff), are (1) mutual engagement; (2) a joint enterprise; and (3) a shared repertoire. Examples of communities of practice might include members of a family, students in a linguistic anthropology class, faculty members in a particular department, a road construction crew, a baseball team, members of a religious congregation, or regulars at a neighborhood bar. Individuals can be members of multiple communities of practice simultaneously or sequentially over a lifespan. A major advantage of the concept of community of practice is that, unlike many sociolinguistic studies that use a concept of speech community based on pre-existing and abstract characteristics such as age, sex, or geographic residence, the concept of community of practice helps researchers produce practice-based, ethnographic studies that illustrate the emergent nature of communities and the inseparability of language from actual social contexts. In such studies, language is just "one of many social practices in which participants engage" (Bucholtz 1999:210). "The community of practice takes us away from the community defined by a location or by a population," Eckert and McConnell-Ginet write. "Instead, it focuses on a community defined by social engagement" (1998:490).

Some wonderful studies have been conducted by scholars describing various communities of practice. Eckert and McConnell-Ginet, for example, identify two main communities of practice in a Michigan high school pseudonymously called "Belten High," at which Eckert conducted ethnographic and sociolinguistic fieldwork in the 1980s (Eckert and McConnell-Ginet 1995, Eckert 1989). The "Jocks" comprise a school-oriented community of practice whose participants engage in extra-curricular activities and embody middle-class values. The "Burnouts" resist schooling and embody working-class values. Eckert and McConnell-Ginet demonstrate how these two class-based communities of practice "define the landscape of identities at Belten" (1995:477). Through close analysis of these students' linguistic and social practices, Eckert and McConnell-Ginet demonstrate how broader social categories such as class, gender, ethnicity, and adulthood are crafted and contested through the everyday interactions of students at the high school. Differences in vowel pronunciation, dress, and behavior characterize the members of these two communities of practice – and yet they are all members as well of an overarching community of practice whose members value "coolness" (even while defining it differently) and consider the Jock-Burnout opposition to be the defining one for the school (1995:478).

Mary Bucholtz's research also involves adolescents, but instead of studying high schoolers who seek to be "cool," she studies "nerds" – those students who define themselves in opposition to Jocks, Burnouts, and any other "cool" group (Bucholtz 1999:211; 2001, 2007). Like Eckert and McConnell-Ginet, Bucholtz finds the concept of community of practice ideal for looking at the complexities of identity formation in teenagers. By carefully analyzing linguistic and social practices, Bucholtz is able to distinguish between two different ways in which nerds construct their social identity. Negative identity practices are those that individuals employ to distance themselves from a rejected identity, such as avoiding slang and nonstandard pronunciation, or avoiding fashionable attire. Positive identity practices are those in which individuals engage in order actively to construct a chosen identity, such as proudly displaying knowledge or engaging in skillful word play (1999:211–212). Rather than analyzing nerds according to pre-ascribed identity categories such as age, gender, race, or class, Bucholtz, through her illuminating application of the concept of community of practice, shows how these categories are emergent in the actual social interactions of the individuals in complex and sometimes contradictory ways, thereby linking micro and macro levels of social and linguistic analysis.

Within anthropology as a whole thus far, the concept of community of practice has been utilized most frequently by scholars in the area of the anthropology of education and the study of language and gender. Some scholars have suggested that the concept lends itself most appropriately to the study of novices and experts, making it especially appropriate for research on adolescents who are learning how to act in culturally appropriate ways in schooling or other contexts, but others have argued that the concept is equally useful in studying any social group (Meyerhoff 2002:539–540).

The concept of community of practice is not without its detractors, however. Some scholars have criticized the approach for lacking a sufficiently robust theorization of power (e.g., Hughes et al. 2007), while others have lamented the lack of attention given to language (both verbal and written) by scholars who analyze communities of practice in fields such as business or education (e.g., Barton and Tusting 2005). Nevertheless, the concept remains a promising alternative to speech community as a way to recognize the emergent and socially embedded nature of all linguistic interactions.

Whichever terms scholars use to designate the groups of language users they study – speech community, speech area, speech network, community of practice, or something else altogether – they have an obligation to their readers to define their terms clearly. From the perspective of linguistic anthropology, any of these terms could generate insightful research as long as the researcher incorporated an awareness of the importance of the multifunctional nature of language, an understanding of the way it indexes social identities and relations, an analysis of the intertwining of social and linguistic practice, and an acknowledgment of the influence of language ideologies on social categories (and vice versa).

6 Multilingualism and Globalization

Consider these residents of central New Jersey whom I have met in my classes at Rutgers University or in my daily interactions around town.[1]

Mary, a second-year college student, was born in the United States to parents who had immigrated to this country from Vietnam, so Vietnamese was her first language. By the time she entered kindergarten, however, she was quite proficient in English as well, though she lacked knowledge of everyday idioms. Because Mary was extremely shy, her kindergarten teacher thought she was less fluent in English than she actually was, so she advised Mary's parents to speak to her at home in English only. Her parents did this, and the result was that by age eight Mary could no longer speak Vietnamese fluently. In Mary's extremely diverse, multilingual high school, teachers used to patrol the hallways and reprimand students who were speaking languages other than English. Mary's passive understanding of Vietnamese remains good, but her conversational ability is poor. Mary wrote the following in a language autobiography essay for one of my classes: "From the age of five, I became a victim of the 'tyranny of the standard' (Morgan 2004:15) imposed by all educational institutions and became a victim of my own language insecurities."

Miguel, a senior in college, was born in the United States, but both of his parents are from Mexico. Miguel has a sister who is four years older than he is and a brother who is five years younger. When Miguel

Living Language: An Introduction to Linguistic Anthropology, First Edition. Laura M. Ahearn.

was born, his mother was still learning English, so the main language spoken in the home was Spanish. Once Miguel started school, he learned English as well but retained his Spanish fluency. His sister also became completely bilingual in Spanish and English. By the time their younger brother was born, however, their mother's English had improved greatly, and the main language spoken in their home shifted to English. As a result, Miguel's younger brother understands Spanish somewhat but cannot speak it. When the family gets together, they speak a mixture of Spanish and English. His sister, who is married to another bilingual speaker of Spanish and English, speaks only English to her children, so they are now monolingual.

Sarah, a bank teller in her twenties, has grandparents who immigrated to the United States from Ireland and Germany, but they spoke Gaelic or German in the home too rarely for Sarah's parents to become fluent in either of these languages, so Sarah was raised in a monolingual English-speaking household. Throughout junior high and high school, Sarah took Spanish for her foreign language requirement, but she never gained more than a basic proficiency. Even that diminished throughout college and beyond because her university did not require students to take any foreign languages, and Sarah chose not to continue taking Spanish. Nevertheless, she speaks in very different ways to her friends, her parents, and her work colleagues (including her boss).

Aaron, who was born in the United States in the 1950s, had four grandparents who immigrated to the United States from various places in Eastern Europe. All of them spoke Yiddish, the language of Jews who lived in shtetls (small villages) in Eastern Europe at the turn of the last century, and had some proficiency in English as well. Aaron's parents both learned Yiddish as children but became completely fluent in English. English was the main language spoken in Aaron's home while he was growing up, though his parents did code-switch into Yiddish sometimes when their parents were around or when they wanted to prevent their children from understanding what they were saying. As a result, Aaron acquired a little bit of passive knowledge of Yiddish. After college, Aaron traveled to Israel, becoming fluent in Hebrew and living there for six years. Upon his return to the United States, however, he married a woman who did not speak Hebrew or Yiddish, so the language they speak in their home, aside from a smattering of Hebrew, Yiddish, and a couple of other languages – and the only language spoken by their daughter – is English.

Min, a fourth-year student in a joint BA/MS/PhD pharmacology program, was born in China with profound hearing loss. Min's mother spent many, many hours teaching her to lip read and speak intelligibly Mandarin Chinese. When Min was nine years old, the family immigrated to the United States, and Min spent the next several years learning how to lip read and speak intelligibly English. When she entered middle school, she was offered a chance to learn American Sign Language (ASL), and within just a few months Min felt as though she had "found" her native language. No longer did she miss what people said when they were turned away from her, and no longer did she have to struggle to be understood. By learning ASL, Min had also become a member of a new "speech" community – the Deaf community (note the intentionally and proudly capitalized "D") – with its own cultural and linguistic practices and different norms for communication and interpretation. While Min prefers this speech community to all others, she still lip reads often and participates regularly in many non-Deaf communities of practice.

When **Douglas** was a toddler, his parents took him to the Dominican Republic for a year while they did volunteer work there. Although he was completely bilingual in Spanish and English by the end of his time there, he quickly lost his fluency in Spanish upon the family's return to the United States, but since reaching adulthood he has tried to regain his Spanish proficiency in order to interact with Spanish-speaking customers in his store. And after Douglas married and had children of his own, he and his wife, who is a monolingual English speaker, decided to send their two children to a bilingual Spanish-English summer camp to help them acquire at least a little bit of Spanish.

How typical are these individuals? How common is it, in other words, for someone to speak more than one language fluently? And is multilingualism (whether in individuals or societies) a "good thing" or a "bad thing"? Language ideologies abound concerning the prevalence and desirability of multilingualism. Some of these views are legitimate personal or political opinions, but others are completely mistaken beliefs. Many people, for example, consider multilingualism to be unusual, especially in the United States. Linguist John R. Edwards refutes this misconception:

> To be bilingual or multilingual is not the aberration supposed by many (particularly, perhaps, by people in Europe and North America who speak a 'big' language); it is, rather, a normal and unremarkable necessity for the majority in the world today. A monolingual perspective is often, unfortunately, a consequence of possession of a powerful 'language of wider communication', as English, French, German, Spanish and other such languages are sometimes styled. (Edwards 1994:1; cf. Romaine 2001:512)

While it is clear that bilingualism (the ability to speak two languages) and multilingualism (the ability to speak two or even more languages)[2] are common, estimates regarding the precise number of people who speak two or more languages around the world are hard to come by because it is surprisingly difficult to determine how many languages are spoken in total, and what even counts as a language. This is the case for several reasons. First, the number of languages spoken in the world is changing all the time because so many languages are dying out (an issue we will explore further in chapter 11). Second, it is estimated that a quarter of the world's languages are spoken by fewer than a thousand people, each making them difficult to find, identify, and study (Lewis, M.P. 2006). Third, globalization has led to increases in migration and developments in communication technologies that allow for transnational flows of ideas, languages, and asymmetries, creating "creolized, mixed idioms of polyglottism" – that is, complex and creative mixtures of languages (Jacquemet 2005:263).

And finally, there are no universally accepted criteria for distinguishing between a "language" and a "dialect." The difference between a way of speaking that gets labeled a language and a way of speaking that gets labeled a dialect often comes down to politics, culture, and history (Lippi-Green 1997). The following famous saying is often attributed to linguist Max Weinreich, though he himself reportedly attributed it to an unnamed high school teacher who attended some of his lectures in the 1940s: "A language is a dialect with an army and a navy."[3] In other words, a way of speaking that is labeled a "language" often has the political support of a nation-state in the form of an edict pronouncing it a national or official language. As a result, linguistic variants are often designated as languages or dialects based not on the amount of overlap they have in vocabulary or grammar, or on mutual intelligibility among their speakers, but on the basis of geopolitics.

For example, Swedish and Norwegian are labeled as two separate languages (the official languages of Sweden and Norway, respectively), and yet their speakers have no trouble understanding one another (Childs 2006). Similarly, although the written scripts of Hindi and Urdu differ, there is a great deal of overlap in spoken Hindi and Urdu, but because of their association with the two different nation-states of India and Pakistan (respectively), and their different literary and cultural histories, Hindi and Urdu are often referred to as separate languages. The Cantonese and Mandarin "dialects" of Chinese, on the other hand, are not mutually intelligible when spoken, though their scripts do overlap. And prior to the break-up of the former Yugoslavia, Serbo-Croatian was considered a single language with separate Eastern and Western "dialects," but after Serbia and Croatia became independent, each declared its language to be separate and different from the other. Even though the speakers of Serbian and Croatian generally have little trouble understanding one another, the governments and citizens of the two countries often claim that they are two completely different languages (Greenberg 2004:1–3), as does the government of Bosnia and Herzegovina for the allegedly separate language of Bosnian (sometimes called Bosniak or Bosniac), which was also formerly called simply Serbo-Croatian. Clearly, when it comes to distinguishing between languages and dialects, considerations of politics, history, ethnic identity, culture, and indigenous rights take precedence over technical linguistic considerations.

There is also confusion and controversy surrounding the term "dialect" because it is often used to describe only those ways of speaking that are of lower status in a given society. In actuality, everyone speaks (at least one) dialect, but speakers of standard dialects – the ways of speaking used by mainstream newscasters, highly educated national figures, and others – tend not to recognize that they, too, speak a dialect; they, too, have an "accent" (Lippi-Green 1997).

In addition to dialects, language researchers also use the term "register" to connote "a linguistic *repertoire* that is associated, culture-internally, with particular social practices and with persons who engage in such practices" (Agha 2004:24; emphasis in the original). Examples of registers include what people metalinguistically label as "polite language," "geek speak," "informal speech," "God talk," "girl talk," or "slang." Even monolingual individuals can generally code-switch among several different registers. Asif Agha explains: "An individual's *register range* – the variety of registers with which he or she is acquainted – equips a person with portable emblems of identity, sometimes permitting distinctive modes of access to particular zones of social life … Differences of register competence are thus often linked to asymmetries of power, socioeconomic class, position within hierarchies, and the like" (Agha 2004:24, emphasis in the original; cf. Agha 2007).

Because it is difficult to determine with any certainty what should be labeled a dialect as opposed to a language, and because factoring in the existence registers makes the calculation even more challenging, it is therefore virtually impossible to arrive at a definitive count of the world's languages. Estimates range from 5,000 (Romaine 2001:512) to approximately 7,000 (Harrison 2007:3) separate languages, with many more variants usually labeled as dialects. These languages are not distributed equally across the countries of the world; linguistic diversity is far greater in some areas than others. For example, K. David Harrison notes that "the 65 inhabited islands of Vanuatu (together about the size of the state of Connecticut) support 109 distinct tongues in a population of just 205,000 people. That is one entire language for every 1,880 speakers" (2007:11). Even in countries where there is far less linguistic diversity, however, there are almost always multiple languages spoken. In this sense, then, every country in the world could be said to be multilingual.

In the United States, for example, the 2000 US census asked several questions about languages spoken in the home and levels of proficiency in these languages, as well as in English.[4] According to the responses on the census, 18 percent (roughly 47 million people) of the respondents aged five and over reported that they spoke a language other than English in the home. This figure has increased from 11 percent in 1980 to 14 percent in 1990, and now 18 percent in 2000. More than half of these latter respondents reported speaking Spanish (approximately 10 percent of the total US population). Of the 18 percent who said they spoke a language other than, or in addition to,

English in the home, 55 percent said they spoke English "very well," 22 percent said "well," 16 percent spoke English but "not well," and 7 percent said they could not speak English at all (US Census Bureau 2000, 2006).

How likely are more recent immigrants to the US to learn English over time, compared to immigrant groups in the past? In other words, is English becoming less dominant, or will contemporary immigrants and their descendants learn English at roughly the same rate as past immigrants and their descendants? Answering this question is not easy because of the nature of census data, the complexity of language use, and the variation across different regions of the United States. According to one group of scholars, however, recent groups of immigrants from Asia are learning English at the same rate as European immigrants a century ago, or even more quickly, resulting in a third generation (those whose grandparents immigrated) that almost always speaks only English (Alba et al. 2002:480). Among Spanish-speaking immigrant groups, the rate appears to be somewhat slower, but this is largely dependent upon whether a second-generation bilingual person marries another person bilingual in Spanish and English (an example of "endogamy," or marrying within one's social group) and whether they reside in a community in which Spanish is commonly spoken. Endogamy alone is not enough to ensure that third-generation individuals will still be able to speak Spanish, but endogamy along with residence in a community in which Spanish is supported can increase the chances that a third-generation individual will be able to speak at least some Spanish. Nevertheless, Alba et al. report that "in all the groups that we could examine, the majority of third- and later-generation children speak only English at home, which implies that, with probably limited exceptions, they will grow up to be English monolinguals who have at most fragmentary knowledge of a mother tongue" (2002:480). This research suggests that English will most likely remain the overwhelmingly dominant language for the foreseeable future. As Dennis Baron notes, "A look at what the 2000 Census tells us about language use in the United States reveals that English continues to be the dominant, and in many cases, the only language of the United States and confirms that warnings about the decline of English are unwarranted" (Baron n.d.:1; cf. Baron 1990:199).

Obtaining an accurate count of the number of people worldwide who speak more than one language fluently is even more challenging than ascertaining this statistic for the United States. Nevertheless, we do know that multilingualism in individuals is, as Edwards noted above, quite common. According to some estimates, half the world's population is probably multilingual, and multilingual individuals are present in practically every country in the world (Grosjean 1982:vii, cited in Romaine 2001:512). And in certain areas, such as the Vaupés region of Colombia described in chapter 5, many people speak four or five languages, and some speak up to ten (Jackson 1974:55). The myth – a very powerful language ideology – of the necessity of "one nation, one language" goes back at least several hundred years to German philosophers such as Johann Gottfried Herder (cf. Bauman and Briggs 2003; Jacquemet 2005:260; Silverstein 1996), but it is belied by the reality of so many multilingual nations and individuals around the world. Although conflicts are sometimes blamed on language differences, there is no evidence in most cases to support the assertion that that the language differences themselves have led to problems. Instead, such conflicts are almost always in actuality about something else, usually "about fundamental inequalities between groups who happen to speak different languages" (Romaine 2001:532).

In some nations, multiple languages are accorded "national" or "official" status. In India, for example, Hindi (written in Devanagari script) is the only "official" language, but English, the language of government proceedings when India was a colony of Britain, continues to have special constitutional status and is the language used for the authoritative texts of all laws (Government of India, Ministry of Law and Justice 2007). In addition to Hindi and English, there are many other languages accorded recognition in the Eighth Schedule of the Constitution of India, amended in 1992 and 2003 to add a number of other languages (cf. Booth 2009a). Currently, the Eighth Schedule lists 22 official languages other than English.[5] And while the Official Language Resolution of 1968 states that "it is the duty of the Union to promote the spread of the Hindi Language and to develop it so that it may serve as a medium of expression for all the elements of the composite culture of India," it also states that "it is necessary in the interest of the educational and cultural advancement of the country that concerted measures should be taken for the full development of these languages" – in other words, for the "full development" of all 22 of the languages listed in the Eighth Schedule (Government of India, Ministry of Home Affairs 1968).

In actual practice, the choice of which language to use in schools, for civil service exams, or in court proceedings remains controversial in India, and language movements have arisen from time to time to argue for the official recognition of one language or another (cf. Booth 2009a; LaDousa 2005), but the example of multilingualism in India – the largest democracy in the world, with over a billion people – proves that linguistic diversity is not antithetical to national unity. In fact, multilingualism is an integral part of India's national identity and a daily fact of life for many of its residents. Suzanne Romaine states:

> The average educated person in Hyderabad [a city in southern India] may use Telugu at home, Sanskrit at the temple, English at the university, Urdu in business, etc. He or she may also know other varieties of Telugu, or Kannada, Tamil or Malayalam for reading, dealing with servants, or other specific purposes. Many south Asians have active control over what amounts to complex linguistic repertoires drawn from different languages and varieties. In societies such as these, multilingualism is not an incidental feature of language use, but a central factor and an organizing force in everyday life. In most parts of India, monolingualism would be problematic relative to the norms and expectations about the number of languages and varieties a person needs in order to manage the everyday things a normal person has to do. (2001:517)

Code-Switching, Code-Mixing, and Diglossia

In multilingual communities, the languages, dialects, or registers that are spoken are often linked to social hierarchies. In other words, linguistic practices index status, and language ideologies develop as a result. Some ways of speaking tend to get labeled prestigious, while others are stigmatized. Since all languages, dialects, and registers are rule-governed, there is nothing inherent in them that makes some "better" than others linguistically; these sorts of judgments are made for social, cultural, political, or historical reasons. For example, in some contexts in the United States, speaking Spanish is looked down upon, and people who speak Spanish in public are sometimes stigmatized. (Many English-Only laws are based on these language ideologies.) In countries such as Mexico, however, it is Spanish that is often accorded higher status compared to indigenous languages such as Mexicano or the many Mayan languages. These sorts of language ideologies are complex, however, and must be studied in their actual social contexts.

When individuals within multilingual communities are themselves multilingual (as opposed to communities in which monolingual speakers of different languages live side by side but are not themselves multilingual), the ways in which these multilingual people switch from language to language can vary in interesting ways. The communities themselves can differ in terms of stability – that is, whether the community continues to be multilingual over a long period of time, as Jackson (1974, 1983) documented for the multilingualism in the Vaupés area of the Amazon, or whether the multilingualism transforms into monolingualism, possibly also resulting in the death of one of the languages involved (Garrett 2004:53; Romaine 2001:522). The communities also vary in terms of the number of languages spoken and the extent to which people shift from one to another on a daily basis. Scholars use terms such as *diglossia*, *code-switching*, and *code-mixing* to describe these linguistic practices, which can refer not just to switching from language to language but also from dialect to dialect or register to register. Some researchers therefore argue that these processes of shifting between and among language variants are more common than previously recognized and could even be said to occur in every community. The more distinct the language varieties, however, the easier the shifting will be to study and the more likely it will be that the speakers will be aware of the practice and accord it special social significance. For these reasons, diglossia, code-switching, and code-mixing have most commonly been researched in communities in which individuals speak two or more languages (Woolard 2004:74).

Diglossia

Diglossia refers to a situation in which "each language or variety in a multilingual community serves a specialized function and is used for particular purposes" (Romaine 2001:519). Although the term has been defined in different ways and applied to many different types of linguistic communities, diglossia typically describes a fairly stable situation involving the compartmentalized use of two "codes" (languages or dialects) that are hierarchically related to each other. One code is labeled as the high status (H) code and the other the low status (L) code. The H code tends to be used in domains and activities in which there is an official purpose, such as giving a public lecture, writing, schooling, or broadcasting. The L code, in contrast, tends to be confined to informal and domestic domains involving the interaction of friends and family. In the initial formulation of diglossia by Charles Ferguson (1959), the two varieties were required to be related to each other linguistically, as, for example, classical and vernacular versions of Greek or Arabic are, but in subsequent analyses, scholars have tended to widen the scope of the term to include more than two variants of one language, or two or more completely different languages altogether (Garrett 2004:54). The common thread evident in most research on diglossia, however, remains the condition of compartmentalization within specific social domains, and most scholars who use the term study language varieties that are associated with high or low prestige. While individuals may switch from one to another of the language varieties, in diglossic situations these shifts most often occur as individuals move from one social setting to another – for example, from home to the workplace.

Code-switching

The sorts of shifts from one language variety to another that occur in a single social setting are often considered to be examples of *code-switching*, "an individual's use of two or more language varieties in the same speech event or exchange" (Woolard 2004:73).[6] Both linguists and linguistic anthropologists have sought to demonstrate the ways in which these switches are systematic rather than random, with linguists focusing on grammatical regularities and linguistic anthropologists focusing on the social meanings and identities that the code-switching indexes. For linguistic anthropologists, code-switching is an ideal subject for exploring all four of the discipline's key terms outlined in chapter 1. Shifts between language varieties will always be *multifunctional* – that is, they will always have multiple potential social meanings and functions. Through regular linguistic and social *practice*, the shifts will come to be associated with some meanings and identities more than others – that is, shifting from one language variety to another will come to *index* particular social relationships, meanings, or hierarchies more than others. Opinions and attitudes about these ways of speaking and the social dynamics they index will develop, and in turn these *language ideologies* will influence people's linguistic and social practices in the future. Thus, code-switching lends itself beautifully to study by linguistic anthropologists.

A compelling example of an illuminating analysis by a linguistic anthropologist of code-switching is Jane Hill's (1995) article, "The Voices of Don Gabriel: Responsibility and Self in a Modern Mexicano Narrative." Hill closely examines a story told by Don Gabriel, who was said to be the last speaker of the indigenous language of Mexicano (the strongly preferred local term for the Uto-Aztecan language also known as Nahuatl or Aztec) in his small town near the Yucatan Peninsula of Mexico. As part of a general interview about his life experiences, Don Gabriel was asked if he had ever suffered any accident or serious illness. "No. No, no accident, no, only they murdered my son," Don Gabriel replied, at which point he launched into a 17-minute narrative about his son's death (Hill 1995:98). Hill's complex analysis looks at many aspects of this narrative, including the multiple voices Don Gabriel uses to tell his story, techniques such as reported speech, intonation, and dysfluencies (hesitations, self-corrections, or other departures from normal fluency). Most relevant to our discussion here is Hill's analysis of Don Gabriel's code-switching between Mexicano and Spanish, for these two languages index Don Gabriel's moral assessments of the two speech communities: "These represent the fundamentally opposed ideological positions of peasant communitarianism and the economics of reciprocity in the Mexicano-speaking community on the one hand, and the pursuit of individual profit in the Spanish-speaking world of the marketplace on the other" (Hill 1995:116). Repeatedly throughout the narrative when Don Gabriel refers to the individualistic, profit-making nature of the Spanish-speaking business world with which his son was involved, his narrative contains dysfluencies that indicate, Hill argues, his discomfort with that set of moral values. In addition, when Don Gabriel needs to make use of Spanish words to describe business, he incorporates them into the voices of others through reported speech or in various other ways makes it clear that his own moral position is "firmly grounded in the peasant communitarian value of reciprocity" (Hill 1995:109). In this analysis, then, we see how a close examination of code-switching can shed light on cultural meanings, moral judgments, and social hierarchies.

Another linguistic anthropologist who has studied code-switching is Bonnie Urciuoli (1991, 1996), whose research on the shifts between Spanish and English by Puerto Ricans in New York City has led to a better understanding of when boundaries between languages (or dialects, registers, etc.) are perceived as firm and distinct as opposed to when the boundaries can be fuzzier or more indistinct. As noted in the summary of Urciuoli's work that appeared in chapter 1, socioeconomic status is an important consideration when studying the social aspects of code-switching. When the economically disadvantaged Puerto Ricans Urciuoli studied were with other equally poor neighbors who were black, racial and ethnic differences took a back seat and the boundaries between Spanish and English became fuzzy, resulting in the Puerto Ricans' switching back and forth fluidly between Spanish and English with their black neighbors. In contrast, when the Puerto Ricans were with white, middle-class people, especially if these people were in positions of authority (such as social workers or school administrators), the boundaries between English and Spanish were perceived to be more rigid because the stakes were typically much higher in these sorts of interactions. Thus, Urciuoli states, "I argue that the bilingual's sense of language boundary, English or Spanish, depends on the dynamics of relationships, on race, class, and gender as much as on ethnicity" (1996:295).

Code-mixing

The question of boundaries between language varieties becomes even more complex when considering shifting that occurs mid-sentence, or even mid-word. Scholars generally use the term *code-mixing* to describe the sort of shifting that involves a greater sense of hybridity and inter-mixture between two or more ways of speaking. An example of this sort of code-mixing can be seen in a common practice among many US Peace Corps volunteers I knew in Nepal who would take a Nepali verb form such as *bokne* ("carry," usually referring to the carrying of a basket on one's back using a tumpline across one's forehead) and add to it an English ending such as "-ing" to create a hybrid Nepali-English word in an otherwise English sentence, as in this hypothetical but typical example:

> I saw her *bokne*-ing the heavy firewood, so I offered to help.
> [*Eng*: I saw her carrying the heavy firewood, so I offered to help.]

Another even more hybrid mixture of Nepali and English can be seen in this actual example recorded by Chelsea Booth[7] of a remark made by a young woman in Darjeeling to her friend Laxmi:

> Laxmi, if you see him, *kurā garne u sanga,* just *sodhne,* "Do you know Anoop?" *Thīk?*
> [*Eng*: Laxmi, if you see him, *have a conversation with him*, just *ask*, "Do you know Anoop?" *Okay*?]

Controversies and language ideologies abound regarding the multifunctionality of this sort of mixing. Some people consider such hybrids as Spanglish (the combination of Spanish and English) or Sheng (the combination of Swahili and English) to be impure and detrimental to the speakers, while others consider such mixing to be creative, possibly even constituting a new language altogether, called a "monolect" or a "fused lect" (Meeuwis and Blommaert 1998; Auer 1999). Peter Auer's (1999) typology consists of three kinds of shifting, best conceived of as a continuum from what he calls "codeswitching"[8] (CS) at one end of the spectrum, through "language mixing" (LM) in the middle, to "fused lects" (FL) at the other end of the continuum. Although Auer himself does not present the continuum visually, it could be represented as in Figure 6.1.

Auer defines code-switching as those shifts from one code to another in which "the contrast between one code and the other (for instance, one language and another) is meaningful, and can be

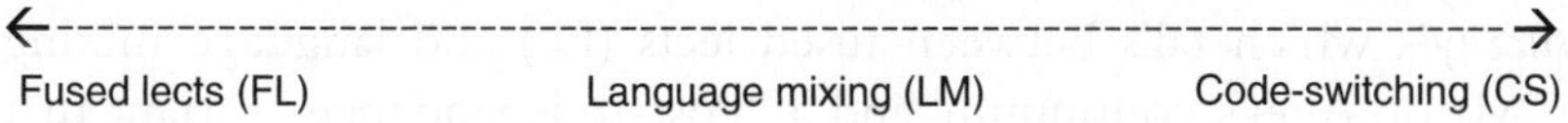

Figure 6.1 Peter Auer's continuum of codeswitching, language mixing, and fused lects.
Source: From Peter Auer (1999:328).

interpreted by participants, as indexing (contextualizing) either some aspects of the situation (discourse-related switching), or some feature of the codeswitching speaker (participant-related switching)" (Auer 1999:310). Language mixing, in contrast, is a more thorough intermixing of codes, to the point that it is the alternation between two codes that "itself constitutes the 'language'-of-interaction" (1999:315). The shifts in language mixing, according to Auer, do not involve the same sort of indexicality and shifts in footing that are involved in code-switching; indeed, the shifts back and forth between the two codes in language mixing do not seem to have any specific discursive function, except insofar as the mixing of the two codes in and of itself might index a particular social identity or set of meanings. At the far end of Auer's continuum is the phenomenon of "fused lects," which he defines as the development of a single code "AB" from two previously separate codes, "A" and "B." The main difference between language mixing and fused lects is one of grammaticalization; certain elements are stabilized or regularized, and there is less fluid shifting back and forth. Moreover, with a fused lect "AB," speakers may be unable to speak either "A" or "B" fluently. The new fusion may or may not develop into a fully recognized "language" in its own right, depending on which language ideologies prevail.

Some researchers, such as Laada Bilaniuk (2005), study shifts between codes – between Ukrainian and Russian in Bilaniuk's case – that span Auer's entire spectrum. These different types of Ukrainian/Russian mixtures are known as *surzhyk* and are generally stigmatized. In her research in Ukraine, Bilaniuk identified five types of Ukrainian/Russian mixtures that depended on factors such as the urban or rural residence of the speakers or the historical time period (pre- or post-Soviet, for example). Bilaniuk locates the five language mixtures along the Auer continuum from fused lects (FL) to language mixing (LM) to code-switching (CS) – and various combinations of these practices. So, for example, she identifies an "Urbanized Peasant" variant of *surzhyk*, which falls between fused lects (FL) and language mixing (LM) on Auer's continuum, and a "Post-Independence" variant that falls between language mixing (LM) and code-switching (CS) on Auer's continuum. In Bilaniuk's careful study, the complexities of linguistic practices and the accompanying language ideologies bring to life the multiple linguistic manifestations and social implications of various kinds of code-switching.

"Heteroglossia" and "Transidiomatic Practice"

To help illuminate the complicated multilingual global landscape, some scholars have coined terms that are intimidating tongue-twisters – and yet in a couple of cases at least, the terms are worth learning and using because they can help us reframe or reorient our study of multilingualism. Heteroglossia, for example, is a term made popular by the Russian literary critic Mikhail Bakhtin many decades ago. Although Bakhtin was mainly analyzing language within novels and other literary genres, much of what he said about language in these contexts has been found to be very helpful for social scientists interested in linguistic practices in real-life social settings.[9] Heteroglossia, in particular, is a concept that sheds light on the complex and fascinating co-existence in any given social context of multiple ways of speaking – whether they are different languages, dialects, or registers (however defined). In "Discourse in the Novel," an essay originally published in the 1930s, Bakhtin argued that language in actual social life is always stratified in multiple ways. Stratification creates different language varieties along the lines of genre, such as the different ways of writing for a popular newspaper versus "high" literature; along the lines of profession, such as different ways of speaking among lawyers, doctors, politicians, or teachers; and along other socially significant dimensions, such as age, education level, or elite status (Bakhtin 1981a:289–290). While Bakhtin calls these ways of speaking "languages," it is clear that he also means to refer to what we would call dialects and registers. Moreover, while he never mentions the term "indexicality," his writings nevertheless describe the processes through which linguistic practices index social identities. In a famous passage, part of which formed the epigraph to chapter 1 of this book, Bakhtin states:

> As a result of the work done by all these stratifying forces in language, there are no "neutral" words and forms – words and forms that can belong to "no one"; language has been completely taken over, shot through with intentions and accents. For any individual consciousness living in it, language is not an abstract system of normative forms but rather a concrete heteroglot conception of the world. All words have the "taste" of a profession, a genre, a tendency, a party, a particular work, a particular person, a generation, an age group, the day and hour. Each word tastes of the context and contexts in which it has lived its socially charged life; all words and forms are populated by intentions. Contextual overtones (generic, tendentious, individualistic) are inevitable in the word. (1981a:293)

There are two opposing forces in language, according to Bakhtin: the "centralizing" (or "centripetal") force used by highly authoritative entities such as governments that want to unify the language and make a unitary, standard way of speaking appear to be obligatory and natural, and the "decentralizing" (or "centrifugal") force that leads to ever greater stratification and ever more variation in socially charged ways of speaking (Bakhtin 1981a:272; Bakhtin 1981b:67). We can see these centralizing and decentralizing forces at work linguistically in many places around the world and also when we look at the global linguistic situation as a whole. Globalization has led in many cases to centralization and standardization in the form of greater use of dominant languages such as English, but it has also led to high rates of migration, resulting in greater decentralization and linguistic diversity in more communities than ever before (cf. Romaine 2001:530–532). Bakhtin was one of the first scholars to appreciate these opposing forces and the social complexity of language.

Another theorist who has helped shed light on multilingualism and globalization is Marco Jacquemet. Like Bakhtin, Jacquemet emphasizes multiplicity, complexity, and social stratification in linguistic practices, but in addition to these features, he also argues that "contemporary studies on language and communication must address the progressive globalization of communicative practices and social formations that result from the increasing mobility of people, languages, and texts" (2005:261). Accelerating rates of migration around the world, accompanied by new communication technologies that enable people to be in touch much more frequently across large distances, call into question, Jacquemet claims, scholarly approaches that assume small-scale, static speech communities based largely on face-to-face interaction. Instead, Jacquemet proposes that researchers of language adopt a different approach:

> [They should try] to account for how groups of people, no longer territorially defined, think about themselves, communicate using an array of both face-to-face and long-distance medias, and in so doing produce and reproduce social hierarchies and power asymmetries. I propose to use the term transidiomatic practice to describe the communicative practices of transnational groups that interact using different languages and communicative codes simultaneously present in a range of communicative channels, both local and distant. (2005: 264–265; emphasis in the original)

An example of people who are engaged in such transidiomatic practices, Jacquemet says, are those who work in call centers in South Asia. As documentaries such as "Diverted to Delhi" demonstrate, the workers at such call centers are given training in "appropriate" accents and cultural practices for the area of the world to which they will be providing customer service. In "Diverted to Delhi," for example, young Indians are shown learning about Australian beaches, favorite sports there, and common Australian phrases so that they can converse in more culturally knowledgeable ways with customers who call from that country (Stitt 2002). "The world is now full of locales where speakers use a mixture of languages in interacting with friends and co-workers, read English and other 'global' languages on their computer screens, watch local, regional, or global broadcasts, and listen to pop music in various languages," Jacquemet writes (2005:266).

Jacquemet provides another example of people who engage in transidiomatic practices – a multilingual Albanian family. After political changes in 1991 allowed Albanians more access to global media and to opportunities for travel and migration, many individuals, such as those in the Xhemali family that Jacquemet describes, became fluent in multiple languages and migrated to the United States or to other countries in Europe for work. In the Adriatic region where Albania is located, multilingualism is not new; what *is* new, however, is "the extraordinary simultaneity and co-presence of these languages produced through a multiplicity of communicative channels, from face-to-face to mass media" (2005:271; cf. Fairclough 2006:3–4). Albanians watch South American soap operas dubbed into Italian, listen to pop music in English, and travel all over the world to work. Consider the multilingual histories of just some of the Xhemali family members (Jacquemet 2005:268):

- Drita, the oldest daughter in the family, left Albania in the early 1990s, migrating first to Germany, then to New York City. She speaks fluent Albanian, German, and English, and can understand and make herself understood in Italian. She is married to an Albanian man, Gencit, who is fluent in Albanian, Greek, English, and Italian.
- Idlir, Drita's brother, also lives in New York City in the same building as Drita. He is married to Helga, a German woman with a German mother and Turkish father. Helga speaks German, English, and Albanian.
- Esmeralda, Drita and Idlir's sister, still lives in Albania and works for an international organization, where she speaks English all day. After work she speaks Albanian and Italian with her friends and surfs the internet in English.

Families such as the Xhemalis who are multilingual and who engage in transnational migration also engage in "transidiomatic practices," according to Jacquemet, because they migrate to multiple countries and communicate through new technologies, leading to complex processes of identity formation and power asymmetries. Such multifunctionality and complexities are the result of recent trends in globalization and must be taken into account by scholars of socially situated language.

Sociolinguist Jan Blommaert (2009) presents a stark example of power asymmetries resulting from incorrect assumptions and pernicious language ideologies held by government officials in the United Kingdom about what the linguistic abilities of a political asylum seeker from Rwanda should be. The asylum seeker, whom Blommaert gives the pseudonym of Joseph Mutingira, had a nightmarish childhood and a horror story of an adolescence that spanned the Rwandan genocide in 1994 and the extremely tumultuous times before and after. His mother, a Tutsi, was murdered when Joseph was five, and his father, a Hutu, was murdered along with the rest of his family shortly thereafter. Joseph escaped his house through a window and spent years in the basement of an uncle, who sent him on dangerous arms-dealing errands. When Joseph was nine or ten years old, he was caught by with a sack of weapons and put in a detention camp, where he was beaten every day, then sent to prison, where he was routinely and very brutally tortured and raped. After four years in prison, in 2001, when Joseph was approximately 14 years old, a woman showed up at the prison and managed to get him released. She then took him to the United Kingdom and disappeared. Joseph started asking strangers for help, and one person took him to the Immigration Service. A cursory interrogation by an immigration official resulted in a declaration of adulthood status for Joseph, as the official believed him to be over 18. This declaration then set into motion a lengthy asylum-seeking process, which resulted in a rejection by Britain's Home Office and a decision to deport Joseph to Uganda.

One of the main grounds for the Home Office's rejection of Joseph's request for political asylum was his "unusual" linguistic profile. Blommaert, drawing on Michael Silverstein's (1996) notion of a "monoglot ideology," claims that the British immigration officials were blinded by this sort of ideology and were therefore operating under the false assumption that everyone from Rwanda should be able to speak Kinyarwanda. While Joseph could speak a few words of this language, he was not at all fluent in it. The reason for this, he explained, was that his parents spoke only English in the home and that he had never attended school in Rwanda because he was in hiding or prison for many years. His interaction with his uncle and various prisoners and guards instead allowed him to acquire another language, Runyankole. The Home Office's rejection letter curiously cited the BBC as an authoritative source on linguistic practices in Rwanda:

> The BBC World Service, however, advises that a genuine Rwandan national from any of the ethnic groups will normally be able to speak Kinyarwanda and/or French. Kinyarwanda, the national language, is the medium of instruction in schools at primary level while French is used at secondary level ... Your lack of basic knowledge of the

> Kinyarwanda language suggests that you are not a genuine national of Rwanda. (Blommaert 2009:420)

Blommaert argues that this decision by Britain's Home Office to deny Joseph political asylum based largely on his unusual linguistic repertoire failed to take into account that Joseph was not living in "normal" times, or that the linguistic situation in almost any nation in the world is more complex than monolingual language ideologies surrounding "national languages" might suggest. "Imposing a strictly national order of things on people who are denationalized or transnationalized is not likely to do them justice," Blommaert concludes (2009:425).

In this chapter, we explored some of the many facets of multilingualism, both at the individual and societal level, and placed these phenomena in the context of an increasingly "globalized" world. Code-switching and code-mixing between or among languages, dialects, or registers provide fascinating opportunities for research on the individual and social dimensions of multilingualism. At a more macro level, studying the stigmatization or valorization of different languages and language policy within various nation-states can shed light on complex political and cultural relationships and values. Studies that consider *both* the micro-level linguistic practices of actual people *and* the macro-level workings of language politics within or across societies have the best chance of adequately analyzing the complexities involved in multilingual communicative interactions.

7

Literacy Practices

Think of all the taken-for-granted ways in which reading and writing saturate our daily lives. Even if we put aside schooling, the most obvious realm in which literacy plays a central role, an average day in the life of a person living in the United States or any number of other countries in the twenty-first century will most likely involve more interactions with written texts than can be counted. "[M]ost social interactions in contemporary society," David Barton and Mary Hamilton proclaim, "are textually mediated" (Barton and Hamilton 2005:14). From cereal boxes, billboards, and newspapers to the internet and words written on clothing, many people engage more frequently with the written word than they realize. And even when people are alone while reading and writing, they are engaged in social activities because reading and writing are enacted and interpreted in culturally and socially specific ways. Moreover, these activities are also bound up with social differences and inequalities. Patricia Baquedano-López writes: "Literacy is less a set of acquired skills and more an activity that affords the acquisition and negotiation of new ways of thinking and acting in the world" (2004:246). And since the social world is not composed of neutral, power-free interactions, James Gee notes that we should therefore not expect this to be true of literacy practices: "The traditional meaning of the word 'literacy' – the 'ability to read and write' – appears 'innocent' and 'obvious.' But, it is no such thing. Literacy as 'the ability to read and write' situates literacy in the

Living Language: An Introduction to Linguistic Anthropology, First Edition. Laura M. Ahearn.

individual person, rather than in society. As such, it obscures the multiple ways in which literacy interrelates with the workings of power" (Gee 2008:31).

Because of the socially embedded nature of reading and writing, these activities present ideal objects of inquiry for linguistic anthropologists. And yet, relatively few linguistic anthropologists have chosen to study literacy. There are of course exceptions, and some of this work will be summarized later in this chapter, but it is fair to say that more linguistic anthropologists have focused on orality rather than literacy – that is, on the ways in which the spoken word reflects and shapes social relations rather than on the ways in which the written word does so. Ideally, scholars should explore both orality and literacy because in almost every instance they are intertwined; written texts directly or indirectly influence many conversations, and verbal interactions can lead eventually to reading or writing of some sort. Consider the following examples in which both orality and literacy are involved:

- Several friends discuss some movie reviews they have read before deciding which movie to attend.
- A woman describes to her lawyer an e-mail she received from someone who is harassing her.
- A man driving in a country where he does not speak the language, and therefore cannot understand the road signs, gets lost, which leads him to ask for directions that he subsequently writes down in his own language.
- New parents anxiously consult parenting how-to books as they debate the best methods for getting their baby to sleep better.
- A man who has lost his job goes in to apply for unemployment insurance and has to consult with someone in the office about how to fill out the forms.
- Several students decide to protest a school policy by launching an online petition and writing a daily blog about the progress of their movement.
- A religious leader gives a sermon based on a passage from the Bible, the Koran, the Vedas, or some other holy text.
- A conversation about an upcoming vacation inspires a man to start a list of all the things he should pack for the trip.

- Several students who have been assigned this chapter to read discuss other examples of the intertwining of literacy and orality in their daily lives.

Given the centrality of literacy in many social interactions around the world, closer attention to reading and writing as forms of social action would enrich the research of many cultural and linguistic anthropologists and other social scientists. This chapter presents an overview of some useful concepts in the study of literacy and a summary of some of the most interesting studies that have been conducted on literacy practices from an ethnographic perspective.

Literacy Events vs. Literacy Practices

Two useful concepts in the anthropological study of reading and writing are "literacy events" and "literacy practices." Shirley B. Heath straightforwardly defines "literacy events" as "occasions in which written language is integral to the nature of participants' interactions and their interpretive processes and strategies" (Heath 2001[1982]:319). The specific examples provided above that interweave orality and literacy are all examples of literacy events. The concept of "literacy event" stresses the situated nature of literacy – literacy events always take place in specific social contexts.

Literacy events should not be studied in isolation from the social relations and cultural norms that prevail in a given society, however. As Heath notes, "literacy events have social interactional rules which regulate the type and amount of talk about what is written, and define ways in which oral language reinforces, denies, extends or sets aside the written material" (1983:386). To analyze these more general "rules" about the significance or interpretation of particular texts in the social contexts in which they are found, the concept of "literacy practice" is very useful. David Barton and Mary Hamilton define literacy practices as "the general cultural ways of utilising written language" (2000:7). They go on to contrast "literacy events" and "literacy practices" as follows: "Literacy events are activities where literacy has a role. Usually there is a written text, or texts, central to the activity, and there may be talk around the text. Events are observable episodes which arise from practices and are shaped by them" (2000:8). Literacy practices, unlike literacy events, are not specific, observable occurrences but rather general norms regarding how written texts tend to be produced, interpreted, or discussed.

Literacy events and practices must be studied together and must be situated within the overall context of social and cultural practices in general. "You can no more cut the literacy out of the overall social practice," James Gee writes, "or cut away the non-literacy parts from the literacy parts of the overall practice, than you can subtract the white squares from a chessboard and still have a chessboard" (Gee 2008:45). This relationship between literacy events and literacy practices is very much in keeping with the emphasis placed on practice from the very beginning of this book; indeed, "practice" was one of the four key terms defined in chapter 1. Just as specific social actions emerge from more general social practices and norms, then recursively loop around to either reinforce or reshape those very practices and norms, so too do literacy events arise from more general literacy practices, which are then either strengthened or reconfigured by those events. In other words, the distinction between literacy events and literacy practices is entirely compatible with practice theory and an approach that views all types of language use as forms of social action.

As an example of how a specific literacy event can influence, and be influenced by, general social norms and literacy practices – culturally acceptable ways, in other words, of using reading and writing – here is a description of a literacy event from my fieldwork on literacy and marriage practices in Nepal in the 1980s and 1990s.[1]

Pema Kumari's letter

When Pema Kumari's marriage was arranged in 1988, she was in the ninth grade, the next-to-last year of high school in Nepal at the time. She and the other young women in her class, all of whom I taught when I was a Peace Corps teacher in their village, were by then the females with the most formal education in the village. The ideas to which Pema Kumari was exposed and the literacy skills that she gained at school turned out to be very influential because they helped her to transform a culturally acceptable practice in which arranged marriage brides were allowed to "resist" their marriages through ineffectual tears and verbal complaints into an action that was unique in the village's history.

Upon learning that she had been given away in marriage, Pema Kumari retreated crying to the attic – the expected token resistance of a soon-to-be arranged-marriage bride. Once there, however, she composed a letter to her father threatening to have him put in jail if he made her go through with the marriage – an act unheard of in Junigau.[2] Others who were there at the time recounted to me how Pema Kumari's father cried as he read the letter aloud to the assembled guests at the pre-wedding feast, after which he reportedly went upstairs to the attic and pleaded with his daughter not to throw away the family's honor. According to differing versions of the story, she either agreed to drop her threat to have her father jailed for marrying her off without her will, or her father proceeded without such an assurance. One woman maintains that it was her own reminders of the inauspiciousness of such actions that convinced Pema Kumari to relent. In any case, the wedding went forward on schedule.

As a teenager, then, Pema Kumari was married to a man who was in the Indian Army. What no one told her at the time, fearing that she would become even more upset, was that he was about to be sent to fight in Sri Lanka. Within a year of her marriage, he was killed in battle there, and Pema Kumari was a widow. Recalling the scene at Pema Kumari's pre-wedding feast, many villagers remarked that she had brought her own bad luck (*karma*) upon herself by using her literacy skills to bring dishonor (*beijjat*) to her family.

After the customary six months of mourning, Pema Kumari was unwilling to remain any longer in the extremely subservient role allotted to her as a widow in her husband's extended family home.[3] She moved back to her parents' home and, without consulting either her parents or her in-laws, she informed the Headmaster that she would be returning to school. Pema Kumari subsequently passed the School Leaving Certificate exam and enrolled in classes at the Tansen campus of Tribuvan University. After she earned her bachelor's degree, she obtained a job in a bank. She continues to live alone in Tansen, supported by her salary and the generous pension provided to her by the Indian Army. Once a year on the anniversary of her husband's death she returns to her husband's home to perform rituals, but otherwise she has almost no contact with her in-laws and very little more with her own parents.

Although Pema Kumari's "literacy event" – the writing of a letter of complaint to her father – did not succeed in preventing her arranged marriage from taking place, through a confluence of factors she did manage to use her literacy skills in a completely novel way, one that drew upon existing social practices that allowed arranged marriage brides to express opposition to their marriages. In the process, she challenged the practice of arranged marriage as no actions before ever had, thus demonstrating how cultural transformation can occur.

Notice how impossible it is to describe this literacy event even as briefly as I have done here without situating it within the context of more general literacy practices in the community and alluding to the broader cultural norms and social practices concerning gender, marriage, and education in Nepal during these years. There is much more that could be said about Pema Kumari, but the inherently social and potentially political nature of an act as simple as writing a letter should be clear from the brief description provided here.

"Autonomous" vs. "Ideological" Approaches to Studying Literacy

Literacy scholars have not always situated acts of reading and writing in terms of broader social and cultural practices in the way I advocate here. Indeed, some researchers and educators still espouse a view that considers literacy to be a neutral technology separate from any particular social context and entailing the identical social or cognitive results. A theoretical debate has been taking place as to how literacy should be defined and studied, and while most linguistic anthropologists consider the debate to have been resolved, it is instructive to review the main issues here, as they shed light on various scholars' and nonscholars' language ideologies regarding the nature of reading and writing.[4]

On one side of the issue are scholars like Jack Goody, who was an early proponent of what Brian Street has called the "autonomous" model of literacy (Goody 1986, 2000; Goody and Watt 1963). Goody and other supporters of the autonomous model maintain that the advent of literacy in a society will cause the *same* social and psychological effects, no matter which society is being studied. These scholars "conceptualise literacy in technical terms, treating it as independent of social context, an autonomous variable whose consequences for society and cognition can be derived from its intrinsic character" (Street 1984:5). Walter Ong, another proponent of the autonomous model, asserts boldly that "without writing, human consciousness cannot achieve its fuller potentials, cannot produce other beautiful and powerful creations. In this sense, orality needs to produce and is destined to produce writing" (Ong 1982:14–15). Ong, Goody, and others who espouse the autonomous model see a "Great Divide" separating "oral" societies from "literate" ones – a gap similar to the one turn-of-the-century anthropologists used to claim existed between "primitive" and "civilized" societies. Most linguistic anthropologists, including myself, find this approach to studying literacy untenable. Moreover, as we saw in chapter 4, scholars such as Scribner and Cole (1981) found no single, overall effect of illiteracy or different types of literacy among the Vai of Liberia but instead showed that each type of literacy was embedded in a set of very different social practices that led to different cognitive effects (1981:234).

Opposing advocates of the "autonomous" model of literacy are those scholars, such as David Barton (Barton and Hamilton 1998; Barton et al. 2000), Keith Basso (1989[1974]), Mike Baynham (1995), Niko Besnier (1995), Jonathan Boyarin (1993), Tamar El-Or (2002), Ruth Finnegan (1988), James Paul Gee (2008), Mastin Prinsloo (Prinsloo and Baynham 2008), and Brian Street (1984, 1993, 2003) who favor an "ideological" model for studying literacies. Besnier describes the goals of this approach as follows: "Rather than seeking an overarching and context-free characterization of the cognitive and social consequences of literacy, proponents of the ideological model focus on the activities, events, and ideological constructs associated with particular manifestations of literacy" (Besnier 1995:5). Scholars advocating this approach examine the specific ramifications of the advent of literacy in each society and claim that there are no universal attributes of so-called literate societies. Advocates of the ideological view of literacy maintain that it is impossible for literacy skills to be acquired neutrally. Many, in fact, speak of "literacies" instead of "literacy" because they want to emphasize the importance of studying the specificities of different literacies. Mike Baynham writes:

> It is important to study from a linguistic base, as the analysis of texts, but we also need the further dimension of literacy as strategic, purposeful activity in social interactions. Beyond this we need to understand literacy as social practice, the way it interacts with ideologies and institutions to shape and define the possibilities and life paths of individuals. (1995:71)

This sort of situated approach to the study of literacy has produced many rich ethnographies over the past few decades.

Some Examples of Situated Literacy Research

The following researchers are some of the many who treat literacy as social practice, just as Baynham advocated. Individually and collectively, they have changed the way many scholars and on-the-ground educators understand social interactions surrounding written texts.

Preschool literacy practices in the southeastern United States

Shirley Brice Heath's long-term ethnographic research in the 1960s and 1970s in the Piedmont Carolinas area in the southeastern United States resulted in one of the most important and widely cited articles on literacy practices, "What No Bedtime Story Means: Narrative Skills at Home and School" (Heath 2001), originally published in *Language in Society* in 1982 and later expanded into a book, *Ways with Words: Language, Life, and Work in Communities and Classrooms* (Heath 1983).[5] Echoing the insights of scholars such as Elinor Ochs and Bambi Schieffelin, who were working on language socialization (see chapter 3) at around the same time, Heath applied the same approach to literacy practices, stating that "ways of taking from books are as much part of learned behavior as are ways of eating, sitting, playing games, and building houses" (Heath 2001:318). Heath therefore considered it essential for researchers to study the many different ways in which preschoolers and adults interacted surrounding written texts in order to understand how these different ways of being socialized into reading and writing had an influence on children's subsequent performance in school.

Heath compared the ways in which parents "socialize their preschool children into a literacy orientation" (2001:323) in three communities:

- *Maintown.* A mainly white "middle-class" community, in which Heath focused on the families of primary-level schoolteachers who had their own preschool children.
- *Roadville.* "A white working-class community of families steeped in four generations in the life of the textile mill" (2001:325).
- *Trackton.* "A working-class black community," whose older generations had worked as farmers on their own or others' land and whose younger generations had more recently found work in the textile mill (2001:325).

Preschoolers in the three communities were introduced to, and socialized into, literacy in ways that differed substantially. The Maintown children Heath studied were encouraged to give attention to books almost from birth on. Their bedrooms often contained bookcases, and their parents read to them regularly, frequently pausing in their reading to ask simple questions about the pictures or story of a book. Adults also talked about books with their preschool children outside of the actual reading time, making links to stories they had read and encouraging their children "to suspend reality, to tell stories that are not true, to ascribe fiction-like features to everyday objects" (2001:321). Well before they entered formal schooling, Maintown children learned formulaic openings for stories and typical narrative tropes, which they used in their own storytelling. They also learned how to be patient listeners as they were read to by adults, speaking up only to answer questions. "A pervasive pattern of all these features is the authority that books and book-related activities have in the lives of both the preschooler and members of their primary network," Heath writes (2001:321). Given this socialization into the specific form of literacy that is so highly valued in most formal educational contexts, it is easy to see that Maintown children entered school well prepared to learn and interact with written texts in the ways that would be expected of them in school.

In Roadville, the white working-class community, Heath found that babies were brought home from the hospital to rooms decorated with "literacy-based stimuli" such as ABCs and nursery rhymes. Adults used books to instruct their children, teaching them labels for items such as balls, dogs, and trucks. Young children were expected to answer simple questions correctly regarding these labels, but then, once children could talk at around age three or so, they were prevented from participating any longer in the reading process and expected to learn to listen quietly. Older preschoolers were given workbooks to practice answering questions about stories and to learn the alphabet, with the emphasis on facts, skills, repetition, and rules. Unlike adults in Maintown, Roadville adults did not extend the content or the habits of literacy beyond bookreading and did not make connections for their children between books and the real world. "Any fictionalized account of a real event is viewed as a *lie*; reality is better than fiction … Thus, children cannot decontextualize their knowledge or fictionalize events known to them and shift them about into other frames" (2001:330; emphasis in the original).

When Roadville children started school, Heath discovered, they usually performed well initially. They often knew some of the alphabet, colors, and shapes, and had acquired other basic skills. They were able to listen quietly to a story and to answer simple questions. They would also do well on workbook exercises that asked them to identify words or letters. But whenever they were asked for their own opinions about a story, or for counter-factual analyses (such as, "What would have happened if Billy had not told the policeman what happened?"), Roadville children most often shrugged their shoulders (2001:330). This inability or unwillingness – more like a culturally based unfamiliarity, Heath argues – with this sort of exercise meant that Roadville children tended to fall behind after the first few years of school. Heath explains:

> Thus their initial successes in reading, being good students, following orders, and adhering to school norms of participating in lessons begin to fall away rapidly about the time they enter the fourth grade. As the importance and frequency of questions and reading habits with which they are familiar decline in the higher grades, they have no way of keeping up or of seeking help in learning what it is they do not even know they don't know. (2001:331)

In contrast to both Maintown and Roadville children, children in Trackton, the black working-class community, were immersed from birth in almost constant human communication, both verbal and nonverbal – but not written. Trackton parents did not read to their children, and their homes did not have any reading materials especially for children. Instead, adults rewarded children for attending to and imitating the verbal and nonverbal behaviors of others, which led children to develop creative and complex abilities to play with language through rhyming and storytelling. Trackton children were left to figure out connections between situations and stories on their own, since their parents, like those in some of the communities described in chapter 3, felt it was unnecessary and inadvisable to simplify their language for them. As a result, the children developed rich verbal repertoires on their own.

When Trackton children started school, they faced totally unfamiliar types of questions and interactions. A few adapted and learned the interactional literacy skills called for in school, but, Heath notes, the majority did not:

> [T]he majority not only fail to learn the content of lessons, but also do not adopt the social-interactional rules for school literacy events. Print in isolation bears little authority in their world. The kinds of questions asked about reading books are unfamiliar. The children's abilities to link metaphorically two events or situations and to recreate scenes are not tapped in school; in fact *these abilities often cause difficulties*, because they enable children to see parallels teachers did not intend and, indeed, may not recognize until the children point them out. (2001:336; emphasis in the original)

In sum, Heath discovered that the ways in which children in these three communities were socialized into both orality and literacy had profound influences on their subsequent school performance. What we learn from Heath's groundbreaking work, Collins and Blot assert, is that orality and literacy cannot be separated. Moreover, they claim, "[T]here is no universality to literacy; instead, there are many literacies. To describe only one set of uses and functions (those associated with school or essayist literacy) is to miss the myriad other uses and functions found among the literacies of communities throughout the world" (Collins and Blot 2003:44; cf. Scribner and Cole 1981).

Love-letter writing in Nepal

Beginning with my years as a Peace Corps teacher in Nepal (1982–1986), and throughout my dissertation fieldwork (1992–1993), and during many subsequent follow-up trips to Nepal, I have always been fascinated by the ways in which literacy practices intersect with emotion, agency, gender, and social change (Ahearn 2001a, 2008).[6] When I first arrived in the village of Junigau in the early 1980s, almost all boys were being sent to the local school for at least a few years, and almost all men could read and write in Nepali at a basic level, either from the formal schooling that they had received or from informal instruction that they had been given as Gurkha soldiers in the British or Indian Army. Among girls and women, however, the situation was very different. Most women in the village were illiterate, and only some families were sending their daughters to the local school. There were evening female literacy classes for teenage girls and married women, however, so by the 1990s most girls and women under the age of 30 or so had at least some ability to read and write.

In my research on this "incipiently literate" community (cf. Besnier 1995), I was very interested to learn what would happen as girls and women acquired literacy skills. How would pre-existing social norms and cultural practices influence how these girls and women used their new skills, and how would the application of their new skills in turn potentially influence these broader norms and practices? What I discovered was that many young, newly literate women in Junigau in the 1990s chose to use their literacy skills in an unanticipated way – to engage in love-letter correspondences, many of which resulted in elopements. Since most marriages up until that time had been arranged by parents, this was a dramatic change.

Because it was not considered appropriate for Junigau men and women to date or spend time alone together, love letters provided them with a way to keep in touch with their sweethearts (see Figure 7.1). They also prolonged courtships, enabling the participants to get to know each other better. Moreover, the mere sending and receiving of love letters marked someone as a particular kind of person – what villagers called a "developed" (*bikāsi*) as opposed to a "backward" (*pichhyāDi*)[7] individual, someone who was capable of creating a particular kind of companionate marriage with a "life friend." Together,

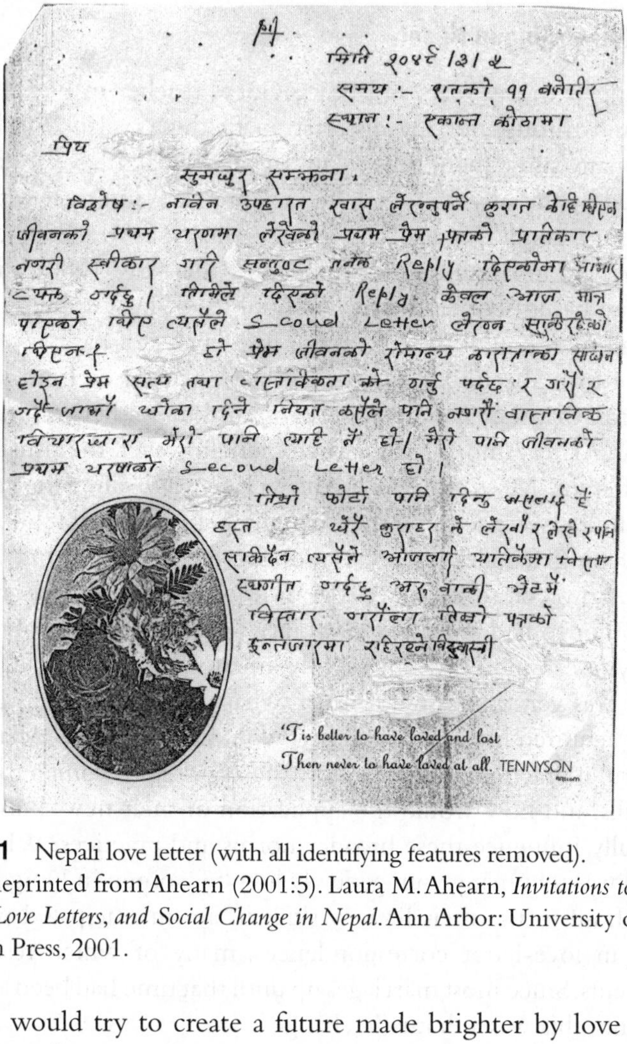
प्रि

मिति २०४९/३/५
समय :- रातको ११ बजेतिर
स्थान :- एकान्त कोठामा

प्रिय
सुमधुर सम्झना।
विशेष :- नाबेन उपहार त खास लेख्नुपर्ने कुरा त केहि थिएन
जीवनको प्रथम चरणमा लेखेको प्रथम प्रेम पत्रको प्रतिकार
नगरी स्वीकार गरी सन्तुष्ट नभै Reply दिएकोमा आभार
व्यक्त गर्दछु। तिमीले दिएको Reply केवल आज मात्र
पाएको थिए त्यसैले Second Letter लेख्न सकिरहेको
थिइन। हो प्रेम जीवनको रोमान्च कहानीका साधन
होइन प्रेम सत्य तथा वास्तविकता को गर्नु पर्दछ र गरौं र
गर्दै जाऔं धोका दिने नियत कसैले पनि नगरौं वास्तविक
विचारधारा मेरो पनि त्यहि नै हो। मेरो पनि जीवनको
प्रथम चरणको Second Letter हो।
तिम्रो फोटो पनि दिनु भएलाई हैं
हस्त धेरै कुराहरु त लेखौं र लेखे र पनि
सकिदैन त्यसैले आजलाई यतिकैमा लेखनी
स्थगीत गर्दछु अरु बाँकी भेटमैं
विस्तार गरौंला तिम्रो पत्रको
इन्तजारमा रहिरहने विश्वासी

'Tis better to have loved and lost
Than never to have loved at all. TENNYSON

Figure 7.1 Nepali love letter (with all identifying features removed).
Source: Reprinted from Ahearn (2001:5). Laura M. Ahearn, *Invitations to Love: Literacy, Love Letters, and Social Change in Nepal.* Ann Arbor: University of Michigan Press, 2001.

the two would try to create a future made brighter by love and by "life success."

Junigau women's literacy practices did not just facilitate a shift away from arranged marriage toward elopement, therefore, but also reflected and helped to shape the new ways in which villagers thought of themselves. Along with these changes, however, came some reinforcement of pre-existing norms, especially in the area of gender relations. While it might seem to readers used to having the right to choose their own spouse that acquiring such a right would inevitably improve someone's life, in fact, the opposite was true for some Junigau women who eloped after love-letter correspondences. In cases where their husbands or in-laws turned out to be abusive, the women found that they had no recourse and no support from their own parents. If they had encountered these kinds of problems after an arranged marriage, most could have returned to their parents' home or expected their parents to intervene on their behalf. Such was not the case for most women who had eloped. Indeed, because most of these women ended up moving into their husbands' extended households as low-status daughters-in-law, their social positioning and daily lives were virtually identical to those of women whose marriages had been arranged – except that they did not have the same recourse if things went poorly. In some respects, therefore, the women's new literacy practices created new and different opportunities and identities, but in other respects, long-standing gender inequalities remained or were even exacerbated.

And literacy practices have continued to shift in Junigau in recent years. For example, during a trip I took to Nepal in early 2010, Junigau residents told me that beginning in 2009, when mobile phones became available to villagers who could afford them, young men and women started talking (but, unlike in the capital city of Kathmandu and many other places in the world, *not* texting) via mobile phone instead of writing out love letters to each other. The implications of this new courtship practice in Junigau remain to be seen.

Instant messaging: more like speech or writing?

New communication technologies offer many exciting research opportunities for scholars interested in literacy. In particular, some of these technologies call into question even further than before the sharp distinction often drawn between verbal and written interactions. Even earlier researchers such as Ruth Finnegan (1988) who argued for the importance of studying orality and literacy in conjunction with each other still considered them analytically separable, albeit integrally interwoven. New communication technologies such as instant messaging, automatic transcription software, and text messaging on mobile phones, however, have blurred the line between speech and writing to the point that, in some instances at least, hybrid forms combining features of both orality and literacy seem to be emerging.

As an example of such hybridity, Graham Jones and Bambi Schieffelin (2009) present some interesting evidence that the examples of Instant Messaging (IM) they studied between 2003 and 2006 became progressively more like speech and less like writing stylistically over these years. IM correspondence takes place on the computer; participants write back and forth to each other in real time on a keyboard. Despite this clearly "written" medium, Jones and Schieffelin (2009:84–85) report that young people using IM regularly referred to their behavior metalinguistically as "talking," "yelling," "saying," or "speaking." This language ideology was evident even in 2003, but what these researchers discovered when they compared the tape recordings and transcripts from both face-to-face and IM conversations from 2003 through 2006 was that the data from 2006 IM exchanges contained many more examples of a certain kind of reported speech characteristic of informal spoken conversations than the 2003 IM exchanges did. "The language ideology that already framed IM as talk by 2003 helped shape the types of stylistic innovations users devised to constitute the activity as such; these innovations, in turn, reinforce the ideological association of IM with informal speech" (Jones and Schieffelin 2009:109).

1 wandawoman (10:20:21 PM): …
2 but my dad was like "OH GOOD I'M SO GLAD YOU
3 WANT TO PAY YOUR OWN RENT!" and I was like
4 oh… okay. :-P

All forms of quotatives (such as "she said…," "I asked her…," etc.) were more numerous in the 2006 IM data compared to the 2003 IM data (see Table 7.1), but the increase in the use of *be* + *like* was especially striking. This development, Jones and Schieffelin report (2009:78), "appears to be associated with users' efforts to reposition IM on the continuum of writing and speaking."

Jones and Schieffelin argue that the increase in *be* + *like* should be viewed as evidence of these young people's creativity with a new form of communication. They also interpret this transformation in IM quotative usage as indicative of the way in which this speech community attempted to set itself apart linguistically as well as socially from other communities of language users. In their conclusion,

Table 7.1 '*Be* + *like*' as a percentage of total quotatives in face-to-face and IM talk (2003 face-to-face n=248; 2003 IM n=35; 2006 face-to-face n=468; 2006 IM n=175; table created from data reported in Jones and Schieffelin 2009:88).

Type of interaction	'*Be* + *like*' as a percentage of total quotatives in 2003	'*Be* + *like*' as a percentage of total quotatives in 2006
Face-to-face conversation	75%	67%
Instant Messaging	6%	50%

Jones and Schieffelin argue strongly against language ideologies that hold *be* + *like* usage in contempt:

> The patterns of language use that we have documented in IM do not support the view that users are 'simplifying' language to make communication easier or more efficient; in fact, users are less concerned with efficiency than with expressivity, seeking to make the language both look as well as 'sound' more like informal talk. To this end, they are mobilizing a collective creativity in accomplishing a specific style of communication. Negative stereotypes about current trends in youth language obscure the purposefulness, care, and artfulness with which young adults like those in our study constitute talk and sociality, while engaging in moral problem-solving activities. The use of *be* + *like* as a quotative marker in the context of Instant Messaging, far from indicating linguistic impoverishment, provides evidence of systematicity in both convention and style. (2009:109)

While the three studies summarized in this section are only a few of the many that treat literacy as a form of social practice, the research by Heath on preschoolers' literacy practices, my own work on love-letter writing in Nepal, and Jones and Schieffelin's study of the use of *be* + *like* in Instant Message exchanges all provide examples of how linguistic anthropologists approach reading and writing as situated, socially embedded practices.

The Not-So-New "New Literacy Studies" and its Critics

All of the scholars whose work was summarized in the previous section insist upon studying literacy as a form of social practice, an approach shared by scholars associated with "New Literacy Studies" (NLS). NLS was initiated by David Barton, James Paul Gee, and Brian Street, among others, and many of the NLS scholars are from the United Kingdom, South Africa, or Europe. For example, the Lancaster Literacy Research Centre, under the directorship of David Barton, is an interdisciplinary group of researchers at Lancaster University in the United Kingdom. Another interdisciplinary group on the Anthropology of Writing is directed by Béatrice Fraenkel and located in Paris at CNRS (Centre National de la Recherche Scientifique), which is part of l'École des Hautes Études en Sciences Sociales. Relatively few NLS scholars at these institutions or elsewhere are anthropologists, and even fewer of them are trained in linguistic anthropology; most have degrees in fields such as applied linguistics, sociolinguistics, English, or education. Nevertheless, the ethnographic focus of their work, as evidenced by the fact that many call themselves "linguistic ethnographers," is very much in keeping with contemporary research priorities in linguistic anthropology, making the dialogue that has begun to take place between NLS scholars and linguistic anthropologists mutually beneficial.

Since the term "New Literacy Studies" was coined decades ago and the approach that considers literacy a social practice is even older, it seems a bit strange to continue calling it "new." James Paul Gee makes the following comments in the third edition of his well-known book, *Social Linguistics and Literacies*:

> It is a problem, of course, to call any enterprise "new," because, of course, it soon becomes "old." Were it not so cumbersome, it would be better to call the field something like "integrated social-cultural-political-historical literacy studies," which names the viewpoint it takes on literacy. However, for better or worse, the term New Literacy Studies has become well known and widely used, so, reluctantly, I will continue to use the term. (2008:150)

As could be expected for any approach that has been around for a quarter of a century, NLS has attracted some criticisms from practitioners and nonpractitioners alike (e.g., Brandt and Clinton 2002; Collins and Blot 2003; Lewis et al. 2007; Maddox 2008; Reder and Davila 2005), the main ones of which can be summarized as follows:

- *Particularism.* The ethnographic approach favored by NLS scholars has produced many rich accounts of literacy practices in specific communities, but these accounts can sometimes be overly particular, some critics maintain, making it difficult, if not impossible, to apply the insights gained from one study to a situation in a different location, or to see how the local and the global are merged in any given context.
- *Losing sight of the materiality of literacy.* In their emphasis on social practice and on what individuals actually do with their reading and writing skills, NLS scholars, some argue, have sometimes failed to recognize the importance of literacy *objects* – the texts themselves, whether they are books, love letters, t-shirts, graffiti on walls, signage in subways, or slogans on billboards. Analysis of the relative permanence of these objects, and their ability to travel across time and space (what Brandt and Clinton 2002 call their "transcontextualing potential"; cf. Barton and Hamilton 2005:23–24) would allow researchers to examine the various "social lives" led by literacy objects (cf. Appadurai 1988), and in so doing would necessarily move the analysis beyond the local context of specific individuals.
- *Under-theorization of power.* Although Brian Street and other NLS scholars were motivated in their initial articulation of the "ideological" vs. "autonomous" approach to literacy by an interest in the non-neutral and power-saturated nature of its use in specific locations around the world, some scholars have criticized their work for not being explicit enough about the workings of power at the micro and macro level.

To the degree that work by NLS scholars suffers from these weaknesses, the problems often stem, in my opinion, from the fact that these researchers often do not have a thorough enough grounding in social theory. This is not to say that the work is without value; on the contrary, many important theoretical insights and many more rich ethnographic descriptions have emerged over the past decades from studies that have looked at literacy events and literacy practices. Moreover, this research has had an extremely valuable impact on educational policy and practice around the world.

Moving forward, however, there is room for research in literacy studies to incorporate the work of certain social theorists while still remaining ethnographically rich in ways that deepen our understanding of literacy. Some long-time NLS scholars (e.g., Barton and Hamilton 2005; Gee 2008; Street 2003, 2007) have been at the forefront of this move toward using aspects of social theory to illuminate local/global connections (and indeed to question the accuracy of conceptualizing local and global as dichotomous variables), the materiality of literacy objects, and the workings of power at the micro and macro levels of society. Two main theoretical avenues have been suggested as paths toward this goal: (1) actor network theory (ANT),[8] and (2) post-structuralist thought. While this is not the appropriate place to provide overviews of these complex bodies of theory, let me say just a few words about the insights some scholars believe they have to offer the field of literacy studies.

Incorporating the insights of ANT as explicated by Bruno Latour (1998, 2005), Michel Callon (1986), and John Law (Law and Hassard 1999) into literacy studies, many proponents claim, would encourage scholars to pay greater attention to texts and other material objects as they circulate through different networks of interaction. Objects are accorded agency in ANT (Latour 2005:72), and some literacy scholars feel that such an approach would be fruitful to apply to their own field of study. ANT would also provide a way to trace the interconnections between local and remote contexts, these scholars maintain, and encourage attention to networks of power. In one form or another, ANT has been adopted (and adapted) by literacy scholars such as Barton and Hamilton (2005), Brandt and Clinton (2002), and Reder and Davila (2005).

An alternative source of theoretical illumination for literacy researchers, according to James Collins and Richard Blot (2003), is French post-structuralist thought. Pierre Bourdieu, Michel de Certeau, Jacques Derrida, and Michel Foucault all provide important analyses of the workings of power in society in ways that are especially apt for scholars interested in studying reading and writing. Drawing on these theorists, Collins and Blot attempt to provide something they argue has been lacking in NLS: "an account of power-in-literacy which captures the intricate ways in which power, knowledge, and forms of subjectivity are interconnected with 'uses of literacy' in modern national, colonial, and postcolonial settings" (2003:66). Lewis et al. (2007) draw upon some of these post-structuralist theorists as well as others to create a "critical sociocultural theory" by focusing on concepts such as "activity," "history," and "communities of practice," which they claim help literacy scholars to incorporate a better understanding of identity, agency, and power into their research.

A final source of theoretical insight for scholars of literacy might be the key concepts introduced in the first chapter of this book – concepts that are themselves derived from various social theorists. Analyzing reading and writing through the lens of *multifunctionality*, *language ideologies*, *practice*, and *indexicality* would enable researchers to appreciate the complex and emergent nature of interactions surrounding written texts. From the perspective of linguistic anthropology, it is most essential to study literacy practices on the ground, in actual social settings, through ethnographic research.

Given the rich ethnographic work that has already been done and the new theoretical directions proposed by these scholars and others, the field of literacy studies has a promising future.

8 Performance, Performativity, and the Constitution of Communities

Consider the following situations, all of which could be analyzed using the concepts of performance and/or performativity, defined in one or more of the various ways we will discuss in this chapter.

1 Two people named Michael (*M*) and Lori (*L*) have a mundane conversation about Lori's work as a musician. The conversation contains a typical number of dysfluencies, repetitions, and false starts. Here is part of their conversation:[1]

> *M*: Okay but, but I thought you said that you were a musician? How do you get around playing your music when you live in an apartment?
>
> *L*: Well, well, I'm lucky because, umm, with the equipment I use – I can use headphones to practice so I don't need to make a lot of noise and, and bother the neighbors.
>
> *M*: Okay, that's good because that's, that's yeah, that, I would think that would be a problem for somebody playing music.

2 On June 16, 2008, octogenarians Phyllis Lyon and Del Martin were pronounced "spouses for life" by San Francisco mayor Gavin

Living Language: An Introduction to Linguistic Anthropology, First Edition. Laura M. Ahearn.

Newsom in the first same-sex wedding to take place in the city after the California Supreme Court legalized same-sex marriage in the state.[2]

3 A Spanish-language version of "The Star Spangled Banner," entitled "Nuestro Himno," was released on April 28, 2006, featuring Latin pop stars such as Ivy Queen, Gloria Trevi, Carlos Ponce, Tito "El Bambino," Olga Tañón and the group Aventura, as well as Haitian American artist Wyclef Jean and Cuban American hip-hop artist Pitbull. Many Spanish-language radio stations played the new version of the national anthem in advance of the pro-immigration rallies scheduled for the following week. Controversies then emerged over issues relating to language and national identity.[3]

As different as these three examples are, they represent only a tiny fraction of the types of situations that could be (and have been) analyzed using the concepts of performance and performativity. These concepts have been important topics of study for many linguistic anthropologists because they provide rich and exciting opportunities for understanding more fully how individuals and communities constitute and express themselves linguistically, socioculturally, politically, aesthetically, and morally. Researchers have differed, however, in how they have defined "performance" and the related term "performativity." Three main approaches can be identified – aligned very roughly with the three examples just presented above:

- *Performance defined in opposition to competence.* In this Chomskyan view held by most linguists (but by few, if any, linguistic anthropologists), a distinction is posited between "competence," defined as the abstract and usually unconscious knowledge that each speaker of a language allegedly has, and "performance," defined as the putting into practice – sometimes imperfectly – of those rules.
- *Performativity.* This refers to the ability of at least some utterances to *do* merely by virtue of *saying* (such as when declaring, "I hereby christen this ship the Queen Elizabeth," is tantamount to naming the ship). This term originated in the speech act theory of philosophers J.L. Austin and J.R. Searle and was important in shifting the conceptualization of language away from an abstract system of phonology, morphology, and syntax toward an understanding of speech as a form

of social action. The concept of performativity has been developed further by the work of scholars such as Judith Butler, who describes gender as a performative process – that is, of continuous acts of "doing" gender rather than a continuous state of being a gender.

- *Performance as a display of verbal artistry.* Linguistic anthropologists have also defined "performances" as events in which performers display special verbal skills for an audience that evaluates the performers in some way. Examples of such performances include political oratories, storytelling sessions, theater performances, songfests, verbal duels, and recitals of poetry, to name just a few of the culturally variable forms of performance studied by linguistic anthropologists.

Most linguistic anthropologists working in the area of performance have primarily followed one of these three approaches, but some have blended or bridged these approaches in creative ways as well (cf. Duranti 1997:14–17). Before presenting some examples of interesting research on performance and performativity, however, let me explain in greater detail each of the three approaches just mentioned.

Performance Defined in Opposition to Competence

Careful readers will recall that chapter 1 introduced Chomsky's distinction between competence and performance. Building on de Saussure's analogous distinction between *langue* (the language system in the abstract) and *parole* (actual speech), Chomsky contrasts the *competence* of a hypothetical "ideal speaker-listener" who knows a "language perfectly and is unaffected by such grammatically irrelevant conditions as memory limitations, distractions, shifts of attention and interest, and errors" (1965:3) with *performance*, which he defines as "the actual use of language in concrete situations" (1965:4). In later writings, Chomsky alludes to "pragmatic competence," which "places language in the institutional setting of its use, relating intentions and purposes to the linguistic means at hand" (2005[1980]:225), but the goal of linguists who study pragmatic competence remains the identification of abstract and universal aspects of language use (Kasher 1991). For Chomsky and the linguists who share his approach to the study of language, competence, or what Chomsky has more recently called "I-language" (for internalized language), is the main focus of their research. They consider everyday language use – performance, or "E-language" (externalized language) – to be uninteresting, unsystematic, or unworthy of study. "Indeed," Cook and Newson write, "Chomsky is extremely dismissive of the E-language approaches: 'E-language, if it exists at all, is derivative, remote from mechanisms, and of no particular empirical significance, perhaps none at all' (Chomsky 1991:10)" (Cook and Newson 2007:13).

Linguistic anthropologists have responded to Chomsky's proposed competence/performance distinction in one of three ways: (1) by redefining what is meant by competence; (2) by reversing the relationship between competence and performance, according performance more centrality and importance than competence; or (3) by rejecting the distinction between competence and performance altogether. Some linguistic anthropologists have combined two or more of these approaches. For example, in a classic article, "On Communicative Competence," Dell Hymes attempts to redefine and expand Chomsky's notion of competence in ways that "transcend the present formulation of the dichotomy of competence:performance" (2001[1972]:62). Hymes does not advocate dispensing with Chomsky's terms altogether, however. It is just as problematic, he argues, for linguists to dismiss performance completely as it is for nonlinguists to valorize only performance. "If some grammarians have confused matters by lumping what does not interest them under 'performance,' as a residual category," Hymes warns, nonlinguists "have not done much to clarify the situation. We have tended to lump what *does* interest us under 'performance,' simply as an honorific designation" (Hymes 1981:81). A better approach, according to Hymes, would be to insist that true communicative competence must include "competency for use" – underlying models and rules, in other words, for actual performance. There are several sectors of communicative competence, according to Hymes, of which the grammatical is only one. "Competence is dependent upon both (tacit) *knowledge* and (ability for) *use*" (Hymes 2001[1972]:64; emphasis in the original). Thus, while expanding Chomsky's original term of competence to include not just grammatical competence but pragmatic or performance-oriented competence, Hymes both undercuts Chomsky's strictly drawn dichotomy and emphasizes the importance of incorporating sociocultural factors into any linguistic analysis.

Performativity

A second way in which linguistic anthropologists have grappled with what it means to perform linguistically is through the influential concept of "performativity." The term was first coined by a philosopher of language, J.L. Austin, in a series of lectures he gave in 1955 that were subsequently published in a famous volume entitled, *How To Do Things With Words* (Austin 1962). Austin's ideas became the basis for speech act theory and were built upon (some would say in an oversimplified and misguided way) by another philosopher, J.R. Searle (1969, 1975). Since then, speech act theory and, more specifically, the notion of performativity have been taken up by scholars in many different fields of study.

In *How To Do Things With Words*, Austin sets out to characterize sentences that merely *say* something – what he called "constatives" (1962:3) – from those that *do* something – what he calls "performatives" (1962:6–7). While constatives are statements that can be clearly determined to be true or false (such as, "It is raining outside today"), performatives, according to Austin, are those utterances that perform an action in the very saying of them (such as, "I promise to study harder on the next exam," or, "I hereby dub thee Knight of the Woeful Countenance"). Performatives in Austin's initial formulation had to begin with "I" and are accompanied by a performative verb, producing phrases such as "I name," "I pronounce," "I warn," "I promise," "I declare," "I appoint," "I order," "I urge," "I apologize," "I congratulate," "I commend," "I challenge," etc. Unlike constatives, which were supposed to have clear truth values, performatives could only be said to be "felicitous" or "infelicitous," depending on whether the statements were uttered in an appropriate context by individuals with the appropriate authority. Performances also had to be uttered correctly according to convention and with the necessary seriousness or intentionality (1962:14–15). For example, if someone said "I do," but the wedding ceremony was performed by someone who did not have the appropriate legal authority, "I do" would be an infelicitous performative.

By the second half of *How To Do Things With Words*, however, Austin has come to the realization that constatives and performatives cannot be neatly distinguished from each other in any consistent way. He therefore decides it is time to make a "fresh start" on the problem and steps back to ask, "When we issue any utterance whatsoever, are we not 'doing something'?" (Austin 1962:91). At this point, Austin's ideas about language overlap quite a bit with those of many linguistic anthropologists today who would answer this question with a resounding "Yes!" because they consider all utterances to be forms of social action in one way or another. Austin himself, however, proceeds in a slightly different direction and brackets for the rest of the book his important insight about the performative underpinnings of all language use.

Instead, Austin (1962:108) divides utterances into the following three categories (which he acknowledges overlap and are not always clearly definable):

- *Locution.* The stating of something. Locutionary acts involve meaning in the traditional sense.
- *Illocution.* The doing of something instantaneously by virtue of stating it. Illocutionary acts involve conventional force rather than meaning and are performative in nature.
- *Perlocution.* The consequences of having stated something. Perlocutionary acts refer to effects rather than to meaning or force.

Unlike some of his followers, however, Austin demonstrates considerable awareness of the complexity and overlap among these categories. By the end of *How To Do Things With Words* he is no longer content to look at sentences in isolation for clues to whether they might constitute action. "Once we realize that what we have to study is *not* the sentence but the issuing of an utterance in a speech situation, there can hardly be any longer a possibility of not seeing that stating is performing an act" (Austin 1962:138). And he concludes that "in general the locutionary act as much as the illocutionary is an abstraction only: every genuine speech act is both" (1962:146). Nevertheless, Austin still ends *How To Do Things With Words* by proposing a taxonomy of five different kinds of illocutionary utterances: (1) verdictives (the giving of a verdict); (2) exercitives (the exercising of powers, rights, or influence); (3) commissives (the committing to doing something); (4) behabitives (involving social behavior such as apologizing, commending, or congratulating); and (5) expositives (explanations of how utterances fit into the conversation, such as replying, conceding, or arguing) (Austin 1962:150–151).

This taxonomy was later challenged by Searle, who proposed his own five classes of illocutionary acts: representatives, directives, commissives, expressives, and declaratives (Searle 1975:10–13).[4] The details of these different categorizations are not worth elaborating upon here; both typologies have been built upon, challenged, or rejected altogether in the decades since they were proposed. Despite the problems that many linguistic anthropologists have identified with the specifics of these categorizations, however, it is important to remember that speech act theory as put forward first by Austin and then by Searle and others advocated a very different way of conceiving of language from that which preceded it. Speech act theorists argued that utterances, rather than merely referring to an already-existing social and material world (Jakobson's referential function), also act upon and even help to constitute the social and material world. This was an influential development in the study of language and a key move toward a better understanding of how the use of language can constitute social action. Indeed, as Kira Hall notes, "[Austin's argument that all utterances are performative] is a revolutionary conclusion, for all utterances must then be viewed as actions, an equation which linguistic anthropologists have of course embraced with fervor" (Hall 2001:180).

While recognizing the importance of Austin's insight that *saying* is *doing* (that speech, in other words, is performative), linguistic anthropologists have criticized speech act theorists for some of the principle aspects of their approach. First, most philosophers and linguists who have written about performativity have assumed the universality of their theories. And yet, linguistic practices, language ideologies, cultural notions of personhood, discursive categories and genres, and ideas about agency have all been shown by anthropologists to be highly variable cross-culturally. Linguistic anthropologists have therefore either rejected speech act theory altogether or have suggested revisions to make it more applicable cross-culturally.

Another anthropological criticism of speech act theory concerns the theory's methodological foundations. Austin and Searle, like most philosophers and many linguists, construct their theories on the basis of intuition or anecdotal personal experience rather than on systematically collected empirical data. A scholar employing such an approach runs the risk of falling prey to unexamined cultural assumptions, language ideologies, and biases – and indeed, this is exactly what anthropologist Michelle Rosaldo argues was the main weakness of Searle's version of speech act theory. In a widely cited article, Rosaldo (1982:212) claims that Searle "falls victim to folk views" when he assumes that meaning resides primarily within autonomous individuals. Rosaldo argues that the Ilongots of the Philippines, in contrast, have very different ideas about meaning, communication, and language, viewing language as thoroughly embedded within webs of social relations. The Ilongots' default type of utterance is not a referential sentence (a "constative," in Austin's original terminology) that reports on an external state of affairs but is instead a directive or command. Moreover, Rosaldo maintains, because Ilongots are disinclined to attribute intentionality to autonomous individuals and are uninterested in giving or receiving promises, they do not have the same categories of performatives that Searle suggests are universal. In particular, Ilongots do not exhibit expressives or commissives, two speech act categories suggested by Searle that involve expressions of individual feelings or intentions. This is because Ilongots, according to Rosaldo,

> [lack]something like our notion of an inner self continuous through time, a self whose actions can be *judged* in terms of the sincerity, integrity, and commitment involved in his or her bygone pronouncements. Because Ilongots do not see their inmost 'hearts' as constant causes, independent of their acts, they have no reasons to 'commit' themselves to future deeds, or feel somehow guilt-stricken or in need of an account when subsequent actions prove their earlier expressions false. (1982:218; emphasis in the original)

Searle's over-emphasis on individual intentions and over-generalizing on the basis of performative verbs within English should be read, Rosaldo claims, not as a convincing case for the universality of speech act theory but rather as Searle's unwittingly culture-specific ethnographic account of his own ideas regarding language, action, and personhood (1982:228).

Many linguistic anthropologists have also rejected the limited and overly simplistic notion of context used by speech act theorists.[5] According to Austin, in order for a performative utterance to work (to be "felicitous," in Austin's words), "*There must exist an accepted conventional procedure having a certain conventional effect, the procedure to include the uttering of certain words by certain persons in certain circumstances*" (Austin 1962:26; emphasis in the original). Despite the centrality of context to speech act theory, many scholars argue that context remains an afterthought to these scholars. R.P. McDermott and Henry Tylbor, for example, claim that speech act theory uses "a soup-in-the-bowl approach to context," the problem with which is that "it allows the assumption that the soup exists independent of the bowl, that the meaning of the utterance remains, if only for a moment, independent of conditions that organize its production and interpretation, that meaning exists 'on the inside territory of an utterance'" (McDermott and Tylbor 1995:230). Instead, these scholars and many others maintain that utterances and their various contexts are mutually constituted; utterances therefore cannot stand alone.

Yet another famous critique of speech act theory emerged from Jacques Derrida's pointed exchange with Searle over the basic principles of the theory (Derrida 1988; Searle 1977, 1994).[6] Derrida, a philosopher and one of the founders of deconstruction within literary criticism, takes issue especially with the role of individual intentionality in speech act theory; indeed, Derrida claims that intentionality is the "organizing center" of Austin's work (Derrida 1988:15). Derrida states that meaning is always and everywhere at least to some degree indeterminate and detached from individuals' intentions. This indeterminacy is crystallized in a term that Derrida coined, *différance*:[7] the "irreducible absence of intention or attendance to the performative utterance" (1988:18–19). Playing with and combining the verbs in French that mean "to defer" and "to differ," Derrida creates the term *différance* to refer to the way in which the meaning of a given word (for example) derives from how it differs from other words that it is *not*. Thus, the meaning of "dog" emerges from its opposition to words like "cat" or "person" – an approach similar to de Saussure's notion of linguistic value. Also, meanings are never singular or permanent, according to Derrida, but emerge in particular contexts that are linked together through the repetition of a term (its "iterability" or "citationality") within those contexts over time.

While this overly brief, overly simplified description of Derrida's deconstructionist literary theory has probably obscured and confused more than it has illuminated, the important and ironic point to note for the purposes of this chapter is that despite Derrida's scathing criticism of Austin's notion of performativity, the concept has become extremely popular among Derridean literary critics as well as researchers in many fields. The widespread use of the concept of performativity has led some scholars, such as David Gorman (1999) and John Searle himself (1994) to bemoan the lack of engagement or familiarity with Austin's actual writings among many literary critics who discuss performativity in their work. Gorman, for example, writes, "In all such work, Austin is repeatedly cited as an inspiration or precedent, but the unasked question is always whether there is any actual *basis* in Austin's thought for using such a generalized notion of performativity as a tool of analysis" (1999:98; emphasis in the original).

While this criticism is often warranted, there are nevertheless many scholars who have used the concept of performativity in interesting and illuminating ways, even if they have not always remained faithful to Austin's original formulation. Let us therefore turn now to a discussion of the work of Judith Butler (1999[1990], 1993, 1997) a scholar who has broadened and redefined the concept of performativity in ways that have been taken up by many linguistic anthropologists as well as by researchers in a variety of other fields.

In applying the concept of performativity to gender, Butler explicitly states that she takes her cue from Derrida (Butler 1999[1990]:xv). But what she borrows from Derrida is not his criticism of Austin but rather his analysis of a short fable by Franz Kafka, "Before the Law" (Derrida 1992).[8] In analyzing Kafka's story, Derrida suggests that the authority of the law is a type of self-fulfilling prophecy; it arises from the acts of those who presuppose the law's importance and from those who attribute a certain force to it because in so doing, they thereby bring the law into existence (Derrida 1992). Similarly, Butler claims that gender is not essentialist, unchanging, or interior to individuals but rather is continuously produced, presupposed, reproduced, and reconfigured through individuals' acts and words:

> Such acts, gestures, enactments, generally construed, are *performative* in the sense that the essence or identity that they otherwise purport to express are *fabrications* manufactured and sustained through corporeal signs and other discursive means. That the gendered body is performative suggests that it has no ontological status apart from the various acts which constitute its reality. (1999[1990]:185; emphasis in the original)

In other words, gender is not something we *have* in an unchanging, essentialistic way but rather something we *do* repeatedly and continuously throughout our lives. According to Butler, people actively create and recreate their gendered identity by wearing certain clothes, using certain phrases or tones of voice, or engaging in certain activities such as sports or sewing. In short, Butler takes Austin's insight that to *say* is to *do* and transforms it into a claim that to *say or do* is to *be*. Rather than being *expressive* of a pre-existing, stable identity, then, gender is *performative*, Butler argues, because people's social and linguistic practices "effectively constitute the identity they are said to express or reveal" (Butler 1999[1990]:192).

Butler's formulation of the performative nature of gender has been enormously influential, not just in gender studies but in other fields as well. Many scholars studying ethnicity, racialization, and other facets of identity formation have also used the concept of performativity in this way, either because they have been influenced by Butler's work or have independently concluded that what they are studying should be understood as an ongoing process of *doing* rather than a static process of *being*. In addition to these scholars who are interested in how performativity might help explain processes of individual identity formation, there are others who apply the concept to the processes of social group formation more generally. Bruno Latour, for example, a well-known anthropologist of science and an advocate of the Actor Network Theory (ANT) approach discussed in chapter 7, argues that all social aggregates are performative because "if you stop making and remaking groups, you stop having groups" (Latour 2005:35).

At times, scholars who use the concept of performativity in a way similar to that of Butler combine that perspective (either knowingly or unknowingly) with a very different sense of performance – that of displaying a particular skill for an audience's evaluation. Performance as display is the third sense of performance/performativity that will be discussed in this chapter and is addressed more fully in the next subsection. "Not everyone writing about 'performance' is always careful to separate senses of 'displayed' or 'framed' performance from that of 'performativity,'" Alaina Lemon writes. But she immediately adds, "Perhaps this is right. Perhaps analytic senses of 'performance' *should* run together where they *are* conflated in practice" (Lemon 2000:24; emphasis in the original). Butler agrees with this sentiment, asserting that a merger of these two quite different uses of the concept of performance/performativity can be productive because they are related "chiasmically"[9] – that is, in a complexly inverted way:

> Moreover, my theory sometimes waffles between understanding performativity as linguistic and casting it as theatrical. I have come to think that the two are invariably related, chiasmically so, and that a reconsideration of the speech act as an instance of power invariably draws attention to both its theatrical and linguistic dimensions … [T]he speech act is at once performed (and thus theatrical, presented to an audience, subject to interpretation), and linguistic, inducing a set of effects through its implied relation to linguistic conventions (1999[1990]:xxvi–xxvii).

We will return to Butler's important but at times frustratingly jargon-laden theories in upcoming chapters on agency and gender. For now, let us explore further the sense of performance involving drama, theatricality, and displays of verbal artistry.

Performance as a Display of Verbal Artistry

A third approach to the study of performance defines the concept as Bauman does in his famous article, "Verbal Art as Performance" – as consisting in "the assumption of responsibility to an audience for a display of communicative competence" (Bauman 2001[1975]:168–169). The presence of an audience is central to this notion of performance. "To pretend that performances of verbal art take place in a social vacuum in which only individual intent matters, that the audience plays no role in shaping such performance, entails a serious failure of method," argues James Wilce (1998:211). Rather, Wilce reminds us, citing Duranti and Brenneis (1986), audiences should be conceived of as co-performers. Even if the audience consists solely of one person (who could theoretically be the performer herself or himself), the evaluation of the virtuosity of the performer(s) is a crucial element in this approach because performance, according to this view, involves heightened attention to *how* something is said (or sung, acted, etc.) – or, in other words, to what Jakobson (recalling the overview presented in chapter 1 of his model of the multifunctionality of language) termed the poetic function of language. This practice is highly reflexive:

> Performance puts the act of speaking on display – objectifies it, lifts it to a degree from its interactional setting and opens it to scrutiny by an audience. Performance heightens awareness of the act of speaking and licenses the audience to evaluate the skill and effectiveness of the performer's accomplishment. (Bauman and Briggs 1990:73)

How does one know that such heightened awareness is called for – in other words, that a performance of verbal artistry is underway? Bauman notes that there are culturally specific ways that particular genres of performance are indexed, or "keyed." Openings such as "Once upon a time …," for example, alert people who are familiar with the cultural practice of storytelling in many English-speaking communities that a story is about to be told. Similarly, an MC's announcement ("Ladies and gentlemen, please join me in welcoming …") serves as a key for other kinds of performances. Even when such formulaic introductory keys are absent, the performance might be made identifiable to the audience members through special seating arrangements or social venues, through special characteristics of the language used, or through special bodily movements or rituals. Some keys that are common cross-culturally include the following (Bauman 2001[1975]:171):

- Special codes, for example, archaic or esoteric language.
- Conventional openings or closings, or explicit statements announcing or asserting performance.
- Poetic or figurative language, such as metaphor.
- Formal stylistic devices, such as rhyme, vowel harmony, or other forms of parallelism.
- Special patterns of tempo, stress, pitch, or voice quality.
- Appeals to tradition.
- Disclaimers of performance.

Each speech community has its own ways of keying performances. Another way of saying this is that each speech community uses keys differently to introduce or invoke performance "frames" (Goffman 1986) – to let people know, in other words, that a performance is taking place. In order to determine which, if any, of these performance keys are used in a given community to trigger a performance frame, a scholar must conduct long-term ethnographic research. Such research is also necessary in order to identify what constitutes performance and what does not among a particular group of people. Is joke-telling a form of performance, for example? How about political oratory, personal narratives, arguments, or recitals of poetry? In every speech community, some speech acts will conventionally involve performance while others may optionally do so or may never do so at all; this can only be determined by studying the culturally specific definitions of, and expectations for, performance. Performances also vary in intensity cross-culturally, and performers may undergo long-term formal training, some informal training, or no training at all. Richard Schechner, a well-known scholar who helped to establish the interdisciplinary field of performance studies, notes that "every genre of performance, even every particular instance of a genre, is concrete, specific, and different from every other – not only in terms of cultural difference but also in terms of local and even individual variation" (2002:162).

What interests linguistic anthropologists the most about performance defined as a display of communicative competence that is evaluated by an audience? As Bauman notes in a recent commentary, for scholars like linguistic anthropologists who focus on how communities are communicatively constituted, "the performance forms of a community tend to be among the most memorable, repeatable, reflexively accessible forms of discourse in its communicative repertoire" (Bauman 2005:149). In other words, because communities are constituted largely through linguistic interactions, studying especially memorable or highlighted forms of communication such as performances will provide insights into how social groups are formed (and re-formed, challenged, reinforced, or disbanded).

In every performance, as in every social interaction, *emergence* takes place. Emergence, which was discussed initially in chapter 1, is a way of talking about instances in which whole is greater than the sum of the parts.[10] "The emergent quality of performance," Bauman states, "resides in the interplay between communicative resources, individual competence, and the goals of the participants, within the context of particular situations" (2001[1975]:179; cf. Mayr 1982; Williams, R. 1977). The heightened attention audience members pay to performers increases the likelihood that emergent, unpredictable outcomes or meanings will occur. The very structure of the performance itself can even be emergent within the actual performance – reinforced, negotiated, or contested as the performance proceeds. Despite the repetitive, ritualized, or predictable nature of many performances, each individual performance takes place in real time, always with the potential emergence of new understandings. Because of the different roles taken by performers and audience members, and because of their different personal histories, there is absolutely no guarantee that they will interpret the event in the same way (Mannheim and Tedlock 1995:13). And even a single individual may construct different understandings of a performance over time as that individual's life circumstances change.

It is also important to note that all performances, whether mundane (such as when the telling of a racist joke falls flat) or extraordinary (such as when soaring political oratory mobilizes people to transform their society), are interwoven with social relations of power and therefore have the potential to reshape or reinforce social hierarchies at the micro or macro level. The concentrated attention given to performers – for example, to singers, actors, or politicians in the broader social context, or to jokesters, college professors, or tellers of personal narratives at the more local level – often enables them to have substantial influence on audience members. Performances can be highly transformative events or, conversely, can strengthen existing social hierarchies.

Performances involving verbal art therefore very clearly link language with cultural practices and social relations. In so doing, they contribute to the fashioning and refashioning of individual identities and social communities. For these reasons, linguistic anthropologists have found the analysis of performance to be a particularly fruitful area of study, as the following examples of research conducted by anthropologists on performance will demonstrate.

Ethnographies of Performance and Performativity

A wonderful example of an analysis that draws on several of the theorists and approaches to performance and performativity mentioned in the first sections of this chapter is Graham Jones and Lauren Shweder's (2003) article, "The Performance of Illusion and Illusionary Performatives: Learning the Language of Theatrical Magic." Jones and Shweder look closely at how a magician teaches an apprentice to perform a particular magic trick involving a handkerchief. The authors argue that the linguistic practices surrounding magic tricks often go unnoticed or unappreciated even though they are central to creating the illusions that make the magic tricks successful. In the lesson Jones and Shweder videotaped, the magician first performed the trick as he would for an audience, constructing a narrative about a ghost named "Splookie" who first lives inside the handkerchief "house" and then makes the handkerchief rise up and "misbehave" in various ways. Out of respect for the standards of secrecy upheld by magicians themselves, Jones and Shweder do not reveal exactly how the trick is accomplished, but they imply that it involves a gimmick and possibly some mechanism or sleight of hand that makes the handkerchief appear to move on its own.

Jones and Shweder's main argument is that the narrative the magician tells while performing this trick is essential to the success of the trick. Talk, the authors maintain, can actually shape the audience's experience of seeing because the narrative of the magician acts, in Bauman's terms, as a key for the performance, triggering a frame that identifies the event not just as a magic trick but as something involving the paranormal in the form of Splookie the ghost. Throughout the trick, Jones and Shweder argue,

> the magician's verbal routine allows an audience to see a potentially uninteresting sequence of gestures as paranormal – to perceive something otherwise unbelievable. In part, the magician accomplishes this effect through the use of performative speech. In the magician's spoken routine, the seemingly descriptive narration of an imaginative world of illusion functions through implicit performativity (Austin 1962) to influence the audience's perception of events. (2003:52)

In addition to this framing of the event as involving a ghost, the magician also creates a coherent plot about the alleged ghost's behavior. In the process, he attributes agency to the ghost, talking to it underneath the handkerchief and accusing it of trying to escape from him. The magician also enlists the audience's input and support at various times during his performance, thereby encouraging them to invest in the story, and therefore buy into the act, by participating in the interaction. When instructing the apprentice in the trick, the magician strongly emphasizes the importance of telling a compelling narrative because this will influence how the audience members view the event.

"The meaning of the magician's talk lies not in its descriptive accuracy," Jones and Shweder assert, "but in the power it has to affect how an audience construes what it sees" (2003:52).

Jones and Shweder directly or indirectly draw on many of the theorists and concepts we have been discussing in this chapter, such as framing and emergence. They also employ Austin's notion of performativity to describe how the magician's narrative calls into being a fictive world that then has the potential to influence what the audience members see (or fail to notice). Words, Jones and Shweder (2003:66) argue, have the power to manipulate vision. In addition to performativity, Jones and Shweder also use the concept of performance as put forward by Bauman and Briggs. They note that a magician's accountability to an audience for the display of virtuosity involves not just physical abilities such as sleight of hand but also verbal skills that construct a narrative and deflect any skeptical comments offered by audience members. In short, Jones and Shweder's article nicely illustrates how several different theoretical approaches to performance and performativity can be productively combined to shed light on actual events.

Another interesting example of an analysis that draws on some of the concepts introduced in this chapter is José Limón's (1989) article about the use of aggressive, highly sexualized jokes among Mexican American men in Texas. Here is Limón's ethnographically rich description of two such interactions:

> At two in the afternoon a periodically unemployed working-class man in Mexican-American south Texas puts hot chunks of juicy barbecued meat with his fingers on an equally hot tortilla. The meat or *carne* has marinated overnight in beer and lemon juice before being grilled. Antoñio, or Toñio, passes the meat-laden tortilla to one of the other eight mostly working-class men surrounding a rusty barbecue grill, but as he does so, the hand holding the food brushes against his own genital area, and he loudly tells the other, *"¡Apaña este taco carnal,'ta a toda madre mi carne!"* (Grab this taco, brother, my meat is a mother!). With raucous laughter all around, I accept the full, dripping taco, add some hot sauce and reach for an ice-downed beer from an also rusty washtub. (1989:471)

> Simón takes Jaime's hand as if to shake it but instead yanks it down and holds it firmly over his own genital area even as he responds to Jaime's

> *"¿Como estas?"* with a loud *"¡Pos, chínga ahora me siento a toda madre, gracias!"* (Well, fuck, now I feel just great, thank you!) There is more laughter which only intensifies when "Midnight" in turn actually grabs and begins to squeeze "el Mickey's" genitals. With his one free hand, for the other is holding a taco, el Mickey tries to pull on Jaime's arm unsuccessfully. Finally in an effort to slip out of Jaime's grip, he collapses to the ground cursing and trying to laugh at the same time and loses his taco in the process. (1989:473)

Limón reviews past scholarly analyses of these sorts of "macho" interactions and finds them to be at best unsatisfactory and simplistic, and at worst objectionably stereotypical. In order to understand how these seemingly crude and aggressive verbal (and sometimes physical) interactions can be understood in their full complexity, Limón applies the concepts of framing and emergence. When these men address one another in this aggressive idiom of sexual violation, they frame these interactions as play – as "relajando" or "llevandosale" (1989:477). They only become actual, open aggression when a novice or stranger fails to recognize the signs, or keys, of a playful performance. Because they are an insiders' way of interacting, these playfully aggressive exchanges offer Mexican American men a way to bond and to build solidarity.

These cultural performances are also multifunctional and have emergent qualities, according to Limón. They allow men who are economically, linguistically, and socially marginalized in the wider society to produce a metaphorical commentary about their own oppression. Their mock aggression indirectly opposes the actual verbal and physical abuse that they experience in these other contexts and therefore has a subversive potential, Limón argues. About the speech play of these Mexican Americans, Limón states, "Created in collective equality, such momentary productions negate the alienating constraints of the historically given social order that exists for *mexicanos* and affirm the possibilities of a different social order" (1989:479). And yet, the emergent potential of these performances includes not only the possibility that alienating effects of this social order might be temporarily overturned but also the possibility that the men will be reminded of the oppression they experience in the wider world. These playful interactions also index, Limón notes, the men's own domination within their patriarchal community and the exclusion of women from these contexts (1989:481). Such interpretations and outcomes are just some of the emergent possibilities of these performances.

The challenge of identifying the many possible interpretations and emergent possibilities of any given performance – or, indeed, any social interaction – has been a central issue in some of my own research. In particular, I became intrigued by a specific woman's festival in Nepal known as Tij. From my first experiences of the yearly festival in the early 1980s when I was a Peace Corps volunteer in the Nepali village of Junigau through my subsequent stints of research there once I became an anthropologist, Tij has always been of interest. The festival is based on Hindu rituals for married women that require them to pray for the long lives of their husbands (and even pray that they die before their husbands). The rituals also require women to atone for having possibly caused men to become ritually polluted by touching them while the women were menstruating or recovering from childbirth. In Junigau, however, the celebration of Tij goes far beyond these rituals, extending weeks in advance and involving feasts for female relatives and many formal and informal songfests at which women sing, men play the drums, and both women and men dance, sometimes even together.

The songfests presented me with the following fascinating paradox: on the one hand, these events are always joyful, with lots of singing, dancing, and laughing; and yet, the lyrics of the songs sung by the women contain heart-wrenchingly melancholy and sometimes defiant lyrics. How can a scholar (or a participant, for that matter) make sense of the seeming contradiction of people lightheartedly singing and dancing to songs with lyrics that could make one cry? Do the participants ignore the lyrics? Or is the lightheartedness merely an act that masks underlying sadness? When the lyrics express opposition to a woman's arranged marriage, or her excruciatingly difficult daily workload, should these be interpreted as expressions of outright opposition to male oppression on the part of the female singers? Or might these lyrics merely enable the women to let off some steam before returning to their traditional gender roles unchanged?

In an attempt to solve this puzzle, consider some of the lyrics of "A Twisted Rope Binds My Waist," a song sung at an informal songfest in Junigau in August 1990. The song starts by saying that a young woman has taken a liking to a "flashy" young man and is presumably planning to elope with him. Instead, her parents arrange a marriage for her and marry her off against her will – not an uncommon occurrence in Junigau and elsewhere in the 1990s, even as the number of elopements was increasing (cf. Ahearn 2001a). Here are some lyrics describing the woman's arranged marriage:[11]

9 I dug and dug with Father's hoe
10 And now they fill bridal litters for me in the courtyard
11 As the bridal litters were filled, I was put into bondage
12 Two pennies' worth of red powder[12] caused me to get caught in the middle

* * *

29 I'll sit on the porch after cutting grass
30 Whose face will I look upon before going inside?
31 If I look upon my lord husband's face, I feel just like a monkey that's eaten salt
32 If I look upon my mother-in-law's face, I feel just like a burning fire

These lyrics do not just contain a woman's defiant voice, however, but many other voices as well. The lyrics are therefore heteroglossic (a term introduced in chapter 6) in a Bakhtinian sense. The woman's own voice is evident in lyrics such as the ones just quoted, and at different points in the song she is defiant, resigned to her fate, or conflicted. But there are also other voices, including a narrator's voice and the father's first-person voice. Here are the song's final four lines, the first two in the father's voice and the final two in the daughter's:

41 Go without crying, without crying, Daughter; you'll hear if we call you home
42 It'll be good to live even in that house
43 If I return home before January/February, you can curse me,
44 But ten times as many curses, Father, go to you[13]

The presence of all these different voices means that multifunctionality and interpretive indeterminacy are built right into the lyrics themselves – it is impossible, in other words, to come up with a single "correct" interpretation of this song.

Even if there were not such richly contradictory voices within the lyrics of this song, there would still be interpretive indeterminacy, however, for every performance contains emergent qualities that are not predictable *a priori* from knowledge of the text and/or its performance. In other words, text and context influence each other reflexively, creating a potentially infinite range of possible interpretations upon which participants, audience members, and scholars may draw, both during the performance and over time (Duranti and Goodwin 1992). This does not mean, however, that such indeterminacy, or what Umberto Eco calls "unlimited semiosis," precludes analysis. Indeed, Eco argues, "the notion of unlimited semiosis does not lead to the conclusion that interpretation has no criteria. To say that interpretation (as the basic feature of semiosis) is potentially unlimited does not mean that it 'riverruns' for the mere sake of itself" (1990:6). It is therefore the job of the linguistic anthropologist to identify these interpretive criteria in particular performances (or everyday interactions) by looking for textual, temporal, sociocultural, and spatial constraints on meaning (cf. Becker 2000).

In short, scholars must learn to be more humble and less authoritative in their assertions regarding the "meaning" of any given performance – or, indeed, of any ordinary interaction. Instead of producing a single, definitive interpretation of an event, I suggest a shift in focus from a search for such definitive interpretations to a search for *constraints* on the interpretive indeterminacy of that event. According to this *practice theory of meaning constraint*, we can *constrain* the range of possible interpretations that might emerge from an event such as a songfest, a jokingly aggressive interaction, or a magician's performance by closely analyzing the words that are uttered while also learning as much as possible about the individual participants, their personal histories and relationships to one another, the general social and cultural norms, and social conflicts, hierarchies, or transformations more broadly. This contextual information, in combination with a close analysis of the words spoken, written, sung, or recited, will enable the researcher to eliminate unlikely interpretations and focus in on the most likely meanings that participants might take away from the event, either immediately or over time as their life circumstances change.

To provide just one example of how these contextual concerns might shape, and be shaped by, the lyrics of "A Twisted Rope Binds My Waist," let us look briefly at the gendered spatial configuration of

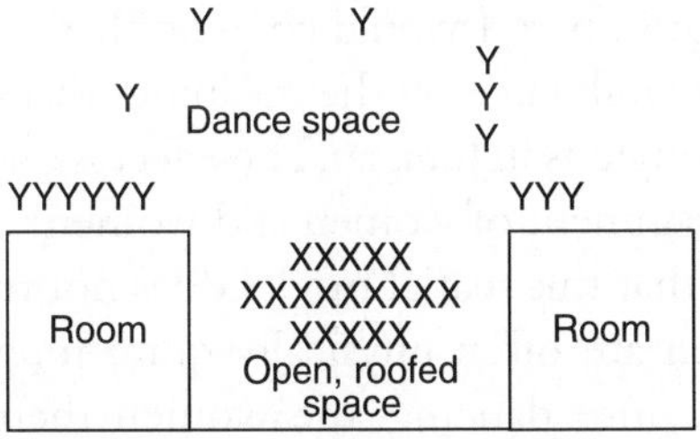

Figure 8.1 Spatial configuration at August 1990 Tij songfest in Junigau (X = woman, Y = man).
Source: Reprinted from Ahearn (1998:67).

the participants during a songfest during which the song was sung in 1990. Women at songfests in Junigau generally all sit closely together, and this was also the case at the Tij songfest analyzed here. Men, on the other hand, place themselves around the outskirts of the courtyard. (See Figure 8.1 for the spatial configuration of the songfest at which "A Twisted Rope Binds My Waist" was performed.) Although the spatial configuration varied quite a bit throughout the songfest, the general pattern remained: women clustered toward the center, men spread out more widely around the edges, encircling the women and the dance space.

The men's encircling of the women could be interpreted as the men's exclusion from the women's singing – the central focus of the event. This is indeed a possible reading of the spatial configuration of the songfest that should be considered. But given the broader array of gendered spatial relations in the village, I would maintain that this interpretation should be put aside, or at least qualified in several ways. There are many spaces within the village and beyond that women are either prohibited from entering, at least at certain times of the month, or during certain events, and many other spaces in which their movements are quite circumscribed.[14] Physical space is certainly not the only, or even the most important, confining factor in Junigau gender relations, but in many respects it is the most visible. In the case of Tij songfests, potentially oppositional song lyrics are sung by women who are confined (or who confine themselves) spatially by men who encircle them. Periodically, one of the men will reach into the group of women to pull one of them (sometimes quite forcibly) out into the dance space. While this spatial pattern undoubtedly acts below the participants' level of awareness for the most part, I would contend that it nevertheless exerts a powerful semiotic influence on the meanings that emerge (or do not emerge) from Tij songfests in Junigau. The effect is one of partial physical and linguistic containment of women and women's words by men.

I hasten to add that this spatial model does not render women passive. Although men are often physically quite rough on the women they try to coerce into dancing, the women themselves sometimes attempt to specify the conditions under which they will allow themselves to be dragged into the dance space. The sequencing of dancers at a Tij songfest thereby becomes a complex choreography that is jointly negotiated by women and men, albeit from unequal social and spatial positions. Thus, Junigau songfests are therefore multifunctional, embodying potentially subversive elements that, given a more conducive environment than the one that has existed over the past several decades in the village, might give rise to oppositional actions that make gender relations more egalitarian.

Such conditions do not, however, seem to be emerging in Junigau, despite numerous transformations in all aspects of life in the village. In fact, during the two days of "official" Tij songfests in 1996, the environment seemed anything but conducive to oppositional readings of Tij lyrics. Young men who had gotten drunk on distilled liquor from outside the village began to fight among themselves, and several times the women had to jump up and move as the groups of fighting men approached. Each time the older men chased the younger men away and urged the women to sit back down and resume singing. Eventually, though, the women, including myself, got tired of rushing to safety whenever the fighting men neared, and the songfests ended much earlier than usual that year. Whether intentionally or unintentionally, the men had displaced the women altogether, truncating their celebration of Tij.[15]

Thus, while the participants in the August 1990 performance of "A Twisted Rope Binds My Waist" might have constructed many different interpretations of the song, in my search for constraints on this interpretive indeterminacy, there are some interpretations that the participants most likely did not construct, either at the time of the performance itself or in the years since then. After applying a practice theory of meaning constraint, I can state with confidence that it would be too simplistic to interpret the song *either* as expressing outright resistance *or* as providing a mere blowing off of steam that serves to rechannel the women unchanged back into their "proper" roles. The multiple voices and shifts in footing within the lyrics themselves argue against such either/or interpretations. Social, cultural, historical, and spatial considerations add contextual richness to the analysis and also strongly suggest that a simplistic interpretation of the song as either resistance to patriarchy or resigned acceptance of it would be misguided.

So what did the song performance "mean" to the participants? I cannot answer this question definitively, but, as I have indicated here, I can rule out some of the least likely interpretations and note some of the possibilities that are emergent within the performance itself. Meanings of performances (or any linguistic interactions) do not reside singularly and statically in the words themselves or in individuals' heads but rather are co-constructed by communities of language users together. Close analysis of the intertwining of texts and contexts can help scholars identify constraints on the range of possible interpretations that might emerge from a given performance.

In this chapter, we explored various uses and definitions of the concepts of performance and performativity. The three main approaches that have most strongly influenced the work of linguistic anthropologists are: (1) performance defined in opposition to competence, as proposed by Chomsky and later refined by Hymes; (2) performativity, as defined in the speech act theory of Austin and Searle and later transformed by Butler, Latour, and other scholars; and (3) performance as a display of verbal artistry that is subject to evaluation by an audience, as elaborated upon by Bauman, Briggs, and others. Linguistic anthropologists have built upon and sometimes combined these approaches in interesting and important ways, drawing on concepts like framing, keying, and emergence to learn how communities use language to create social actions performatively, and how they use performances to help define or redefine themselves as a community.

In the process of this analysis, we have touched upon the relationship between language and gender, race, ethnicity, power, agency, and social change. These will be the central themes of the final part of the book.

Part III Language, Power, and Social Differentiation

9

Language and Gender

Consider the following two questions:

- If you could systematically record every word spoken on a given day by 200 female college students and 200 male college students, as Matthias Mehl and his colleagues did, which speakers do you think would be more talkative on average?
- Which of the following conversations[1] was spoken by an all-female group and which by an all-male group of US high school students? These students were debating the importance for survivors of a plane crash in a desert of items such as sunglasses, a compass, a gun, a first aid kit, and so on.

Group A

S: wouldn't you need the sunglasses?
C: yeah, that's what I think
S: because it would be really hot and protect yourself from the sun and you'd be able to see more
G: yeah, but if you're trying to live, does it matter [whether you can see?
C: [you can go *blind*
G: exactly, but if you're trying to survive, does it really matter?
C: (*sounding irritated*) I wouldn't [want to go *blind*
S: [it does, because if you

were blind you wouldn't be able to see what you were doing and you would end up dying anyway. You'd have less chance of surviving anyway.

G: yeah, but you're not likely to go blind unless you're looking right up into the sun.

Group B

C: (*pointing*) right, what did you put?
M: compass.
C: (*pointing*) what did you put?
T: I put sunglasses
C: right, I put the parachute (*gives long explanation for choosing it*)
Other voices: mirror, mirror. … the torch
C: and you could use a gun, couldn't you? You could shoot –
H: you could shoot the pilot
C: right. So has anyone changed their mind? (*pointing*) What do you think?
H: I say compass
T: I think sunglasses are quite important because you have to be able to see what it says on the compass for a start (laughter from the group)
H: you could just go like that (mimes shading eyes) shut your eyes for a moment
C: right. You go (*pointing*) Say why you thought the first aid kit.

In answering these questions, you probably drew on your firsthand experiences of how males and females use language, as well as (consciously or unconsciously) various language ideologies concerning the gendered nature of communication, especially whether men or women are more talkative, cooperative, or competitive in daily conversations. We will return to each of these cases in the pages that follow.

In addition to examining the research that enables us to answer the two questions that open this chapter, we will also explore many other researchers' findings and look more broadly at the relationship of language to gender, addressing in particular the following questions:

- What is gender, and how does it relate to language?
- Do men and women speak alike or differently?
- Do women and men of all ages and all ethnic, racial, and cultural backgrounds share the same gendered differences in their language use?

- How can we separate myths (that is, powerful but factually incorrect language ideologies) from reality in the area of language and gender, and why are these myths so influential?

In the process of addressing these questions, we will review the two studies cited above regarding the relative talkativeness of male and female college students and the cooperative or competitive nature of groups of male and female high school students engaged in a problem-solving exercise. These studies and others shed light on the fascinating complexities of language and gender. First, however, let us discuss what gender is and how it relates to language.

What is Gender, and How Does it Relate to Language?

Upon hearing that a baby has been born, many people immediately ask, "Is it a boy or a girl?" Right from birth, therefore (if not sooner, since prenatal tests often reveal the sex of the baby long before birth), the gendered categorization of the person begins. This categorization is usually dichotomous – that is, the child is said to be *either* a girl *or* a boy – and the process of categorization seems so obvious, so "natural," that many people take it totally for granted and immediately begin acting upon assumptions about how girls and boys are said to behave (Livia and Hall 1997; McElhinny 2003a). It is worth reflecting, however, on some of the many complexities and assumptions that underlie this seemingly simple act of sex assignment.

One way that some scholars have sought to clarify sex and gender is to say that the term "sex" refers to a person's biological existence as either a female or male human being, and the term "gender" refers to a person's cultural or social identity as either a woman or a man (or a girl or a boy) in a particular society at a particular historical moment. In this view, one's sex is immutable and given at birth, whereas one's gender identity can change, depending on what cultural practices of masculinity or femininity a person might choose to enact at different times.

Many scholars have challenged this sex = biology and gender = culture distinction, however. As Penelope Eckert and Sally McConnell-Ginet write, "there is no obvious point at which sex leaves off and gender begins, partly because there is no single objective biological criterion for male or female sex" (2003:10). Sex is based a complex combination of anatomy (in the form of internal and external genitalia and reproductive organs), hormones (testosterone and estrogen are only two of the many important hormones that affect sexual characteristics), and chromosomes (usually, but not always, XX or XY). Anomalies in any of these areas can result in what is known as an "intersexed" individual – a phenomenon that is more common than many people realize because it is often taboo to discuss babies who are not easily categorized as either male or female at birth. Estimates of the frequency of intersexed individuals vary tremendously, but there seem to be between 1 in 30,000 to about 1 in 1,000 babies who are born with sexually ambiguous genitalia, many of whom are considered candidates for surgical interventions of one kind or another (Preves 2003:2; Bing and Bergvall 1996:8). In addition to these babies, many more individuals (estimates range between 1 and 4 percent of all births) are born with hormonal or chromosomal anomalies that only become evident later in childhood or during puberty (Blackless et al. 2000:151; Preves 2003:2; Eckert and McConnell-Ginet 2003:11). The fact that these individuals are usually deemed so abnormal as to require medical interventions points to the cultural power of the dichotomous gender ideology that is dominant in so many countries – a power that is now being resisted by a growing movement of intersexed individuals who are fighting to have the right to be accepted as they are (cf. Chase 2008). Thus, many scholars consider both sex and gender to be concepts that are influenced by cultural and social norms and practices.

For the purposes of this chapter, we will consider gender to be built upon a set of culturally and historically specific practices that amplify, simplify, and give meaning to perceived or actual biological differences. Penelope Eckert and Sally McConnell-Ginet (2003:31–32) identify the following four characteristics as central to the concept of gender:

- *Gender is learned.* As is the case with other sociocultural practices, children either unconsciously adopt or are consciously instructed in gender-appropriate behavior that varies across societies and throughout historical time.
- *Gender is collaborative.* Although it is individuals who engage in gendered activities, these activities are learned in, and acquire

meaning from, social contexts. Gender, like other aspects of identity such as race or ethnicity, is a joint accomplishment that is constructed in and through interactions with others.

- *Gender is not something we have, but something we do.* Judith Butler's concept of the performativity of gender, discussed in chapter 8, asserts that people continuously reinforce or reconfigure their gender identities. Gender, according to Butler, is not a static and unchanging element of someone's identity but rather an ongoing process of *doing* that involves choices in how that person dresses, acts, and speaks. "The fact is," Eckert and McConnell-Ginet write, "that gender requires work, and when aspects of gender are not consistently performed at all levels of society they can wither away" (2003:32).
- *Gender involves asymmetry.* Eckert and McConnell-Ginet are joined by many other social scientists in their insistence that inequality is built into gender at a very fundamental level. Men and women, and masculine and feminine ways of acting or speaking, are rarely considered simply different; there are usually value judgments that accompany such assessments of gendered difference. Men, and those things that are deemed masculine, are not always more prestigious; there is complexity and variability depending on the particular social context. Moreover, there are multiple masculinities and femininities even within one society, so judgments about prestige or appropriateness will also vary. What is often the case, however, is that those qualities associated with men and masculinity tend to be taken for granted – tend to be the default ways of behaving or speaking, in other words. Scholars, drawing on the important linguistic concept of markedness, call these masculine practices "unmarked." They are taken as the norm for all humans, and anything that departs from them, such as perceived feminine ways of speaking or acting, are considered different or "marked."

Markedness also helps to illuminate gender as it appears in the realm of grammar. The use of masculine generic pronouns, for example, is supposed to enable the speaker to refer to anyone – male or female. Consider the following sentence: "If a student wants to do well, _____ should study hard for the test." According to many prescriptive grammarians, the appropriate pronoun for the blank in the following sentence is "he" because the masculine pronoun in English is unmarked and therefore supposed to encompass a more generic meaning than the feminine pronoun. In recent years, however, this prescription has been challenged by editors and even some English teachers. "Using *he*, *his*, and *him* as common-sex pronouns is now widely considered sexist, if not misleading," declares the classic reference book, *The Chicago Manual of Style*, continuing on to claim, "A good writer can usually recast the sentence to eliminate the need for any personal pronoun at all." Thus, instead of writing something like, "Some boy or girl left his {or her, or their} lunch box on the bus," a writer might instead write, "Some child left a lunch box on the bus."[2] And, similarly, a sentence such as, "If a student wants to do well, _____ should study hard for the test," could be converted into the plural ("If students want to do well, they should study hard for the test") or recast without a personal pronoun ("Students who want to do well should study hard for the test"). Writers and editors espousing different language ideologies will therefore advocate different approaches to the use or avoidance of masculine generics in English.

In a fascinating ethnographic and linguistic study of the use by women of masculine generics in Hebrew and Arabic, Amalia Sa'ar reveals that female speakers of both these languages in Israel often use masculine grammatical forms as generics to refer to themselves and their female addressees (Sa'ar 2007:408). For example, one 34-year-old Hebrew-speaking fashion designer made this remark to Sa'ar to explain why she had become self-employed: "'One day you♂ suddenly realize♂ that you♂ are♂ a mother and all you♂ wish♂ to do is stay home with the children'" (2007:413).[3] Similarly, an 80-year-old Arabic-speaking woman answered her neighbor's question, "How have you been?" with the following: "'Very poorly♂ lately; I don't know♂ what it is – my health is not good'" (2007:415). Sa'ar found that the women who used these masculine grammatical forms generally did so unconsciously. When she brought this practice to their attention, they had several different kinds of reactions. Some women felt it helped them participate in pubic or professional spheres to use masculine grammatical forms. Others thought it was a function of their particular dialect of Hebrew or Arabic. If gender is, as Judith Butler claims, something that we do rather than something that we have, Sa'ar asks, then what gender are these women "doing"?

Masculinity? Femininity? A combination? A redefinition of one or both of these genders? Sa'ar concludes that whatever sort of gender is being performed when women use masculine generics, it would serve their interests far better if they were to begin using feminine grammatical forms, both to refer to themselves and to address mixed- and same-sex groups generically because, Sa'ar claims, "Generalized feminine talk brings the female gender to the forefront, instead of denying it" (2007:426).

Grammatical gender involves much more than the use of generic pronouns, however. The 7,000 or so languages in the world encode gender grammatically in many different ways (including not at all). The grammatical categories of some languages require speakers to assign a gender when using a personal pronoun, such as "she" or "he" in English, whereas the grammatical categories of other languages, such as the dialect of Nepali spoken in the village of Junigau, where I have conducted fieldwork, does not assign gender at all in any personal pronoun – but does assign several different levels of social status in second- and third-person pronouns. Sometimes grammatical gender involves not just personal pronouns but all nouns, as in Spanish or French. In other languages, there are pronouns and/or noun classes that extend beyond "masculine" or "feminine," such as German, in which a "neuter" category of nouns and pronouns exists. This "neuter" category does not always correlate with social gender, however, as can be seen by the fact that the German word for girl, *Mädchen*, takes the neuter article "das" rather than the feminine article, "die." Another example of noun classifications that extend beyond "masculine" and "feminine" is the one mentioned in chapter 4 of the four classes of nouns in Dyirbal, an endangered indigenous language of Australia (Lakoff 1987:93; Dixon 1982):

1 *Bayi*: (human) males; animals
2 *Balan*: (human) females; water; fire; fighting
3 *Balam*: nonflesh food
4 *Bala*: everything not in the other classes.

There is no simple one-to-one mapping, therefore, of grammatical and social gender onto each other. Researchers have shown, however, that what might appear to be an arbitrary gender categorization of items or individuals in a particular language often seems anything but arbitrary to speakers of that language (McElhinny 2003b:848). As we saw in chapter 4, grammatical categories can powerfully influence how people make connections and groupings in real-world actions. It may very well be the case, therefore, that for languages that group terms in gender categories that link women with water, fire, and fighting, as in Dyirbal, for example, speakers might be predisposed (but *not* required in a deterministic way, remember) to view these items as linked in some way. Still, the relationship between social and grammatical gender is so complex that it is far more useful to take a broader approach to the study of language and gender rather than to focus exclusively on how particular languages encode gender grammatically.[4]

Indeed, Elinor Ochs (1992) made an important contribution to the study of language and gender when she noted that a large part of the way that language and gender are connected involves indirect rather than direct indexicality. As one of the book's four key terms, indexicality is especially useful in studying the relationship between language and gender because it helps us understand which linguistic features, styles, or discourses index, or "point to," gendered identities or practices. In her classic 1992 article, "Indexing Gender," Ochs states that although few features of any language directly and exclusively index gender, many features, communicative styles, and stances more indirectly and complexly index gender by alluding to, and helping to constitute, other domains of social reality, which then relate to gender (1992:343). This sort of indirect indexicality would work differently in each particular community of practice.

For example, Ochs describes two very different styles of linguistic interaction between mothers and their children – in white, middle-class communities in the United States, and in Western Samoa. As readers will remember from chapter 3, the white, middle-class American mothers that Ochs studied tended to accommodate to their children, using simplified language and treating them as more competent conversational partners than they were capable of being. Western Samoan mothers, in contrast, refused to accommodate to their children in these ways, preferring instead to reserve such linguistic accommodation for high-status foreigners who had trouble speaking Samoan. Both sets of mothers used accommodation in the form of simplified language to nonfluent speakers – but they did so with two very different groups of conversation partners. Ochs argues that because accommodation is universally associated with the actions of lower-ranking individuals in the presence of higher-status individuals, the uses in two different communities of practice to two different groups of individuals (children vs. foreigners) lead to the constitution of two different social identities. In the United States, Ochs maintains, children are socialized into viewing mothers as accommodating, addressee-oriented, and relatively low in status, whereas in Samoa, it is the children who are socialized to become accommodating themselves (Ochs 1992:344–345). Thus, the same linguistic practice – accommodation to a nonfluent speaker – indirectly indexes two very different social identities in these two societies (cf. Bucholtz and Hall 2004:476).

Do Men and Women Speak Alike or Differently?

Language ideologies concerning the alleged differences in how women and men speak have created a multi-million-dollar self-help industry consisting of books, workshops, and career seminars that purport to explain these differences and advise readers or clients as to what, if anything, to do about them. Books such as Deborah Tannen's *You Just Don't Understand: Women and Men in Conversation*, for example, assume categorical, dichotomous, essential differences in the ways that men and women speak. Women, according to Tannen, are much more likely to engage in "rapport talk" – that is, talk that cooperatively establishes and maintains social relationships. Men, on the other hand, according to Tannen, tend to use "report talk" – talk that conveys straightforward information rather than emotion or gossip (Tannen 1990:74ff).

While Tannen is a well-respected sociolinguist who has conducted her own research in several different areas, in *You Just Don't Understand* she relied primarily on anecdotal evidence from her own experiences as well as some early work done in the area of language and gender research in the 1970s and 1980s. In much of this early work, gendered differences in communicative styles were simply assumed rather than investigated systematically. Men, these researchers (e.g., Maltz and Borker 1982) asserted, were more likely to compete for the floor and to

"And do you, Deborah Tannen, think they know what they're talking about?"

Figure 9.1 Cartoon referring to author Deborah Tannen's ability to understand gendered language. Tannen writes about the communication between men and women.
Source: From The New Yorker, March 20, 1995. © Peter Steiner/The New Yorker Collection/www.cartoonbank.com

interrupt when others were speaking, while women spoke more cooperatively, asking more questions, linking their comments to others' comments, and rarely interrupting. Scholars in these early years of language and gender research largely accepted that these sorts of fundamental differences existed, and then they proceeded to advocate various approaches for dealing with such allegedly different gendered communicative styles. Some suggested that women should take assertiveness training to learn how to speak like men. Others advised women and men that such differences were akin to cross-cultural differences and could therefore best be dealt with through attempts at greater understanding and tolerance. And still others felt that differences in communicative style reflected deep gender inequalities in society and prescribed actions to remedy these injustices. But what all these early scholars in the field of language and gender assumed was the existence of dramatic across-the-board differences in how women and men talked.

In recent years, however, this basic assumption of the existence of substantial gender differences in communicative style has been challenged. Psychologist Janet Hyde, a researcher who specializes in meta-analyses – that is, analyses of multiple studies on a given topic – has put forward a Gender Similarities Hypothesis. According to Hyde (2005), the gender differences model that dominates the popular media is inaccurate at best and harmful at worst when it comes to most variables, including alleged gender differences in communication. Among the variables on which Hyde conducted meta-analyses were those involving verbal and nonverbal behaviors among males and females of various ages. As Table 9.1 indicates, almost all of these behaviors showed gender differences that were close to zero or very small. In the studies that Hyde analyzed, only two communicative behaviors, spelling and smiling, showed moderate differences (both in this case favoring females), and none showed large differences. "Stated another way," Hyde writes, "within-gender variability is typically much larger than between-gender variability" (2007:260).

As Hyde herself readily admits, the nuances of particular contexts are by necessity glossed over in these large meta-analyses, and it is exactly these sorts of nuances that are of greatest interest to linguistic anthropologists. And yet, there is a benefit to considering these large-scale quantitative analyses in conjunction with smaller, more ethnographically rich studies.

Consider the issue of the relationship between gender and talkativeness, for instance. Hyde's meta-analysis relies upon an earlier meta-analysis done by two other psychologists on 73 different studies that quantified in some way the amount of talk produced by males and females (Leaper and Smith 2004). All 73 of these studies were con-

Table 9.1 Findings of Hyde's meta-analyses regarding gender differences in communicative behavior, adapted from Hyde (2005:583–586) and Cameron (2007b:43).

Area of research	Number of studies analyzed	Size of gender difference (with females [F] or males [M] favored)
Reading comprehension	23	Close to zero (F)
Verbal reasoning	5	Close to zero (F)
Vocabulary	44	Close to zero (F)
Affiliative speech	46	Small (F)
Assertive speech	75	Small (M)
Conversational interruption	70	Small (M)
Self-disclosure	205	Small (F)
Speech production	12	Small (F)
Talkativeness	73	Small (F)
Smiling	418	Moderate (F)
Spelling	5	Moderate (F)

Source: Adapted from Hyde (2005:583–586) and Cameron (2007b:43).

ducted among children 17 years of age or younger (mostly preschoolers and children in the middle years of childhood), and they varied in terms of where the study took place (home, school, laboratory) as well as who the conversation partners were for the children (other children or adults). On average, across all these different contexts, girls produced slightly more talk than boys, though the researchers termed this difference "negligible" (Leaper and Smith 2004:993). A later meta-analysis on talkativeness among adults in 63 different studies also found a "negligible" difference, though in the opposite direction. "Contrary to prediction, men tended to talk significantly more than women," the authors concluded (Leaper and Ayres 2007:353; cf. Holmes 1998; James and Drakich 1993).

A more recent study was undertaken by Matthias Mehl and his colleagues in order to study talkativeness not just in particular contexts or conversations, as previous studies such as those analyzed by Leaper and his colleagues had documented, but among large groups of people for extended periods of time (Mehl et al. 2007). As Mehl and his colleagues reported in the prestigious journal *Science*, they were concerned about wildly inaccurate assertions regarding the relative talkativeness of women and men that were circulating in the media. One source for these erroneous figures was a popular book on "the female brain" that alleged that women spoke an average of 20,000 words per day while men spoke only an average of 7,000 words (Brizendine 2006). These figures, Mehl reported, had struck linguist Mark Liberman as implausible, and in columns in *The Boston Globe* as well as in the wonderful blog, Language Log, Liberman fact-checked them and found them to be based on absolutely no research at all but rather on unscientific estimates.[5]

Mehl and his colleagues conducted a study of almost 400 college students – the study mentioned at the outset of this chapter – in order to measure gender differences in the average number of words spoken over the course of the research subjects' waking hours (Mehl et al. 2007). The college students (divided roughly equally between women and men) were rigged up with digital recorders that were programmed to record for 30 seconds every 12.5 minutes. The students could not tell when they were being recorded. The researchers then transcribed all the words spoken by the participants and extrapolated from these figures to estimate the total number of words spoken over the course of an average day for these individuals. The findings showed that female college students spoke an average of 16,215 words per day, while men spoke an average of 15,669 words per day – but this difference was not statistically significant. "Thus," write Mehl and his co-authors, "the data fail to reveal a reliable sex difference in daily word use. Women and men both use on average about 16,000 words per day, with very large individual differences around this mean … We therefore conclude, on the basis of available empirical evidence, that the widespread and highly publicized stereotype about female talkativeness is unfounded" (Mehl et al. 2007:82).

Before considering what might account for the discrepancy between common language ideologies regarding gender differences in talkativeness and actual empirical research, let us examine another area in which there are widespread assumptions about gendered communicative styles – the competitive vs. cooperative (or "affiliative" vs. "assertive") nature of men's and women's speech. The large-scale meta-analyses by Hyde (2005) and Leaper and Ayres (2007) found differences in this area that accorded with popular language ideologies that depict women as using talk more cooperatively and men as using talk more competitively – but these differences, which showed up on average across dozens of separate studies, were "small" or "negligible."

A look at more in-depth research in which talk is analyzed in actual social contexts illuminates some of the complexities that get erased in larger quantitative studies and in many of the earlier research that assumed the existence of essential gender differences. For example, Marjorie Harness Goodwin has conducted extremely detailed, long-term analyses of the linguistic and social interactions in several groups of children – most notably, a mixed-age, mixed-sex group of African American children in Philadelphia, and a racially and ethnically mixed group of girls from their fourth through sixth grade in Los Angeles (Goodwin 1990, 2006). Goodwin audio- or videotaped hundreds of hours of naturally occurring interactions while these children played among themselves and with other boys and girls. In her two books about these children's social worlds, she interweaves close analysis of "talk-in-interaction" with insights gathered from ethnographic fieldwork – a very different methodology from that which is generally employed by child psychologists or sociolinguists (Goodwin 2006:15). Rather than conducting interviews or psychological tests, Goodwin immerses herself in the actual social worlds of the children as much as possible and presents them as agents who construct their own social relationships and hierarchies through talk (1990:283).

Goodwin's long-term ethnographic and linguistic fieldwork enables her to understand some of the complexities of children's social worlds and leads her to oppose simplistic, dualistic representations of girls as cooperative and boys as competitive. In her first study of the children of Maple Street in Philadelphia, *He-Said-She-Said: Talk As Social Organization Among Black Children*, Goodwin (1990) conducts close conversation analysis and concludes that in some of the girls' activities, such as making rings out of glass bottle rims, the girls cooperate and use supportive talk. In other pastimes, however, such as pretend play, "he-said-she-said" arguments, or fabricated conflicts known as "instigating," the girls are anything but cooperative. In these interactions, their talk displays competition and asymmetry, often using the same sorts of directives and other linguistic forms that boys use during their play. And when the girls and boys on Maple Street played together, there was a mixture of linguistic forms and social interactions. Thus, Goodwin argues, the notion of "separate worlds" or "separate cultures" for boys and girls was not at all borne out by her research. Moreover, the stereotype of girls as always affiliative, nonconfrontational, and egalitarian within their same-sex play groups was also contradicted by the actions of the girls she studied. "Not only do girls establish hierarchical arrangements among members of their groups, but they also differentiate themselves and establish implicit rankings by forming coalitions against particular girls" (Goodwin 1990:133). The variety in forms of talk and forms of social organization among these girls and boys speaks to the need, Goodwin asserts, for studies of language and gender to be "grounded in detailed analysis of specific contexts of use" (1990:137). The contribution that a focus on specific activities and communities of practice makes to linguistic research on gender, Bonnie McElhinny notes, is that it shifts the research question away from what the differences are in men and women's (or boys' and girls') speech – a question that makes unwarranted assumptions about the existence of differences and also serves to perpetuate and exaggerate the dichotomous nature of gender categories – to research questions involving "when, whether, and how men and women's speech are done in similar and different ways" (McElhinny 2003a:29).

In her second ethnography, *The Hidden Life of Girls: Games of Stance, Status, and Exclusion*, Goodwin (2006) describes the linguistic and social interactions of several different groups of children. In her analysis of the actions and words of one particular group of ethnically and racially mixed fourth- to sixth-grade girls in a private school in Los Angeles, she documents how they confronted the boys and several school officials, demanding to have the right to play on the soccer field that the boys had been monopolizing at recess. The girls also complained to the vice principal about a male aide who had been siding with the boys. Eventually, the girls managed to change the school's policy so that access to the soccer and football fields was shared between the boys and girls, and a sign-up process was implemented. For the next year or so, the girls' participation in team sports increased dramatically, but then, according to Goodwin, their interest waned because the boys often refused to pass the ball to them, and some boys even sexually harassed the girls through actions such as pinching their nipples while they were playing soccer. Goodwin concludes,

> Despite problems, the girls did succeed in initiating a new moral order on their own terms. The overtly political activity of the girls countering the boys challenges the view of girls as non-competitive and displays quite dramatically their engagement in issues of justice and fairness; it also provides a view of girls as wielders of authority and instruments of change. (2006:106)

Other examples of research that illuminates complex linguistic and social interactions among girls and contradicts the stereotype of girls as cooperative and egalitarian can be found in the work of Penelope Eckert. In an article entitled, "Cooperative Competition in Adolescent 'Girl Talk,'" Eckert (1993) shows how six high school girls use a conversation to co-construct the social norms against which the girls judge and compete against one another. Drawing on Bourdieu's concept of symbolic capital, which refers to the status acquired by those who are able to speak in highly valued ways in appropriate contexts, Eckert argues that because of the gender dynamics in the high school she studied in the 1980s, the girls acquired symbolic capital largely through their relationships with particular kinds of boys. In the conversation Eckert analyzes in her "Cooperative Competition" article, a group of girls, most of whom have not seen one another since junior high school, compete only indirectly because they perceive a conflict between the goal of being "successful" and the goal of being "likable" (1993:37). Moreover, the meanings of these two words are also up for interpretation during the conversation. The girls discuss the different paths they have taken in high school, their differing attitudes toward using go-betweens instead of asking boys out themselves, the pros and cons of dating "popular" boys, and the advisability of marrying within or outside of one's religion. On all these topics, the girls perform intricate linguistic and social negotiations that allow them to compete against one another without appearing to do so. Eckert concludes, "Therefore, their noncompetitive performance in this interaction, which allows each girl to display her understanding of human nature and her ability to resolve conflict and create community, can be seen as part of the competition" (1993:37).

Despite the competitiveness in this conversation, which contradicts language ideologies in which females are portrayed as more cooperative by nature, the girls Eckert studied do engage in a social and linguistic practice stereotypically associated with girls and women: gossip, or "girl talk." Indeed, Eckert argues that because females in the United States during the 1980s often accrued social status by virtue of the males they dated or married, girls and women had good reasons to use gossip to assess one another's prestige. Thus, in the community of practice Eckert studied (a high school in Michigan during the 1980s), gossip was a gendered form of communication that both reflected and reinforced inequalities between males and females.

Gossip, however, like almost all other linguistic forms and genres, is not the sole province of one gender. As Deborah Cameron compellingly demonstrates in her article, "Performing Gender Identity: Young Men's Talk and the Construction of Heterosexual Masculinity" (Cameron 1997), even a fairly mundane conversation among several male college students can involve gossip. Cameron defines gossip as the discussion of people who are known to the participants but who are not currently present in which the focus is on critically examining these individuals' appearance, dress, social behavior, and sexual mores. Gossip usually affirms the solidarity of an in-group by constructing absent others as an out-group, whose behavior is minutely examined and found wanting (1997:51, 54; cf. Besnier 2009). Using this definition of gossip, the men in the conversation Cameron studied were certainly gossiping.

There is an interesting twist to Cameron's analysis, for it is actually a re-analysis of a conversation tape-recorded and analyzed by a male student of hers for a class assignment. In the student's original analysis of the conversation, in which he himself was a participant, along with several of his male friends, the student argued that the conversation was an example of typically masculine talk because the topics discussed included sports, women, and alcohol. Cameron agreed that these topics were present, but she also saw something else as well – aspects of the conversation that did not conform to the prevailing language ideologies about differences in how men and women talk. The student's analysis – like the analyses of all scholars, whether well-seasoned researchers or amateurs – was "*partial*: it was shaped by expectations that caused some things to leap out of the record as 'significant,' while other things went unremarked," Cameron declared (1997:47; emphasis in the original). While the male student considered the content of the conversation to involve mainly gender-typical subjects such as "wine, women, and sports" (the title the student chose for his paper), Cameron, on the other hand, argued that the conversation dwelled more on typically "feminine" topics, such as clothing and bodily appearance. And in the area of linguistic form, the conversation "must be judged as highly cooperative," Cameron argues (1997:55), because of the latching (when participants link their utterances immediately onto the previous participant's utterance), repetitions, and multiple tokens of hearer support. Take, for example, this segment of the conversation (Cameron 1997:53–54):[6]

BRYAN: uh you know that really gay guy in our Age of Revolution class who sits in front of us? he wore shorts again, by the way, it's like 42 degrees out he wore shorts again [laughter] [Ed: That guy] it's like a speedo, he wears a speedo to class (.) he's got incredibly skinny legs [Ed: it's worse] you know=
ED: =you know like those shorts women volleyball players wear? it's like those (.) it's l[ike

BRYAN: [you know what's even more ridicu[lous? when
ED: [French cut spandex]

BRYAN: you wear those shorts and like a parka on …
(*5 lines omitted*)

BRYAN: he's either got some condition that he's got to like have his legs exposed at all times or else he's got really good legs=
ED: =he's probably he'[s like
CARL: [he really likes

BRYAN: =he
ED: =he's like at home combing his leg hairs=
CARL: his legs=

BRYAN: he doesn't have any leg hair though= [*yes* and oh
ED: =he *real*[*ly* likes

ED: his legs=

AL: =very long very white and very skinny

BRYAN: those ridiculous Reeboks that are always (indeciph)
and goofy white socks always striped= [tube socks
ED: =that's [right

ED: he's the antithesis of man

Despite the ways in which the form and content of this conversation contradict language ideologies regarding gendered styles of talk, Cameron does not claim that these men are subverting or challenging gender norms in any way. Indeed, they seem mainly to be concerned with performing a gender identity that is highly normative in its heterosexual masculinity. In this sense, Cameron agrees with her student's analysis. And yet, the participants in the conversation achieve this goal of reasserting their normative gender identities through linguistic practices that have been associated with femininity rather than masculinity – gossip about others' clothing and behavior, and linguistic forms that are cooperative rather than competitive in nature. It is therefore unhelpful, Cameron concludes, "for linguists to continue to use models of gendered speech which imply that masculinity and femininity are monolithic constructs, automatically giving rise to predictable (and utterly different) patterns of verbal interaction" (1997:62).

An excellent example of the complexities and variations inherent in gendered language use can be found in Kira Hall's (1995) analysis of the ways in which phone sex operators in San Francisco used stereotypically ultra-feminine styles in order to cater to their clients' expectations and language ideologies. Just as Cameron's study of the speech of college men reminds us that no linguistic forms or conversational topics are unique to one sex, so too does Hall's study remind us that even when individuals are using language in ways that accord with gendered language ideologies, the meanings behind their words, and the power dynamics associated with their interactions, can be quite complex and varied. Hall explains that the phone sex operators she studied (who included 11 women of different ethnicities and sexual orientations, and one bisexual Mexican American man who portrayed himself as a female heterosexual to his callers) used linguistic features often labeled as "feminine" and "powerless," such as raising the pitch of their voices and using multiple adjectives to describe their clothes and bodies, thereby depicting themselves in their phone conversations with their paying male customers as submissive and engaging in stereotypically feminine activities. Their linguistic styles closely resembled that of this prerecorded phone sex message, in which a woman describes her new job as a phone sex operator:[7]

> oo::f:: – i'm so ((in breathy voice)) excited. – i just got a hot new job. (0.8) well, – ((in slight Southern accent)) i've been bored lately. .hh – i live in a small town and my husband travels a lot, (0.5) i have lots of time on my hands. – .hhh of course, i've always managed to stay busy. (0.4) lots of girlfriends, you know, – ((whispered)) i love to shop, – i ((laugh)) ^pract^ically live at the mall it seems. (Hall 1995:192)

As submissive and reinforcing of certain stereotypes as these sorts of messages are, Hall maintains that the phone sex operators viewed their use of these linguistic features as powerful and considered themselves to be in a superior position within the conversations. "The operators who participated in the study reported that they are completely in control of each conversation: they initiate and dominate the conversational exchange; they are creators of the fantasy story line and scenario; they can decide what kind of fantasies they will entertain, and they can terminate the conversation with a simple flick of the index finger" (Hall 1995:204). And yet, these workers in the phone sex industry also admitted that using this language and catering to the fantasies of their male callers could feel degrading and restricting, and several seemed worried that they might reinforce negative and inaccurate stereotypes of women through their conversations. Nevertheless, these phone sex operators also felt that it would be "ridiculous" to attribute any power to their male callers. Hall concludes, therefore, that language, gender, and power should be analyzed within particular communities of practice; doing so will allow for greater nuance in understanding and representing these complexities.

Hall's conclusion in the specific case of phone sex operators in San Francisco applies equally well to the question posed at the outset of this section: do men and women speak alike or differently? There is no single answer to this question that would be applicable across all contexts. Men and women (or boys and girls) sometimes speak in similar ways, and sometimes speak differently from each other – it all depends on who is speaking to whom, when, where, and to what audiences. Many received notions, or language ideologies, concerning the alleged differences in how women and men speak have been disproved by the research of scholars such as Deborah Cameron, Marjorie Harness Goodwin, Janet Hyde, and Matthias Mehl. We will return at the end of this chapter to consider why such assumptions of gender difference in communicative styles continue to be so prevalent despite the large amount of research countering them. First, however, it is important to consider some cross-cultural examples because as eye-opening as the mostly US-based research surveyed in this section has been in illuminating the complexities and refuting the misconceptions surrounding gendered language use, the studies that have been conducted elsewhere in the world help us understand even better the wide range of linguistic styles both within the United States and elsewhere and remind us of the need to situate all research in specific social and historical contexts.

Do Women and Men of All Ages and All Ethnic, Racial, and Cultural Backgrounds Share the Same Gendered Differences in their Language Use?

Lest the language ideologies dominant in the United States and some other countries be mistaken for a universal set of assumptions (correct or incorrect) about the existence and character of gender differences in language, studies from other societies remind us of the diversity not just in how individuals actually talk (as opposed to how they are assumed to talk) but also in the cultural norms and assumptions themselves.

In a classic article (Keenan [Ochs] 1974) about the linguistic practices of Malagasy-speaking women and men in Madagascar, for example, Elinor Ochs describes a very different set of language ideologies concerning gendered communicative styles than those that prevail in most of the United States and Europe. Whereas many Americans and Europeans (including scholars!) assume that women are, or should be, more cooperative and polite than men, the people with whom Ochs worked in Madagascar in the 1970s assumed exactly the reverse. The two overarching Malagasy speech genres, *resaka* (ordinary, direct, everyday speech) and *kabary* (ceremonial, oratorical, indirect speech) were therefore thought to index femininity and masculinity, respectively. Women, Ochs claimed,

> are associated with direct criticism and haggling in markets. They are able to put others on the spot, to confront others with possibly offensive information where man cannot or prefer not. Women tend to be direct and open in manner. Men tend to conduct themselves with discretion and subtlety. Women dominate situations where directness is called for. Men, on the other hand, dominate situations where indirectness is desirable. (Keenan [Ochs] 1974:139)

Because women were more willing to confront others directly, men often used them to intervene in social conflicts. On the whole, however, Ochs reports that the most highly valued style involved indirectness and avoidance of affront, and so women in Madagascar were looked down upon because of their direct linguistic practices and the language ideologies that led people to judge these practices as appropriate only for children and the unsophisticated.

Don Kulick points out that the gendered patterns Ochs uncovered in Madagascar are by no means unique. Indeed, as Steven Feld, Bambi Schieffelin, and others have noted, similar practices can be found in places like Papua New Guinea. Kulick's own research analyzes how language, gender, and emotion are interwoven in culturally specific ways by the villagers of Gapun in Papua New Guinea. Anger, in particular, is viewed in Gapun as the province mainly of women, at least in its explicit articulation through a speech genre villagers call the *kros*. A *kros*, Kulick explains, is a manifestation of the negative dimension of the self that Gapuners call *hed*, which, as we saw in the discussion in chapter 3 of Kulick's work on language socialization, makes people "individualistic, irascible, selfish, unbending, haughty, and proud" (1992:19). Women are considered less capable of controlling their *hed* than men, and one result of this perceived inability is that it is only women villagers who will engage in an angry, obscene shouting match known as a *kros*. Far from being the cooperative, consensus-seeking, accommodative speakers that some scholars (e.g., Maltz and Borker 1982; Tannen 1990) have assumed all women are, the women in Gapun, much like the women of Madagascar whom Ochs studied, use a much more direct, confrontational, and even vulgar style in their disputes, as can be seen in this excerpt from a typical *kros* between two sisters, Sake and Erapo, who were arguing because Sake had caught Erapo's son red-handed as he was shooting coffee beans at Sake's pig:[8]

Sake:	No good rotten big black hole!
Erapo:	Smelly cunt bloody bastard!
Sake:	I was talking to Erapo [sarcastic]. I was talking good about the rubbish [i.e., the coffee beans], Erapo gets up and swears at me. Fucking cunthole bastard you! (Kulick 1998:93)

The *kros* continues on in this vein for quite some time, Kulick reports, and ends in threats of physical violence. In contrast to this sort of confrontation, the styles of communication favored by men in Gapun emphasize cooperation and the importance of community. Anger is generally concealed in the talk that goes on in the men's house, even when there is a conflict between two of the participants. In such cases, the anger is eventually revealed, but only in a very tentative and temporary fashion, after which it is recontextualized and reconcealed. The dominant language ideology in Gapun values this kind of controlled expression of anger, followed by an immediate resuppression of this emotion that Gapuners consider so dangerous. The gendered nature of these linguistic expressions of emotion demonstrates the need to study such interactions ethnographically as they occur in actual social interactions.

Even in cultural contexts in which the language ideologies concerning gendered differences in linguistic practices are more in keeping with those that are predominant in the United States and Europe, the same need to study the specificities of these ideologies and practices applies. For Japan, for instance, Miyako Inoue reports that the extremely distinctive "Japanese women's language," assumed to exist by many Japanese and non-Japanese alike, serves as a powerful language ideology in which women and men are said to speak differently at all levels of language, including extra-linguistic features such as very high pitch, and discursive practices such as being soft-spoken, polite, gentle, and empathetic. "But here," Inoue writes, "is a little public secret: the very simple, yet obstinately disregarded, fact is that most women in Japan do not have access to – did not systematically learn and cannot skillfully produce – the speech forms identified as women's language in their habitual speech repertoire" (Inoue 2006:3). So, why then is there an "almost theological avowal" of dramatic gender differences in linguistic practices in Japan?

Through a detailed analysis, Inoue debunks the myth of allegedly ancient roots of "Japanese women's language," tracing its origins instead to a particular historical era in the not-so-distant past: the late Meiji period (1888–1912), a time when Japan was engaged in dramatic social changes involving modernization, capitalism, and nationalism. Far from being an ancient, widespread, traditional way that all Japanese women actually spoke, the grammatical forms and discursive styles now considered to be "Japanese women's language" began in the late nineteenth century, Inoue argues, as "schoolgirl speech," which, male commentators of the time claimed, was "vulgar" and "lazy" because it omitted honorifics and used different utterance endings (Inoue 2006:57). Ironically, however, other male writers of the time saw this style as suitable for the kinds of novels that they wanted to write – novels that incorporated dialogue and reported speech, much as Western novels of the time did. Thus, what was initially a stigmatized form of talk that was said to have been used among a small set of upper-class schoolgirls in the late nineteenth century came to be employed in novels, newspaper reports, advertisements, and other print media to represent the way that all Japanese women spoke (or were supposed to speak). Over time, through reading and eventually hearing on the TV and radio this "Japanese women's language," many people in Japan came to associate this way of speaking with femininity, Japaneseness, and modernity. Inoue calls this process one of *indexical inversion* because "it actively constructs the very reality that it claims to be representing" (2006:51). Often, Inoue writes, language "does not wait until the category it refers to or indexes is 'out there'"; instead, as she shows in the case of "Japanese women's language," indexicality is involved in the very creation of the category of modern Japanese women (2006:107). Then, through repeated linguistic practice influenced by language ideologies, the ways that Japanese women actually speak come to be informed by ideas about how they should speak, which then in turn come to be influenced by how women actually speak. Inoue's research therefore provides an illuminating case study of the performative and recursive nature of indexicality.

Some Thoughts on Myths and Realities

Much of this chapter has been devoted to debunking some widespread myths – that is, some inaccurate language ideologies. Across all of the research we have explored, we see that language and gender are related in complex and variable ways. Far from being reducible to simplistic and dualistic generalizations stating something like, "All women speak like Venusians, and all men speak like Martians," the realities of the relationship between language and gender must be determined by studying actual language use, and ideas surrounding that language use, in actual communities of practice.

Let us return now to the second question posed at the outset of the chapter: which group of high school students studied by Judith Baxter (2006:164, 170) was composed solely of girls, and which solely of boys? Recall that the teenagers were discussing what items would be most useful to survivors of a plane crash in a desert. Can the characteristics of these two groups' discussions reveal their composition? As Deborah Cameron, author of *The Myth of Mars and Venus: Do Men and Women Really Speak Different Languages*, notes in her analysis of these two conversations (2007b:61–64), compelling arguments could be made for either Group A as the all-girls group and Group B as the all-boys group, or vice versa. For example, it could be said that Group B's discussion was more cooperative; Speaker C politely solicits suggestions from the other group members, and there is no overt conflict. In contrast, Group A's members could be said to interact more competitively, with open conflict emerging as Speaker G challenged the other speakers and participants interrupted one another. Such an analysis might encourage someone who assumed women's communicative styles were more cooperative and less competitive than men's to conclude that Group A was made up of boys and Group B of girls.

On the other hand, even though Group B's discussion displayed more cooperative features in some respects, in other respects it seemed

"What I don't, like, get is how she, like, figured out I was, like, having an affair with, like, the babysitter."

Figure 9.2 Cartoon showing how certain linguistic forms can index social identities.
Source: © Danny Shanahan/The New Yorker Collection/www.Cartoonbank.com

to involve more hierarchy and structure. Speaker C did solicit other group members' input, but Speaker C also seems to be assuming a leadership role in a businesslike fashion. No one does this in Group A. It could be said, therefore, that Group A is more cooperative and less competitive than Group B. If so, someone in agreement with Tannen's (1990) and Maltz and Borker's (1982) generalizations regarding gendered linguistic practices might conclude that Group A was made up of girls and Group B of boys.

In fact, Group A was indeed made up of girls, and Group B was made up of boys. But, Cameron states,

> if you do not already know which group is which, it is difficult to deduce it from linguistic evidence alone. Each group's conversation contains both 'competitive' and 'cooperative' elements … Once you know C is a boy, though, it is tempting to use that information to resolve the ambiguity – in other words, to interpret his behaviour as on balance more 'directive' than 'facilitative'. The claim that boys' talk is more competitive can thus become a self-fulfilling prophecy. (2007b:64)

If the realities of language and gender are really so complex and varied, however, why are the language ideologies concerning female talkativeness or male verbal competitiveness that can be found in the vignettes presented by Tannen (1990) and others so recognizable to us? Cameron (2007b) explains that it happens because of the tendency of all people to rely at least in part on stereotyping when processing information. It is not just ignorant or prejudiced people who stereotype, Cameron states, but everyone because stereotyping provides us with convenient shortcuts in determining what people are like and how we should treat them. The downside, however, is that such stereotypes "can reinforce unjust prejudices, and make us prone to seeing only what we expect or want to see" (Cameron 2007b:14). When we see someone who fits our preconceptions – say, a woman who is extremely talkative, for example – we easily "supply the cultural script that makes them meaningful and 'typical'" (Cameron 1997:48). When we encounter someone who does not fit a particular stereotype, however, we tend either not to notice or to explain the case away as an aberration.

Why should we care if one or more of our gendered language ideologies might be inaccurate or at least overly simplistic? There are many real-world implications of inaccurate language ideologies – in the workplace, in family life, in court cases, and in interpersonal relationships. Women, men, and children all suffer when gendered assumptions regarding communicative styles and identities are inaccurate or overly rigid. What the research described in this chapter clearly demonstrates is that complexity and variability best characterize the relationship of language to gender. We will come to a similar conclusion in the next chapter after exploring the ways in which language relates to race and ethnicity.

10 Language, Race, and Ethnicity

Multiple dimensions of difference and inequality can shape, and be shaped by, language use. Gender (discussed in the previous chapter), socioeconomic class, age, regional identity, caste, and profession are just a few of the many types of social variation that can intersect with linguistic practice – often in complex, overlapping ways. This chapter focuses on two other common forms of social differentiation as they are instantiated in, and molded by, linguistic practices: race and ethnicity. Some of the issues we will address in this chapter include the following:

- *The rule-governed nature of African American English (AAE).* Contrary to many inaccurate representations of AAE as "sloppy" standard English, scholars have been demonstrating for decades the regularities at every linguistic level for AAE, just as they have been for all other dialects, registers, and languages. How does this scholarship relate to the key terms of the book, especially language ideologies and indexicality?
- *The Ebonics controversy.* When the Board of Education in Oakland, California, declared in December 1996 that students in the district "possess and utilize a language described in various scholarly approaches as 'Ebonics' (literally Black sounds) or Pan African Communication Behaviors or African Language Systems," and that this way of speaking is "genetically-based and not a dialect of

English" (Baugh 2000:43–44), a huge controversy emerged that revealed the very different language ideologies held by scholars, celebrities, and various members of the public regarding African American English. What can we learn from this controversy?

- *Racist language*. In the movie, "Terminator 2: Judgment Day," the character played by Arnold Schwarzenegger is taught various expressions, such as "Hasta la vista, baby," that are supposed to make him sound more like a "real person" rather than a robotic cyborg. Is this sort of Mock Spanish (Hill 1998:683) an instance of racist language? What kinds of linguistic practices constitute racism?
- *Language and racial/ethnic identities*. In the United States, people often belong to, or interact with, multiple races and ethnic groups. Moreover, mass media and other elements of popular culture expose individuals to the linguistic practices associated with various races and ethnic groups. How do these complexities play out in actual social contexts?

Before turning to these questions, it is first necessary to define "race" and "ethnicity" in at least a provisional way so that it is clearer what we are studying when we begin to explore language, race, and ethnicity.

Defining Race and Ethnicity

Many misconceptions surround the concept of race. Jane Hill, a well-known linguistic anthropologist and the former President of the American Anthropological Association, maintains that most white Americans share a largely inaccurate "folk theory" of race and racism, one of the main components of which is a belief in "race" as a basic category of human biological variation, combined with a belief that each human being can be assigned to a race, or sometimes to a mixture of races (Hill 2008:6–7). Hill argues that this folk theory is widespread and taken for granted – but mistaken in most respects, according to the vast majority of anthropologists and other social scientists. Indeed, the official statement on race of the American Anthropological Association begins with these two paragraphs:[1]

> In the United States both scholars and the general public have been conditioned to viewing human races as natural and separate divisions within the human species based on visible physical differences. With the vast expansion of scientific knowledge in this century, however, it has become clear that human populations are not unambiguous, clearly demarcated, biologically distinct groups. Evidence from the analysis of genetics (e.g., DNA) indicates that most physical variation, about 94%, lies *within* so-called racial groups. Conventional geographic "racial" groupings differ from one another only in about 6% of their genes. This means that there is greater variation within "racial" groups than between them. In neighboring populations there is much overlapping of genes and their phenotypic (physical) expressions. Throughout history whenever different groups have come into contact, they have interbred. The continued sharing of genetic materials has maintained all of humankind as a single species.
>
> Physical variations in any given trait tend to occur gradually rather than abruptly over geographic areas. And because physical traits are inherited independently of one another, knowing the range of one trait does not predict the presence of others. For example, skin color varies largely from light in the temperate areas in the north to dark in the tropical areas in the south; its intensity is not related to nose shape or hair texture. Dark skin may be associated with frizzy or kinky hair or curly or wavy or straight hair, all of which are found among different indigenous peoples in tropical regions. These facts render any attempt to establish lines of division among biological populations both arbitrary and subjective.

As definitive as the AAA's statement is about the lack of a consistent biological basis for the concept of race, it should not be read as arguing that race does not exist. Race is clearly an important social category that influences people's life trajectories and identities. Many scholars in fact view it as a, or even *the*, central organizing principle in the United States. But the social fact of race does not support the folk theory described by Hill above.[2] Reflect for a moment upon the following paradox: because of the so-called "one-drop rule," a white woman in the United States can give birth to a black child, but a black woman cannot give birth to white child. Such reflection should lead to an appreciation for the social foundations of the concept of race (Ignatiev 1995:1).

A brief review of American history and a few cross-cultural examples demonstrate the ways in which race, rather than being a primordial biological essence, is better thought of as a process of racialization or racial formation. As Michael Omi and Howard Winant write in their well-known book, *Racial Formation in the United States*:

> *[R]ace is a concept which signifies and symbolizes social conflicts and interests by referring to different types of human bodies.* Although the concept of race invokes biologically based human characteristics (so-called 'phenotypes'), selection of these particular human features for purposes of racial signification is always and necessarily a social and historical process. (1994:55; emphasis in the original)

Thus, just as the concept of gender, discussed in the previous chapter, allows us to understand the various cultural and social meanings people associate with perceived or actual biological differences in reproductive hormones, chromosomes, or genitalia, so, too, does the concept of race provide us with insight into the cultural and social meanings people associate with other kinds of perceived or actual biological differences, such as skin color or hair type.

At one point in the history of the United States, for example, many groups now unquestioningly considered "white" were initially not included in this privileged category.[3] Benjamin Franklin, for example, wrote in the eighteenth century that Swedes and Germans were "swarthy," and he did not include them among the "white people," who consisted, according to Franklin, solely of the English and the Saxons. "This example," Jane Hill comments, "shows how what seem to us today like fundamental perceptions may be of very recent historical origin … Contemporary White Americans can no longer see 'swarthiness' among Swedes, and find it astonishing that anyone ever did so" (Hill 2008:14).

The Swedes were not the only group not to be included among "white people" in the past. Irish immigrants to the United States, for example, were at first subject to discrimination and oppression, much as they had been in Ireland, and were excluded from white society, but over time they and other European immigrant groups allied themselves together in opposition to African Americans as they formed the American (white) working class (Ignatiev 1995:183–184). Jews have undergone a similar process, according to Karen Brodkin: "In the last hundred years, Jews in the United States have been shuttled from one side of the American racist binary to the other" (1998:175). At the turn of the last century, Jews in Europe and the United States "were considered a separate, inferior race, with a distinguishable biological identity justifying discrimination and even genocide" (Ferber 2007:113). Even now, Abby Ferber notes, contemporary white supremacists define Jews as nonwhite. One white supremacist publication, *The New Order*, states that Jews are "not a religion, they are an Asiatic *race*, locked in mortal conflict with Aryan man" (Ferber 2007:112; emphasis in the original). Ferber describes the process she went through while researching white supremacists as one in which she at first took for granted her unmarked, privileged status as a white American. As she read more and more hateful, anti-semitic materials written by contemporary white supremacists, however, Ferber became more aware of the many people who do not automatically accept her whiteness, and this has provided her, she says, some degree of insight (albeit partial) into the experiences of nonwhite people in the United States.

The parameters and nuances of racial classifications in countries other than the United States have been studied by anthropologists and other social scientists for many years. In Brazil, for example, scholarly debates have focused on the meanings of multiple Brazilian racial categories that intersect in complicated ways with class, gender, and sexuality.[4] In Nepal, the country I know best ethnographically, there is nothing like the black–white binary commonly attributed to the United States, and until recently, the concept of "race" was not mentioned in public debates at all. Instead, caste, ethnicity, and religion have been the most salient forms of social differentiation for Nepalis. During the 1990s, however, a group of activists from various Tibeto-Burman ethnic groups drew upon outdated social science research from the last century to posit three main races in the world (Hangen 2005, 2009). Susan Hangen, an anthropologist who has conducted fieldwork on this topic in Nepal, reports that a politician in eastern Nepal stated the following during one of his speeches in 1997:

> We are a Mongol community, we are not a caste either; we are Mongol. For example, in this world there are three types of people. One is white with white skin like Americans, for example like sister here

> [referring to me] … The other has black skin and is called Negro. The other is called the red race like us: short like us; stocky like us; with small eyes and flat noses like us. (2005:49)

By invoking this outdated tripartite racial classification, the politician was attempting to unite a number of linguistically and culturally diverse ethnic groups, such as Rais, Magars, Limbus, Gurungs, and Sherpas, under the umbrella of one political party, the Mongol National Organization (MNO). The hope was that unifying these disparate but similarly disadvantaged groups would help them oppose Nepal's high-caste Hindu ruling groups. One person told Hangen, "We didn't know that we were Mongols until the MNO came here" (2005:49). Hangen's research is a fascinating example of the complexities, contradictions, and cross-cultural differences involved in the concept of race.

Several other anthropologists of Nepal have conducted research on how certain Nepali ethnic groups have come into being.[5] Arjun Guneratne (2002), for example, has studied the formation of a single Tharu ethnic identity. The Tharus are considered to be (and consider themselves to be) the aboriginal residents of the Terai, a strip of jungle that runs across the southern border of Nepal with India (Guneratne 2002:39). They have long shared the ethnonym (the name given to an ethnic group) "Tharu," but they do not all share a single language or set of cultural practices. In fact, most Tharus have much more in common linguistically and culturally with non-Tharus living near them than they have with Tharus from other parts of Nepal. The Nepali state, however, grouped all Tharus together in its key classification of all castes and ethnic groups in 1854, and in more recent times, Tharu elites have created an organization designed to promote a pan-Tharu ethnic identity. Thus, Guneratne argues, "a common ethnic identity does not have to be predicated on a shared culture" (2002:10). Instead, according to Guneratne, ethnic formation is more accurately studied as a phenomenon having to do with economics, politics, and nation-state formation. Cultural elements are often foregrounded, posited, or brought into existence as part of this ethnicizing process, but the origins are often material rather than purely cultural, Guneratne maintains (2002:200). "Ethnic groups are thus not fixed phenomena but are constantly being created and re-created anew; objective realities such as differences of language, territory, religion, and custom are transformed into the basis of a subjective consciousness or self-awareness," he writes (2002:11).

Bonnie Urciuoli approaches the process of ethnicization differently in her research on Puerto Ricans in New York City, contrasting ethnicization with racialization and situating both within the context of class and gender identities in the United States. According to Urciuoli (1996), racial discourses "frame group origin in natural terms." Ethnic discourses, in contrast, "frame group origin in cultural terms" (1996:15). Racialized people, Urciuoli writes, are considered out of place; they are dirty, dangerous, and unwilling or unable to participate constructively in the nation-state. In contrast, the cultural differences said to be characteristic of ethnicized people are considered safe, ordered, and "a contribution to the nation-state offered by striving immigrants making their way up the ladder of class mobility" (1996:16). Within this landscape of social inequality and exclusion, Urciuoli states that language differences are often racialized. That is, an inability to speak English, or an inability to speak English "without an accent" (cf. Lippi-Green 1997), marks someone as disorderly and unlikely to experience social mobility – as someone, in other words, who does not fully belong in the United States.

No matter how race and ethnicity are defined or studied, language is central to the ways in which these forms of social differentiation are conceptualized and actually experienced. Let us turn now, therefore, to a closer look at the linguistic features and rule-governed nature of African American English, which, according to William Labov (2010:15) and Marcyliena Morgan (2002:3), is perhaps the most closely studied nonstandard dialect in the world (though the terms "nonstandard" and "dialect" have political implications that we will discuss further below).

The Rule-Governed Nature of African American English

To the ears of many Americans, the speech variety known as African American English (AAE, also known as African American Vernacular English [AAVE], Black English [BE], Black English Vernacular [BEV], and Ebonics) sounds like incorrect or sloppy Standard American English (SAE). As the well-known linguist Geoffrey Pullum notes: "The majority of English speakers think that AAVE is just English with two added factors: some special slang terms and a lot of grammatical mistakes. They are simply wrong about this" (1999:41). AAE, like all other languages and dialects around the world, is rule-governed. In other words, AAE is a linguistic system that has its own phonology, morphology, syntax, semantics, and pragmatics. Many of AAE's features are shared with other dialects of English, such as the regional variant of English spoken in the southern United States, or Cockney English, which is spoken mostly by working-class Londoners.

Not all African Americans speak AAE, and even among those who do speak AAE there are regional differences and of course many different language ideologies regarding the advantages, disadvantages, and meanings associated with speaking AAE. There are also, however, broadly overarching similarities among AAE speakers in all regions of the United States. For example, although AAE speakers in Texas, Louisiana, and Pennsylvania pronounce the vowel sounds in the words "hair" and "here" differently (Green 2002:1–2), they share similar rules for the use of the habitual, invariant verb "be," though the rates of usage of these sorts of grammatical structures vary depending on the relative amounts of residential and educational segregation in states such as California, Georgia, and Pennsylvania (Labov 2010:20).

Some African Americans speak absolutely no African American English. There is of course nothing biological in people who are identified by themselves or others as African Americans that makes them speak AAE. Rather, AAE is a language variant that, like all other language variants, is learned in particular social settings. Thus, African Americans such as President Barack Obama, for example, who was raised by his SAE-speaking white mother and grandparents, can speak the standard dialect in a way that is indistinguishable from others of all backgrounds who speak the same dialect. Many African Americans can code-switch between SAE and AAE, appropriately adjusting their speech styles to the particular social context much as bilingual individuals code-switch between two different languages for different addressees, and there are more "standard" variants of AAE that some individuals use in certain circumstances. Such code-switching can help build subtle alliances or identities or can index unequal power relations among speakers (Morgan 2002:73–74).

So, what are some of the rules and patterns of AAE that are often mistaken for incorrect SAE? Let us look at some of the most frequently commented upon linguistic features of AAE: the use of invariant or habitual "be"; copula deletion; double negatives; the reduction of final consonants; and pronouncing the word "ask" as "aks."[6]

Invariant or habitual "be"

Perhaps one of the most widely stigmatized and misinterpreted features of AAE is the use of "be" in its unconjugated, or invariant, form. Sentences such as "He be singin" (Pullum 1999:46) or "He be talkin when the teacher be talkin" (Baugh 1999:6) do not indicate a failure to conjugate the verb "to be." Instead, the invariant "be" does important grammatical work in these sentences because it indicates habitual behavior or a usual state of being. Replacing the "be" in such sentences with "is" or "are" would change the meaning. Thus, "She be happy" would indicate a perpetual state of happiness, whereas "She is happy" (or simply, "She happy" – see the next section on copula deletion) would indicate only a momentary feeling of happiness.

The invariant "be" is only one of a whole class of auxiliaries that enable AAE speakers to choose among a much wider array of moods and aspects in their verb forms than are available to SAE speakers. The use of such aspectual and preverbal markers as "come," "go," "done," and "steady" provide AAE speakers with semantic possibilities and nuanced eloquence that cannot easily be translated into any other dialect of English (Labov 2010:20; Green 1998). Such verb forms are often overlooked or misunderstood by standard English speakers because they sound just like standard English words, and yet their usages and meanings are totally different – and totally rule-governed.

Non-AAE-speaking individuals who attempt to come up with examples of AAE often misuse the invariant "be." Examples of such grammatical errors – that is, sentences that would be ungrammatical within the rules of AAE – abounded during the 1996–1997 Ebonics controversy, which we will discuss below. Geoffrey Pullum (1999:53–54) describes two such grammatically incorrect usages of the invariant "be" that appeared during the Ebonics controversy, both of which were part of a fictional conversation that distinguished African American (but non-AAE-speaking) columnist William Raspberry constructed between an imaginary AAE-speaking taxi driver and an imaginary alter ego of Raspberry himself. The first mistaken use of the invariant "be" occurs in this sentence: "What you be talkin' about, my man?" Pullum notes that Raspberry clearly means for the taxi driver to be asking, "What are you talking about right now?" But because the invariant "be" indicates habitual action, the meaning to native AAE-speakers is something more like, "What do you habitually talk about?" The second mistaken use of the invariant "be" in this made-up dialogue is this sentence from the taxi driver: "I don't be offerin' you my grub." Again, from the context, the intended meaning clearly refers to the present time, not to habitual action – something more like, "I am not offering you my food right now," rather than, "In general, I don't offer you my food."

William Raspberry was not the only African American columnist to write inaccurately or disparagingly about AAE. *New York Times* columnist Brent Staples did so as well in a column printed on January 24, 1997 and reprinted in Baugh (2000:x–xi). The ambivalence or even outright hostility toward AAE felt and expressed by some African Americans can be interpreted as an example of what Pierre Bourdieu calls misrecognition – the failure to recognize that the status accorded the standard variety of English is arbitrary and merely a function of politics and power. Many African Americans, however, fully recognize that SAE is the prestige dialect solely because its speakers are the group with the most prestige socially, politically, and economically in the United States. John Baugh, for example, states the following: "Pragmatic reality forces the burden of adjustment on groups who are outside positions of influence and power. It does little good to claim that street speech is a valid dialect – which it is – when the social cost of linguistic and other differences can be so high" (Baugh 1983:122, cited in Lippi-Green 1997:185).

Copula deletion

Another common grammatical feature of AAE that causes confusion among some non-AAE-speakers is copula deletion – in other words, the omission of the conjugated form of "to be." So, in AAE it is perfectly grammatical to say, "She happy," rather than "She is happy." This is not a random or haphazard omission; copula deletion follows rigorous rules, even though they operate largely below the level of awareness in the minds of most AAE speakers. These rules are similar to the ones in SAE that let speakers know when it is appropriate to use a contraction. For example, it is grammatical in SAE to use a contraction in the sentence, "She's happy," but not in the sentence "I know how happy she is" because contraction is not allowed when the verb is accented or emphasized, as it is at the end of a sentence. Just as the sentence "I know how happy she's" would be ungrammatical in SAE, so, too, would copula deletion be ungrammatical in the AAE sentence "I know how happy she ___" because copula deletion in AAE, like contraction in SAE, follows careful and rigorous (though usually unconscious) rules.

Many other languages in the world, including Russian, Hebrew, Arabic, and Swahili, to name just a few, feature copula deletion in some or all of the tenses of the verb "to be." In the Hebrew sentence, *hu babayit* ("He [is] in the house/at home"), for example, the form of the verb "to be" that we use in SAE for this purpose is omitted. This is not sloppy Hebrew – in fact, to attempt to insert some sort of present-tense form of the verb "to be" in this sentence in Hebrew would be ungrammatical. The directly analogous sentence in AAE is, "He at home." An AAE speaker who utters this sentence is being no more ungrammatical than a Hebrew speaker who utters *hu babayit*.

Double negatives

Double or even triple negatives are another grammatical form that can be found in AAE, as well as in many other languages and in other dialects of English. Working-class Londoners who speak the Cockney dialect regularly use double negatives, for example, and examples from popular culture, such as the classic Rolling Stones hit from the 1960s, "(I Can't Get No) Satisfaction," are common. But are double negatives automatically ungrammatical or illogical, as some claim? Jenny Cheshire (1998:119–120) traces the use of multiple negatives in English back many centuries and notes that such usages were common in Chaucer and Shakespeare, as can be seen in these two examples:

But nevere gronte he at no strook but oon. (Chaucer, *Canterbury Tales*)
[But he never groaned at any of the blows except one.]

I have one heart, one bosom, and one truth
And that no woman has; nor never none
Shall mistress be of it, save I alone. (Shakespeare, *Twelfth Night* III.i.172–174)

Multiple negatives seem to have fallen out of favor, according to Cheshire, during the eighteenth century when grammarians attempted to set a prescribed way of speaking and writing English for "polite" or "cultivated" members of society. Over time, double negatives came to be stigmatized, at least in certain communities of practice.

It is an accident of history, however, that has stigmatized double or multiple negatives. In many languages such as French, Spanish, Russian, Arabic, and Hungarian (to mention only a few), *not* using a double negative is ungrammatical. In French, for example, *je ne veux rien* means "I don't want anything," with *ne* ("not") and *rien* ("nothing") as the two negatives. Just as to say, "I don't want nothing" in standard English would be ungrammatical, to leave out the second negative in any of these languages – or in AAE – would be ungrammatical.

Some people argue that using two negatives is "illogical" because two negatives is a positive according to formal logic or mathematical principles. But if this were so, then the use of three negatives, as in the sentence, "I can't get nothin' from nobody," would go back to being a negative and would no longer "violate" these principles. Clearly, this sentence would be as objectionable as ones with only two negatives to the prescriptivists who want to impose the grammatical rules of one dialect of English (the standard one) on all other dialects. While there may be many good reasons for preferring standard English over other dialects of English in certain instances, nevertheless, as Labov (1972a) famously demonstrated decades ago in his classic article, "The Logic of Nonstandard English," logic and grammaticality are not among them. The preference of one dialect over another is one based on social, political, or economic factors – it cannot be based on linguistic factors because all dialects are equally logical and grammatical.

The reduction of final consonants

AAE differs from other dialects of English not just in its morphology and syntax but also in its phonology. Again, according to the language ideologies of some people, these differences in pronunciation are considered haphazard, sloppy, or unsuccessful attempts to achieve the SAE pronunciation. As Pullum (1999:50–51) outlines in detail, however, the phonology of AAE is also rule-governed and therefore highly regular. Contrary to the belief, for instance, that AAE speakers "drop their consonants right and lef'," Pullum explains that there is a very specific rule that determines when final consonant reduction is permissible in AAE. To understand the rule that applies in these cases, it is necessary to know that "stop consonants" include the letters p, t, k, b, d, and g.[7] It is also necessary to understand that some consonants are voiceless and therefore involve no vibration of the vocal cords. The stop consonants p, t, and k are voiceless, as are other non-stop consonants, such as s, f, and sh. Voiced consonants, in contrast, involve the vibration of the vocal cords, such as the stops b, d, and g, as well as other consonants such as j, v, or z, to name just a few. Okay – now we are ready for the phonological rule that governs the permissibility of final consonant reduction in AAE:

> *A stop consonant at the end of a word may be omitted (and usually is) if it is preceded by another consonant of the same voicing.* (Pullum 1999:51; emphasis added)

According to this rule, Pullum notes, AAE speakers would not drop the final consonant in words such as *dump*, *belt*, and *sink* because although they all end in stops, the p, t, and k stops are all voiceless, while the sounds that precede them in these words are voiced. Only the words that follow the rule above are eligible for final consonant reduction in AAE. Thus, a word like *left* may be pronounced as *lef'* by a speaker of AAE because the final voiceless stop, t, is preceded by an equally voiceless f sound. Similarly, *old* can be pronounced *ol'* in AAE because the final voiced stop, d, is preceded by an equally voiced l sound (Pullum 1999:51). Although this phonological rule operates below the level of awareness of most AAE speakers, they have no trouble implementing it consistently. For many SAE speakers, however, the rule is imperceptible and therefore assumed to be absent. This assumption is mistaken.

Pronouncing the word "ask" as "aks"

AAE also contains a few idiosyncratic phonological features, some of which it shares with other dialects of English. One of these is the pronunciation of the word "ask" as "aks." Even though the *Oxford English Dictionary* establishes that the variation between these two pronunciations goes back hundreds of years, many SAE speakers, Rosina Lippi-Green notes, characterize the use of the pronunciation "aks" as "the most horrendous of errors" (1997:179). And yet, this pronunciation is shared by other English dialects. (Indeed, my daughter's pale-skinned, strawberry blond kindergarten teacher used "aks" regularly.) Critics, such as a call-in viewer of the "Oprah Winfrey Show" in 1987, say things like, "I guess what I'd like to say is that what makes me feel that blacks tend to be ignorant is that they fail to see that the word is spelled A-S-K, not A-X. And when they say *aksed*, it gives the sentence an entirely different meaning" (Lippi-Green 1997:180). And yet, as Lippi-Green demonstrates, there is a "large-scale lack of correspondence between sound and symbol in English" (1997:180). The call-in viewer herself provides several examples of this, Lippi-Green notes, when she fails to aspirate the *h* in *what* and pronounces *spelled* as *spelt* and *different* as *difərnt*. Also, instead of pronouncing every sound in *sentence*, she put a glottal stop in the middle of the word, as many SAE speakers do, producing something that sounds more like *se-əns*. So, pronouncing "ask" as "aks" is one of many, many examples of instances when speakers pronounce English words differently from how they are spelled.

Despite the decades of research that have demonstrated the existence within AAE of all of these (and many other) rule-governed phonological, morphological, and syntactic features, according to the language ideologies of many people, AAE remains a highly stigmatized dialect of English. "The real problem with black English," Lippi-Green concludes, "is a general unwillingness to accept the speakers of that language and the social choices they have made as viable and functional" (1997:201). Most scholars (e.g., Labov 2010) believe that AAE will continue to be stigmatized as long as African Americans themselves suffer discrimination.

The Ebonics Controversy

On December 18, 1996, the Board of Education in Oakland, California, passed a resolution declaring that students in the district "possess and utilize a language described in various scholarly approaches as 'Ebonics' (literally Black sounds) or Pan African Communication Behaviors or African Language Systems," and that this way of speaking is "genetically-based and not a dialect of English" (Baugh 2000:43–44). The Board of Education therefore resolved that the Superintendent should set up:

> the best possible academic program for imparting instruction to African-American students in their primary language for the combined purposes of maintaining the legitimacy and richness of such language whether it is known as "Ebonics," "African Language Systems," "Pan-African Communication Behaviors" or other description, and to facilitate their acquisition and mastery of English language skills. (Baugh 2000:44)

The Board of Education concluded its resolution by declaring that special funding should be allocated to this program, and that the Superintendent should apply for additional state and federal funds earmarked for this purpose. Many commentators assumed that the main goal of the Board was to acquire federal Title VII funds allocated for bilingual education, though the Board subsequently denied this (Baugh 2000:48).

In passing this resolution, the Oakland Board set off a firestorm of debate, much of it ill-informed but extremely interesting linguistically, centering largely on the following questions:

1 Is AAE (or "Ebonics," as the School Board called it) a dialect of English, or a separate language?
2 How should speakers of AAE and other nonstandard linguistic variants be taught SAE in school? Should AAE be used in educational materials in order to facilitate the acquisition of SAE proficiency, much as bilingual education programs use materials in the students' native languages in order do the same thing?

To these two questions, which were extensively debated at the time, we might add a third: what can we learn about language and race in the United States nowadays by looking back to the Ebonics controversy of 1996–1997?

First, the issue of the status of AAE, or "Ebonics,"[8] as a language or a dialect is a contentious one. As was discussed already in chapter 6, there is no set of agreed-upon criteria that will determine whether a way of speaking constitutes a dialect or a language. One cannot say, for example, that if two ways of speaking share at least 68 percent of their vocabulary and 74 percent of their grammar, they are dialects, and if not, they are separate languages. No such metric exists. Instead, the distinction is often a political one that is enmeshed in relations of power and inequality. Ways of speaking associated with nation-states or the groups in a given society with the highest prestige or wealth are generally termed languages or "standard" dialects, while the ways of speaking of less prestigious minority groups that do not control a nation-state are generally considered "mere" dialects, and often "nonstandard" dialects at that. Thus, Mandarin and Cantonese are considered two dialects of Chinese even though they are mutually unintelligible, while Serbian and Croatian, or Hindi and Urdu, or Swedish and Norwegian, are called separate languages, even though their speakers generally have no trouble understanding one another. There is clearly no easily applied measure of linguistic relatedness that accurately and uncontroversially determines whether two ways of speaking should be labeled languages or dialects.

Thus, the status of AAE as a separate language versus a dialect of English is a social and political matter that has little to do with linguistic facts. Scholars who study the history and origins of AAE fall on both sides of this debate. John Baugh, for example, an eminent African American linguist whose work on linguistic profiling will be discussed below, writes the following: "Any suggestion that American slave descendants speak a language other than English is overstated, linguistically uninformed, and – frankly – wrong" (Baugh 2000:41). Geneva Smitherman, on the other hand, another distinguished sociolinguist and educator, disagrees, using AAE itself to state her opinion: "Yeah, uhm sayin 'language,' cause I think it is a language" (2005:50).

There is also debate among scholars as to whether AAE owes its distinctive linguistic features more to creoles such as Gullah or Jamaican Creole, or to various dialects of English – or to a combination of influences (Green 2002:8ff). All scholars working on AAE acknowledge, however, that AAE owes its distinctiveness to the legacy of slavery in the United States. All scholars also agree that AAE, whatever it is called, is rule-governed – just like all other linguistic systems in the world. At the January 1997 meeting of the Linguistic Society of America, a resolution on the Ebonics issue was unanimously passed that stated the following: "What is important from a linguistic and educational point of view is not whether AAVE is called a 'language' or a 'dialect' but rather that its systematicity be recognized" (Baugh 2000:118).

Turning to the second question about how or whether AAE should be used in schools to facilitate the acquisition among AAE-speaking students of the standard dialect of English, it is important to note the serious educational crisis that the Oakland Board of Education was trying to address (however ineffectively or controversially) in its December 1996 resolution. As John Rickford (2005) reminds us, the Oakland school district was not alone in experiencing extremely high rates of failure and drop-out among its African American population. Other school districts throughout the United States faced similar disparities in school performance at the time – and still do today. The question remains how to address these educational disparities. Although this issue is far beyond the scope of this book, involving as it does complex issues of poverty, racial discrimination, and residential segregation, among other possible contributing factors, the extent to which speaking a nonstandard, stigmatized linguistic variant such as AAE contributes to school problems deserves to be studied further (cf. Labov 2010; Rickford 2005).

Some scholars and educators advocate using some AAE in the classroom in order to help students understand more explicitly the differences between AAE and SAE so that they can more easily master SAE. Such scholars (e.g., Labov 2010) maintain that the students who participate in these kinds of programs are likely to be successful in learning SAE and in developing pride in the linguistic practices of their homes. These debates parallel similar debates in the field of bilingual education – which, although they subsequently denied it, was exactly what the Oakland Board of Education was trying to point out in its resolution.

As a result of the barrage of criticism aimed at the Oakland Board of Education, the Board adopted a revised resolution in January 1997 that

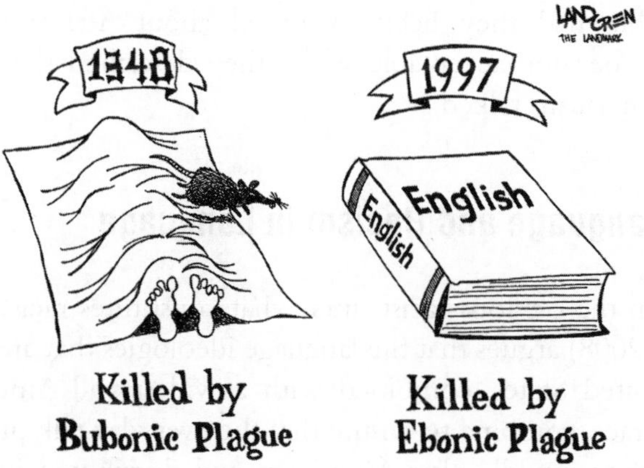

Figure 10.1 "The Ebonic Plague," January 2, 1997. Political cartoon that appeared in the wake of the Ebonics controversy.
Source: Don Landgren Jr.

removed the most controversial phrases, such as "genetically based," and more strongly stated the goal of moving students "from the language patterns they bring to school to English proficiency" (Baugh 2000:44–45). Nevertheless, the Ebonics controversy overall did nothing to improve the educational outcomes of AAE-speaking students in Oakland and elsewhere. No extra money was allocated to helping them become proficient in SAE, and no new AAE-related programs were funded.

Overall, however, were there other benefits that resulted from the public debate over Ebonics in 1996–1997? It is difficult to say, but since many of the commentaries printed in newspapers and broadcast on TV and radio during that time period repeated inaccurate linguistic statements, it is hard to argue that the public became better informed about language and race as a result of the controversy. Moreover, the vehemence and viciousness of some of the cartoons and jokes that made fun of Ebonics as a term and linked it to the Ebola virus and other plagues (see Figure 10.1) probably did more to reinforce racist stereotypes than challenge them. While many public commentators and private individuals had thoughtful things to say about the complexities of the issue, and while many individuals also eloquently described their ambivalences and anguish regarding race, language, education, and economic success, others used the Ebonics controversy as a way to channel their prejudices. Opinions that would have been unacceptable had they been expressed about African Americans themselves became acceptable when they described the way some African Americans talked.

Racist Language and Racism in Language

Aside from the obvious racist slurs, what constitutes racist language? Jane Hill (2008) argues that the language ideologies that are dominant in the United States, combined with a widespread American folk theory of race, combine to ensure that the everyday talk produced by average white, middle-class Americans and distributed in respected media "continues to produce and reproduce White racism" (2008:47). Far from being an element of the past, Hill maintains, racism "is a vital and formative presence in American lives, resulting in hurt and pain to individuals, to glaring injustice, in the grossly unequal distribution of resources along racially stratified lines, and in strange and damaging errors and omissions in public policy both domestic and foreign" (2008:47–48). And this racism, Hill suggests, is largely produced in and through everyday talk – not through the obvious racist slurs that most people today condemn (though these of course contribute), but through unintentional, indirect uses of language that reinforce racist stereotypes.

As an example of this sort of covert racist discourse, Hill discusses Mock Spanish, which she argues is a way of racializing Spanish speakers in the United States. In order to understand how Mock Spanish can act in this way, according to Hill, it is first necessary to understand a key element of the American folk theory of race and racism. In addition to the mistaken belief, analyzed earlier in this chapter, that race is a biological entity, Hill also maintains that many Americans hold an equally mistaken view of racism: that it is a quality of individuals, and only of those few individuals who are virulently racist, such as white supremacists (Hill 2008:6–7). Instead, Hill argues (and many other scholars agree), racism is more a function of institutions, norms, and practices that facilitate the production of racist effects, so even when individuals do not intend to be racist or discriminatory, their actions may have these effects because of the institutions and norms they act within.

So, what is Mock Spanish? An example that Hill provides is from the film "Terminator 2: Judgment Day," in which Arnold Schwarzenegger plays a robot hero sent from the future to protect a little boy who will one day grow up to save humanity. The little boy, a character named John Connor, tries to teach the Terminator how to sound more "real" and "American" through the use of Mock Spanish phrases such as "No problemo" and "Hasta la vista, baby" (Hill 1998:683; 2008:144–145). Hill provides another example in the form of a hypothetical invitation to go out for a beer: "Let's get together and crack a few cervezas" (2008:42). Other examples include using the Spanish word for tomorrow, mañana, or other Spanish words or phrases in everyday English conversations.

Hill acknowledges that the users of Mock Spanish are not in any way being intentionally racist. On the contrary, she says, they believe that they are being humorous, cosmopolitan, and even respectful of Spanish speakers. "I have never found any evidence that they are not completely sincere in these objections, and I believe that the racializing functions of Mock Spanish are genuinely invisible to them," she asserts (2008:42). And yet, Hill also strongly maintains that Mock Spanish elevates whiteness and pejoratively racializes Spanish speakers through a process of indirect indexicality (cf. Urciuoli 1991, 1996). Unlike the direct indexicality involved in Mock Spanish, which explicitly indexes the speaker as humorous or cosmopolitan and is usually fully acknowledged by the speaker, indirect indexicality implicitly indexes negative stereotypes of Mexicans and other Latin Americans as treacherous, lazy, politically corrupt, or sexually loose (1998:683). Hill argues that people who use Mock Spanish must have access to these stereotypes in order to use and interpret the jokes or phrases. For example, someone who says, "Mañana, mañana," when answering a question about when s/he will complete a job is indirectly indexing the purported laziness of Mexicans. And the famous "Hasta la vista, baby," uttered by the Terminator, indexes the alleged treacherousness of Spanish speakers, Hill suggests. Without awareness of these racialized stereotypes, the Mock Spanish jokes would not be funny and the Mock Spanish phrases would not be intelligible. And when these stereotypes are invoked in this sort of indirect indexicality, Hill argues, the stereotypes are reinforced.

There are undoubtedly many such instances of covert racist discourse in Mock Spanish – and in Mock AAE or Mock Asian (also called

"Yellow English," see Reyes and Lo 2009) – that are illuminated in a valuable way by Hill's analysis. Nevertheless, her approach suffers from a weakness that she herself readily admits (2008:47): her analysis of Mock Spanish is based largely on examples from movies, newspapers, and other forms of mass media rather than from actual everyday conversations. Because we know that language is always multifunctional, I am sure that further analysis of Mock Spanish utterances in actual social contexts would yield a more complex set of meanings than simply covert racism. Utterances often accomplish many social tasks simultaneously, so it is not difficult to imagine instances of Mock Spanish that not only directly index the speaker's humor and indirectly index negative stereotypes but also challenge or parody those stereotypes in some way, for example. Hill alludes to some of the subversive potential in Mock Spanish and other similar linguistic practices (1998:685–686); it will be up to future researchers to investigate these phenomena further.

Other researchers have already begun to explore how other forms of racism are emergent in actual conversations. According to Valentina Pagliai (2009:553), racism is not a quality that individuals have in a static way but rather something that they *do* – that is, rather than being inherently racist individuals, Pagliai argues, some people enact racism through their behavior and conversations. In her research, therefore, Pagliai looks at how racialization occurs interactionally through the ways in which participants in a conversation agree with other speakers (or fail to disagree) when racist comments are made. For example, in this excerpt from a conversation that took place in a barber shop in Tuscany, Italy, the participants co-construct a negative, racialized assessment of immigrants, building on one another's at first subtle indications of disapproval in a deepening of the negative stance, leading to this increasingly racist set of remarks (Pagliai 2009:559–560):[9]

Giuseppe: illnesses, syphilis, who knows what they don't carry
Fabbri: all kinds of things
Giuseppe: malaria
Fabbri: dirt
Giuseppe: they bring dirt
Fabbri: of course
Giuseppe: everything

Pagliai calls this tendency to co-construct an increasingly racist discourse a "spiral effect," which she explains occurs because when speakers receive a positive reception for their mildly negative comments, they are emboldened to make more blatantly negative and eventually outright racist remarks. Thus, Pagliai argues, "The role of conversational agreement cannot be understated. It inevitably works at reinforcing racializing or racist discourses already present in the society, by reproducing them and creating consent around them" (2009:576).

Another way in which racism operates in language is through the process of what John Baugh (2003) calls "linguistic profiling." Focusing mainly on fair access to housing cases, Baugh has conducted experiments in which he called landlords two different times to inquire about the availability of an apartment, the first time using SAE, and the second time using AAE. (Baugh is able to code-switch seamlessly between the two.) In over one hundred calls, Baugh found that his AAE voice (or "guise," since this was a form of a matched guise test) received less than half the number of calls back from the landlords.[10] As obvious as it is that we all make judgments about someone's voice on the phone – as young or old, gay or straight, female or male, and as black, Latino, Asian, or white, perhaps – it is quite difficult to prove this kind of discrimination in court. Moreover, there is a risk that the concept of linguistic profiling could be used against an innocent person. But Baugh's research shows definitively yet another way in which, consciously or unconsciously, racism can be enacted through language.

In a similar set of experiments, Rubin (1992) and Rubin and Smith (1990) conducted matched guise tests with undergraduates (Hill 2008:12). All their research participants heard the same four-minute tape-recorded lecture featuring a woman who was a native speaker of English, but half of the students were shown a slide of a white woman while they listened to the lecture and were told that this was the speaker, while the other half were shown a slide of an East Asian woman. The students in the latter group tended to report that the speaker had a foreign accent, and they even did significantly worse on a comprehension quiz on the material in the lecture – even though these students had heard exactly the same lecture as the students who were shown the photo of a white woman while they listened to the lecture! Clearly, racial categories and racialized language ideologies can influence perceptions even without our being aware of the process.

Language and Racial/Ethnic Identities

There are many fascinating uses of language that are associated with racial and ethnic identity formation. In addition to the rule-governed phonological, morphological, and syntactic features of AAE, for example, there are also distinctive semantic and pragmatic features of AAE – different ways, in other words, that language is used in social settings by AAE speakers compared to SAE speakers (Smitherman 1998). Scholars have studied AAE-specific oral traditions such as the call-and-response patterns often found in African American churches, gospel music, and hip-hop; linguistic practices such as "signifying," which involves indirectness and cultural allusions; "instigating," the fabricated conflicts Goodwin (1990) studies among African American girls in Philadelphia; and, most famously perhaps, "the dozens," which is a competition between two speakers, usually young African American males, involving humor and ritualized insults. African American beauty parlors and barber shops have also been sites for social and linguistic research on the intersections among language, race, and identity formation. Among scholars working in these sites within linguistic anthropology is Lanita Jacobs-Huey (2006), who conducted a fine-grained cultural and linguistic analysis of hair care professionals in the African American community. Jacobs-Huey's book also contains reflections on the ways in which hair, gender, race, and language all contribute to the process of identity formation among African Americans and "native" anthropologists such as herself (2006:129–147).

Some recent research by scholars explores communities in which race and language are intertwined in unexpected or hybrid ways. For example, Cecilia Cutler (2003) looks at how some white, middle-class teenagers in the New York area have adopted elements from AAE in their speech as a result of their affiliation with hip-hop. Many of these young people develop hybrid and shifting identities, thereby demonstrating the "subtle and intriguing process by which linguistic (and cultural) patterns unexpectedly diffuse across cultural boundaries" (Cutler 2003:213). They may, however, Cutler suggests, eventually revert in adulthood to the more prestigious and economically advantageous SAE that was their native form of English, but while they are adolescents, they acquire a different form of prestige from adopting the "Hip-Hop Speech Style." Such linguistic practices raise complicated and interesting questions about identity formation, authenticity, and racialized language use.

Another promising approach to research on language, race, and ethnicity is evident in the volume *Beyond Yellow English: Toward a Linguistic Anthropology of Asian Pacific America*, edited by Angela Reyes and Adrienne Lo (2009). As these scholars note, Asian Americans are "uniquely racialized" in the US context. They comprise an extremely diverse group of ethnicities, socioeconomic backgrounds, and linguistic practices, and yet they are often lumped together as "model minorities" and "honorary whites," or else as "forever foreign" (2009:7). Linguistically, Asian Americans are often indistinguishable from other groups that use SAE; scholars have found very little evidence of ethnically specific speech variants among these individuals. And yet, just as Guneratne noted with regard to the absence of a single Tharu language not inhibiting the formation of a single Tharu ethnic identity in Nepal, Reyes and Lo argue that a distinctive ethnic dialect is not necessary for the formation of an ethnic identity.

Often, the identities that emerge through linguistic and cultural performances and practices are complex, multifaceted ones. Mary Bucholtz (2009), for example, describes how two female Laotian American high schoolers in San Francisco made different choices in the ethnic identities they crafted agentively, and also exhibited different linguistic practices that operated largely unconsciously but powerfully to affiliate them with different groups in the high school. One of the young women, Nikki, was a former member of the Crips gang and still dressed and spoke using the cultural and linguistic styles associated with gangs. Much like the young white people Cutler studied who borrowed from AAE in their speech, Nikki also used elements of AAE – though AAE was even more deeply enmeshed in her language use than was the case among the young people Cutler studied, as could be seen in her AAE-influenced grammatical features. For example, Nikki used AAE's habitual "be" in the sentence in which she reported her mother's remark upon learning she was involved in a gang: "I know what you be doing" (Bucholtz 2009:30). In addition, she used copula deletion in this utterance (Bucholtz 2009:28):

Nikki: and it's like,
when you in a gang,
right,
(.) you have a little clique,=
=your own clique,=
=right.

In contrast to Nikki, Ada, the other Laotian American teenager Bucholtz came to know at the high school, decided that "the perpetuation of the model-minority stereotype was far less harmful than the very immediate dangers of gang culture" (2009:32). Thus, in her dress and language, Ada affiliated more with middle-class white students – the "nerds" of Bucholtz's earlier (1999) study – avoiding gang-related attire and speaking SAE, even though she, like Nikki, came from a working-class refugee family and was not yet quite fluent in English.

In these two case studies, Bucholtz demonstrates the importance of looking closely at actual linguistic and cultural practices in order to understand more fully how ethnic identities are emergent in social interactions. She also shows how, even though many Asian Americans may not speak a distinctive ethnic dialect, it is nonetheless extremely fruitful to see how these individuals "do" ethnicity through their linguistic practices.

Conclusion

In this chapter, we have explored the often controversial, sometimes indirect, but always fascinating ways in which language relates to race and ethnicity. The rule-governed nature of AAE can be seen in the various phonological, morphological, and syntactic features of the AAE linguistic system – though many people still mistakenly consider AAE to be an imprecise or lazy attempt to speak SAE. The Ebonics controversy of 1996–1997 brought into the public realm many opinions and conflicts that had simmered below the surface for years in what Bourdieu would call *doxa*, as opposed to the for/against debates of orthodoxy and heterodoxy of public discourse. The overt and covert racism that could be seen in some of the comments, cartoons, and conversations during the Ebonics controversy can still be found in other linguistic practices today – in some Mock Spanish (or Mock AAE or Mock Asian), for example, and more subtly in conversational co-constructions in which one participant agrees with, or at least decides not to disagree with, the racist comments of another participant, as Valentina Pagliai has shown.

Because race and ethnicity are so fraught, and also so intertwined with other dimensions of difference, inequality, and identity, such as gender, class, age, and region, it is absolutely crucial that research on these topics involves close attention to language use and, whenever possible, long-term ethnographic fieldwork, because these are the methods that are best able to shed light on the complex and controversial areas of language, power, and agency in the contemporary world.

11

Language Death and Revitalization

As part of an article on endangered languages that appeared in *The New Yorker* magazine in 2005, journalist Elizabeth Kolbert made an appointment to interview Chief Marie Smith Jones, the last remaining full-blooded member of the Eyak nation and the last remaining native speaker of the Eyak language. When Kolbert arrived at Chief Smith Jones's apartment in Anchorage, Alaska, however, no one answered the door. It turned out that Chief Smith Jones had decided she did not want to be interviewed after all. When the Chief heard that Kolbert, upon the advice of a friend of the Chief's, had brought some halibut, however, she changed her mind and allowed an interview that ended up lasting several hours. Chief Smith Jones, whom Kolbert described as an 87-year-old woman with wispy white hair, a face covered in fine wrinkles, and wrists no wider than a child's, had strong emotions about the imminent loss of her language, which would inevitably accompany her own death. When Kolbert asked her how she felt about the loss of her native language, Chief Smith Jones answered, "How would you feel if your baby died? If someone asked you, 'What was it like to see it lying in the cradle?' So think about that before you ask that kind of question" (Kolbert 2005:46).

Chief Marie Smith Jones died on January 21, 2008, at the age of 89, and the Eyak language died with her.

Living Language: An Introduction to Linguistic Anthropology, First Edition. Laura M. Ahearn.

Many other last speakers of endangered languages all over the world have passed away in recent decades. Here are just a few of the final speakers of some of these languages (Nettle and Romaine 2000:1–2).

Arthur Bennett, the last person who knew more than a few words of Mbabaram, an Aboriginal language, died in 1972 in north Queensland, Australia. Linguist R.M.W. Dixon describes his search for the remaining speakers of Mbabaram in his memoir, and reports that Arthur Bennett was at first unconvinced when Dixon told him Mbabaram was so important he would make sure it was put in a museum. "You know what we call 'dog'?" Dixon reports that Bennett asked him. Dixon continues: "I waited anxiously. 'We call it *dog*.' My heart sank …" (Dixon 1984:107). Eventually, however, Bennett agreed to help Dixon with his research on Mbabaram.

Ned Maddrell, the last native speaker of Manx, a Gaelic language spoken on the Isle of Man, located in the Irish Sea between Great Britain and Ireland, died in 1974. Although Manx no longer has any native speakers, it is being learned as a second language in many schools on the Isle of Man, and is the medium of instruction in at least one primary school on the island (Hinton and Hale 2001:103, 299).

Pat Gabori, whose traditional name is Kabararrjingathi bulthuku, was in 2010 one of only eight remaining speakers of Kayardild, an Aboriginal language spoken on Bentinck Island, Australia. Nicholas Evans reports (2010:xv–xvi) that Pat Gabori, who was elderly and blind when Evans last saw him, loved to talk for hours about hunting, intricate tribal genealogies, and sacred spaced on Bentinck Island. His comprehensive knowledge of tribal law allowed him to make a valuable contribution as a witness in a recent Aboriginal court case to obtain recognition of traditional sea rights.

Laura Fish Somersal, the last speaker of Wappo, a Native American language formerly spoken in the area north of San Francisco, died in 1990. The only reason Somersal retained her Wappo fluency, according to researchers who recently published a Wappo grammar (Thompson et al. 2006) based on information provided by Somersal, was that Somersal was excused as a child from attending the Bureau of Indian Affairs school in her area because she had to stay home to take care of her blind mother. Had she attended school, she would have become literate – but she also would have been forced to speak only English and would probably have lost her fluency in Wappo. This was fortunate for the researchers' study of Wappo, they report, "but not good for Laura."[1]

Tevfic Esenç, who lived on a farm in Turkey, had already decided years before he died in 1992, what he wanted inscribed on his gravestone: "This is the grave of Tevfic Esenç. He was the last person able to speak the language they call Ubykh."

Putting a human face on the abstract crisis known as language endangerment, language extinction, or language death helps to shed light on some of the actual experiences and feelings of the last speakers of the many languages of the world thought to be close to disappearing. What is it like to speak a language with ten or fewer speakers? Linguist K. David Harrison, who has traveled around the world documenting endangered languages, says that for people like Vasya Gabov of Siberia, who is one of the last speakers of the Ös language, it means feeling isolated and having very few opportunities to speak one's language. It also means feeling nearly invisible, surrounded by speakers of a much larger, much more dominant language who do not even acknowledge the existence of other languages. It can also mean forgetting words and grammatical rules because of a lack of opportunities to speak one's native language in actual social contexts. "In this situation, one shared by speakers of thousands of small languages worldwide, it becomes hard to be heard, hard not to forget, hard not to become invisible" (Harrison 2007:4–5).

In this chapter, we take a close look at the phenomenon of language death, as well as at some language revitalization efforts. First, we review various estimates of the extent of the crisis and also explore some of the advantages and disadvantages for different audiences of attempting to quantify the number of languages in danger of disappearing. We also discuss the various reasons for the extinction of so many languages. Then we ask what dies when a language dies – what, in other words, does it mean for a language to become "extinct"? Is it comparable to the extinction of a biological species? What are the implications of using these kinds of metaphors to describe language endangerment? Finally, we will look at some case studies of language revitalization programs, exploring some of the logistical and ethical dilemmas involved in documenting and revitalizing endangered languages.

Enumerating the Crisis: How Many Dying Languages Are There?

In a much-cited overview of the status of endangered language around the world, linguist Michael Krauss admits that "statistics on language viability are very hard to come by" (Krauss 1992:4). For one thing, many of the places around the world with the highest concentration of languages are in remote places that have not been thoroughly, or even partially, surveyed by scholars. In addition, many governments are either unaware of, or actively hostile to, speakers of languages aside from the ones recognized by the state, so government figures often cannot be relied upon. Moreover, many languages have already disappeared over the past millennia; there is no way of knowing anything about these, since most had no script associated with them and therefore disappeared without a trace. And of course, as we have noted several times in this book already, there is a fundamental dilemma regarding the enumeration of languages (endangered or otherwise): there is no agreed-upon set of criteria that would distinguish a language from a dialect, other than the one with which linguist Max Weinreich is credited – that a language has an army and a navy, whereas a dialect does not. In addition, there are many hybrid linguistic variants that call into question the very existence of any bounded entity that could be termed either a language or a dialect. The "socially charged life" of language, as Bakhtin called it, is far messier than the shelves of published grammars of individual languages would lead one to believe.

The great poet and scholar A.K. Ramanujan acknowledged that "the chief difficulty of translation is its impossibility" (1989:47) – and then proceeded to discuss how best to translate a poem. Similarly, many linguists have acknowledged the difficulties (and even the impossibility) of ever coming up with an accurate number of languages in the world – and then have gone ahead and produced estimates. One of the most frequently consulted sources for this information is *Ethnologue: Languages of the World* (Lewis 2009), a database of the world's languages compiled by the Summer Institute of Linguistics, a Christian group dedicated to documenting as many languages as possible, partly in order to translate the Bible into each language. *Ethnologue* estimates

Table 11.1 Ten most commonly spoken languages in the world (Lewis 2009).

Language	Speakers (in millions)
1. Chinese (Mandarin)	1,213
2. Spanish	329
3. English	328
4. Arabic	221
5. Hindi	182
6. Bengali	181
7. Portuguese	178
8. Russian	144
9. Japanese	122
10. German	90.3

Source: From Lewis (2009). Used by permission, © SIL, *Ethnologue: Languages of the World*, 16th edition.

that there were 6,909 languages in the world as of 2009. The distribution of speakers among these languages is quite striking: 389 (nearly 6 percent) of the world's languages have at least a million speakers and account for 94 percent of the world's population. The remaining 94 percent of languages are spoken by only 6 percent of the population.[2] And just the top ten most commonly spoken languages – a little more than one tenth of one percent of all languages – are spoken by almost half of the world's population (see Table 11.1).

Moreover, languages are not spread evenly across the globe. Instead, there are "hotspots of language diversity" (Harrison 2007:10–13) and relative linguistic deserts. For example, in all of Saudi Arabia, there are estimated to be only nine languages spoken, six of which are variants of Arabic. In contrast, in Papua New Guinea, a country a quarter of the size of Saudi Arabia, an estimated 860 languages are spoken (Grenoble and Whaley 1998:vii). Similarly, the 65 inhabited islands of Vanuatu in the South Pacific, together roughly the size of Connecticut, support 109 different languages, which works out to about one language for every 1,880 speakers (Harrison 2007:11).

Even more challenging, perhaps, than coming up with the total number of languages currently spoken around the world is the task of assessing which ones are likely to survive and which ones are endangered. Scholars have come up with various criteria and classifications, such as the following commonly used ones proposed by Michael Krauss (1992:4–7):

- *Safe languages*. Those languages that have official government support and/or large numbers of speakers. If the threshold is placed at 100,000 speakers in order for the language to be considered "safe," Krauss states that only 600 or so of the 6,000 languages he estimates exist – only 10 percent of all the world's languages, in other words – are "safe."
- *Endangered languages*. Those languages that, although they are still being learned by children, will cease to be learned by children in the next century if present conditions persist.
- *Moribund languages*. Those languages that have ceased to be learned by children, and are therefore almost certainly doomed to extinction.
- *Dead or extinct languages*. Those languages that are no longer spoken by anyone, even if there are written materials or recordings in those languages.

Michael Krauss (1992:5), drawing on his own work with many endangered languages, provides the following often-cited numbers for the situation as it was in 1992:

- In Alaska, only two of the 20 Native languages (Central Yupik Eskimo and Siberian Yupik Eskimo of St Lawrence Island), or only 10 percent, are still being learned by children.
- Among the languages of the northern minorities of Siberia, only three of the 30, again only 10 percent, are still being learned by children.
- For all of the United States and Canada together, 149 of the 187, or 80 percent, of the Native languages are moribund.
- In Central and South American, the situation is less dire, with about 50 of 300 of the indigenous Meso-American and 110 of 400 of the indigenous South American languages considered moribund.
- In Australia, 90 percent of the estimated 250 Aboriginal languages are moribund, with most of the remaining ones very close to extinction.

Overall, though it is virtually impossible to know for sure, Krauss states that since only 10 percent of the world's languages can be considered "safe," many of the rest are in danger of becoming extinct. He therefore estimates that as many as half of the world's languages may disappear in the next hundred years (1992:6).

This figure is alarming, and many linguists, public officials, and ordinary citizens have committed themselves to attempting to stem the tide of language death. Organizations such as the Endangered Language Fund, the National Science Foundation, the National Endowment for the Humanities, and the Summer Institute of Linguistics have supported research and documentation efforts, as well as revitalization efforts on the part of communities and individuals. Some of these programs will be described later in this chapter. First, though, it is important to take a step back and look critically for a moment at the tendency toward enumeration, even though such numerical estimates are, as we have already noted, at best partial and at worst utterly misleading.

What are the problematic assumptions underlying the desire to count the number of endangered languages, and the number of speakers each endangered language has? Jane Hill (2002:127–128; cf. Duchêne and Heller 2007) names several. First, although she acknowledges that numbers can be powerful "calls to action" that have been used to mobilize activists to reverse the trend toward language death, and although Hill herself has been involved in such efforts, she warns that journalists and the mass media are soundbite oriented and cannot or will not devote enough time or space to explaining the difficulties or subtleties involved in quantifying languages or speakers. Second, Hill warns that numbers and statistics that are meant for one kind of audience – speakers of dominant languages, perhaps, who have the power to do something about the extinction of smaller languages – can have very negative effects when heard by a very different kind of audience – the speakers of endangered languages themselves. Hill reminds her readers that numbers have often been used by colonial powers in the past as one means of control, what Foucault would call governmentality through enumeration. Speakers of endangered languages are often fearful, she warns, that numbers can be (and have been) held against them, and they can therefore become fearful or resentful.

Some speakers of endangered languages can also feel that scholars' estimates of the number of speakers of their languages – of "native" speakers, or "partial" speakers, or "bilingual" speakers – is disrespectful to them. Often, younger speakers attempt to reclaim their ancestral languages, "often through heroic work with linguistic archives," but are not considered "real" speakers of the language by researchers (Hill 2002:128). Thus, enumeration can end up alienating the very individuals in a community who are the most highly motivated to preserve a language.

Most troubling, Hill maintains, are the language ideologies that underpin the drive toward enumeration in language endangerment studies. Among these language ideologies are ones we have discussed earlier in the book, such as the assumption of monolingualism – what Michael Silverstein (1996) has called the "culture of monoglot standardization" – which can be complicated in areas where languages are endangered because the norm in such places is often complex multilingualism. Speakers of endangered languages can also be put off, Hill warns, by assumption of the "pricelessness" of their languages and assertions by language activists and scholars that such languages "belong" to all of humanity. We will have more to say about these language ideologies and others later in the chapter.

What Dies When a Language Dies?

How significant is it that the native languages from which English borrowed words such as moose, raccoon, and the name of the state Massachusetts are all dead? What dies when a language dies? Many scholars working in the field of language endangerment have mourned the passing of even a single language by remarking upon the richness that is present in any one of the world's thousands of languages. Marianne Mithun, for example, a linguist who specializes in North American indigenous languages, most of which are moribund or already extinct, writes:

> There is not a language in North America that fails to offer breathtakingly beautiful intricacy. For descendants of speakers to discover this beauty can profoundly enrich their lives, much like the discovery of music, literature, or art, if not more … Language represents the most creative, pervasive aspect of culture, the most intimate side of the mind.

> The loss of language diversity will mean that we will never even have the opportunity to appreciate the full creative capacities of the human mind. (1998:189)

K. David Harrison, another linguist who works on endangered languages all over the world, lists three areas of loss if we fail to safeguard and document languages at risk of extinction: (1) the erosion of the human knowledge base, especially local ecological knowledge; (2) the loss of cultural heritage; and (3) failure to acquire a full understanding of human cognitive capacities (2007:15–19). With regard to the first area of loss, Harrison notes that an estimated 87 percent of the world's plants and animals have not yet been identified or studied by modern scientists. If we are to hope that a cure to cancer or other horrible diseases might be found in the Amazon, or in Papua New Guinea, or if we want to learn about more sustainable forms of agriculture from people who have been living in harmony in their environments for many hundreds of years, then we should recognize, Harrison writes, that "most of what humankind knows about the natural world lies completely outside of science textbooks, libraries, and databases, existing only in unwritten languages in people's memories" – that is, mostly in unwritten endangered languages (2007:15). Of course, some of this knowledge can be communicated in a different language, assuming the person speaking the endangered language is bilingual, but oftentimes there is a "massive disruption of the transfer of traditional knowledge across generations" when a group switches from an endangered language to a dominant language (2007:16). Particular languages are often especially rich in certain areas of the lexicon, such as reindeer herding, botany, or fishing, that are the most important to the speakers of those languages, and a great deal of ecologically specific knowledge is encoded in that language that goes along with those particular cultural practices. It is not surprising, then, that much of that knowledge is not passed on when the language (and often the way of life as well) dies.

The second area of loss that Harrison describes is the loss of cultural heritage that can accompany the loss of a language. Myths, jokes, wordplay, wise sayings, and other forms of verbal art are just some of the cultural practices that can be lost when a language becomes extinct. "Language is the most massive and inclusive art we know, a mountainous and anonymous work of unconscious generations," the famous linguistic anthropologist Edward Sapir declared (1949[1933], cited in Crystal 2000:40). Even when myths or sayings are translated into another language, there is always something lost. Trying to preserve the whole corpus of an endangered language's verbal art is virtually impossible, even with modern technology such as videotaping, for once a language disappears, the linguistic practices specific to the speakers of that language also disappear.

The third area of loss Harrison identifies is the ability to acquire a full understanding of the capabilities of the human mind. Linguists and cognitive scientists make assumptions about what the human brain can and cannot do based on experiments and existing data. One source of such data is the group of languages that have been studied by linguists. Whenever a language is analyzed for the first time, scholars look to see what patterns it shares grammatically with other languages in the world and which features it has that might be unique. The more languages that die, the more likely it is that the conclusions scholars draw about the limits of human cognition might be mistaken. For example, the language of Urarina, which is spoken by only 3,000 people in the Amazon rainforest of Peru, has a very unusual word order for its sentences. Unlike English, which generally uses the Subject – Verb – Object (S-V-O) word order, as in sentences such as, "The girl rode the bike," Urarina uses the Object – Verb – Subject (O-V-S) word order, which would have a literal translation for this sentence as, "The bike rode the girl." O-V-S word order is extremely rare among the world's languages. "Were it not for Urarina and a few other Amazonian languages," Harrison writes, "scientists might not even suspect it were possible. They would be free to hypothesize – falsely – that O-V-S word order was cognitively impossible, that the human brain could not process it" (2007:19).

Similarly, Kayardild, the Australian Aboriginal language spoken by Pat Gabori, who was described at the outset of this chapter, does not have one of the grammatical features – a restriction on the use of noun affixes to express tense – that Steven Pinker and other Chomskyan linguists have said were universal across all languages. "Kayardild shows us how dangerous it is to talk about 'universals' of language on the basis of a narrow sample that ignores the true extent of the world's linguistic diversity" (Evans 2010:xvi).

David Crystal, a prolific linguist who has written on many topics, including language death, presents five answers to the question, "Why should we care if a language dies?" (Crystal 2000:32–67). His answers provide a slightly different angle on language loss but make many of the same arguments that Harrison does. Here are Crystal's five reasons for why we should care if a language dies:

1 Because we need diversity.
2 Because language expresses identity.
3 Because languages are repositories of history.
4 Because languages contribute to the sum of human knowledge.
5 Because languages are interesting in themselves.

Throughout these arguments, Crystal, like many other scholars, explicitly likens the extinction of a language to the extinction of a biological species. In nature, genetic diversity ensures that at least some species will be able to adapt to changes in the environment. For similar reasons, Crystal argues, cultural and linguistic diversity is important. Some scholars go even further than Crystal, stating that biological and linguistic diversity are intrinsically linked. Nettle and Romaine, for example, talk of "biolinguistic diversity – the rich spectrum of life encompassing all the earth's species of plants and animals along with human cultures and their languages" (2000:13). Should we be less concerned, they ask, about the passing of Taiap (the language studied by Don Kulick, discussed in chapters 3 and 9) than the passing of the California condor? In fact, they conclude, these two kinds of extinction are not just metaphorically connected but actually connected, for in order to preserve biodiversity, the people whose environments are at risk must be enlisted to help. Since they are the ones with the most knowledge about that environment, they must be empowered, Nettle and Romaine argue, to control these natural resources themselves. It is peripheral rural communities, they claim, "who are in the environments where the biodiversity is, who are poor and marginalized by unsustainable development, and who are the stewards of most linguistic and cultural diversity. To a very significant extent, common cause can be made among development, biodiversity, and linguistic diversity" (Nettle and Romaine 2000:165).

But some scholars have recently critiqued the use of biological analogies in the rhetoric surrounding language endangerment. Shaylih

Muehlmann (2007:15), for instance, claims that these discourses essentialize language, nature, and indigenous people in ways that mask the complexities of situations that often involve multilingualism and marginalization. Indigenous people are on the one hand valorized and held up as "stewards," Muehlmann argues, and on the other hand exoticized and treated in a simplistic, often disrespectful manner, with assumptions being made about their preferences, life goals, and interests. People are made into "icons rather than agents" (Muehlmann 2007:22; cf. Hoffman 2008:50). It can sometimes be the case, in other words, that indigenous people who speak endangered languages are used as symbols in an endeavor that, while well-intentioned, might actually be more in the interests of the powerful, such as scholars, development workers, or government officials, than in the interests of the speakers themselves.

Deborah Cameron (2007a) has also cautioned against the assumptions and language ideologies underlying endangered languages rhetoric. While she does not deny the seriousness of potential language loss, she finds it very troubling that languages are unproblematically equated with endangered animal species. She also takes exception to statements such as this one, which was made by the Chairman of the US National Endowment for the Humanities, Bruce Cole, in a press release announcing the decision by the NEH and the National Science Foundation to fund language documentation projects jointly: "Language is the DNA of a culture, and it is the vehicle for the traditions, customs, stories, history, and beliefs of a people. A lost language is a lost culture" (Cole, cited in Cameron 2007a:274). This sort of rhetoric, Cameron maintains, borrows the authority of modern genetics to make an argument whose origins lie back in the eighteenth and nineteenth centuries. The one nation/one language/one people ideology espoused by German philosophers such as Johann Gottfried von Herder and William von Humboldt underpins many of the discourses surrounding language endangerment, Cameron asserts, even among scholars and activists with good intentions who otherwise hold very different views of language. This language ideology assumes no internal dissent within a group of people, no multilingualism, and no change over time that does not come from the outside. This "monoglot ideology" (Silverstein 1996) is a homogenous, static view of language and culture that has long since been discarded in linguistic and cultural anthropology. Moreover, Cameron warns, it is not that different from the language ideology espoused by the Nazis in Germany, who also held an essentialistic view of peoples, languages, and nations. The Nazis even tried to preserve certain German dialects and Celtic languages, Cameron notes. Of course, she does not equate those working in endangered language preservation today with Nazis; she is simply pointing out that the connection between "speaking A" and "being A" is much more complicated and fluid than some of the rhetoric would suggest (Cameron 2007a:280). The multifunctionality of all language guarantees that the way in which one speaks can index multiple identities simultaneously, and any given identity can have many different kinds of links (or no link at all) to a particular language.

Alexandra Jaffe (2007) discovered the problems with too simplistic an approach to language and identity in her research on Corsican. Revitalization efforts that emphasized a purist, homogeneous view ended up stigmatizing many habitual language practices, such as code-switching between French and Corsican. Also, not all Corsicans can speak Corsican, so this language ideology ended up causing feelings of linguistic insecurity and cultural inauthenticity among Corsicans who were not fluent speakers of the language. Eventually, Jaffe notes, a "polynomic" language ideology came to dominate Corsican preservation efforts. This ideology is pluralist and anti-purist in nature, allowing for many different varieties of Corsican to exist and not stigmatizing anyone for their level of proficiency or their code-switching (2007:65).

Perhaps the clearest indication of the problematic nature of the some of the language ideologies underpinning the discourses on language endangerment is the use of the very same language ideologies to support claims of language endangerment for languages that are clearly not endangered, such as English (Schmidt 2007; Duchêne and Heller 2007). The "English Only" movement, some scholars argue, has borrowed the rhetoric of language endangerment to suggest that English must be made the official language of the United States, or else it will be overrun by other languages (Baron 1990). Like all other languages, English is always changing, but it is in no danger of becoming extinct (see Figure 11.1). The normal changes that are constantly taking place in any spoken language cause shifts over time that can make the version of the language spoken decades or centuries earlier

Figure 11.1 Cartoon depicting normal and inevitable changes in a language over time.
Source: "Zits" by Jerry Scott and Jim Borgman, December 10, 1998. Reproduced with kind permission of Dan Piraro and Bizarro.com. Distributed by King Features Syndicate.

almost unintelligible to contemporary speakers; the English spoken in the Middle Ages is a good example of this. Similarly, some so-called "dead" languages such as Latin or Ancient Greek never became extinct in the ways described in this chapter but rather gradually evolved into other languages (Italian and Spanish, for example, in the case of Latin, and Modern Greek in the case of Ancient Greek). While our focus in this chapter is on languages that are truly in danger of extinction, it is certainly interesting to note that English, the third most commonly spoken language out of the thousands of languages in the world, can be perceived by some to be under threat.

Why Do Languages Die?

The processes by which a language becomes extinct are on one level quite simple: either the speakers of that language all die, or they all stop transmitting their language to their children. In actual cases, however, the factors are usually more complicated. All the speakers of a language can be killed by natural causes, such as the eruption of a volcano on the island of Sumbawa in the Indonesian archipelago in 1815 that caused the death of all the speakers of the Tamboran language (Nettle and Romaine 2000:51). Or human actions may result in language death, as was the case after a peasant uprising in El Salvador in 1932 led to the targeting and killing of 25,000 Indians. Those

Indians who were not killed during this period stopped using their native languages for fear of reprisals (Nettle and Romaine 2000:6). Many native languages also became extinct as a result of colonialism, when their speakers died directly from violence or, more indirectly, through exposure to new germs. Languages have also been lost when their speakers have had to relocate for economic or political reasons.

Most of the time, however, the process of language death is more gradual and less overtly violent. Language contact occurs, and the speakers of the less dominant language economically, politically, or socially either decide or are forced to shift to the more dominant language. An "ideology of contempt" (Grillo 1989:173–174, cited in Dorian 1998:7) may come to characterize the less dominant language, and its speakers no longer wish to be associated with it. As we saw in chapter 3 with Taiap, the transition can be unintentional, with parents not realizing that they were transmitting to their children the negative language ideologies they had toward the endangered language (Kulick 1992). The end result is that children are exposed to less and less of the endangered language, and the negative attitudes they often absorb in the process make them ill-disposed toward using the language if they do acquire it.

In some cases, the shift is painful, involving a great deal of psychological, if not physical, violence. In many US Bureau of Indian Affairs schools, for example, children of Native Americans were taken away from their parents and forbidden to speak their native languages. In other schools, such as those in Wales in the nineteenth century, children were forced to wear a wooden badge (in other schools, it was just a button or a piece of paper) called a "Welsh Not" if a teacher caught them speaking their native language. They were then told to transfer the "Welsh Not" badge to any other student who was speaking Welsh. Whoever had the badge at the end of the week was punished with flogging (Nettle and Romaine 2000:140–141; Crystal 2000:84–85).

As a language is in the process of dying out, it often undergoes simplification in its grammar and lexicon. Speakers have fewer opportunities to use the language and so either forget or do not acquire a large vocabulary. Grammatical structures can also be lost or simplified. For example, in Dyirbal, an endangered Aboriginal language in Australia, there used to be a four-part classification of nouns. (See chapter 4 for a discussion of the four categories.) Nowadays, however, young people are less familiar with the ancestral myths and cultural practices that motivated the four-part classification, and they are less fluent in Dyirbal, having attended school mostly in English, and so they have replaced the four-part system of noun classification with a two-part one. It is still different from English and retains some of the features of the older system, but it has become much simpler to use (Nettle and Romaine 2000:66–69).

As a language dies, it disappears from various domains of use. For some languages, this is a top-down process in which the language is no longer used in public domains or official institutions but is retained, at least for a while, in the home. For other languages, the process is a bottom-up one in which the language is no longer used in the home or in everyday contexts but is kept in official and public domains. The languages mentioned at the outset of this chapter in reference to the last speakers of Mbabaram, Manx, Kayardild, Wappo, and Ubykh are examples of top-down language loss because the language disappeared from public, ceremonial contexts first and was retained only in informal, everyday settings. Languages that have experienced bottom-up loss are mostly those in which sacred texts or religious ceremonies continue to be read or performed in the endangered language, while the language of other domains shifts to something else. Hebrew experienced bottom-up language loss for most of the 2,000 years of the Jewish diaspora. During these years, Hebrew continued to be used mostly by Jewish men as they studied sacred texts and performed religious rituals, but for all other purposes, other languages were used, either the local languages of the area where the Jews lived, or alternative Jewish languages that emerged, such as Yiddish or Ladino.

Of course, Hebrew did not eventually die out, unlike many other endangered languages, which brings us to the final question of this chapter: can languages be brought back from the brink?

Can Endangered Languages Be Saved?

Hebrew is a fascinating, and in many ways unique, case. Its speakers were scattered around the world after the destruction of the Second

Temple in Jerusalem in 70 CE and were subject to persecution in the form of pogroms and eventually the Holocaust, which caused the death of six million Jews. In addition, some Jews assimilated partially or totally into the societies in which they lived, giving up Hebrew altogether. For many Jews, however, Hebrew remained in use in religious contexts, mainly by men, and so it never really became "extinct" in the way that so many indigenous languages have. Nevertheless, Hebrew was not used for any everyday conversations for almost 2,000 years (Hinton 2001; Kuzar 2001).

In the late eighteenth and early nineteenth century, some Jews began to return to their ancestral home in Palestine in the hope of one day re-establishing a Jewish state there. The question of which language should be the official language of the new state arose, and the main debate was between Hebrew, the language of the Jewish religion's sacred texts, and Yiddish, the Jewish language that emerged in Eastern Europe. Yiddish, which was written using the Hebrew alphabet, was a combination of Hebrew, German, and other languages, as well as its own unique words and grammatical structures (Jacobs 2005; Weinreich 2008). The language ideologies held by many Jews at the end of the nineteenth century considered Hebrew to be a language of high prestige, while Yiddish was stigmatized as a lowly language fit only for everyday, non-sacred contexts. Given these ideologies, it is not surprising that Hebrew was chosen to be the official language of the new state of Israel. The process of revitalizing and adapting Biblical Hebrew for use in the modern era was an involved one, with Eliezer Ben-Yehuda coining thousands of new words. Biblical Hebrew was his main source for roots, but there were many words needed for contemporary usage of the language that had to be created from scratch. Ironically, whereas once Hebrew was endangered and Yiddish was spoken by millions of people, now Hebrew is spoken by millions of people and Yiddish is endangered. Still, there is a rich literature in Yiddish, and efforts to preserve the language are growing rapidly (Lansky 2004; Shandler 2005).

No other language has thus far succeeded in being brought back from the brink to the extent that Hebrew has, most likely because of the unique circumstances that surrounded Hebrew's disappearance from everyday conversations and then its return under the aegis of a new nation-state, but many language revitalization efforts are underway around the world. In some cases, there are no longer any speakers of the language left, but sometimes descendants of a "sleeping language" (Hinton 2001:413) find written or recorded materials and attempt to learn the language. When speakers of an endangered language are still alive, they are sometimes brought into the language preservation effort as teachers or leaders. Collaborative, community-based programs can succeed in some cases in raising the prestige associated with endangered languages, thereby improving the chances that people will want to keep speaking their language and keep teaching it to their children. Indeed, one of the 2010 MacArthur Foundation "Genius" grant recipients was Jessie Little Doe Baird, a linguist who is attempting to revive Wampanoag (or Wôpanâak), a language spoken by Native Americans in New England up until about 150 years ago. The recognition of Baird should bring additional prestige to the Wampanaoag Language Reclamation Project and many other such efforts. Unfortunately, as Muehlmann notes, "we cannot conclude that saving languages or rainforests will reverse the social processes that marginalize some groups in the first place" (2007:31).

Conclusion

Language endangerment is a subject that can be illuminated in valuable ways using the insights and methods of linguistic anthropology. The four key terms introduced in the first chapter of this book can lead us toward a deeper understanding of this phenomenon. Remembering that language is always *multifunctional* can help prevent simplistic, if well-intentioned, efforts that assume a one-to-one mapping of languages onto ethnic or national identities. Habitual linguistic *practices* can create patterns related to the cultural norms and social meanings associated with endangered languages. These practices in turn often *index* particular identities, hierarchies, or values. The *language ideologies* that emerge from this process of indexicality can affect the likelihood of a language's survival.

At the root of language endangerment, wherever it manifests itself around the world, are issues related to social power and individual or collective agency. We turn in the next and final chapter of the book, therefore, to a discussion of these matters, which must inform any investigation of language in actual social contexts.

12

Conclusion: Language, Power, and Agency

Thus far in this book we have discussed numerous aspects of language use in real-life social contexts. In many of the case studies offered in the previous chapters, power of some sort, as expressed in or through language, has played an important role, even though we may have focused on other aspects of the cases at hand. Recall, for example, the following research described in earlier parts of this book.

- In her ethnography, *Exposing Prejudice: Puerto Rican Experiences of Language, Race, and Class*, Bonnie Urciuoli (1996) argues that the boundaries between Spanish and English in a New York Puerto Rican community are fuzzy when the socioeconomic status of the speakers is similar, as when Puerto Ricans are speaking with their African American neighbors. In contrast, when there are stark differences in the socioeconomic statuses of Puerto Ricans and the people with whom they are speaking, as when they are talking to white middle-class or upper-middle-class professionals, then the boundaries between Spanish and English are much more clearly demarcated.
- In many of the law school classrooms that Elizabeth Mertz studied, authoritative exchanges occurred between professors and students (such as the dialogue cited near the end of chapter 3), powerfully directing students toward a new way of reading, thinking, and being (2007a:125).

- When researcher Steven Levinson took a walk with Dan, a speaker of the indigenous Australian language called Guugu Yimithirr, he witnessed an example of the power of grammatical features within a language to influence perception and help to constitute the social and material world. Because of the way spatial reckoning works grammatically in Guugu Yimithirr, Dan was able to calculate his spatial position effortlessly in an absolute rather than relative sense. Levinson walked with Dan all day long to reach a set of caves with ancient paintings in them and described what happened next: "We are sitting in the cave entrance, and disoriented myself, I ask him to point back to base. He does so without hesitation, right through the hillside we are sitting on. I check with an accurate prismatic compass, and ask him for other locations. Checking later on maps, it turns out that he is spot on – absolutely dead accurate, as far as my compass can discriminate" (Levinson 2003b:5).
- In her study of the socially stigmatized group labeled "nerds," Mary Bucholtz (1999) looks at identity formation and power-laden relationships in a high school community of practice. Bucholtz shows how macro-level categories such as race, class, and gender are emergent in the micro-level social interactions of the individuals in complex and sometimes contradictory ways. Even the most mundane conversations, therefore, can (and should) be analyzed, Bucholtz argues, in order to arrive at a deeper understanding of how social statuses, identities, and hierarchies are maintained or transformed.
- Jan Blommaert's (2009) research on political asylum seekers in the United Kingdom presents a stark example of power asymmetries resulting from incorrect assumptions on the part of government officials about what the linguistic abilities of a political asylum seeker from Rwanda should be. The asylum seeker, whom Blommaert gives the pseudonym of Joseph Mutingira, had a nightmarish childhood and adolescence that spanned the genocide in 1994 and extremely tumultuous times before and after. Blommaert claims that Mutingira's application for political asylum was denied because of the officials' mistaken assumptions and deeply ingrained language ideologies.
- Shirley Brice Heath's classic book, *Ways with Words: Language, Life, and Work in Communities and Classrooms* (Heath 1983), describes the

long-term, life-altering effects of the differences in how families from different communities socialize their preschool children with regard to written texts. Heath looked at both race and class dimensions to these differences and concluded that because the mostly white middle-class families of Maintown introduced their children to ways of interacting with books that were quite similar to school practices, the Maintown children entered school well prepared to learn and interact with books in the ways that would be expected of them in school. Children from the other two communities, Trackton and Roadville, were at a disadvantage when they reached school because they did not go through the same socialization process with regard to written texts.

- Graham Jones and Lauren Shweder's (2003) article, "The Performance of Illusion and Illusionary Performatives: Learning the Language of Theatrical Magic," looks closely at how a magician can create a powerful illusion through both verbal and nonverbal actions. Talk in particular, Jones and Shweder argue, can actually shape the audience's experience of seeing because the narrative of the magician activates a frame in audience members that identifies the event not just as a magic trick but as something involving the paranormal in the form of Splookie the ghost.
- Laura Fish Somersal, who died in 1990, was the last speaker of the Native American language of Wappo (Thompson et al. 2006). As noted in chapter 11, Somersal might not have retained her native Wappo if she had attended the Bureau of Indian Affairs (BIA) school in her area because it was official BIA policy to force students to speak only English. The long history of colonization and oppression that has characterized relationships between the US government and Native Americans has helped to make 80 percent of Native North American languages extinct or moribund (Krauss 1992:5).

Each of these examples illustrates in one or more different ways how power relations can be enacted in, by, and through language. Closely tied to this question is the way in which agency – the socioculturally mediated capacity to act – is an essential aspect of, and counterpart to, power. In a sense, then, we have been building throughout this book toward the central focus of this concluding chapter. Scholars interested in exploring any of the topics treated in earlier chapters of this book will benefit from grounding their analyses in the social theory most relevant to language, power, and agency. We therefore turn first to examine language and power theoretically and then add agency into the mix and consider the complicated, interconnected nature of language, agency, and power.

What is Power?

"Power" is a term used frequently in both everyday conversations and dense theoretical treatises. There is far too much written by scholars on the nature of power (social, political, economic, etc.) than can be reviewed here, but it is important to situate our discussion of power within the social theories that will be most helpful and relevant to the study of language in actual social contexts. These theories can be dense, but familiarity with their basic tenets will enrich and deepen any analysis of actual linguistic interactions. Analyses that are not directly informed by such social theory often end up being indirectly informed by taken-for-granted and inaccurate assumptions regarding social power. The three approaches I have chosen to highlight in this concluding chapter are the ones that have been used most frequently and most helpfully by linguistic anthropologists to shed light on power and language: (1) the concept of hegemony as put forward by Raymond Williams, building on the work of Antonio Gramsci; (2) Michel Foucault's writings on power relations and discourse; and (3) the work of practice theorists such as Sherry Ortner, Anthony Giddens, and especially Pierre Bourdieu.[1]

Hegemony

One of the most useful terms for our purposes in understanding how power intersects with language is *hegemony*. According to Raymond Williams, a cultural Marxist who builds on the work of Antonio Gramsci, hegemony refers to a dynamic system of domination based not so much on violence or the threat of violence, or merely on the economic control of the means of production, but rather on political, cultural, and institutional influence. "That is to say," Williams writes, "it is not limited to matters of direct political control but seeks to describe a more general predominance which includes, as one of its key features, a particular way of seeing the world and human nature and relationships" (1983:145). Having military power or economic wealth can certainly lead to power, but social status and cultural dominance can also come from other sources, and hegemony is a term that helps us understand this process. Hegemony is saturated with the specific forms of inequality belonging to particular societies at particular historical moments, according to Williams, and is "... in the strongest sense a 'culture', but a culture which has also to be seen as the lived dominance and subordination of particular classes" (1977:110). Emphasizing the dynamic nature of any "lived hegemony," Williams reminds us that "it does not just passively exist as a form of dominance. It has continually to be renewed, recreated, defended, and modified. It is also continually resisted, limited, altered, challenged by pressures not all its own" (1977:112). In other words, Williams concludes, while any lived hegemony is always by definition dominant, it is never total or exclusive (1977:113).

Thus, although hegemonic ways of acting, talking, feeling, or being may seem overwhelmingly obligatory or simply "the (only) way things are done," Williams reminds us that these practices can change over time. There is always room within a given hegemonic system to resist or transform it. How are hegemonic ideas or practices reinforced or challenged? At least partially through language. For this reason, the concept of hegemony is a useful one as we move forward in this concluding chapter to explore the relationships among language, power, and agency.

Foucault's power relations and discourse

The extremely influential French theorist Michel Foucault wrote prolifically and complexly about many aspects of power. Rather than conceiving of power as a thing or an entity possessed by individuals or institutions, Foucault's approach involves looking at *power relations*. Unlike relationships of *violence*, Foucault claims, which involve direct and immediate actions on bodies or things (such as breaking, destroying, bending, or hurting), relationships of *power* involve *actions upon others' actions*. Power in this relational sense, Foucault argues,

> is a set of actions on possible actions; it incites, it induces, it seduces, it makes easier or more difficult; it releases or contrives, makes more

> probable or less; in the extreme, it constrains or forbids absolutely, but it is always a way of acting upon one or more acting subjects by virtue of their acting or being capable of action. (1994b:138)

Foucault distinguishes power relations both from violence on the one hand and from voluntary consent on the other. Power is therefore, he argues, less like an open confrontation or a mutual engagement than a form of "government" – that is, the governing of one person by another through the structuring of that person's field of possible actions. The person whose actions are thus constrained or shaped remains "free," Foucault claims, with the potential to struggle or flee. Power and freedom are not mutually exclusive but are instead interwoven in a complex manner in his theory (1994b:139). Over time, Foucault maintains, power relations can result in "domination," which he defines as "a general structure of power … a strategic situation, more or less taken for granted and consolidated, within long-term confrontation between adversaries" (1994b:143). The term Foucault uses to describe such complex forms of power that are constituted by institutions, procedures, and knowledge is "governmentality." Much of Foucault's writing involves a survey of European history and institutions to analyze particular governmental apparatuses and systems of knowledge (1994a:244).

Just as the concept of hegemony as put forward by Raymond Williams emphasizes the processual, dynamic nature of power, so too do Foucault's power relations direct attention to processes and actions. Even more pertinent to the subject of this chapter, Foucault notes that, "Power relations are exercised, to an exceedingly important extent, through the production and exchange of signs" – that is, through systems of communication (1994b:136). Power relations are thus deeply embedded within everyday social and linguistic interactions.

There have been numerous critiques of Foucault's definition of power, many of them focusing on the problematic implications it has for human agency (Bartky 1995; Hoy 1986). Even though Foucault states that, "Where there is power, there is resistance," he continues on to say, "and yet, or rather consequently, this resistance is never in a position of exteriority in relation to power" (Foucault 1978:95). The problem is that Foucault only vaguely explains how power is enforced or personified, and the processes of resistance remain similarly opaque. Instead, he focuses on much larger-scale "discourses" – the sets of rules and practices that allow people to produce meaningful statements in given societies at particular historical moments. For Foucault, a discourse – we might even capitalize the term as Discourse – could be said to be hegemonic. Stuart Hall describes Foucault's concept of discourse as follows:

> Discourse, Foucault argues, constructs the topic. It defines and produces the objects of our knowledge. It governs the way that a topic can be meaningfully talked about and reasoned about. It also influences how ideas are put into practice and used to regulate the conduct of others. Just as a discourse 'rules in' certain ways of talking about a topic, defining an acceptable and intelligible way to talk, write, or conduct oneself, so also, by definition, it 'rules out', limits and restricts other ways of talking, of conducting ourselves in relation to the topic or constructing knowledge about it. (2001:72)

Within linguistic anthropology there is much more attention to discourses (with a lower-case "d") at the micro level than to Foucault's Discourse (with an upper-case "D") at the macro level, but the two different approaches can be profitably combined, since large-scale power relations are emergent in small-scale everyday linguistic interactions.

Practice theory and power

Readers should recall that *practice*, a concept introduced in chapter 1, is one of the four key terms of this book (the other three being *multifunctionality*, *language ideologies*, and *indexicality*). Practice, which both reflects and shapes social structures of power, is, according to Sherry Ortner, any form of human action or interaction that reverberates with "features of inequality, domination, and the like in its particular historical and cultural setting" (1989:11–12; see also Ortner 1984). Not all practice theorists have foregrounded issues related to power, however. In fact, Ortner criticizes practice theorists such as Pierre Bourdieu and Anthony Giddens for being relatively uninterested in questions of power (Ortner 2006a:17). While this is somewhat true of Giddens (1979), it is less true of other practice theorists such as Marshall Sahlins (1981), and even less true, I would claim, of Bourdieu, at least in his writings about language. Indeed, Bourdieu's book, *Language and Symbolic Power* (1991), is quite centrally concerned with criticizing the influence within anthropology and sociology of the Saussurean model that "treats language as an object of contemplation rather than as an instrument of action and power" (Bourdieu 1991:37).

We shall return to Bourdieu's analysis of language and power in a moment, but first it is necessary to review some aspects of his more general social theory. In chapter 1, we discussed Bourdieu's notion of the *habitus*, which refers to a set of predispositions or habits within individuals. These predispositions are shaped by the social structures from which they emerge, and they lead the individuals to produce actions and representations that will either reproduce or transform those social structures (Bourdieu 1977:78). Bourdieu's concept of *habitus* provides insight into how we can both shape and be shaped by our social and cultural surroundings. By emphasizing how we are *predisposed*, not *predetermined*, to act, think, and speak in certain ways, Bourdieu allows for the influence of social structures on our behavior while still leaving room for the possibility that we might act in opposition to the structures and norms that have influenced us. In this sense, the *habitus* is similar to Williams's notion of hegemony. The *habitus* has an endless capacity to generate thoughts, perceptions, expressions, and actions – but this "conditioned and conditional freedom," Bourdieu argues, "is as remote from a creation of unpredictable novelty as it is from a simple mechanical reproduction of the initial conditionings" (1977:95). Ortner (1989:198) uses the term "loosely structured" to describe people who are thus neither completely free agents nor completely predetermined robots. The thoughts and actions generated by the *habitus* lead to differing outcomes within actual, concrete, real-life situations; sometimes the results of *habitus*-generated actions reinforce the status quo and sometimes they transform it. Although Ortner and others (myself included) have criticized Bourdieu for emphasizing social reproduction more than social transformation, his approach to practice theory is valuable because it provides us a deeper understanding of how and why social inequalities can be reproduced, reinforced, or sometimes challenged.

Bourdieu's concept of *habitus*, and his practice theory in general, can be strengthened significantly by taking into account critiques that have been offered by scholars such as Asif Agha (2007:229–231) and Brenda Farnell (2000). Agha faults Bourdieu for claiming that the *habitus* is instilled in individuals in a top-down manner and is not transmitted through language. "There is every reason to think," Bourdieu writes, "that the factors which are most influential in the formation of the habitus are transmitted without passing through language and consciousness, but through suggestions inscribed in the most apparently insignificant aspects of the things, situations and practices of everyday life" (Bourdieu 1991:51). In contrast, Agha claims that "far from being 'transmitted without passing through language' the social life of the habitus is mediated by discursive interactions" (Agha 2007:229). In other words, it is through everyday verbal *and* nonverbal interactions – "one communicative event at a time," Agha argues – as well as through multiple metalinguistic processes (speech about language that assigns it social prestige or stigma) that the *habitus* is produced.[2]

Farnell (2000) also criticizes Bourdieu for proposing a disembodied notion of the *habitus* that seems to be a set of habitual practices that get inculcated in people unconsciously. Instead, Farnell suggests a more concrete, dynamic, and embodied process of social and linguistic actions. She illustrates the utility of this more grounded approach by providing examples from her fieldwork among the Nakota (Assiniboine) people of Montana, some of whom still use Plains Indian Sign Language, or "sign talk," in their storytelling and rituals, and when communicating with the deaf or elderly. "In contrast with Bourdieu's talk *about* the body," Farnell writes (2000:412), "in the form of third-person descriptions of normative practices that are activated by the dispositions of a *habitus*, we have talk *from* the body, accounts of persons enacting their bodies using vocal signs and action signs in dialogic interactional processes."

Rather than undercutting Bourdieu's usefulness as a theorist, Agha and Farnell's critiques of some of Bourdieu's concepts can sharpen his theoretical insights and make them even more relevant to scholars interested in linguistic analysis. In addition to the concept of *habitus*, Bourdieu proposes another concept to describe the ways in which power differentials can be maintained or even exacerbated through habitual nonverbal behavior communicating value judgments about "appropriate" dress, bearing, manners, or posture. Bourdieu calls this *body* (or sometimes *bodily*) *hexis*, and once a particular *bodily hexis* is internalized, it can be very difficult to change. As we saw in chapter 3 when we discussed language socialization, children absorb more than just new words and grammatical structures as they are learning their native language(s); they also absorb culturally appropriate (and often gender-specific) ways of holding their bodies when they stand, sit, walk, or talk. This "hidden persuasion of an implicit pedagogy" is capable, Bourdieu says, of "instilling a whole cosmology, an ethic, a metaphysic, a political philosophy, through injunctions as insignificant as 'stand up straight' or 'don't hold your knife in your left hand'" (1977:94).

An extremely important aspect of bodily hexis is the overall way of using the mouth, or what Bourdieu, following Pierre Guiraud, calls "articulatory style," in which "the bodily hexis characteristic of a social class determines the system of phonological features which characterizes a class pronunciation" (Bourdieu 1991:86). In other words, accents and dialects index social class positioning as well as many other forms of social difference and dominance, and Bourdieu links these differences in pronunciation to the *habitus* and to bodily hexis. "Language," Bourdieu remarks, "is a body technique, and specifically linguistic, especially phonetic, competence is a dimension of bodily hexis in which one's whole relation to the social world, and one's whole socially informed relation to the world, are expressed" (1991:86).

Another concept of Bourdieu's that can be very useful in explaining ongoing social inequality as well as occasional social change is the notion of *doxa* – that which is taken for granted, that which is "commonsense," that which literally goes without saying (Bourdieu 1977:166–167). *Doxa* includes every social norm or cultural value that lies outside of the "universe of discourse or argument"; people do not debate *doxa* because it does not occur to them that there could be other ways of thinking or acting. Bourdieu contrasts *doxa* with two alternatives: *orthodoxy* and *heterodoxy*. Both orthodoxy and heterodoxy exist within the universe of discourse or argument. Orthodoxy, defined by Bourdieu, is opinion in favor of the status quo and the current alignment of powers. Heterodoxy is the opposite – that is, opinion that is against the status quo (see Figure 12.1).

Take, for example, the question of gay marriage. Not too long ago in the United States (and still in many countries), it used to be a part

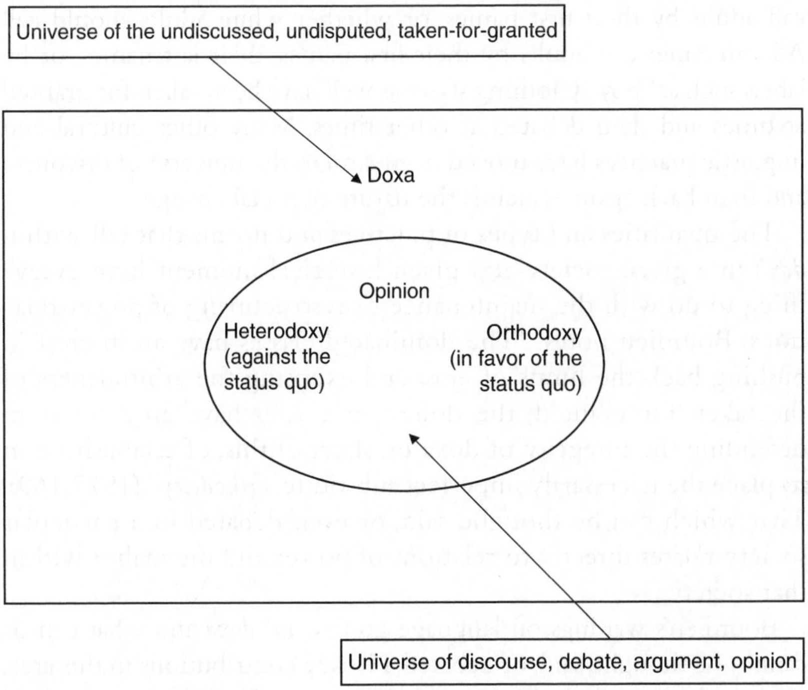

Figure 12.1 *Doxa* as that which is taken for granted and therefore outside the universe of discourse.
Source: Adapted from Bourdieu (1977:168). Used with permission of Cambridge University Press.

of *doxa* that marriage was an institution that could be entered into only by one woman and one man. In recent years, however, that taken-for-granted assumption has come to be challenged. The issue, in Bourdieu's terms, has left the realm of *doxa* and entered the universe of discourse, and arguments have ensued. People now take positions in favor or against the marriage of two women or two men, whereas in the past it never occurred to many in the United States that the institution of marriage might change. Other examples include how women and men wear their hair in particular societies at particular historical moments – long, short, braided, similar to each other or very different, etc. Forms of address (calling older people by their first names instead of by "Mrs.," "Ms.," or "Mr.") have also been taken for granted for certain periods of time, and then changed, with some arguments pro or con regarding whether, for example, children should call adults by their first names, or whether white adults should call African American adults by their first names, their last names, or by labels such as "boy." Clothing styles as well have been taken for granted at times and then debated at other times. Many other cultural and linguistic practices have moved from *doxa* to the universe of discourse and then back again – such is the nature of social change.

The quantities and types of practices and norms that fall within *doxa* in a given society at a given historical moment have everything to do with the maintenance or restructuring of power relations. Bourdieu notes: "The dominated classes have an interest in pushing back the limits of *doxa* and exposing the arbitrariness of the taken for granted; the dominant classes have an interest in defending the integrity of doxa or, short of this, of establishing in its place the necessarily imperfect substitute, *orthodoxy*" (1977:169). That which can be thought, said, or even debated in a particular society relates directly to relations of power and inequality within that society.

Bourdieu's writings on language go beyond *doxa* and what can or cannot be thought, said, or debated. His key contributions in this area, presented primarily in his book, *Language and Symbolic Power*, extend his theoretical framework of practice theory to include an analysis of linguistic practices, thereby bringing questions of power and inequality to the fore. "[O]ne must not forget," Bourdieu writes, "that the relations of communication *par excellence* – linguistic exchanges – are also relations of symbolic power in which the power relations between speakers or their respective groups are actualized" (1991:37).

Drawing on terms used in economics such as *linguistic market*, *profit of distinction*, and *symbolic capital*, Bourdieu offers a way of understanding how linguistic practices can be imbued with power differentials.[3] Power relations emerge, according to Bourdieu, when the *linguistic habitus* (which is a subset of the predispositions comprising the overall *habitus*) comes into contact with the *linguistic market* (on which different ways of speaking circulate – styles, registers, accents, dialects, and languages). While this concept of *linguistic market* is quite similar in some respects to Bakhtin's notion of heteroglossia, which was discussed in chapter 6, Bourdieu more explicitly than Bakhtin points to the varying levels of prestige associated with different ways of speaking. For Bakhtin, "All words have the "taste" of a profession, a genre, a tendency, a party, a particular work, a particular person, a generation, an age group, the day and hour" (Bakhtin1981a:293). But for Bourdieu, in contrast, there is a *profit of distinction* to be gained from speaking in socially valued ways. The specifics of the local linguistic market will determine the outcome, so a highly educated professor, for example, may speak in a way that is well received in a doctor's office, thereby ensuring that the professor's child is given preferential treatment. The same professor, however, may be ridiculed when speaking with a group of teenagers, even – or especially – when s/he attempts to speak as the teens do.

Different class positions, educational or professional backgrounds, and ethnic, racial, or regional identities both shape and reflect the different communicative repertoires individuals have (cf. Agha 2007). Those who are able to speak in highly valued ways in appropriate contexts have what Bourdieu calls *linguistic* or *symbolic capital*. This sort of capital is related to ordinary economic capital (money or wealth of some sort), but not necessarily in a simplistic one-to-one way. The more economic capital one has, the more likely one will be able to acquire symbolic capital in the form of mastery of the standard dialect or competence in multiple registers or languages. In turn, such mastery can often (but not always) result in greater professional success and more economic capital.

In a contribution that ties in nicely with one of this book's key concepts, that of language ideologies, Bourdieu describes how different levels of *symbolic capital* can turn into *symbolic dominance* and even *symbolic violence*. When individuals in a society are not proficient in the most highly valued ways of speaking (such as English in the United States, especially Standard American English), they do not benefit from the access such proficiency often provides to prestigious schools, professions, or social groups (cf. Lippi-Green 1997). And yet, speakers of stigmatized variants (for example, in the United States these might include speakers of nonstandard varieties of English such as African American English or Appalachian English) frequently buy into the system of evaluation that ranks Standard American English as superior. These people's own language ideologies, in other words, stigmatize the ways in which they themselves speak. This acceptance of differing social values accorded various ways of speaking is in actuality a *misrecognition*, according to Bourdieu, because the differential levels of prestige constitute an arbitrary ranking. Every language or dialect is as good *linguistically*, even though not socially, as every other.

In support of this insight that there is a *misrecognition*, or misunderstanding, of the nature of the varying levels of prestige associated with different languages or dialects, Bourdieu draws upon the work of Labov that we discussed in chapter 5, which shows that even though New Yorkers speak in many different ways, they participate in a set of shared norms, or language ideologies, that evaluate some ways of speaking as "better" than others (Labov 1972b; Bourdieu 1991:52). The result of this *misrecognition* is *symbolic violence*. And yet, by participating in these shared norms, Bourdieu controversially adds, individuals who cannot speak in the most prestigious ways are nevertheless at least somewhat complicit in their own subjugation. "All symbolic domination presupposes, on the part of those who submit to it, a form of complicity which is neither passive submission to external constraint nor free adherence to values," he writes (Bourdieu 1991:51). In this respect, Bourdieu's approach to *symbolic violence* is similar to Foucault's assertion that relations of power involve actions upon others' actions and therefore display a complex interweaving of consent and coercion (Foucault 1994b:139; cf. Ahearn 1994).

All three of these approaches to power within social theory – the concept of hegemony, Foucault's writings on power relations and discourse, and the work of practice theorists, especially Pierre Bourdieu – differ in substantial ways from the approach to power taken by most linguists. Most linguists, even including many sociolinguists, avoid talking about power altogether, preferring instead to treat language, as Bourdieu's criticism noted above claims, "as an object of contemplation rather than as an instrument of action and power" (Bourdieu 1991:37; cf. Gal 2006).

Despite the assumption often made by linguists that language is apolitical and can therefore be studied apolitically with no reference at all to differential levels of social power, the field of linguistics has itself been deeply implicated in colonialism's project of conquest and control, according to linguistic anthropologist Joseph Errington. For hundreds of years in Africa, Asia, and other places of European colonization, linguists produced dictionaries, grammars, orthographies, and other works that "made languages objects of knowledge, so that their speakers could be made subjects of power" (Errington 2008:3). Linguists who documented these non-European languages were never "just linguists," Errington argues. Instead, they were involved in using native languages for religious missionary work or as part of a "civilizing" enterprise that facilitated European control (Errington 2008:6). This is not to say that linguists did not generate useful empirical knowledge; they of course did, as Hill (2009) and others note. But neither language itself nor the study of language can ever be entirely divorced from relations of power.

Judith Irvine and Susan Gal (2000) persuasively demonstrate the linkages between language and power in an important and widely cited article that encourages scholars to study how ways of speaking come to be labeled as different from one another. How does a particular language come to be considered a language historically and politically? How, in other words, does a language like Macedonian come to be considered separate from Greek or Bulgarian? How does Serbo-Croatian come to be divided into several separate languages, such as Serbian, Croatian, and Bosnian? And what is the relationship between Urdu and Hindi, which in many places are indistinguishable verbally but which have two different writing systems and are the official languages of two different nation-states (Pakistan and India, respectively)?

Irvine and Gal provide several case studies of this sort of linguistic differentiation to illustrate the ways in which language ideologies influence both the participants (that is, the speakers) and the observers (that is, the scholars). For example, they describe how the Senegalese languages of Fula, Wolof, and Sereer were influenced by the ideologies of European linguists, ethnographers, and colonizers in the nineteenth and twentieth centuries. "The way these languages were identified, delimited, and mapped, the ways their relationships were interpreted, and even the ways they were described in grammars and dictionaries were all heavily influenced by an ideology of racial and national essences," Irvine and Gal write (2000:47). Although most linguists today consider Fula, Wolof, and Sereer to be three distinct but related languages forming a "Senegal group" spoken by people in overlapping geographical areas, Irvine and Gal report that a hundred years ago the linguistic and ethnic terrain was understood very differently (2000:48).

Fula was considered by linguists to be unrelated to Wolof and Sereer, and Sereer was thought to include several Cangin languages from what is today thought to be a very different language group.

Why such a change in the understanding of these languages? Irvine and Gal argue that the answer it was not so much because of better scholarship or improved data but instead because, "There have also been changes in what observers expected to see and how they interpreted what they saw" (2000:48). Nineteenth-century linguists and ethnographers assumed that linguistic classifications could be used to judge evolutionary rankings of groups. (White Europeans were of course at the top of this ranking, and various African groups clustered toward the bottom.) They also assumed that ethnic groups were monolingual and that a "primordial relationship" existed that linked languages with territories, nations, tribes, and peoples. In the case of Fula, Wolof, and Sereer, racial and linguistic ideologies led nineteenth-century linguists to consider the Fula language and its speakers (who were often lighter skinned than the others and who tended to espouse a more orthodox Islam) to be of higher status and intelligence. The Wolof language was deemed "less supple, less handy" than Fula, and its speakers less intelligent. The Sereer language, nineteenth-century linguists claimed, was "the language of primitive simplicity" (Irvine and Gal 2000:55).

While it is easy to fault previous generations of scholars for being blinded by their ideologies, Irvine and Gal caution that such ideologically influenced scholarship continues today, for, "There is no 'view from nowhere,' no gaze that is not positioned" (2000:36). Moreover, ideologically laden judgments about languages made in past centuries have had consequences that have affected how certain languages have changed, whether they have become extinct, how scholars have written grammars and dictionaries, and how political territories and identities have been claimed or mapped out. These consequences continue to affect linguistic, social, and political practices around the world, according to Irvine and Gal.

Linguistic differentiation – the labeling of a way of speaking as different from or opposed to some other way of speaking – involves three kinds of semiotic processes, Irvine and Gal maintain: (1) iconization; (2) fractal recursivity; and (3) erasure. Other linguistic anthropologists have begun to identify these processes in many different linguistic and geopolitical situations, so they are important to summarize here (Irvine and Gal 2000:37–39).

- *Iconization*. Recall from chapter 1 the discussion of Peirce's three kinds of signs: *icons*, *indexes*, and *symbols*. An *icon* is a sign that refers to its object by means of similarity, such as how a "choo choo" refers to a train, or a photograph of a person relates to the person herself. *Iconization* is a process in which linguistic features appear to be similar in some way to individual speakers or whole groups. In the case of the Senegalese languages discussed by Irvine and Gal, for example, Sereer was (mistakenly) thought by linguists to be a "primitive" language with extremely simple vocabulary and grammatical forms; this characterization was applied to the speakers of the language as well, who were, Irvine and Gal report, also considered "primitive."
- *Fractal recursivity*. When an opposition or contrast that operates at one level is projected onto another level, Irvine and Gal call this process *fractal recursivity*. An excellent example of this is provided by Stacy Pigg, who describes how her inquiries about shamans (traditional healers) in Nepal led her to a deeper understanding of how shamans are "handy symbols in the construction of 'modernity'" (Pigg 1996:161). Whenever Pigg asked a Nepali about shamans in the area, the Nepali would claim that local shamans in that particular area (wherever she was) were not really that traditional; for "real" shamans, Pigg was always instructed to go to a place that was more "remote," "traditional," or "backward" (1996:160). Eventually, Pigg realized that her respondents were constructing themselves as more "modern" than the other places they mentioned. Just as she herself represented to them the "modern" or "developed" West in opposition to the "backward" Nepal (and I can confirm that the Nepali terms for "developed" and "backward" are often used by Nepalis themselves in this way), so too did city dwellers represent themselves as more "developed" in opposition to villagers. In turn, village dwellers, no matter how remote the village, would always present themselves as more "developed" than villagers living even further from the capital city, Kathmandu. This is a perfect example of Irvine and Gal's *fractal recursivity*.

- *Erasure*. Language ideologies can render certain linguistic features, activities, or even people invisible. Irvine and Gal call this process *erasure*. In the Senegalese example described above, nineteenth-century linguists ignored or simplified complex grammatical features in Sereer because these complexities did not fit their preconceived notion of the language as "primitive." The multilingualism of many Senegalese at the time and the overlapping nature of the linguistic terrain were also subject to erasure by nineteenth-century linguists. Similarly, the monoglot ideology dominant in the United States makes the actual linguistic diversity of the country invisible – another example of erasure. "Because a linguistic ideology is a totalizing vision, elements that do not fit its interpretive structure – that cannot be seen to fit – must either be ignored or transformed," Irvine and Gal argue (2000:38).

In all three of these processes – iconization, fractal recursivity, and erasure – linguistic differentiation is interwoven with macro-level power dynamics. But power does not just operate at macro levels. In addition to the large-scale social, political, and historical processes that Errington, Irvine, and Gal analyze, relations of power also operate at the more micro levels of language. In a short but very helpful essay on power, Susan Philips (2001) argues that "in anthropology today, the constitution of social reality is itself considered a form of power. Within this view, the power of language lies in its reality-creating capacity" (2001:190). Philips identifies two other approaches to understanding the reality-creating power of language in addition to the language ideologies involved in the large-scale socio-historical processes described above: discourse and linguistic structure. First, she points to Capital-D Discourse, both in the sense of micro-level face-to-face interactions and also in Foucault's broader sense of discourse as a form of power to which we are all subordinated. Recent analyses of medical discourse by linguistic anthropologists provide good examples of how these two approaches can be merged to arrive at a better understanding of how globally circulating discursive forms and local discursive traditions intersect in actual clinical encounters (Wilce 2009:209).

Second, Philips points to the structure of language itself as an important location to study the reality-constituting power of language.

Chapter 4 described many examples of how grammatical categories and semantic domains within particular languages can predispose speakers of those languages to see or think about the world in specific ways. These three areas – socio-historical processes, discourse, and linguistic structure – are three important and interrelated sites for studying the power of language to constitute reality. Philips describes their interrelationship as follows: "[T]he creation of social realities through the deployment of language structures in discourse is the process through which broader socio-historical power relations are sustained and transformed through time" (2001:192).

Agency

With all the discussion in the foregoing pages of rather abstract, large-scale power relations, it is easy to lose sight of the fact that power is instantiated in the actions and words of actual people in real-life social settings. The concept of *agency* was developed by social theorists as a corrective to an over-emphasis on abstract social structures, and so we turn now to a discussion of agency, especially as it is enacted in and through language.[4]

Agency is itself an abstract concept that scholars often define inadequately, if at all, but it has nevertheless become a widely used term across the humanities and social sciences. Before turning to definitional issues, it is worthwhile to ask why so many scholars in so many fields are currently interested in the concept of agency. Ellen Messer-Davidow (1995:23) poses this question directly, asking, "Why agency now?" While there are undoubtedly many answers to this question, one is that there is a clear connection between the emergence of interest in approaches that foreground practice on the one hand, and the social movements of the 1960s and 1970s on the other (Ortner 1984:160). In addition, the social upheavals in central and eastern Europe in the late 1980s and early 1990s directly led many scholars to articulate more clearly their ideas about human agency and social structures (e.g., Sztompka 1991). As a result of witnessing or participating in actions aimed at transforming society, then, many academics began to investigate how linguistic and social practices can either reproduce or transform the very structures that shape them.

It is because questions about agency are so central to contemporary political and theoretical debates that the concept arouses so much interest – and why it is so crucial to define the term clearly. Let me therefore present a provisional definition: *Agency refers to the socioculturally mediated capacity to act.*

This barebones definition leaves a great deal unspecified, but it serves as a starting point for further elaboration of the concept. Scholars interested in the concept might ask the following kinds of questions in order to flesh out their particular usages more precisely:

1 Must all agency be human? Can nonhuman primates, machines, technologies, spirits, or signs exercise agency, as some researchers have suggested?
2 Must agency be individual, or can agency also be supra-individual – the property, perhaps, of families, faculties, institutions, or labor unions? Some scholars, such as Wertsch et al. (1993) and advocates of Actor Network Theory (ANT) such as Latour (2005), advocate a non-individualistic notion of agency. Drawing on Vygotsky (1978, 1987) and paraphrasing Bateson (1972), Wertsch et al., for example, argue that agency "extends beyond the skin" because it is frequently a property of groups and involves "mediational means" such as language and tools (Wertsch et al. 1993:352).
3 Conversely, can agency be sub-individual, as when someone feels torn within herself or himself – the property therefore of "dividuals," to borrow the term used by McKim Marriott, Val Daniel, Bonnie McElhinny, and others (Daniel 1984:42; Marriott 1976; McElhinny 1998:181)?
4 What does it mean to be an agent of *someone else*?
5 Must agency be conscious, intentional, or effective? What does it *mean* for an act to be conscious, intentional, or effective?

No matter how scholars choose to answer these questions, two oft-assumed synonyms for agency – "free will" and "resistance" – must immediately be ruled out if agency is understood as referring to the sociocultural capacity to act. First, agency cannot be considered a synonym for free will because such an approach ignores or only gives lip service to the social nature of agency and the pervasive influence of culture on human intentions, beliefs, and actions. Even Charles Taylor, a philosopher whose writings on language and agency are extremely thought provoking, locates agency inside the mental processes of particular individuals rather than within broader social processes when he connects agency with "second-order desires," "strong evaluation," and "a vocabulary of worth" (Taylor 1985). Similarly, Ludwig Wittgenstein, the famous philosopher of language to whom linguistic anthropologists increasingly look for inspiration, fails to theorize adequately the sociocultural nature of language and action. While Wittgenstein (1958) recognizes the degree to which language and social forms are intertwined, he leaves the details of this interrelationship unexplained. Practice theorist Anthony Giddens notes this shortcoming in Wittgenstein's work on language and action, stating, "Wittgensteinian philosophy has not led towards any sort of concern with social change, with power relations, or with conflict in society" (1979:50).

Second, agency should not be considered a straightforward synonym for resistance. Labeling as agency *only* those actions that resist the status quo is characteristic of the work of some anthropologists, many scholars in subaltern studies, and, until recently, most feminist theorists in a number of fields. According to these researchers, in order to demonstrate agency, a person must resist existing power differentials. While one can certainly understand the impulse behind equating agency with resistance, agency should not be reduced to it. Oppositional agency is only one of many forms of agency.

Cultural anthropologists and feminist theorists such as Saba Mahmood have recently been challenging this equation of agency with resistance. In her book on the women's mosque movement in Cairo, Egypt, Mahmood (2005) argues strongly for a notion of agency that does not unreflectively reproduce culturally specific Western notions of personhood, oppression, and freedom. I agree entirely with Mahmood when she writes, "I am not interested in offering *a* theory of agency, but rather I insist that the meaning of agency must be explored within the grammar of concepts within which it resides" (2005:34; emphasis in the original). Other feminist scholars have suggested that "negative agency" is an appropriate term to describe how some women, such as the Huli of Papua New Guinea, refuse "to use their bodily energies in the ways expected of them" (Wardlow 2006; cf. Kratz 2000). Given these cross-cultural variations in the nature and types of agency, anything more precise than a barebones definition of agency runs the risk of over-generalizing notions that are actually culturally or linguistically specific.

A central task for scholars is therefore to ask themselves how conceptions of agency may differ from society to society, and how these conceptions might be related to notions of personhood and causality. Andrew Pickering suggests that "within different cultures human beings and the material world might exhibit capacities for action quite different from those we customarily attribute to them" (1995:245). Robert Desjarlais presents an illustration of this within the United States itself in his study of a homeless shelter in Boston, in which he argues that the forms of agency he observed among the shelter's residents emerged out of a specific sociocultural context. Agency did not exist prior to that context, Desjarlais maintains, but arose from within the social, political, cultural, and linguistic dynamics of the homeless shelter during a particular time period (Desjarlais 1997:204). Likewise, among the Anakalang of Indonesia, Webb Keane notes, "The relevant locus of agency – living individual, disembodied ancestor, household, faction, clan, interclan alliance – is subject to ongoing construction and transformation … Much of the work of power aims at, and is registered in, such construction and transformation" (Keane 1997:7–8). Claudia Strauss (2007) offers another example of varying ideas about responsibility and agency in the wake of the 1999 Columbine High School shooting in Colorado, in which two students killed 12 other students, a teacher, and themselves. Strauss demonstrates that "the cultural model of persons as autonomous agents, while certainly very important in the contemporary United States, is just one of a number of cultural models Americans use to explain human action" (Strauss 2007:807–808).[5]

Many of the scholars who have written about agency have attempted to subdivide agency into different types or categories. Ortner, for example, proposes two different but closely interrelated types of agency: the agency of (unequal) power and the agency of projects. The first kind of agency involves domination or resistance to domination and is therefore to a large degree defined by the terms of the dominant group, while the second kind of agency "is about (relatively ordinary) life socially organized in terms of culturally constituted projects that infuse life with meaning and purpose" (2006b:147).

In agency of projects, Ortner directs us to look for how people attempt to sustain their own culturally constituted projects, often in the face of overwhelming power differentials in the form of colonialism or racism. Kockelman (2007) also identifies two types of agency: "residential agency" (involving power and choice) and "representational agency" (involving knowledge and consciousness). Likewise, Duranti (2004) has identified two different dimensions of agency in language: the performance of agency (which he subdivides further into "ego-affirming" and "act-constituting") and the grammatical encoding of agency.

All of these attempts to define, subdivide, and categorize types of agency are very useful for scholars interested in analyzing language. Duranti's two dimensions are particularly helpful. The first, the performance of agency, refers to the performative aspects of language that we discussed in chapter 8. The second, the grammatical encoding of agency, is also very important to understand, as it is central to questions of agency in language, and so we turn now to this topic.

The Grammatical Encoding of Agency

Any discussion of agency and language must consider how grammatical categories in different languages distinguish among types of subjects, actors, or agents, for as we saw in chapter 4, such categories, "to the extent that they are obligatory and habitual, and relatively inaccessible to the average speaker's consciousness, will form a privileged location for transmitting and reproducing cultural and social categories" (Hill and Mannheim 1992:387). While each language has its own set of linguistic resources that can be used to exercise, attribute, or deny agency, there are also some features that seem to be present in every language (Comrie 1981). According to R.M.W. Dixon (1994:6), for example, all languages work in terms of three basic relations – *S*, *A*, and *O* – defined as follows:

S – *S*ubject of an intransitive verb (e.g., *Sita* went to Kathmandu)
A – *A*gent, or subject, of a transitive verb (e.g., *Parvati* loves Shiva)
O – *O*bject of a transitive verb (e.g., Maya ate *rice*).

Semantically, there are various roles the subject of a sentence can take, such as the following (Duranti 1994:122–123; cf. Duranti 2004:460; Keenan [Ochs] 1984):

Agent	*Pabi* read the book
Actor	*Shiva* danced
Perceiver	*Tika* heard the news
Instrument	*The stone* broke the window
Patient/Undergoer	*The old woman* died.

These semantic roles can be treated in various ways grammatically. Defining the linguistic subject in a way that applies to all languages turns out to be a challenging and controversial topic over which linguists differ (Comrie 1981:98–101). In the majority of languages, including most of the languages of Europe, the subjects of transitive and intransitive verbs are treated the same way grammatically, while the object of a transitive verb is treated differently. This pattern is known as *accusativity*. In about a quarter of the world's languages, however, a complementary pattern obtains in which the subject of an intransitive verb and the object of a transitive verb are treated the same way syntactically, while the subject of a transitive verb is treated differently. This pattern is known as *ergativity* (Bittner and Hale 1996; Dixon 1994).[6] In ergative languages, there is usually a grammatical marker that distinguishes Agents (of transitive verbs) from Subjects (of intransitive verbs) and Objects (of transitive verbs). This results in the potential for very different notions of subjectivity obtaining in ergative and accusative languages. Whether or not these differences exist must be determined empirically, for there is no automatic correspondence between grammatical and social agency.

Some languages have "split" grammatical systems in which speakers follow an accusative pattern in some cases and an ergative pattern in other cases. A related sort of split appears in languages that have grammatical systems in which the subjects of some intransitive verbs are categorized with transitive subjects, while the subjects of other intransitive verbs are categorized with intransitive subjects. In Guaraní, for example, the word for "I" used with more agentive intransitive verbs, such as "go" and "get up," is the same word for "I" used with the transitive verb "bring" (Mithun 1991:511). A completely different word for "I" is used with less agentive intransitive verbs, such as "to be" – the same word that is used for the direct object pronoun "me." In these languages, attributions of agency are built right into their semantic and syntactic structures.

How can the grammatical details regarding Agent, Subject, and Object in particular languages be relevant to scholars interested in the social aspects of agency? Derbyshire (1987:319) reports that in many Amazonian languages, when a highly ranked person in a transitive clause is the subject, the accusative pattern is followed, whereas when the higher ranked person is the object, the ergative pattern is followed. In English, Marianne LaFrance (1992) has shown that when subjects are asked to supply plausible scenarios of events that might have preceded and followed a set of sentences alternating male and female subjects and objects, they demonstrate a linguistic bias against women that she calls "the disappearing agent effect." Her findings indicate that if a sentence is phrased such that a female is described as doing something or feeling something, especially with respect to a male, then she fades from causal view, but when she is on the receiving end of someone else's actions, then the subject or source of these events, rather than she herself, is highlighted (LaFrance 1992:341). While these responses were elicited rather than taken from naturally occurring conversations, an ethnographically informed investigation of this phenomenon would demonstrate exactly how these linguistic usages reflect, reinforce, and sometimes reconfigure status hierarchies in the society.

Alessandro Duranti's *From Grammar to Politics: Linguistic Anthropology in a Western Samoan Village* (1994) provides just such an ethnographically rich example of how attention to what may seem like highly technical, esoteric grammatical forms can shed light on human agency. Duranti maintains that the Samoans' use of ergative markers reveals how they attribute agency socially, especially in cases of praise or blame. Powerful individuals are more likely to use the ergative marker when they want to accuse someone of a malicious act, whereas less powerful individuals try to resist such accusations by suggesting alternative linguistic definitions of events. Duranti's "grammar of praising and blaming" demonstrates how agency is expressed in, and shaped by, the linguistic forms that a socially and linguistically embedded speaker uses. Through this sort of close linguistic analysis, the links between micro and macro levels of power and agency become evident.

Talk About Agency: Meta-Agentive Discourse

Another way of analyzing power and agency in language is to look for how people *talk about agency* – how they talk about their own actions and others' actions, how they attribute responsibility for events, how they describe their own and others' decision-making processes. I have long been fascinated by this kind of talk about agency – what I have called "meta-agentive discourse," piggybacking onto the term "meta-pragmatic discourse," as used by Michael Silverstein (1976, 1993, 2001), Debra Spitulnik (2001), and others. Such talk about agency can be found in everyday mundane conversations, in narratives and life stories, in politicians' speeches, and in many other oral and written genres, including Nepali love letters, which we will discuss further below. Meta-agentive discourse can also be found in scholars' own writings (this book included, of course).

Analyzing this meta-agentive discourse can provide insight into people's own theories of agency. An example of such work can be found in Christopher McCollum's (2000) study of two different kinds of narratives he elicited from middle-class couples in the United States: (1) how they ended up with their current romantic partners, and (2) how they ended up in their current careers. In the first type of narrative, people often presented the process by which they met and fell in love with their current romantic partners as one involving fate or chance. They just happened to go to a singles bar or answer a personal ad, they claimed, even though they "had not been looking" to get involved with anyone. In the second type of narrative, in contrast, the same individuals presented themselves as much more agentive in the process of arriving at their current professional position. They told of making active choices to major in a particular subject or apply for a certain job, even though there may have been at least some degree of luck or privilege involved in who mentored them, where they went to school, and how they happened to be hired at one place rather than another. A close analysis of meta-agentive discourse can thus bring to light differences in people's theories of agency in various areas of their lives.

Another example of how a study of meta-agentive discourse, combined with a grammatical analysis and grounded in long-term ethnographic research, can provide a deeper understanding of people's conceptualizations of their own and others' actions comes from my own work on love-letter writing in Nepal (Ahearn 2001a, 2008). As I noted briefly in chapter 7, love-letter writing only became possible in the Nepali village of Junigau in the 1990s because it was during that decade that most of the young women became literate, and they put their literacy skills to an unexpected use: writing love letters. The letters were about much more than love, however; they were saturated with "development discourse" (cf. Escobar 1995; Pigg 1992, 1996). The practice of sending and receiving of love letters came to be interpreted by Junigau residents in the 1990s as indexing a certain kind of person – a "developed" (*bikāsi*) person as opposed to a "backward" (*pichhyāDi*) person (and they used these exact terms).

Many social, economic, and political changes were taking place in Nepal in general and Junigau in particular during the 1990s. For our purposes here, the most relevant changes came in the ways that people conceptualized causality or responsibility for events – in other words, their theories of agency. To oversimplify quite a bit but to give a basic idea of the trend, more and more Junigau residents in the 1990s attributed events to particular individuals rather than to fate. This trend was not unidirectional, nor was it without complexities, as we shall see in the letters of Shila and Vajra excerpted below, but the trend was very evident, both to villagers themselves, who commented explicitly on the change during the years I lived in the village.

Before presenting some of Shila and Vajra's love letters, some background on their relationship is important.[7] I met Shila on the very first day I arrived in Junigau in 1982. At that time she was a lively, skinny, mischievous little girl of 12 or so who had long since been pulled out of school in order to help her widowed mother. From time to time Shila would attend evening female literacy classes, but often she was kept busy at home or in the fields. I met Vajra a few days after my arrival in Junigau when I started teaching at the village school. He was one of my brightest students in seventh grade English, and he eventually went on to study at the campus in the district center. In those years I never imagined that the studious, painfully shy Vajra and the vivacious, popular Shila would ever be attracted to each other. Nevertheless, by the summer of 1990, when they were both in their early twenties, it was clear to everyone in the village, including me, that they were courting.

Vajra and Shila had known each other their whole lives, but both say that it was only after they worked together on the construction of a youth club building in 1990 that they began to notice each other. In a December 1992 interview, Vajra described how afraid he used to be of girls and women; if one accidentally brushed against him, he said, he felt a current (*karant*) of electricity. Eventually, however, as his parents increased their pressure on him to marry, Vajra started thinking of what kind of person he would like his life friend (*lāiph phrend*) to be. In explaining how his courtship with Shila got started, however, Vajra eschewed agency, instead claiming that love "just happens" to people. In the same conversation, Vajra then went on to describe a phenomenon I have heard echoed in many villagers' accounts of how they started their courtships. Infatuation starts with a *dekhā dekh* – an exchange of glances. No one has to *do* anything. Thus, the village agentive theory regarding romantic love is that it is something that happens *to* people rather than something for which they themselves are responsible. Love, like other types of emotion, "befalls" or "is felt by" people (*lāgyo*). In this respect, Junigau residents' approach to agency (or lack thereof) in the realm of love resembles the research by McCollum summarized above for couples in the United States.

By the end of summer in 1990 there were many public occasions at which Shila and Vajra were quite evidently exchanging more than glances. Shila was usually the aggressor at these events, mercilessly teasing Vajra when he declined to dance or was too shy to even look at her. Shila wrote the following letter to Vajra right around this time in their courtship:[8]

> Mother's Brother's Son, why have we started to love and love each other, have such affection for each other? I can't figure out why. Why, oh, why? If I don't see you, this heart/mind of mine starts to worry even more: where will I see you? Where will I meet you? What is that, what is that? I don't know myself .... In this life of [seemingly] two days' length, it seems to me [that one is always asking] when and how. It seems that what one says won't necessarily happen.[9]
>
> Sometimes sunshine, sometimes rain; sometimes a river flows, sometimes it dries up. Sometimes laughter, sometimes tears; sometimes suffering, sometimes joy. This is what a person's life is like. Once a person has

> been born, s/he must do all kinds of things, but even ....? And I ....? Maybe it's because I'm extremely unlucky, I don't know – why is it that really bad things always come to me? Even when I do something well, it turns out badly. If I speak well, it comes out wrong. And to you I speak extremely badly, don't I? You might say that it doesn't seem so to you. But how meanly I have treated you! And while speaking to you, how I have spit upon you! How meanly I have treated you and spoken to you, you probably thought, haven't you ....?
>
> But don't think that way, okay? No, then again, for whatever reason when I say to myself that I won't say it, then just like that, from my mind and mouth .... [your] name comes out. Why is it that when I say I won't say something, it comes out of this mouth of mine anyway? It probably has made you extremely angry, right? ...
>
> .... May we be successful, I say. What is your wish ....? Of course, even when there are wishes and desires, no one knows anything about the time and circumstances under which they will be fulfilled.
>
> But some people say that if it's their lot in life, [whatever it is] they'll do it. But it seems to me that it's up to each person's own wishes .... Even without my telling you this, you would be knowledgeable about it.

In a close analysis I conducted recently of Shila and Vajra's letters, I found a gendered difference in their conceptions of their own and others' actions – both in their explicit talk about agency in their letters and in their implicit grammatical choices. While they both mix individualistic and fatalistic notions of action in their letters, as Shila does in the letter quoted above, Shila tends to emphasize the more fatalistic notions and tends to claim that it is not possible to achieve what one wants to achieve in life. Vajra, on the other hand, often states that any and all obstacles can be overcome. Listen to just a few examples of the many that contain meta-agentive discourse in the letters – first, two from Shila's letters:

Here is an example from a letter written by Shila in July 1990 (Letter #18, 2047–4–8):[10]

> But what to do? A person probably doesn't get to survive just because s/he says, 'I will survive,' and a person probably doesn't get to die just

> because s/he says, 'I will die.' And so, even though I've said, 'I'm an unfortunate one; I'll die,' I haven't been able to die. How very, very much suffering and sadness, how many thousands of troubles and difficulties, how many thousands of obstacles I've borne! And even though they have burnt up this heart/mind inside me and turned it into ashes and stones, I find that I'm obliged to go on living in this human world......? Let's see what this human world will be, ..., I write. If whatever one said became true, I would .... you today. What to do? It seems to me that whatever one says does not necessarily become true.

And here is another excerpt from a letter written by Shila in September 1990 (Letter #27, 2047–6–12):

> I find that the world is like this: how many wishes, how many desires, how many interests, how many hopes there keep on being, but – what to do? – because of conditions and obstacles they get lost by themselves. And yet I find that it's necessary to go on living. You'll probably say, "What kinds of conditions and obstacles are there, after all?" you'll probably say, but – what to do? – it's not possible to cut one's chest open to show the obstacles and conditions that have arisen.

And indeed, Vajra writes frequently of being able to overcome all obstacles and of his belief that nothing was impossible. Here is an excerpt from a letter that Vajra wrote in June 1990 (Letter #12, 2047–3):

> Because one is human, one has to do all kinds of things – one has to walk, one has to talk. Why wouldn't all kinds of circumstances befall one in whatever group/class?? In that way, one has to be able to become part of one's family/race/group. That alone is called a human life. Whoever can mold time and circumstances during one's own lifetime – that alone is the human condition.
>
> These days nothing is impossible in this world. A person can do anything. I offer a prayer today to Shree Pashupatibaba that just as our love develops more and more fully, so too may it grow and develop fully in the future, may it be able to blossom and blossom. I also say today that love is for the purpose of spending one's whole life together forever; [I don't say that love is] for the purpose of separation.

And here are excerpts from two different letters that he wrote in August 1990 (Letter #21, 2047–4–15; and Letter #22, 2047–4–25):

> It seems to me that if anyone challenges us, we shouldn't retreat/run away; rather, after we show that person, s/he will give up. To laugh and to talk is in the nature of human beings. In the face of pure love, any power in the world must go down to defeat in the end, as much love as there is.
>
> Whenever doing anything some obstacles will always arise, but just because those obstacles arise, should we not do it? It will be necessary to complete the work with a lot of effort in order to overcome those obstacles. After beginning any kind of work, it will certainly be completed in the end; it shouldn't be left off in the middle. It must be completed. With any kind of work, what kind of circumstance is it if one talks and talks about it, then leaves it off in the middle without finishing it? Looking at what kind of manner that is, [it looks] so bad.

In Vajra's letters, therefore, we see a theory of agency that leans toward attributing to people in general and certainly to himself and Shila the ability to achieve their goals and to overcome any obstacles that arise. In Shila's letters, in contrast, there are more mentions of limitations, constraints, and fate. Many of the statements of both Vajra and Shila are gendered in very interesting ways. Although this is a partial analysis, what is clear is that there is a definite difference in Shila and Vajra's meta-agentive discourse in the letters. Their explicit remarks about their own and others' capacity to act in the world are indeed quite different.

Power and Agency in/through/by/of Language

As we have seen in this chapter and throughout the book, when language use is considered a form of social action, issues surrounding power and agency become central. When clear definitions of these concepts are provided, social theory can have direct relevance to the study of language in real-life social contexts. The work of social theorists such as Pierre Bourdieu, Sherry Ortner, Raymond Williams, and

Michel Foucault, for example, can help to deepen linguistic analyses of actual interactions. In turn, these kinds of close studies of language use can illuminate for social theorists the ways in which large-scale power relations emerge from micro-level communicative events.

The 12 chapters of this book, organized into three parts, have each demonstrated the benefits of treating language use as a form of social action that is embedded in relations of power. In the introductory chapter, four key terms were presented to help elucidate the linguistic anthropological approach to language: *multifunctionality*, *language ideologies*, *practice*, and *indexicality*. These terms have acted as a set of lenses through which the topics covered in the 12 chapters of the book could be viewed. The first part of the book, "Language: Some Basic Questions," introduced methods and approaches undergirding linguistic anthropology, focusing in particular on how linguistic anthropologists carry out their research (chapter 2), how they study language acquisition and socialization in children, adolescents, and adults (chapter 3), and how they understand the complex ways in which language, thought, and culture are related (chapter 4).

In the second part of the book, "Communities of Speakers, Hearers, Readers, and Writers," the emergent nature of communities of practice provided a starting point for discussions of speech communities (chapter 5), multilingual communities (chapter 6), literacy practices within various communities around the world (chapter 7), and the importance of performance and performativity for the constitution of communities (chapter 8).

In the final part of the book, "Language, Power, and Social Differentiation," the ways in which language use is enmeshed with relations of power and agency were made explicit by focusing on language and gender (chapter 9), language, race, and ethnicity (chapter 10), language endangerment and death (chapter 11), and language power, and agency (chapter 12).

What I hope has become increasingly clear throughout the book is that linguistic anthropology as a discipline provides scholars in many different fields who are interested in social and linguistic practices with the analytical tools and insights for investigations that extend far beyond any given utterance. As diverse and as open to borrowing from other disciplines as the field is, linguistic anthropologists share a commitment to *language as a non-neutral medium* (Duranti forthcoming).

As the Russian literary critic M.M. Bakhtin famously noted, "The word in language is half someone else's … Language is not a neutral medium that passes freely and easily into the private property of the speaker's intentions; it is populated – overpopulated – with the intentions of others" (1981a:293–294). Understanding the complex and inherently social nature of language requires an approach that takes into account the ways in which linguistic practices and language ideologies both shape and reflect power relations, cultural identities, and social norms. Linguistic anthropology provides such an approach to "living language."

Notes

Chapter 1 The Socially Charged Life of Language

1 This incident is taken from Bucholtz (2007:243–244). The names used are pseudonyms, most of which were chosen by the participants themselves.
2 The case of Taiap's endangered status is analyzed in Kulick (1992).
3 A more deeply contextualized analysis of this ritual can be found in Ahearn (2001a:90–93).
4 The soup bowl analogy is taken from McDermott and Tylbor (1995). For illuminating discussions of context, see the various contributions to Duranti and Goodwin (1992).
5 Such an approach is *in itself* an act that is thoroughly embedded in a historically specific, socially influenced understanding of language. As Michael Silverstein (2006:276) notes: "The carving out and theoretical stabilization of *langue* [language considered as an abstract set of grammatical rules] from among all the partial facts of language in use has been, to be sure, a Western cultural project of immense importance to vast projects of domination and control of 'nature,' of people, of communication, and of the legitimation of certain qualities of mind at the expense of others."
6 Indeed, to look only at decontextualized, abstract grammar, according to Asif Agha, amounts to "fetishizing restricted data about fragments of language" (2007:8). "As with any fad," Agha writes, "the time for this one has come and gone" (Agha 2007:7). Michael Tomasello, a cognitive psychologist and the co-director of the Max Planck Institute for

Evolutionary Anthropology agrees: "Universal grammar was a good try," he states, "and it really was not so implausible at the time it was proposed, but since then we have learned a lot about many different languages, and they simply do not fit one universal cookie cutter" (Tomasello 2005:641). Nicholas Evans and Stephen Levinson (2009) argue in convincing detail that there are "vanishingly few," if any, true universals across all languages and that in fact diversity itself, present at every level of linguistic organization, may be the only universally shared aspect of all languages. "The claims of Universal Grammar," Evans and Levinson write, "are either empirically false, unfalsifiable, or misleading in that they refer to tendencies rather than strict universals" (2009:429).

7 These abbreviations, copied from an actual pattern for an Irish knit sweater, are probably as foreign to non-knitters as linguists' jargon is to non-linguists. A brief gloss of the abbreviations is as follows: k = knit stitch; p = purl stitch; T R = twist to the right; T L = twist to the left.

8 Of Madame Defarge's knitted list of names and crimes, her husband remarks: "It would be easier for the weakest poltroon that lives, to erase himself from existence, than to erase one letter of his name or crimes from the knitted register of Madame Defarge" (Dickens 2000 [1859]:179).

9 Jakobson borrowed the term "phatic" from the famous social anthropologist Bronislaw Malinowski, who coined it in a 1923 essay, "The Problem of Meaning in Primitive Languages," where he defined "phatic communion" as follows: "There can be no doubt that we have here a new type of linguistic use – *phatic communion* I am tempted to call it, actuated by the demon of terminological invention – a type of speech in which ties of union are created by a mere exchange of words … Once more language appears to us in this function not as an instrument of reflection but as a mode of action" (Malinowski 1994[1923]:10).

10 Language ideologies have also been called linguistic ideologies and ideologies of language. There are subtle differences in the intellectual histories of these terms, but in the interests of consistency and simplicity, I will refer only to language ideologies here.

11 The section on practice is adapted from Ahearn (2001a).

12 Some of the social theorists most commonly associated with practice theory are Pierre Bourdieu, Michel de Certeau, Anthony Giddens, Sherry Ortner, and Marshall Sahlins. Within linguistic anthropology, Bonnie McElhinny and Shaylih Muehlmann have written about "discursive practice theory" (McElhinny and Muehlmann 2006), and William Hanks proposes a "practice approach to language" (Hanks 2005).

13 Peirce's semiotics consists of far more than this tripartite typology, but to do justice to his wide-ranging philosophy would take up the rest of this book (and then some). For lucid explanations of Peirce's philosophy and for analyses that are influenced by Peirce, see the work of Vincent Colapietro, E. Valentine Daniel, Webb Keane, Paul Kockelman, Elizabeth Mertz, Richard Parmentier, Michael Silverstein, and James M. Wilce.

14 For this reason, such words are sometimes called "shifters" (Silverstein 1976).

Chapter 2 The Research Process in Linguistic Anthropology

1 For more information on grounded theory, see Glaser (1992), Strauss (1987), and Morse et al. (2009).

2 Bernard (2006:451–453) distinguishes between qualitative or quantitative *data* and qualitative or quantitative *analysis*. Thus, data, according to Bernard, can be either qualitative or quantitative in nature and can be analyzed either qualitatively or quantitatively. While this distinction might be useful for certain kinds of research, for our purposes here it is helpful to make a more basic distinction between research that involves the counting of something (quantitative) and research that does not (qualitative).

3 Sometimes participant observation is called "doing ethnography" (though "ethnography" is a term that literally refers to the writing about various peoples or ethnic groups). "Ethnographic research," a phrase and approach increasingly popular in fields outside anthropology, can refer to many different kinds of research methods, usually including participant observation.

4 What to call the people anthropologists study has become a controversial issue. In the past, many cultural anthropologists used the term "informants," but this term has fallen out of favor among many scholars because of its negative connotations. Instead, some anthropologists use "research subjects," "research participants," "consultants," or "interlocutors." In more participatory research, the term "collaborators" is sometimes used. Some scholars prefer not to use any of these labels, instead referring to specific individuals by name or to groups of individuals as "the residents of X" or "the people with whom I spoke." The controversy surrounding these terms relates to ethical issues that will be discussed further below.

5 It is estimated that up to 40 percent of the world's languages will disappear in the next hundred years (Harrison 2007). We will explore the complex issues surrounding language death later in the book.

6 A fascinating story on National Public Radio's show Morning Edition about research documenting "linguistic profiling" provides an example of a variation on the matched guise test method to determine racial prejudice based on how someone speaks: www.npr.org/templates/story/story.php?storyId=1128513, accessed November 8, 2010.
7 See the special issue of *American Ethnologist* from November 2006 for a group of articles on how IRB review has affected cultural anthropologists.
8 www.aaanet.org/committees/ethics/ethcode.htm, accessed November 8, 2010
9 www.aaanet.org/committees/ethics/ethcode.htm, accessed November 8, 2010
10 Examples of case studies involving ethical dilemmas anthropologists have faced can be found on the AAA's website at www.aaanet.org/committees/ethics/ethical_currents.htm, accessed November 8, 2010.
11 Sometimes also called "engaged" or "public" anthropology, applied research is that which is not mainly for the purposes of increasing knowledge about a subject but rather is in the service of some institution or group of people, such as a nonprofit organization, a multinational corporation, a community group, or a Native American tribe. The distinction between "applied" and "pure" research is historically contingent, however, and has been called into question as either dated, irrelevant, or misleading. Edelman and Haugerud (2005:2), for example, write: "Mostly gone are musty oppositions between 'applied' and 'mainstream' or 'academic' anthropology."

Chapter 3 Language Acquisition and Socialization

1 Ochs and Schieffelin were not creating a subfield out of thin air, of course. In their entry on language acquisition in the *Encyclopedia of Language and Education* (Ochs and Schieffelin 2008), they survey some of the early cross-cultural work on the development of communicative competence in children and discuss how it influenced their formulation of a new field of research.
2 An ergative marker is a particle that is placed on the subject of a transitive verb. The subject of an intransitive verb has no such marking.
3 Don Kulick returned recently to Gapun, however, and reported that the teenagers he saw there appeared to be speaking a version of Taiap that they adapted and simplified within their adolescent peer groups

(Kulick, personal communication). Kulick plans to investigate this interesting development in a future trip to Gapun.

4 The transcription conventions Mertz uses include underlining for emphasis, measurements of pauses in parentheses in hundredths of seconds, a period within parentheses for a very short pause, and double brackets for backchannel sounds such as laughter.

Chapter 4 Language, Thought, and Culture

1 This semiotic approach owes much to the work of Charles Sanders Peirce, whose tripartite concept of the linguistic sign and contributions to our understanding of indexicality were introduced in chapter 1.

2 See Lucy (1992) for a detailed review of the contributions of Boas, Sapir, and Whorf to scholarship on the relationship of language to thought and culture.

3 See Malotki (1983) and Duranti (1997:61) for challenges to Whorf's claims, and see Lucy (1996:43) for a rebuttal.

4 The difficult and politically charged nature of distinguishing languages from dialects will be discussed in chapter 6.

5 See Geoff Pullum's (1991) book for an amusing essay that builds upon Martin's article. There are also numerous postings regarding "snowclones" ("just as the Eskimos have N words for snow, so the X (should) have M words for Y") on the Language Log blog: http://languagelog.ldc.upenn.edu/nll, accessed November 20, 2010. As the many insightful postings on this blog indicate, Martin's debunking of this myth more than 20 years ago has failed to stanch the flow of ill-conceived references to "Eskimo words for snow."

6 See Silverstein (1985) for a discussion of how changing language ideologies over the centuries led to the dropping of "thou/thee." Also, while most Southerners consider "y'all" to be plural only and consider Northerners' usages of the term to refer to only one person clear indications of their outsider status, some linguists have presented more complex views of "y'all" (also spelled "ya'll") in actual discourse (Ching 2001) and as a vocative (Hyman 2006).

7 Kay and Maffi (1999) argue that these languages are at the earliest point in the evolutionary development of color terminology. Their assumption is that as these languages change over time, they will begin to partition the color domain, and they will do so in the order that Kay and others have suggested. See Everett (2005:627–628) for

a description of the apparent lack of color terms in Pirahã; and Deutscher (2010:41ff.) for an overview of the work of a "boldly original" thinker, Lazarus Geiger, who proposed a color sequence in 1867 that was remarkably similar to the one that Berlin and Kay proposed a hundred years later.

8 These scholars are quick to claim, however, that Whorfian effects are not without an underlying foundation of universality, as these two passages illustrate: (1) "We take our present findings to be compatible with such Whorfian results, provided one allows that the variation of category boundaries itself is constrained by universal forces" (Regier et al. 2005:8390). (2) "These judgments were shown to be influenced by language-specific lexical boundaries in a comparison of English speakers with speakers of Tarahumara, an unaffiliated language of Mexico that lacks a lexical distinction between green and blue. Demonstrations such as these, which show that differences in color naming between languages can influence nonlinguistic behavior toward colors should not, however, be taken as evidence that color naming varies without constraint across the world's languages" (Kay 2005:51).

9 Cf. Levinson (1996, 2003a, 2003b); Levinson and Wilkins (2006); and Evans (2010:163–169).

10 Levinson's research has been challenged by Li and Gleitman (2002), who claim to have been able to induce both absolute and relative responses in a group of American college students by manipulating the conditions of the task. Levinson's (2003a:40–41) rebuttal to Li and Gleitman not only chastises them for their naive assumptions ("Simple Nativism") regarding linguistic diversity and cognitive universalism but also asserts that Li and Gleitman were invoking an "intrinsic" response, not an absolute one with their manipulations. See Levinson (2003b:197–206) and Levinson et al. (2002) for a description of the follow-up experiments Levinson and his colleagues conducted to refute Li and Gleitman's claims.

11 The // symbol in Hai//om indicates a lateral click sound similar to what a rider might say to a horse before saying "giddy up" (Evans 2010:243).

12 Bowerman (1996); Bowerman and Choi (2003); McDonough et al. (2003).

13 See Lucy (1992, 1996, 1997); Lucy and Gaskins (2003).

14 See the commentators at the end of Everett's (2005) *Current Anthropology* article and Nevins et al. (2007) for some responses to Everett's claims. For Everett's rebuttal to Nevins et al. (2007), see Everett (2007).

Chapter 5 Communities of Language Users

1 Gumperz's definition of "speech community" has evolved over the years. For an overview of the development of this concept in his thinking, see Patrick (2002:579–582), Duranti (1997:72–83), and Gumperz (1996:362–364). Other helpful overviews and critiques of the concept of speech community include Irvine (1987), Morgan (2004), and Rampton (2000).

2 See Ahearn (2001a) for a very different approach to analyzing love letters. Whereas Santa Ana and Parodí use hypothetical love letters that were written specifically for the study using two different writing styles in order to elicit judgments about formal or informal registers, my own study involved the analysis of actual love letters in their real-life social and linguistic contexts. In order to conduct this kind of research, ethnographic methods such as participant observation were essential. Santa Ana and Parodí, like other sociolinguists, ask different research questions and employ different research methods in their attempts to answer their questions.

3 See also Gomez-Imbert (1996) for a piece on linguistic relativity in the multilingual setting of the Vaupés that in many respects echoes, but in some areas also departs from, Jackson's analysis.

4 On the distinction between *Sprachbund* and *Sprechbund*, see Jackson (1974:55), Gal (2006:182), and Patrick (2002:584).

5 Within linguistic anthropology, the field of language and gender research has most wholeheartedly embraced the notion of community of practice for reasons suggested by Miriam Meyerhoff (2002:539).

Chapter 6 Multilingualism and Globalization

1 These are all real people, though I have used pseudonyms here. All have given permission to have their linguistic biographies summarized here.

2 Because "multilingual" refers to the use of two or more languages, in the remainder of the chapter I use it instead of the more cumbersome phrase "bilingual or multilingual" to refer to any individual who speaks more than one language and any community in which more than one language is spoken.

3 For an account of the search for the originator of this famous aphorism, see the Wikipedia article on the topic at http://en.wikipedia.org/wiki/A_language_is_a_dialect_with_an_army_and_navy, accessed August 13, 2009.

4 The data reported in this paragraph all come from the US Census Bureau's 2000 census. All of the information the Census Bureau collected about language use and proficiency is self-reported and should therefore be interpreted with caution. The US census, like all censuses, is also the subject of debates and controversies regarding its methods and analyses. The Modern Language Association (MLA) has used the information collected by the US Census Bureau on language to create a series of interactive maps of the United States, available online at www.mla.org/map_main, accessed November 22, 2010.

5 These languages are Assamese, Bengali, Bodo, Dogri, Gujarati, Hindi, Kannada, Kashmiri, Konkani, Maithili, Malayalam, Manipuri, Marathi, Nepali, Oriya, Punjabi, Sanskrit, Santhali, Sindhi, Tamil, Telugu, and Urdu (Government of India, Ministry of Law and Justice 2007:330, *Constitution of India*, Articles 344 and 351).

6 Notice that the use of "code" in this term sidesteps the need to decide whether a particular way of speaking constitutes a language or not. The term can therefore be used to describe shifts between or among languages, dialects, registers, or any other speech varieties (Romaine 2001:523).

7 Chelsea Booth (personal communication, October 1, 2009). See also Booth (2009a, 2009b).

8 Some scholars, including Auer, omit the hyphen in "code-switching," so I have retained Auer's usage when quoting him directly.

9 For an interesting overview of the controversy surrounding the authorship of works attributed to Bakhtin and others in his circle, and for a comparison between differing emphases placed on aspects of Bakhtin's work by Russian as opposed to European and US scholars, see Steinglass (1998).

Chapter 7 Literacy Practices

1 This passage is adapted from Ahearn (2001b:58-60). More information about changing courtship and marriage practices in Nepal, including love-letter writing, can be found in that book. All the names mentioned in this passage are pseudonyms.

2 The Nepali legal code requires the informed consent of both the bride and the groom. See Gilbert (1992:748). In practice, however, arranged marriage brides in Junigau in the 1980s and 1990s were rarely even informed of their impending marriages, never mind asked to consent. For more about consent and coercion in Junigau marriages, see Ahearn (1994).

3 Widowhood in Junigau and elsewhere in South Asia is often extremely stigmatized. Unlike in more orthodox, high-caste Hindu villages, widows

in Junigau do sometimes remarry, especially if they are young and childless. Nevertheless, remarriage does not erase the stigma of widowhood. See Bennett (1983) and Galvin (2006) on the status of widows in Nepal.

4 See Besnier (1995), Brandt and Clinton (2002), Collins (1995), Collins and Blot (2003), Gee (2008), Reder and Davila (2005), and Street (2003) for excellent reviews and critiques of this debate. The first part of the overview that follows here is adapted from Ahearn (2001a:46–48).

5 Even Collins and Blot, who criticize some of the early works of scholars such as Heath, are nevertheless extravagant in their praise of Heath's book: "*Ways with Words* is a major accomplishment, one that has yet to be surpassed in depth or influence" (2003:44). The original article was: Heath, S.B. (1982) What no bedtime story means: narrative skills at home and school. *Language in Society* 11(1):49–76.

6 This section is adapted from Ahearn (2001a).

7 That Junigau villagers themselves use such dichotomies as developed/backward or modern/traditional speaks to the complexities and ironies inherent in what Gupta (1998) calls "the postcolonial condition." As Stacy Pigg notes, "Whether or not this [traditional/modern] dichotomy serves us well in social analysis, the fact is that these terms are thriving in the world we aim to describe and interpret. We need, then, to track the terms of the discourse of modernity as people adopt, deploy, modify, and question it" (Pigg 1996:163–4). See also Collier (1997:213) on how "modernity" and "tradition," are best seen as subtraditions of a wider post-Enlightenment European culture.

8 "Actor network theory" is sometimes also called "actant network theory" (both phrases are written alternately with one, two, or no hyphens), "enrolment theory," or "the sociology of translation." For a set of clarifications or responses from Bruno Latour to common misunderstandings of ANT see Latour (1998). Here Latour states, "There is no model of (human) actor in ANT nor any basic list of competences that have to be set at the beginning because the human, the self and the social actor of traditionnal [sic] social theory is not on its agenda."

Chapter 8 Performance, Performativity, and the Constitution of Communities

1 Taken verbatim from www.betteratenglish.com/real-english-conversations-noisy-neighbors, accessed November 10, 2009.

2 www.msnbc.msn.com/id/25188169, accessed November 10, 2009.

3 www.washingtonpost.com/wp-dyn/content/article/2006/04/27/AR2006042702505.html, accessed November 10, 2009.
4 In Searle's later work, he changed "representatives" to "assertives" (Searle and Vanderveken 1985). See Duranti (1997:223ff.) for an explanation of these five categories and a critique of speech act theory.
5 For an important anthology on context, see Duranti and Goodwin (1992).
6 Actually, "pointed" is probably too mild a term for the Searle–Derrida debate, which is widely noted for the hostility and derision expressed on both sides. As Gayatri Spivak, a translator of Derrida and a famous post-colonial scholar in her own right, put it, Searle uses a "tone of high disdain" when replying to Derrida, while Derrida puts on a "mocking show of elaborate patience" (1980:29) and engages in "high class tomfoolery" in response (1980:45).
7 Note that the spelling of this word is *différance*, not *différence*.
8 Derrida quotes the entire short fable by Kafka in his own essay. See Derrida (1992:183–184).
9 Butler is notorious for her jargon, and "chiasmically" is just one example. Because I dislike using such inaccessible and sometimes off-putting terms, let me try to define "chiasmically" here. "Chiasma" (or just "chiasm," with an adjectival form of "chiasmic" or "chiastic") is a term that originates with the Greek letter Chi, or "X," and refers to a crossing over. The term is used in biology to indicate the crossing over of something like the nerves within the optic nerve, or the crossing over of genetic material between chromosomes. "Chiasma" is also a literary term that refers to an inverted parallelism within a verse of poetry or the Bible, for example, or within an entire literary work. A structure such as ABC – CBA, for example, would be a chiasma. Robert Alter, the famous literary critic of the Bible, identifies many chiasms (he uses the shorter term) in the Bible (Alter 1987), such as in Genesis, where there is light in darkness and darkness in light (Fokkelman 1987:60), or in the Hebrew play on words in Ecclesiastes 7:1, *shem tov mi-shemen tov* – "A good name is better than precious ointment" (Williams, J.G. 1987:279–280).

Having defined certain aspects of the term "chiasma," however, it is still not entirely clear what Butler means when she says that performance and performativity are related "chiasmically," though it appears to have something to do with the complex relationship between language and the body. Thus, in *Undoing Gender*, Butler clarifies the remark I have quoted in the text: "In my view, performativity is not just about speech acts. It is also about bodily acts. The relation between the two is complicated, and I called it a "chiasmus" in *Bodies that Matter*. There is always a dimension of bodily life that cannot be fully represented, even as it works as the condition and activating condition of language" (Butler 2004:198–199).

10 An excellent analysis of the concept of emergence can be found in Mannheim and Tedlock (1995:8–15). Other perspectives can be found in Bauman (2001[1975]); Bauman and Briggs (1990); Caton (1990: 260–261); Mayr (1982); Sherzer (1990:10); Urban (1991:23–28); and Williams, R. (1977:123).

11 See Ahearn (1998) for the complete Nepali and English lyrics, and for a much fuller analysis of both the lyrics and details of the performance and performers. The summary presented here borrows directly from that article in some places and diverges from it in others. For another analysis of Tij songfests from a different part of Nepal where women composed their own song lyrics and were incorporating explicitly political ideas into their Tij songs, see Holland and Skinner (1995).

12 Red powder, or *sindur*, is placed in the part of a woman's hair at a crucial moment in the wedding ceremony.

13 In this bitter accusation the woman uses the honorific form of "you" to address her father, even though she used the more familiar (but not the lowest) form when questioning her father earlier in the song.

14 See my other ethnographic work for more details on gender relations in Junigau (Ahearn 1994, 2001a).

15 I have attended Tij songfests several times since 1996, and this sort of displacement has occurred frequently. Unlike women in other Nepali villages, the women in Junigau have not banned alcohol – a popular goal of many women's groups during the ten-year Maoist insurgency (1996–2006).

Chapter 9 Language and Gender

1 These conversations from Baxter (2006:164, 170) were excerpted and discussed in Cameron (2007b:61ff.). Single brackets indicate overlapping utterances.

2 The Chicago Manual of Style Online, section 5.43. At www.chicagomanualofstyle.org/ch05/ch05_sec043.html, accessed June 1, 2010.

3 Note that the words with the masculine symbol directly following them have masculine grammatical forms in the original Hebrew or Arabic.

4 See Deutscher (2010:194–216) for an overview of research by Susan Ervin-Tripp, Lera Boroditsky, Lauren Schmidt, and Toshi Konishi on the ways in which grammatical gender can influence thought.

5 Mark Liberman wrote many posts on the invalidity of Brizendine's statistics on Language Log. A representative post is this one from December 11, 2006: "Sex Differences in 'Communication Events' Per Day?" accessed at http://158.130.17.5/~myl/languagelog/archives/003894.html on April 27, 2010. Deborah Cameron also reviews the Brizendine controversy in her book, *The Myth of Mars and Venus: Do Men and Women Really Speak Different Languages?* (Cameron 2007:19–20).

6 Cameron uses "=" as the symbol for latching. Square brackets indicate overlapping utterances. A period within parentheses indicates a pause.

7 Hall's transcription conventions are described in Hall (1995:211) and include hhh for exhalations (the more *h's*, the longer the exhalation), ... hhh for inhalations (again, the more *h's*, the longer the inhalation), lengths of pauses in tenths of seconds within single parentheses, a hyphen for short pauses of less than 0.2 seconds, double parentheses for nonverbal movements and extra-linguistic commentary, underlining for syllabic stress, and rising arrows for higher pitch. Hall uses no capitalization in the utterances she transcribes.

8 Underlined utterances were spoken in Taiap, the indigenous language. Non-underlined utterances were spoken in Tok Pisin, the national language of Papua New Guinea. Brackets contain situational context and nonverbal actions.

Chapter 10 Language, Race, and Ethnicity

1 These paragraphs are taken from the American Anthropological Association's "Statement on 'Race,'" published on May 17, 1998 and available online at www.aaanet.org/stmts/racepp.htm, accessed June 18, 2010. Emphasis in the original.

2 Even recent research showing clusters of genetic characteristics that tend to group according to continents can be interpreted in many ways, with some scholars calling the divisions "arbitrary" (e.g., Thompson 2006). Indeed, the authors of an article in *Science* (Rosenberg et al. 2002) acknowledge that humans across all populations are overwhelmingly more similar than different. They also note that within-group genetic variation accounts for 93 to 95 percent of all human genetic diversity and state that the proportion of genetic differences between members of different human populations "only slightly exceeds" that between unrelated members of the same human population (Rosenberg et al. 2002:2381). "Because most alleles are widespread," they conclude, "genetic differences among human populations derive mainly from

gradations in allele frequencies rather than from distinctive 'diagnostic' genotypes" (Rosenberg et al. 2002:2384).

3 For a few key works in the growing field of whiteness studies, see Allen (1994), Brodkin (1998), Hartigan (1997), Ignatiev (1995), Trechter and Bucholtz (2001), and Waterston (2006).

4 For a taste of some of these debates, see Baran (2007), Goldstein (1999), Roth-Gordon (2007), Sansone (2004), and Sheriff (2004).

5 On the Thakali, see Fisher (2001), and on the Tamang, see Holmberg (1989). On the Muluki Ain of 1854, the law that classified hierarchically all castes and ethnic groups in Nepal, see Höfer (1979).

6 This overview only scratches the surface of the research that has been conducted on the grammatical and phonological patterns of AAE; for a more detailed analysis, see the work by scholars such as Lisa Green (2002), William Labov (1972a, 2010), and Marcyliena Morgan (2002), as well as those whose research is included in the volume edited by Mufwene et al. (1998).

7 To simplify matters, I have not included the phrase "the sounds usually represented in English by the letters…" Clearly, these sounds and others in English can sometimes be represented by different letters. The International Phonetic Alphabet would be a more precise way of representing these sounds, but for our purposes here, I hope this simplification will help those who are not well-versed in phonology to understand the rule that governs the permissibility of final consonant reduction in AAE.

8 For an explanation of the origins of the term "Ebonics," see Smitherman (2005:50–51) and Baugh (2000:15ff). I follow the practice of many other linguists and linguistic anthropologists in using the term African American English (AAE) rather than "Ebonics" because of the lack of clarity regarding whether Ebonics refers only to the speech variety spoken by most African Americans, or more broadly to the many languages and dialects that emerged from various mixtures of African and European languages, such as Hatian Creole, West African Pidgin English, and Dutch Creole, as well as African American English. I therefore only use "Ebonics" to refer to the debate that occurred in 1996–1997.

9 I have simplified the transcription format here, omitting the original Italian and various nonverbal gestures. For the full conversation in its original form, see Pagliai (2009).

10 Baugh reported these results in a story on National Public Radio on linguistic profiling on September 5, 2001. At www.npr.org/templates/story/story.php?storyId=1128513, accessed June 25, 2010.

Chapter 11 Language Death and Revitalization

1 Quote taken from a University of California at Santa Barbara press release, available online at www.ia.ucsb.edu/pa/display.aspx?pkey=1577, accessed June 29, 2010.
2 Cited on *Ethnologue*'s website, www.ethnologue.com/ethno_docs/distribution.asp?by=size, accessed June 29, 2010.

Chapter 12 Conclusion: Language, Power, and Agency

1 The following three sections are adapted from Ahearn (2001a and 2001b).
2 See Kockelman (2007) for an alternative critique of Bourdieu that seeks to apply a Peircean approach to the process of *habitus* formation.
3 In borrowing these terms from economics, Bourdieu also opens himself up to criticisms of economic reductionism. For a rebuttal of these criticisms, see Thompson (1991:15–16).
4 Parts of this section have been adapted from Ahearn (2001b) and Ahearn (2010).
5 A central dilemma for theorists who want to define agency more precisely than the barebones "socioculturally mediated capacity to act" definition is the question of intentionality. If intentional, goal-directed action is added to this skeletal definition, then the question arises as to what it means to intend to do something. Giddens (1979:55–57), Ortner (2006b:134–135), Duranti (1988, 2004, 2006b), and Kockelman (2007) have all written about agency and intentionality.
6 Accusative languages are sometimes known as "nominative-accusative," while ergative languages are sometimes called "ergative-absolutive." Some "split" languages are known as "stative-active" (Duranti 2004:460ff.).
7 This overview of Shila and Vajra's relationship is condensed from Ahearn (2001a, chapter 6).
8 A complete translation of Shila and Vajra's entire love-letter correspondence, and all of the love letters written by another man who eventually married a woman from Junigau, are available online at the University of Michigan Press's website: www.press.umich.edu/pdf/0472097849-appa.pdf and www.press.umich.edu/pdf/0472097849-appb.pdf, accessed November 28, 2010. The extracts in this chapter were translated by the author in *Invitations to Love: Literacy, Love Letters, and Social Change in*

Nepal (Ahearn 2001a) and are included here with permission of the University of Michigan Press.

9 The many ellipses (multiple dots in a row) are in the original letter as written by Shila. An analysis of the possible meanings of these ellipses can be found in Ahearn (2001a, chapter 6).

10 The Nepali calendar differs from our own. Each year starts in mid-April, and the year is roughly 56 years ahead of ours. This notation indicates the date on which the letter was written – on the eighth day of the fourth month of the year 2047 – correlating approximately to the end of July 1990.

References

Agha, A. (2004) Registers of language. In Duranti, A. (ed.), *A Companion to Linguistic Anthropology*. Oxford: Blackwell, pp. 23–45.

Agha, A. (2007) *Language and Social Relations*. Cambridge: Cambridge University Press.

Ahearn, L.M. (1994) Consent and Coercion: Changing Marriage Practices among Magars in Nepal. PhD dissertation, University of Michigan.

Ahearn, L.M. (1998) "A twisted rope binds my waist": locating constraints on meaning in a Tij songfest. *Journal of Linguistic Anthropology* 8(1):60–86.

Ahearn, L.M. (2001a) *Invitations to Love: Literacy, Love Letters, and Social Change in Nepal*. Ann Arbor: University of Michigan Press.

Ahearn, L.M. (2001b) Language and agency. *Annual Review of Anthropology* 30:109–137.

Ahearn, L.M. (2008) Fateful literacy: new meanings, old ideologies, and some unexpected consequences of Nepali love letter writing. In Prinsloo, M. and Baynham, M. (eds.), *Literacies: Global and Local*. Amsterdam: John Benjamins, pp. 93–116.

Ahearn, L.M. (2010) Agency and language. In Verschueren, J., Östman, J.-O., and Jaspers, J. (eds.), *Handbook of Pragmatics*. Amsterdam: John Benjamins, pp. 28–48.

Aikhenvald, A.Y. (2004) *Evidentiality*. Oxford: Oxford University Press.

Alba, R., Logan, J., Lutz, A., and Stults, B. (2002) Only English by the third generation? Loss and preservation of the mother tongue among the grandchildren of contemporary immigrants. *Demography* 39(3):467–484.

Allen, T.W. (1994) *The Invention of the White Race*. Vol. 1: *Racial Oppression and Social Control*. New York: Verso.

Alter, R. (1987) Introduction. In Alter, R. and Kermode, F. (eds.), *The Literary Guide to the Bible*. Cambridge, MA: Harvard University Press, pp. 11–35.

Appadurai, A. (ed.) (1988) *The Social Life of Things: Commodities in Cultural Perspective*. Cambridge: Cambridge University Press.

Astington, J.W. and Jenkins, J.M. (1999) A longitudinal study of the relation between language and theory-of-mind development. *Development Psychology* 35(5):1311–1320.

Auer, P. (1999) From codeswitching via language mixing to fused lects: towards a dynamic typology of bilingual speech. *International Journal of Bilingualism* 3(4):309–332.

Austin, J.L. (1962) *How To Do Things With Words: The William James Lectures Delivered at Harvard University in 1955*. London: Oxford University Press.

Bakhtin, M.M. (1981a) Discourse in the novel. In Bakhtin, M.M., *The Dialogic Imagination: Four Essays*, ed. M. Holquist. Trans. C. Emerson and M. Holquist. Austin: University of Texas Press, pp. 259–422.

Bakhtin, M.M. (1981b) From the prehistory of novelistic discourse. In Bakhtin, M.M., *The Dialogic Imagination: Four Essays*, ed. M. Holquist. Trans. C. Emerson and M. Holquist. Austin: University of Texas Press, pp. 41–83.

Baquedano-López, P. (2004) Literacy practices across learning contexts. In Duranti, A. (ed.), *A Companion to Linguistic Anthropology*. Oxford: Blackwell, pp. 245–268.

Baran, M. (2007) "Girl, you are not *Morena*. We are *Negras*!": questioning the concept of "race" in southern Bahia, Brazil. *Ethos* 35(3):383–409.

Baron, D. (n.d.) English Spoken Here? What the 2000 Census Tells Us about Language in the USA. At http://www.english.illinois.edu/-people-/faculty/debaron/essays/espoken.htm, accessed August 11, 2009.

Baron, D. (1990) *The English-Only Question: An Official Language for Americans?* New Haven, CT: Yale University Press.

Bartky, S.L. (1995) Agency: what's the problem? In Gardiner, J.K. (ed.), *Provoking Agents: Gender and Agency in Theory and Practice*. Urbana: University of Illinois Press, pp. 178–193.

Barton, D. and Hamilton, M. (1998) *Local Literacies: A Study of Reading and Writing in One Community*. New York: Routledge.

Barton, D. and Hamilton, M. (2000) Literacy practices. In Barton, D., Hamilton, M., and Ivanic, R. (eds.), *Situated Literacies: Reading and Writing in Context*. New York: Routledge, pp. 7–15.

Barton, D. and Hamilton, M. (2005) Literacy, reification and the dynamics of social interaction. In Barton, D. and Tusting, K. (eds.), *Beyond Communities Of Practice: Language, Power And Social Context*. Cambridge: Cambridge University Press, pp. 14–35.

Barton, D., Hamilton, M., and Ivanič, R. (eds.) (2000) *Situated Literacies: Reading and Writing in Context.* New York: Routledge.

Barton, D. and Tusting, K. (eds.) (2005) *Beyond Communities of Practice: Language, Power and Social Context.* Cambridge: Cambridge University Press.

Basso, K.H. (1989[1974]) The ethnography of writing. In Bauman, R. and Sherzer, J. (eds.), *Explorations in the Ethnography of Speaking,* 2nd edn. Cambridge: Cambridge University Press, pp. 425–432.

Basso, K.H. (1996) *Wisdom Sits in Places: Landscape and Language Among the Western Apache.* Albuquerque: University of New Mexico Press.

Bates, E. and MacWhinney, B. (1989) Functionalism and the competition model. In *The Cross-Linguistic Study of Sentence Processing.* Cambridge: Cambridge University Press, pp. 3–76.

Bateson, G. (1972) *Steps to an Ecology of Mind: A Revolutionary Approach to Man's Understanding of Himself.* New York: Ballantine.

Baugh, J. (1983) *Black Street Speech: Its History, Structure, and Survival.* Austin: University of Texas Press.

Baugh, J. (1999) *Out of the Mouths of Slaves: African American Language and Educational Malpractice.* Austin: University of Texas Press.

Baugh, J. (2000) *Beyond Ebonics: Linguistic Pride and Racial Prejudice.* Oxford: Oxford University Press.

Baugh, J. (2003) Linguistic profiling. In Makoni, S., Smitherman, G., Ball, A.F., and Spears, A.K. (eds.), *Black Linguistics: Language, Society and Politics in Africa and the Americas.* New York: Routledge, pp. 155–168.

Bauman, R. (2001[1975]). Verbal art as performance. In Duranti, A. (ed.), *Linguistic Anthropology: A Reader.* Oxford: Blackwell, pp. 165–188.

Bauman, R. (2005) Commentary: indirect indexicality, identity, performance. *Journal of Linguistic Anthropology* 15(1):145–150.

Bauman, R. and Briggs, C.L. (1990) Poetics and performance as critical perspectives on language and social life. *Annual Review of Anthropology* 19:59–88.

Bauman, R. and Briggs, C.L. (2003) *Voices of Modernity: Language Ideologies and the Politics of Inequality.* Cambridge: Cambridge University Press.

Baxter, J. (2006) "Do we have to agree with her?" How high school girls negotiate leadership in public contexts. In Baxter, J. (ed.), *Speaking Out: The Female Voice in Public Contexts.* New York: Palgrave Macmillan, pp. 159–178.

Baynham, M. (1995) *Literacy Practices: Investigating Literacy in Social Contexts.* London: Longman.

Becker, A. (2000) *Beyond Translation: Essays toward a Modern Philology.* Ann Arbor: University of Michigan Press.

Bennett, L. (1983) *Dangerous Wives and Sacred Sisters: Social and Symbolic Roles of High-Caste Women in Nepal*. New York: Columbia University Press.

Berlin, B. and Kay, P. (1969) *Basic Color Terms: Their Universality and Evolution*. Berkeley: University of California Press.

Bernard, H.R. (2006) *Research Methods in Anthropology: Qualitative and Quantitative Approaches*, 4th edn. Walnut Creek, CA: Altamira Press.

Besnier, N. (1995) *Literacy, Emotion, and Authority: Reading and Writing on a Polynesian Atoll*. New York: Cambridge University Press.

Besnier, N. (2009) *Gossip and the Everyday Production of Politics*. Honolulu: University of Hawai'i Press.

Bialystok, E. (2010) Global-local and trail-making tasks by monolingual and bilingual children: beyond inhibition. *Developmental Psychology* 46(1):93–105.

Bialystok, E. and Viswanathan, M. (2009) Components of executive control with advantages for bilingual children in two cultures. *Cognition* 112: 494–500.

Bilaniuk, L. (2005) *Contested Tongues: Language Politics and Cultural Correction in Ukraine*. Ithaca, NY: Cornell University Press.

Bing, J.M. and Bergvall, V.L. (1996) The question of questions: beyond binary thinking. In Bergvall, V.L., Bing, J.M., and Freed, A.F. (eds.), *Rethinking Language and Gender Research: Theory and Practice*. London: Longman, pp. 1–30.

Bittner, M. and Hale, K. (1996) Ergativity: toward a theory of a heterogeneous class. *Linguistic Inquiry* 27(4):531–604.

Blackless, M., Charuvastra, A., Derryck, A., et al. (2000) How sexually dimorphic are we? Review and synthesis. *American Journal of Human Biology* 12:151–166.

Blommaert, J. (2009) Language, asylum, and the national order. *Current Anthropology* 50(4):415–441.

Bloomfield, L. (1984[1933]) *Language*. Chicago: University of Chicago Press.

Bonvillain, N. (2000) *Language, Culture, and Communication: The Meaning of Messages*, 3rd edn. Upper Saddle River, NJ: Prentice-Hall.

Booth, C.L. (2009a) Country is my mother, language is my soul. *Anthropology News* 50(7):50.

Booth, C.L. (2009b) "An ocean of culture": language ideologies and the social life of language in multilingual Darjeeling, India. *Texas Linguistic Forum: Proceedings of the 17th Annual Symposium about Language and Society, Austin* 53:8–17.

Bourdieu, P. (1977) *Outline of a Theory of Practice*. Trans. R. Nice. Cambridge: Cambridge University Press.

Bourdieu, P. (1991) *Language and Symbolic Power*, ed. J.B. Thompson. Trans. G. Raymond and M. Adamson. Cambridge, MA: Harvard University Press.

Bowerman, M. (1996) The origins of children's spatial semantic categories. In Gumperz, J.J. and Levinson, S.C. (eds.), *Rethinking Linguistic Relativity*. Cambridge: Cambridge University Press, pp. 145–176.

Bowerman, M. and Choi, S. (2003) Space under construction: language-specific spatial categorization in first language acquisition. In Gentner, D. and Goldin-Meadow, S. (eds.), *Language in Mind: Advances in the Study of Language and Thought*. Cambridge, MA: MIT Press, pp. 387–427.

Boyarin, J. (ed.) (1993) *The Ethnography of Reading*. Berkeley: University of California Press.

Brandt, D. and Clinton, K. (2002) Limits of the local: expanding perspectives on literacy as a social practice. *Journal of Literacy Research* 34(3):337–356.

Briggs, C.L. (1986) *Learning How to Ask: A Sociolinguistic Appraisal of the Role of the Interview in Social Science Research*. Cambridge: Cambridge University Press.

Briggs, C.L. (1998) "You're a liar – you're just like a woman!": Constructing dominant ideologies of language in Warao men's gossip. In Schieffelin, B.B., Woolard, K.A., and Kroskrity, P.V. (eds.), *Language Ideologies: Practice and Theory*. Oxford: Oxford University Press, pp. 229–255.

Briggs, C.L. (2007) Anthropology, interviewing, and communicability in contemporary society. *Current Anthropology* 48(4):551–580.

Brizendine, L. (2006) *The Female Brain*. New York: Morgan Road.

Brodkin, K. (1998) *How Jews Became White Folks, and What That Says About Race in America*. New Brunswick, NJ: Rutgers University Press.

Bucholtz, M. (1999) "Why be normal?": language and identity practices in a community of nerd girls. *Language in Society* 28:203–223.

Bucholtz, M. (2000) The politics of transcription. *Journal of Pragmatics* 32:1439–1465.

Bucholtz, M. (2001) The whiteness of nerds: superstandard English and racial markedness. *Journal of Linguistic Anthropology* 11(1):84–100.

Bucholtz, M. (2007) Word up: social meanings of slang in California youth culture. In Monaghan, L. and Goodman, J.E. (eds.), *A Cultural Approach to Interpersonal Communication: Essential Readings*. Oxford: Wiley-Blackwell, pp. 243–267.

Bucholtz, M. (2009) Styles and stereotypes: Laotian American girls' linguistic negotiation of identity. In Reyes, A. and Lo, A. (eds.), *Beyond Yellow English: Toward a Linguistic Anthropology of Asian Pacific America*. Oxford: Oxford University Press, pp. 21–42.

Bucholtz, M. and Hall, K. (2004) Theorizing identity in language and sexuality research. *Language in Society* 33:469–515.

Bucholtz, M. and Hall, K. (2008) All of the above: new coalitions in sociocultural linguistics. *Journal of Sociolinguistics* 12(4):401–431.

Butler, J. (1993) *Bodies that Matter: On the Discursive Limits of "Sex"*. New York: Routledge.

Butler, J. (1997) *Excitable Speech: A Politics of the Performative.* New York: Routledge.

Butler, J. (1999[1990]) *Gender Trouble.* New York: Routledge.

Butler, J. (2004) *Undoing Gender.* New York: Routledge.

Callon, M. (1986) Some elements of a sociology of translation: domestication of the scallops and the fishermen of St. Brieuc Bay. In Law, J. (ed.), *Power, Action and Belief: A New Sociology Knowledge.* London: Routledge & Kegan Paul, pp. 196–233.

Cameron, D. (1997) Performing gender identity: young men's talk and the construction of heterosexual masculinity. In Johnson, S. and Meinhof, U. (eds.), *Language and Masculinity.* Oxford: Blackwell, pp. 47–64.

Cameron, D. (1999) Linguistic relativity: Benjamin Lee Whorf and the return of the repressed. *Critical Quarterly* 41(2):153–156.

Cameron, D. (2007a) Language endangerment and verbal hygiene: history, morality, and politics. In Duchêne, A. and Heller, M. (eds.), *Discourses of Endangerment.* London: Continuum, pp. 268–285.

Cameron, D. (2007b) *The Myth of Mars and Venus: Do Men and Women Really Speak Different Languages?* Oxford: Oxford University Press.

Caton, S. (1990) *Peaks of Yemen I summon: Poetry as Cultural Practice in a North Yemeni Tribe.* Berkeley: University of California Press.

Chase, C. (2008) "Cultural practice" or "reconstructive surgery"? US genital cutting, the intersex movement, and medical double standards. In Ehrenreich, N. (ed.), *The Reproductive Rights Reader: Law, Medicine, and the Construction of Motherhood.* New York: New York University Press, pp. 47–56.

Cheney, D.L. and Seyfarth, R.M. (1990) *How Monkeys See the World: Inside the Mind of Another Species.* Chicago: University of Chicago Press.

Cheney, D.L. and Seyfarth, R.M. (1998) Why animals don't have language. In Peterson, G. (ed.), *The Tanner Lectures in Human Values.* Vol. 19. Salt Lake City: University of Utah Press, pp. 173–210.

Cheney, D.L. and Seyfarth, R.M. (2007) *Baboon Metaphysics: The Evolution of a Social Mind.* Chicago: University of Chicago Press.

Cheshire, J. (1998) Double negatives are illogical. In Bauer, L. and Trudgill, P. (eds.), *Language Myths.* New York: Penguin, pp. 113–122.

Chicago Manual of Style Online, 15th edn. Chapter 5: *Grammar and Usage*, by B.A. Garner. Section 5.43, Antecedents of different genders. At http://www.chicagomanualofstyle.org/ch05/ch05_sec043.html, accessed June 1, 2010.

Childs, G.T. (2006) What's the difference between dialects and languages? In Rickerson, E.M. and Hilton, B. (eds.), *The Five-Minute Linguist: Bite-Sized Essays on Language and Languages*. Oakville, CT: Equinox, pp. 16–20.

Ching, M.K.L. (2001) Plural *you/ya'll* variation by a court judge: situational use. *American Speech* 76(2):115–127.

Chomsky, N. (1965) *Aspects of the Theory of Syntax*. Cambridge, MA: MIT Press.

Chomsky, N. (1968) *Language and Mind*. New York: Harcourt, Brace and World.

Chomsky, N. (1975) Knowledge of language. In Gunderson, K. (ed.), *Language, Mind and Knowledge*. Minneapolis: University of Minneapolis Press, pp. 299–320.

Chomsky, N. (1991) Linguistics and adjacent fields: a personal view. In Kasher, A. (ed.), *The Chomskyan Turn*. Oxford: Blackwell, pp. 3–25.

Chomsky, N. (1999) On the nature, use, and acquisition of language. In Ritchie, W.C. and Bhatia, T.K. (eds.), *Handbook of Child Language Acquisition*. San Diego, CA: Academic Press, pp. 33–54.

Chomsky, N. (2005[1980]) *Rules and Representations*. New York: Columbia University Press.

Cipollone, N., Keiser, S.H., and Vasishth, S. (1998) What do you know when you know a language? In *Language Files: Materials for an Introduction to Language and Linguistics*, 7th edn. Columbus: Ohio State University Press.

Ciscel, M.H. (2007) *The Language of the Moldovans: Romania, Russia, and Identity in an Ex-Soviet Republic*. Lanham, MD: Lexington Books.

Cohn, C. (1987) Sex and death in the rational world of defense intellectuals. *Signs* 12(4):687–718.

Collier, J.F. (1997) *From Duty to Desire: Remaking Families in a Spanish Village*. Princeton: Princeton University Press.

Collins, J. (1995) Literacy and literacies. *Annual Review of Anthropology* 24:75–93.

Collins, J. and Blot, R.K. (2003) *Literacy and Literacies: Texts, Power, and Identity*. Cambridge: Cambridge University Press.

Comrie, B. (1981) *Language Universals and Linguistic Typology: Syntax and Morphology*. Oxford: Basil Blackwell.

Cook, V. and Newson, M. (2007) *Chomsky's Universal Grammar: An Introduction*. Oxford: Wiley-Blackwell.

Crago, M.B., Allen, S.E.M., and Hough-Eyamie, W.P. (1997) Exploring innateness through cultural and linguistic variation. In Gopnik, M. (ed.),

The Inheritance and Innateness of Grammars. Oxford: Oxford University Press, pp. 70–90.

Creese, A. (2008) Linguistic ethnography. In King, K.A. and Hornberger, N.H. (eds.), *Encyclopedia of Language and Education*, 2nd edn. Vol. 10: *Research Methods in Language and Education*. New York: Springer, pp. 229–241.

Crystal, D. (2000) *Language Death*. Cambridge: Cambridge University Press.

Cutler, C. (2003) "Keepin' it real": white hip-hoppers' discourses of language, race, and authenticity. *Journal of Linguistic Anthropology* 13(2) 211–233.

Daniel, E.V. (1984) *Fluid Signs: Being a Person the Tamil Way*. Berkeley: University of California Press.

Demuth, K. (1986) Prompting routines in the language socialization of Basotho children. In Schieffelin, B.B. and Ochs, E. (eds.), *Language Socialization Across Cultures*. Cambridge: Cambridge University Press, pp. 51–79.

Demuth, K. (1992) The acquisition of Sesotho. In Slobin, D.I. (ed.), *The Crosslinguistic Study of Language Acquisition*. Vol. 3. Hillsdale, NJ: Lawrence Erlbaum, pp. 557–638.

Derbyshire, D.C. (1987) Morphosyntactic areal characteristics of Amazonian languages. *International Journal of American Linguistics* 53:311–326.

Derrida, J. (1988) *Limited Inc*. Evanston, IL: Northwestern University Press.

Derrida, J. (1992) Before the law. In *Acts of Literature*, ed. D. Attridge. New York: Routledge, pp. 183–220.

Desjarlais, R. (1997) *Shelter Blues: Sanity and Selfhood Among the Homeless*. Philadelphia: University of Pennsylvania Press.

Deutscher, G. (2010) *Through the Language Glass: Why the World Looks Different in Other Languages*. New York: Metropolitan Books, Henry Holt.

Dickens, C. (2000[1859]) *A Tale of Two Cities*. New York: Penguin Classics.

Dixon, R.M.W. (1982) *Where Have All the Adjectives Gone?* Berlin: Walter de Gruyter.

Dixon, R.M.W. (1984) *Searching for Aboriginal Languages: Memoir of a Field Worker*. Chicago: University of Chicago Press.

Dixon, R.M.W. (1994) *Ergativity*. New York: Cambridge University Press.

Dorian, N.C. (1998) Western language ideologies and small-language prospects. In Grenoble, L.A. and Whaley, L.J. (eds.), *Endangered Languages: Current Issues and Future Prospects*. Cambridge: Cambridge University Press, pp. 3–21.

Duchêne, A. and Heller, M. (eds.) (2007) *Discourses of Endangerment*. London: Continuum.

Duranti, A. (1988) Intentions, language, and social action in a Samoan Context. *Journal of Pragmatics* 12:13–33.

Duranti, A. (1994) *From Grammar to Politics: Linguistic Anthropology in a Western Samoan Village*. Berkeley: University of California Press.

Duranti, A. (1997) *Linguistic Anthropology*. Cambridge: Cambridge University Press.

Duranti, A. (ed.) (2001) *Key Terms in Language and Culture*. Oxford: Blackwell.

Duranti, A. (2003) Language as culture in US anthropology: three paradigms. *Current Anthropology* 44:323–347.

Duranti, A. (2004) Agency in language. In Duranti, A. (ed.), *A Companion to Linguistic Anthropology*. Oxford: Blackwell, pp. 451–473.

Duranti, A. (2006a) Transcripts, like shadows on a wall. *Mind, Culture, and Activity* 13(4):301–310.

Duranti, A. (2006b) The social ontology of intentions. *Discourse Studies* 8(1):31–40.

Duranti, A. (Forthcoming) Linguistic anthropology: language as a non-neutral medium. In Mesthrie, R. (ed.), *Cambridge Handbook of Sociolinguistics*.

Duranti, A. and Brenneis, D. (eds.) (1986) The audience as co-author. Special issue of *Text* 6(3).

Duranti, A. and Goodwin, C. (eds.) (1992) *Rethinking Context: Language as an Interactive Phenomenon*. Cambridge: Cambridge University Press.

Eckert, P. (1989) *Jocks and Burnouts: Social Categories and Identity in the High School*. New York: Teachers College Press.

Eckert, P. (1993) Cooperative competition in adolescent "girl talk." In Tannen, D. (ed.), *Gender and Conversational Interaction*. New York: Oxford University Press, pp. 32–61.

Eckert, P. and McConnell-Ginet, S. (1992) Think practically and look locally: language and gender as community-based practice. *Annual Review of Anthropology* 21:461–490.

Eckert, P. and McConnell-Ginet, S. (1995) Constructing meaning, constructing selves: snapshots of language, gender, and class from Belten High. In Hall, K. and Bucholtz, M. (eds.), *Gender Articulated: Language and the Socially Constructed Self*. New York: Routledge, pp. 469–507.

Eckert, P. and McConnell-Ginet, S. (1998) Communities of practice: where language, gender, and power all live. In Coates, J. (ed.), *Language and Gender: A Reader*. Oxford: Blackwell, pp. 484–494.

Eckert, P. and McConnell-Ginet, S. (2003) *Language and Gender*. Cambridge: Cambridge University Press.

Eco, U. (1990) *The Limits of Interpretation*. Bloomington: Indiana University Press.

Edelman, M. and Haugerud, A. (2005) Introduction: The anthropology of development and globalization. In Edelman, M. and Haugerud, A. (eds.),

The Anthropology of Development and Globalization. Oxford: Blackwell, pp. 1–74.

Edwards, J.R. (1994) *Multilingualism*. New York: Routledge.

El-Or, T. (2002) *Next Year I Will Know More: Literacy and Identity among Young Orthodox Women in Israel*. Trans. H. Watzman. Detroit, MI: Wayne State University Press.

Errington, J. (2008) *Linguistics in a Colonial World: A Story of Language, Meaning, and Power*. Oxford: Wiley-Blackwell.

Escobar, A. (1995) *Encountering Development: The Making and Unmaking of the Third World*. Princeton: Princeton University Press.

Evans, N. (2010) *Dying Words: Endangered Languages and What They Have To Tell Us*. Oxford: Wiley-Blackwell.

Evans, N. and Levinson, S. (2009) The myth of language universals: language diversity and its importance for cognitive science. *Behavioral and Brain Sciences* 32:429–492.

Everett, D.L. (2005) Cultural constraints on grammar and cognition in Pirahã. *Current Anthropology* 46(4):621–646.

Everett, D.L. (2007) Cultural constraints on grammar in Pirahã: a reply to Nevins, Pesetsky, and Rodrigues (2007). Unpublished manuscript accessed at http://ling.auf.net/lingbuzz/000427 on April 19, 2007.

Fader, A. (2007) Reclaiming sacred sparks: linguistic syncretism and gendered language shift among Hasidic Jews in New York. *Journal of Linguistic Anthropology* 17(1):1–22.

Fader, A. (2009) *Mitzvah Girls: Bringing Up the Next Generation of Hasidic Jews in Brooklyn*. Princeton: Princeton University Press.

Fairclough, N. (2006) *Language and Globalization*. New York: Routledge.

Farnell, B. (2000) Getting out of the *habitus*: an alternative model of dynamically embodied social action. *Journal of the Royal Anthropological Institute* 6:397–418.

Ferber, A.L. (2007) What white supremacists taught a Jewish scholar about identity. In Anderson, M.L. and Collins, P.H. (eds.), *Race, Class, and Gender: An Anthology*, 6th edn. Belmont, CA: Thomson Wadsworth, pp. 111–115.

Ferguson, C.A. (1959) Diglossia. *Word* 15:325–340.

Figueras-Costa, B. and Harris, P. (2001) Theory of mind development in deaf children: a nonverbal test of false-belief understanding. *Journal of Deaf Studies and Deaf Education* 6(2):92–102.

Finnegan, R. (1988) *Literacy and Orality: Studies in the Technology of Communication*. Oxford: Basil Blackwell.

Fisher, W.F. (2001) *Fluid Boundaries: Forming and Transforming Thakali Identity in Nepal*. New York: Columbia University Press.

Fokkelman, J.P. (1987) Exodus. In Alter, R. and Kermode, F. (eds.), *The Literary Guide to the Bible.* Cambridge, MA: Harvard University Press, pp. 56–65.

Foucault, M. (1978) *The History of Sexuality.* Vols. 1 and 2. New York: Pantheon.

Foucault, M. (1994a) Governmentality. In Rabinow, P. and Rose, N. (eds.), *The Essential Foucault: Selections from the Essential Works of Foucault, 1954–1984.* New York: The New Press, pp. 229–245.

Foucault, M. (1994b) The subject and power. In Rabinow, P. and Rose, N. (eds.), *The Essential Foucault: Selections from the Essential Works of Foucault, 1954–1984.* New York: The New Press, pp. 126–144.

Gal, S. (2006) Linguistic anthropology. In Brown, K. (ed.), *Encyclopedia of Language and Linguistics,* 2nd edn. Vol. 7. Oxford: Elsevier, pp. 171–185.

Galvin, K.-L. (2006) *Forbidden Red: Widowhood in Urban Nepal.* Washington State University Press.

Garfinkel, H. (1967) *Studies in Ethnomethodology.* Englewood Cliffs, NJ: Prentice-Hall.

Garrett, P.B. (2004) Language contact and contact languages. In Duranti, A. (ed.), *A Companion to Linguistic Anthropology.* Oxford: Blackwell, pp. 46–72.

Gaudio, R.P. (2001) White men do it too: racialized (homo)sexualities in postcolonial Hausaland. *Journal of Linguistic Anthropology* 11(1):36–51.

Gee, J.P. (2008) *Social Linguistics and Literacies: Ideology in Discourses,* 3rd edn. New York: Routledge.

Gentner, D. and Goldin-Meadow, S. (2003) Whither Whorf. In Gentner, D. and Goldin-Meadow, S. (eds.), *Language in Mind: Advances in the Study of Language and Thought.* Cambridge, MA: MIT Press, pp. 3–14.

Giddens, A. (1979) *Central Problems in Social Theory: Action, Structure and Contradiction in Social Analysis.* Berkeley: University of California Press.

Gilbert, K. (1992) Women and family law in modern Nepal: statutory rights and social implications. *New York University Journal of International Law and Politics* 24(2):729–758.

Givón, T. (1985) Function, structure, and language acquisition. In Slobin, D.I. (ed.), *The Crosslinguistic Study of Language Acquisition.* Vol. 2: *Theoretical Issues.* Hillsdale, NJ: Lawrence Erlbaum, pp. 1005–1027.

Glaser, B. (1992) *Basics of Grounded Theory Analysis.* Mill Valley, CA: Sociology Press.

Goffman, E. (1981) Footing. In Goffman, E., *Forms of Talk.* Philadelphia: University of Pennsylvania Press, pp. 124–159.

Goffman, E. (1986) *Frame Analysis: An Essay on the Organization of Experience.* Boston, MA: Northeastern University Press.

Goldstein, D. (1999) "Interracial" sex and racial democracy in Brazil: twin concepts? *American Anthropologist* 101(3):563–578.

Gomez-Imbert, E. (1996) When animals become "rounded" and "feminine": conceptual categories and linguistic classification in a multilingual setting. In Gumperz, J.J. and Levinson, S.C. (eds.), *Rethinking Linguistic Relativity*. Cambridge: Cambridge University Press, pp. 438–469.

Goodwin, M.H. (1990) *He-Said-She-Said: Talk As Social Organization Among Black Children*. Bloomington: Indiana University Press.

Goodwin, M.H. (2006) *The Hidden Life of Girls: Games of Stance, Status, and Exclusion*. Oxford: Blackwell.

Goody, J. (1986) *The Logic of Writing and the Organization of Society*. Cambridge: Cambridge University Press.

Goody, J. (2000) *The Power of the Written Tradition*. Washington, DC: Smithsonian.

Goody, J. and Watt, I. (1963) The consequences of literacy. *Comparative Studies in Society and History* 5(3):306–326, 332–345.

Gorman, D. (1999) The use and abuse of speech-act theory in criticism. *Poetics Today* 20(1):93–119.

Government of India, Ministry of Home Affairs (1968) *The Official Language Resolution*. At http://www.rajbhasha.gov.in/dolresolutioneng.htm, accessed August 27, 2009.

Government of India, Ministry of Law and Justice (2007) *The Constitution of India* (as modified up to December 1, 2007). At http://lawmin.nic.in/coi/coiason29july08.pdf, accessed August 27, 2009.

Green, L.J. (1998) Aspect and predicate phrases in African-American Vernacular English. In Mufwene, S.S., Rickford, J.R., Bailey, G., and Baugh, J. (eds.), *African-American English: Structure, History and Use*. New York: Routledge, pp. 37–68.

Green, L.J. (2002) *African American English: A Linguistic Introduction*. Cambridge: Cambridge University Press.

Greenberg, R.D. (2004) *Language and Identity in the Balkans*. Oxford: Oxford University Press.

Grenoble, L.A. and Whaley, L.J. (eds.) (1998) *Endangered Languages: Current Issues and Future Prospects*. Cambridge: Cambridge University Press.

Grillo, R.D. (1989) *Dominant Languages: Language and Hierarchy in Britain and France*. Cambridge: Cambridge University Press.

Grosjean, F. (1982) *Life with Two Languages: An Introduction to Bilingualism*. Cambridge, MA: Harvard University Press.

Gumperz, J.J. (2001[1968]) The speech community. In Duranti, A. (ed.), *Linguistic Anthropology: A Reader*. Oxford: Blackwell, pp. 43–52.

Gumperz, J.J. (1996) Introduction to Part 4. In Gumperz, J.J. and Levinson, S.C. (eds.), *Rethinking Linguistic Relativity*. Cambridge: Cambridge University Press, pp. 359–373.

Guneratne, A. (2002) *Many Tongues, One People: The Making of Tharu Identity in Nepal*. Ithaca, NY: Cornell University Press.

Gupta, A. (1998) *Postcolonial Developments: Agriculture in the Making of Modern India*. Durham, NC: Duke University Press.

Hall, K. (1995) Lip service on the fantasy lines. In Hall, K. and Bucholtz, M. (eds.), *Gender Articulated: Language and the Socially Constructed Self*. New York: Routledge, pp. 183–216.

Hall, K. (2001) Performativity. In Duranti, A. (ed.), *Key Terms in Language and Culture*. Oxford: Blackwell, pp. 180–183.

Hall, S. (2001) Foucault: power, knowledge and discourse. In Wetherell, M., Taylor, S., and Yates, S.J. (eds.), *Discourse Theory and Practice: A Reader*. Thousand Oaks, CA: Sage, pp. 72–81.

Hangen, S. (2005) Race and the politics of identity in Nepal. *Ethnology* 44(1):49–64.

Hangen, S. (2009) *The Rise of Ethnic Politics in Nepal: Democracy in the Margins*. New York: Routledge.

Hanks, W.F. (1991) Foreword. In Lave, J. and Wenger, E., *Situated Learning: Legitimate Peripheral Participation*. Cambridge: Cambridge University Press, pp. 13–24.

Hanks, W.F. (1996) *Language and Communicative Practices*. Boulder, CO: Westview.

Hanks, W.F. (1999) Indexicality. *Journal of Linguistic Anthropology* 9(1–2): 124–126.

Hanks, W.F. (2005) Explorations in the deictic field. *Current Anthropology* 46(2):191–220.

Harding, S.F. (1987) Convicted by the Holy Spirit: the rhetoric of fundamental Baptist conversion. *American Ethnologist* 14(1):167–181.

Harrison, K.D. (2007) *When Languages Die: The Extinction of the World's Languages and the Erosion of Human Knowledge*. Oxford: Oxford University Press.

Hartigan, J., Jr. (1997) Establishing the fact of whiteness. *American Anthropologist* 99(3):495–505.

Heath, S.B. (1983) *Ways with Words: Language, Life, and Work in Communities and Classrooms*. Cambridge: Cambridge University Press.

Heath, S.B. (2001[1982]) What no bedtime story means: narrative skills at home and school. In Duranti, A., *Linguistic Anthropology: A Reader*, Oxford: Blackwell, pp. 318–342.

Hill, J.H. (1995) The voices of Don Gabriel: responsibility and self in a modern Mexicano narrative. In Tedlock, D. and Mannheim, B. (eds.), *The Dialogic Emergence of Culture*. Urbana: University of Illinois Press, pp. 97–147.
Hill, J.H. (1998) Language, race, and white public space. *American Anthropologist* 100(3):680–689.
Hill, J.H. (2002) "Expert rhetorics" in advocacy for endangered languages: who is listening, and what do they hear? *Journal of Linguistic Anthropology* 12(2):119–133.
Hill, J.H. (2005) Intertextuality as source and evidence for indirect indexical meanings. *Journal of Linguistic Anthropology* 15(1):113–124.
Hill, J.H. (2008) *The Everyday Language of White Racism*. Oxford: Wiley-Blackwell.
Hill, J.H. (2009) Review of *Linguistics in a Colonial World: A Story of Language, Meaning, and Power*. *Language in Society* 38(1):108–111.
Hill, J.H. and Mannheim, B. (1992) Language and world view. *Annual Review of Anthropology* 21:381–406.
Hinton, L. (2001) Sleeping languages: can they be awakened? In Hinton, L. and Hale, K. (eds.), *The Green Book of Language Revitalization in Practice*. San Diego, CA: Academic Press, pp. 419–423.
Hinton, L. and Hale, K. (eds.) (2001) *The Green Book of Language Revitalization in Practice*. San Diego, CA: Academic Press.
Höfer, A. (1979) The caste hierarchy and the state in Nepal: a study of the Muluki Ain of 1854. *Khumbu Himal* 13(2). Innsbruck: Universitätsverlag Wagner.
Hoffman, K.E. (2008) *We Share Walls: Language, Land, and Gender in Berber Morocco*. Oxford: Wiley-Blackwell.
Holland, D. and Skinner, D. (1995) Contested ritual, contested femininities: (re)forming self and society in a Nepali women's festival. *American Ethnologist* 22(2):279–305.
Holmberg, D.H. (1989) *Order in Paradox: Myth, Ritual and Exchange among Nepal's Tamang*. Ithaca, NY: Cornell University Press.
Holmes, J. (1998) Women talk too much. In Bauer, L. and Trudgill, P. (eds.), *Language Myths*. New York: Penguin Books, pp. 41–49.
Holmes, J. and Meyerhoff, M. (1999) The community of practice: theories and methodologies in language and gender research. *Language in Society* 28:173–183.
Hoy, D.C. (ed.) (1986) *Foucault: A Critical Reader*. Oxford: Blackwell.
Hughes, J., Jewson, N., and Unwin, L. (2007) Introduction: Communities of practice: a contested concept in flux. In Hughes, J., Jewson, N., and Unwin, L. (eds.), *Communities of Practice: Critical Perspectives*. New York: Routledge, pp. 1–16.

Hyde, J.S. (2005) The gender similarities hypothesis. *American Psychologist* 60(6):581–592.

Hyde, J.S. (2007) New directions in the study of gender similarities and differences. *Current Directions in Psychological Science* 16(5):259–263.

Hyman, E. (2006) The *all* of *you-all*. *American Speech* 81(3):325–331.

Hymes, D. (1974) *Foundations in Sociolinguistics*. Philadelphia: University of Pennsylvania Press.

Hymes, D. (1981) Breakthrough into performance. In Hymes, D., *In Vain I Tried to Tell You: Essays in Native American Ethnopoetics*. Philadelphia: University of Pennsylvania Press, pp. 79–141.

Hymes, D. (2001[1972]). On communicative competence. In Duranti, A. (ed.), *Linguistic Anthropology: A Reader*. Oxford: Blackwell, pp. 53–73.

Ignatiev, N. (1995) *How the Irish Became White*. New York: Routledge.

Inoue, M. (2006) *Vicarious Language: Gender and Linguistic Modernity in Japan*. Berkeley: University of California Press.

Irvine, J.T. (1987) Domains of description in the ethnography of speaking: a retrospective on the "speech community." In *Performance, Speech Community, and Genre*, Working Papers and Proceedings of the Center for Psychosocial Studies, 11. Chicago, Center for Psychosocial Studies [now the Center for Transcultural Studies], pp. 13–24. At http://www.sas.upenn.edu/transcult/pubwor11.html, accessed November 15, 2010.

Irvine, J.T. (1989) When talk isn't cheap: language and political economy. *American Ethnologist* 16:248–267.

Irvine, J.T. and Gal, S. (2000) Language ideology and linguistic differentiation. In Kroskrity, P.V. (ed.), *Regimes of Language: Ideologies, Polities, and Identities*. Santa Fe, NM: School of American Research Press, pp. 35–83.

Jackson, J. (1974) Language identity of the Colombian Vaupés Indians. In Bauman, R. and Sherzer, J. (eds.), *Explorations in the Ethnography of Speaking*. New York: Cambridge University Press, pp. 50–64.

Jackson, J.E. (1983) *The Fish People: Linguistic Exogamy and Tukanoan Identity in Northwest Amazonia*. Cambridge: Cambridge University Press.

Jacobs, N.G. (2005) *Yiddish: A Linguistic Introduction*. Cambridge: Cambridge University Press.

Jacobs-Huey, L. (2006) *From the Kitchen to the Parlor: Language and African American Women's Hair Care*. Oxford: Oxford University Press.

Jacquemet, M. (2005) Transidiomatic practices: language and power in the age of globalization. *Language and Communication* 25:257–277.

Jaffe, A. (1999) *Ideologies in Action: Language Politics on Corsica*. New York: Mouton de Gruyter.

Jaffe, A. (2007) Discourses of endangerment: contexts and consequences of essentializing discourses. In Duchêne, A. and Heller, M. (eds.), *Discourses of Endangerment*. London: Continuum, pp. 57–75.

Jakobson, R. (1960) Linguistics and poetics. In Sebeok, T.A. (ed.), *Style in Language*, Cambridge, MA: MIT Press, pp. 350–377.

James, D. and Drakich, J. (1993) Understanding gender differences in amount of talk: a critical review of the research. In Tannen, D. (ed.), *Gender and Conversational Interaction*. New York: Oxford University Press, pp. 281–312.

Jones, G.M. and Schieffelin, B.B. (2009) Enquoting voices, accomplishing talk: uses of *be+ like* in instant messaging. *Language in Communication* 29(1):77–113.

Jones, G.M. and Shweder, L. (2003) The performance of illusion and illusionary performatives: learning the language of theatrical magic. *Journal of Linguistic Anthropology* 13(1):51–70.

Kasher, A. (1991) Pragmatics and Chomsky's research program. In Kasher, A. (ed.), *The Chomskyan Turn*. Oxford: Blackwell, pp. 122–149.

Kay, P. (1999) Color. *Journal of Linguistic Anthropology* 9(1–2):32–35.

Kay, P. (2005) Color categories are not arbitrary. *Cross-Cultural Research* 39(1):39–55.

Kay, P. and Kempton, W. (1984) What is the Sapir-Whorf hypothesis? *American Anthropologist*, 86(1):65–79.

Kay, P. and Maffi, L. (1999) Color appearance and the emergence and evolution of basic color lexicons. *American Anthropologist* 101(4):743–760.

Keane, W. (1997) *Signs of Recognition: Powers and Hazards of Representation in an Indonesian Society*. Berkeley: University of California Press.

Keenan [Ochs], E. (1974) Norm-makers, norm-breakers: uses of speech by men and women in a Malagasy community. In Bauman, R. and Sherzer, J. (eds.), *Ethnography of Communication*. Cambridge: Cambridge University Press, pp. 125–143.

Keenan [Ochs], E.L. (1984) Semantic correlates of the ergative/absolutive distinction. *Linguistics* 22:197–223.

Kockelman, P. (2007) Agency: the relation between meaning, power, and knowledge. *Current Anthropology* 48(3):375–401.

Kolbert, E. (2005) Letter from Alaska: last words, a language dies. *The New Yorker*, June 6, pp. 46–48, 58–59.

Kratz, C.A. (2000) Forging unions and negotiating ambivalence: personhood and complex agency in Okiek marriage arrangement. In Masolo, D.A. and Karp, I. (eds.), *African Philosophy as Cultural Inquiry*. Bloomington: Indiana University Press, pp. 136–171.

Krauss, M. (1992) The world's languages in crisis. *Language* 68(1):4–10.

Kroskrity, P.V. (2000a) Language ideologies in the expression and representation of Arizona Tewa ethnic identity. In Kroskrity, P.V. (ed.), *Regimes of Language: Ideologies, Polities, and Identities*. Santa Fe, NM: School of American Research Press, pp. 329–359.

Kroskrity, P.V. (2000b) Regimenting languages: language ideological perspectives. In Kroskrity, P.V. (ed.), *Regimes of Language: Ideologies, Polities, and Identities*. Santa Fe, NM: School of American Research Press, pp. 1–34.

Kuczaj, S.A., II, and Hendry, J.L. (2003) Does language help animals think? In Gentner, D. and Goldin-Meadow, S. (eds.), *Language in Mind: Advances in the Study of Language and Thought*. Cambridge, MA: MIT Press, pp. 237–275.

Kulick, D. (1992) *Language Shift and Cultural Reproduction: Socialization, Self, and Syncretism in a Papua New Guinean Village*. Cambridge: Cambridge University Press.

Kulick, D. (1998) Anger, gender, language shift, and the politics of revelation in a Papua New Guinean village. In Schieffelin, B.B., Woolard, K.A., and Kroskrity, P.V. (eds.), *Language Ideologies: Practice and Theory*. Oxford: Oxford University Press, pp. 87–102.

Kuzar, R. (2001) *Hebrew and Zionism: A Discourse Analytic Cultural Study*. Berlin: Mouton de Gruyter.

Labov, W. (1972a) The logic of nonstandard English. In Labov, W., *Language in the Inner City: Studies in the Black English Vernacular*. Philadelphia: University of Pennsylvania Press, pp. 201–240.

Labov, W. (1972b) *Sociolinguistic Patterns*. Philadelphia: University of Pennsylvania Press.

Labov, W. (2010) Unendangered dialect, endangered people: the case of African American Vernacular English. *Transforming Anthropology* 18(1):15–27.

LaDousa, C. (2005) Disparate markets: language, nation, and education in North India. *American Ethnologist* 32(3):460–478.

LaFrance, M. (1992) When agents disappear: how gender affects the implicit causality of interpersonal verbs. In Hall, K., Bucholtz, M., and Moonwomon, B. (eds.), *Locating Power: Proceedings of the Second Berkeley Women and Language Conference*, April 4 and 5. Berkeley: Berkeley Women and Language Group, pp. 338–343.

Lakoff, G. (1987) *Women, Fire, and Dangerous Things: What Categories Reveal about the Mind*. Chicago: University of Chicago Press.

Lansky, A. (2004) *Outwitting History: The Amazing Adventures of a Man Who Rescued a Million Yiddish Books*. Chapel Hill, NC: Algonquin Books.

Latour, B. (1998) On actor network theory: a few clarifications. At http://www.nettime.org/Lists-Archives/nettime-l-9801/msg00019.html, accessed August 2, 2009.

Latour, B. (2005) *Reassembling the Social: An Introduction to Actor-Network-Theory*. Oxford: Oxford University Press.

Lave, J. and Wenger, E. (1991) *Situated Learning: Legitimate Peripheral Participation*. Cambridge: Cambridge University Press.

Law, J. and Hassard, J. (1999) *Actor Network Theory and After.* Oxford: Blackwell.

Leaper, C. and Ayres, M.M. (2007) A meta-analytic review of gender variations in adults' language use: talkativeness, affiliative speech, and assertive speech. *Personality and Social Psychology Review* 11(4):328–363.

Leaper, C. and Smith, T.E. (2004) A meta-analytic review of gender variations in children's language use: talkativeness, affiliative speech, and assertive speech. *Developmental Psychology* 40(6):993–1027.

Lee, B. (1997) *Talking Heads: Language, Metalanguage, and the Semiotics of Subjectivity.* Durham, NC: Duke University Press.

LeMaster, B. (2006) Language contraction, revitalization and Irish women. *Journal of Linguistic Anthropology* 16(2):211–228.

Lemon, A. (2000) *Between Two Fires: Gypsy Performance and Romani Memory from Pushkin to Postsocialism.* Durham, NC: Duke University Press.

Leslie, A.M. (2001) Theory of mind. In Smelser, N.J. and Baltes, P.B. (eds.), *International Encyclopedia of the Social and Behavioral Sciences.* New York: Elsevier, pp. 15652–15656.

Levinson, S.C. (1996) Relativity in spatial conception and description. In Gumperz, J.J. and Levinson, S.C. (eds.), *Rethinking Linguistic Relativity.* Cambridge: Cambridge University Press, pp. 177–202.

Levinson, S.C. (2003a) Language and mind: let's get the issues straight! In Gentner, D. and Goldin-Meadow, S. (eds.), *Language in Mind: Advances in the Study of Language and Thought.* Cambridge, MA: MIT Press, pp. 25–46.

Levinson, S.C. (2003b) *Space in Language and Cognition: Explorations in Cognitive Diversity.* Cambridge: Cambridge University Press.

Levinson, S.C. and Wilkins, D.P. (eds.) (2006) *Grammars of Space: Explorations in Cognitive Diversity.* Cambridge: Cambridge University Press.

Levinson, S.C., Kita, S., Haun, D.B., and Rasch, B.H. (2002) Returning the tables: language affects spatial reasoning. *Cognition* 84(2):155–188.

Lewis, C., Enciso, P., and Moje, E.B. (eds.) (2007) *Reframing Sociocultural Research on Literacy: Identity, Agency, and Power.* Mahwah, NJ: Lawrence Erlbaum.

Lewis, M.P. (2006) How many languages are there in the world? In Rickerson, E.M. and Hilton, B. (eds.), *The Five-Minute Linguist: Bite-Sized Essays on Language and Languages.* Oakville, CT: Equinox, pp. 11–15.

Lewis, M.P. (ed.) (2009) *Ethnologue: Languages of the World*, 16th edn. Dallas, TX: SIL International. Online version at http://www.ethnologue.com, accessed November 15, 2010.

Li, P. and Gleitman, L. (2002) Turning the tables: language and spatial reasoning. *Cognition* 83:265–294.

Limón, J.E. (1989) *Carne, carnales*, and the carnivalesque: Bakhtinian *batos*, disorder, and narrative discourses. *American Ethnologist* 16(3):471–486.

Lippi-Green, R. (1997) *English with an Accent: Language, Ideology, and Discrimination in the United States*. New York: Routledge.

Livia, A. and Hall, K. (1997) Introduction: "It's a girl!": bringing performativity back to linguistics. In Livia, A. and Hall, K. (eds.), *Queerly Phrased: Language, Gender, and Sexuality*. Oxford: Oxford University Press, pp. 3–18.

Lucy, J.A. (1992) *Language Diversity and Thought: A Reformulation of the Linguistic Relativity Hypothesis*. Cambridge: Cambridge University Press.

Lucy, J.A. (ed.) (1993) *Reflexive Language: Reported Speech and Metapragmatics*. Cambridge: Cambridge University Press.

Lucy, J.A. (1996) The scope of linguistic relativity: an analysis and review of empirical research. In Gumperz, J.J. and Levinson, S.C. (eds.), *Rethinking Linguistic Relativity*. Cambridge: Cambridge University Press, pp. 37–69.

Lucy, J.A. (1997) Linguistic relativity. *Annual Review of Anthropology* 26: 291–312.

Lucy, J.A. and Gaskins, S. (2003) Interaction of language type and referent type in the development of nonverbal classification preferences. In Gentner, D. and Goldin-Meadow, S. (eds.), *Language in Mind: Advances in the Study of Language and Thought*. Cambridge, MA: MIT Press, pp. 465–492.

Maddox, B. (2008) Literacies, identities and social change: interdisciplinary approaches to literacy and development. *Journal of Development Studies* 44(6):769–778.

Mahmood, S. (2005) *The Politics of Piety: The Islamic Revival and the Feminist Subject*. Princeton: Princeton University Press.

Malinowski, B. (1994[1923]) The problem of meaning in primitive languages. In Maybin, J. (ed.), *Language and Literacy in Social Practice*. Avon, UK: Multilingual Matters, pp. 1–10.

Malotki, E. (1983) *Hopi Time: A Linguistic Analysis of the Temporal Concepts in the Hopi Language*. Berlin: Mouton.

Maltz, D.N. and Borker, R.A. (1982) A cultural approach to male–female miscommunication. In Gumperz, J.J. (ed.), *Language and Social Identity*. Cambridge: Cambridge University Press, pp. 196–216.

Mannheim, B. and Tedlock, D. (1995) Introduction. In Tedlock, D. and Mannheim, B. (eds.), *The Dialogic Emergence of Culture*. Urbana: University of Illinois Press, pp. 1–32.

Marriott, M. (1976) Hindu transactions: diversity without dualism. In Kapferer, B. (ed.), *Transaction and Meaning: Directions in the Anthropology of Exchange and Symbolic Behavior*. Philadelphia: Institute for the Study of Human Issues, pp. 109–142.

Martin, L. (1986) "Eskimo words for snow": a case study in the genesis and decay of an anthropological example. *American Anthropologist* 88: 418–423.

Marx, K. (1978[1852]) The Eighteenth Brumaire of Louis Bonaparte. In *The Marx-Engels Reader*, 2nd edn., ed. R.C. Tucker. New York: Norton, pp. 594–617.

Mayr, E. (1982) *The Growth of Biological Thought: Diversity, Evolution, and Inheritance*. Cambridge, MA: Belknap Press.

McCollum, C.C. (2000) The Cultural Patterning of Self-Understanding: A Cognitive-Psychoanalytic Approach to Middle-Class Americans' Life Stories. PhD dissertation, Duke University.

McDermott, R.P. and Tylbor, H. (1995) On the necessity of collusion in conversation. In Tedlock, D. and Mannheim, B. (eds.), *The Dialogic Emergence of Culture*. Urbana: University of Illinois Press, pp. 218–236.

McDonough, L., Choi, S., and Mandler, J.M. (2003) Understanding spatial relations: flexible infants, lexical adults. *Cognitive Psychology* 46:229–259.

McElhinny, B. (1998) Genealogies of gender theory: practice theory and feminism in sociocultural and linguistic anthropology. *Social Analysis* 42(3):164–189.

McElhinny, B. (2003a) Theorizing gender in sociolinguistics and linguistic anthropology. In Holmes, J. and Meyerhoff, M. (eds.), *The Handbook of Language and Gender*. Oxford: Blackwell, pp. 21–42.

McElhinny, B. (2003b) Three approaches to the study of language and gender. *American Anthropologist* 105(4):848–852.

McElhinny, B. and Muehlmann, S. (2006) Discursive practice theory. In Brown, K. (ed.), *Encyclopedia of Language and Linguistics*, 2nd edn. Vol. 3. Oxford: Elsevier, pp. 696–699.

Meeuwis, M. and Blommaert, J. (1998) A monolectal view of code-switching: layered code-switching among Zairians in Belgium. In Auer, P. (ed.), *Code-Switching in Conversation: Language, Interaction and Identity*. New York: Routledge, pp. 76–98.

Mehl, M.R., Vazire, S., Ramírez-Esparza, N., et al. (2007) Are women really more talkative than men? *Science* 317:82.

Mertz, E. (2007a) *The Language of Law School: Learning to Think Like a Lawyer*. New York: Oxford University Press.

Mertz, E. (2007b) Semiotic anthropology. *Annual Review of Anthropology* 36:337–353.

Messer–Davidow, E. (1995) Acting otherwise. In Gardiner, J.K. (ed.), *Provoking Agents: Gender and Agency in Theory and Practice*. Urbana: University of Illinois Press, pp. 23–51.

Meyerhoff, M. (2002) Communities of practice. In Chambers, J.K., Trudgill, P., and Schilling-Estes, N. (eds.), *The Handbook of Language Variation and Change*. Oxford: Blackwell, pp. 526–548.

Milroy, L. (1987) *Language and Social Networks*, 2nd edn. Oxford: Blackwell.

Milroy, L. (2002a) Introduction: Mobility, contact and language change – working with contemporary speech communities. *Journal of Sociolinguistics* 6(1):3–15.

Milroy, L. (2002b) Social networks. In Chambers, J.K., Trudgill, P., and Schilling-Estes, N. (eds.), *The Handbook of Language Variation and Change*. Oxford: Blackwell, pp. 549–572.

Mithun, M. (1991) Active/agentive case marking and its motivations. *Language* 67(3):510–546.

Mithun, M. (1998) The significance of diversity in language endangerment and preservation. In Grenoble, L.A. and Whaley, L.J. (eds.), *Endangered Languages: Current Issues and Future Prospects*. Cambridge: Cambridge University Press, pp. 163–191.

Moerman, M. (2007) Talking culture: ethnography and conversation analysis. In Monaghan, L. and Goodman, J.E. (eds.), *A Cultural Approach to Interpersonal Communication: Essential Readings*. Oxford: Wiley-Blackwell, pp. 119–133.

Morgan, M. (2002) *Language, Discourse and Power in African American Culture*. Cambridge: Cambridge University Press.

Morgan, M. (2004) Speech community. In Duranti, A. (ed.), *A Companion to Linguistic Anthropology*. Oxford: Blackwell, pp. 3–22.

Morse, J.M., Stern, P.N., Corbin, J., et al. (2009) *Developing Grounded Theory: The Second Generation*. Walnut Creek, CA: Left Coast Press.

Muehlmann, S. (2007) Defending diversity: staking out a common global interest? In Duchêne, A. and Heller, M. (eds.), *Discourses of Endangerment*. London: Continuum, pp. 14–34.

Mufwene, S.S., Rickford, J.R., Bailey, G., and Baugh, J. (eds.) (1998) *African–American English: Structure, History and Use*. New York: Routledge.

Munnich, E. and Landau, B. (2003) The effects of spatial language on spatial representation: setting some boundaries. In Gentner, D. and Goldin-Meadow, S. (eds.), *Language in Mind: Advances in the Study of Language and Thought*. Cambridge, MA: MIT Press, pp. 113–155.

Nader, L. (1972) Up the anthropologist: perspectives gained from studying up. In Hymes, D.H. (ed.), *Reinventing Anthropology*. New York: Pantheon Books, pp. 284–311.

Nettle, D. and Romaine, S. (2000) *Vanishing Voices: The Extinction of the World's Languages*. Oxford: Oxford University Press.

Nevins, A., Pesetsky, D., and Rodrigues, D. (2007) Pirahã exceptionality: a reassessment. Unpublished manuscript accessed at http://ling.auf.net/lingBuzz/000411 on April 19, 2007.

Ochs, E. (1979) Transcription as theory. In Ochs, E. and Schieffelin, B. (eds.), *Developmental Pragmatics*. New York: Academic Press, pp. 43–72.

Ochs, E. (1988) *Culture and Language Development: Language Acquisition and Language Socialization in a Samoan Village*. Cambridge: Cambridge University Press.

Ochs, E. (1992) Indexing gender. In Duranti, A. and Goodwin, C. (eds.), *Rethinking Context: Language as an Interactive Phenomenon*. Cambridge: Cambridge University Press, pp. 335–358.

Ochs, E. and Schieffelin, B. (1995) The impact of language socialization on grammatical development. In Fletcher, P. and MacWhinney, B. (eds.), *The Handbook of Child Language*. Oxford: Blackwell, pp. 73–94.

Ochs, E. and Schieffelin, B. (2001[1984]) Language acquisition and socialization: three developmental stories and their implications. In Duranti, A. (ed.), *Linguistic Anthropology: A Reader*. Oxford: Blackwell, pp. 263–301.

Ochs, E. and Schieffelin, B. (2008) Language socialization: an historical overview. In Duff, P. and Hornberger, N. (eds.), *Encyclopedia of Language and Education*. Vol. 8: *Language Socialization*. New York: Springer, pp. 3–15.

Omi, M. and Winant, H. (1994) *Racial Formation in the United States: From the 1960s to the 1990s*. New York: Routledge.

Ong, W.J. (1982) *Orality and Literacy: The Technologizing of the Word*. London: Methuen.

Ortner, S.B. (1984) Theory in anthropology since the sixties. *Comparative Studies in Society and History* 26(1):126–166.

Ortner, S.B. (1989) *High Religion: A Cultural and Political History of Sherpa Buddhism*. Princeton: Princeton University Press.

Ortner, S.B. (2006a) Introduction: Updating practice theory. In Ortner, S.B., *Anthropology and Social Theory: Culture, Power, and the Acting Subject*. Durham, NC: Duke University Press, pp. 1–18.

Ortner, S.B. (2006b) Power and projects: reflections on agency. In Ortner, S.B., *Anthropology and Social Theory: Culture, Power, and the Acting Subject*. Durham, NC: Duke University Press, pp. 129–153.

Pagliai, V. (2009) Conversational agreement and racial formation processes. *Language in Society* 39:549–579.

Patrick, P.L. (2002) The speech community. In Chambers, J.K., Trudgill, P., and Schilling-Estes, N. (eds.), *The Handbook of Language Variation and Change*. Oxford: Blackwell, pp. 573–597.

Peirce, C.S. (1955) *Philosophical Writings of Peirce*, ed. J. Buchler. New York: Dover.

Peterson, C.C. and Siegal, M. (2000) Insights into theory of mind from deafness and autism. *Mind and Language* 15(1):123–145.

Philips, S.U. (2001) Power. In Duranti, A. (ed.), *Key Terms in Language and Culture*. Oxford: Blackwell, pp. 190–192.

Pickering, A. (1995) *The Mangle of Practice: Time, Agency, and Science*. Chicago: University of Chicago Press.

Pigg, S.L. (1992) Inventing social categories through place: social representations and development in Nepal. *Comparative Studies in Society and History* 34(3):491–513.

Pigg, S.L. (1996) The credible and the credulous: the question of "villager's beliefs" in Nepal. *Cultural Anthropology* 11(2):160–201.

Pinker, S. (1994) *The Language Instinct: How the Mind Creates Language*. New York: William Morrow.

Plunkett, K. (1995) Connectionist approaches to language acquisition. In Fletcher, P. and MacWhinney, B. (eds.), *The Handbook of Child Language*. Oxford: Blackwell, pp. 36–72.

Preves, S.E. (2003) *Intersex and Identity: The Contested Self*. Piscataway, NJ: Rutgers University Press.

Prinsloo, M. and Baynham, M. (eds.) (2008) *Literacies, Global and Local*. Philadelphia: John Benjamins.

Pullum, G.K. (1991) *The Great Eskimo Vocabulary Hoax, and Other Irreverent Essays on the Study of Language*. Chicago: University of Chicago Press.

Pullum, G.K. (1999) African American Vernacular English is not Standard English with mistakes. In Wheeler, R.S. (ed.), *The Workings of Language*. Westport, CT: Praeger, pp. 39–58.

Pye, C. (1990) The acquisition of ergative languages. *Linguistics* 28:1291–1330.

Ramanujan, A.K. (1989) On translating a Tamil poem. In Warren, R. (ed.), *The Art of Translation: Voices from the Field*. Boston, MA: Northeastern University Press, pp. 47–63.

Rampton, B. (2000) Speech community. Working Papers in Urban Language and Literacies, Paper 15. At http://www.kcl.ac.uk/content/1/c6/01/42/29/paper15.pdf, accessed November 17, 2010.

Reddy, M.J. (1979) The conduit metaphor: a case of frame conflict in our language about language. In Ortony, A. (ed.), *Metaphor and Thought*, Cambridge: Cambridge University Press, pp. 284–324.

Reder, S. and Davila, E. (2005) Context and literacy practices. *Annual Review of Applied Linguistics* 25:170–187.

Regier, T., Kay, P., and Cook, R.S. (2005) Focal colors are universal after all. *Proceedings of the National Academy of Sciences* 102(23):8386–8391.

Reyes, A. and Lo, A. (eds.) (2009) *Beyond Yellow English: Toward a Linguistic Anthropology of Asian Pacific America*. Oxford: Oxford University Press.

Rickford, J.R. (2005) Using the vernacular to teach the standard. In Ramirez, J.D., Wiley, T.G., de Klerk, G., et al. (eds.), *Ebonics: The Urban Education Debate*, 2nd edn. Clevedon, UK: Multilingual Matters, pp. 18–40.

Romaine, S. (2001) Multilingualism. In Aronoff, M. and Rees-Miller, J. (eds.), *The Handbook of Linguistics*. Oxford: Blackwell, pp. 512–532.

Rosaldo, M.Z. (1982) The things we do with words: Ilongot speech acts and speech act theory in philosophy. *Language in Society* 11:203–237.

Rosenberg, N.A., Pritchard, J.K., Weber, J.L., et al. (2002) Genetic structure of human populations. *Science*. Dec 20, 298(5602):2381–2385.

Roth-Gordon, J. (2007) Racing and erasing the *Playboy*: slang, transnational youth subculture, and racial discourse in Brazil. *Journal of Linguistic Anthropology* 17(2):246–265.

Rubin, D.L. (1992) Nonlanguage factors affecting undergraduates' judgments of nonnative English-speaking teaching assistants. *Research in Higher Education* 33:511–531.

Rubin, D.L. and Smith, K.A. (1990) Effects of accent, ethnicity, and lecture topic on undergraduates' perceptions of non-native English-speaking teaching assistants. *International Journal of Intercultural Relations* 14: 337–353.

Sa'ar, A. (2007) Masculine talk: on the subconscious use of masculine forms among Hebrew- and Arabic-speaking women in Israel. *Signs: Journal of Women in Culture and Society* 32(2):405–429.

Sacks, H., Schegloff, E.A., and Jefferson, G. (1974) A simplest systematics for the organization of turn-taking for conversation. *Language* 50:696–735.

Sahlins, M. (1981) *Historical Metaphors and Mythical Realities: Structure in the Early History of the Sandwich Islands Kingdom*. Ann Arbor: University of Michigan Press.

Sansone, L. (2004) Three views on color and race in Brazil. *American Anthropologist* 106(3):600–606.

Santa Ana, O. and Parodí, C. (1998) Modeling the speech community: configuration and variable types in the Mexican Spanish setting. *Language in Society* 27(1):23–51.

Sapir, E. (1949[1924]) The grammarian and his language. In Mandelbaum, D.G. (ed.), *Selected Writings of Edward Sapir in Language, Culture and Personality*. Berkeley: University of California Press, pp. 150–159.

Sapir, E. (1949[1929]) The status of linguistics as a science. In Mandelbaum, D.G. (ed.), *Selected Writings of Edward Sapir in Language, Culture and Personality*. Berkeley: University of California Press, pp. 160–166.

Sapir, E. (1949[1933]) Language. In Mandelbaum, D.G. (ed.), *Selected Writings of Edward Sapir in Language, Culture and Personality*. Berkeley: University of California Press, pp. 7–32.

Sapir, E. (1964[1931]). Conceptual categories in primitive languages. In Hymes, D.H. (ed.), *Language in Culture and Society: A Reader in Linguistics and Anthropology*. New York: Harper & Row, p. 128.

Saussure, F. de (1986[1916]) *Course in General Linguistics*, ed. C. Bally, A. Sechehaye and A. Riedlinger. Trans. R. Harris. La Salle, IL: Open Court.

Schechner, R. (2002) Performance studies in/for the 21st century. *Anthropology and Humanism* 26(2):158–166.

Schegloff, E.A. (2007) *Sequence Organization in Interaction: A Primer in Conversation Analysis*. Vol. 1. Cambridge: Cambridge University Press.

Schick, B., Villiers, J. de, Villiers, P. de, and Hoffmeister, R. (2007) Language and theory of mind: a study of deaf children. *Child Development* 78(2):376–396.

Schieffelin, B. (1990) *The Give and Take of Everyday Life: Language Socialization of Kaluli Children*. Cambridge: Cambridge University Press.

Schmidt, R., Sr. (2007) Defending English in an English-dominant world: the ideology of the "Official English" movement in the United States. In Duchêne, A. and Heller, M. (eds.), *Discourses of Endangerment*. London: Continuum, pp. 197–215.

Scribner, S. and Cole, M. (1981) *The Psychology of Literacy*. Cambridge, MA: Harvard University Press.

Searle, J.R. (1969) *Speech Acts: An Essay in the Philosophy of Language*. Cambridge: Cambridge University Press.

Searle, J.R. (1975) A classification of illocutionary acts. *Language in Society* 5:1–23.

Searle, J.R. (1977) Reiterating the differences: a reply to Derrida. *Glyph* 1:198–208.

Searle, J.R. (1994) Literary theory and its discontents. *New Literary History* 25(3):637–667.

Searle, J.R. and Vanderveken, D. (1985) *Foundations of Illocutionary Logic*. Cambridge: Cambridge University Press.

Seyfarth, R.M. and Cheney, D.L. (1997) Behavioral mechanisms underlying vocal communication in nonhuman primates. *Animal Learning and Behavior* 25:249–267.

Shandler, J. (2005) *Adventures in Yiddishland: Postvernacular Language and Culture*. Berkeley: University of California Press.

Sheriff, R.E. (2004) Review of *Blackness Without Ethnicity: Constructing Race in Brazil*. *Journal of Latin American Anthropology* 9(2):461–463.

Sherzer, J. (1990) *Verbal Art in San Blas: Kuna Culture through its Discourse*. Cambridge: Cambridge University Press.

Silverstein, M. (1976) Shifters, verbal categories and cultural description. In Basso, K.H. and Selby, H.A. (eds.), *Meaning in Anthropology*. Albuquerque: School of American Research, pp. 11–57.

Silverstein, M. (1979) Language structure and linguistic ideology. In Clyne, P., Hanks, W., and Hofbauer, C. (eds.), *The Elements: A Parasession on Linguistic Units and Levels*. Chicago: Chicago Linguistic Society, pp. 193–247.

Silverstein, M. (1985) Language and the culture of gender: at the intersection of structure, usage, and ideology. In Mertz, E. and Parmentier, R. (eds.), *Semiotic Mediation: Sociocultural and Psychological Perspectives*. Orlando: Academic Press, pp. 219–259.

Silverstein, M. (1993) Metapragmatic discourse and metapragmatic function. In Lucy, J. (ed.), *Reflexive Language: Reported Speech and Metapragmatics*. New York: Cambridge University Press, pp. 33–58.

Silverstein, M. (1996) Monoglot "standard" in America: standardization and metaphors of linguistic hegemony. In Brenneis, D.L. and Macaulay, R.K.S. (eds.), *The Matrix of Language: Contemporary Linguistic Anthropology*. Boulder, CO: Westview, pp. 284–306.

Silverstein, M. (2001) The limits of awareness. In Duranti, A. (ed.), *Linguistic Anthropology: A Reader*. Oxford: Blackwell, pp. 382–401.

Silverstein, M. (2006) How we look from where we stand. *Journal of Linguistic Anthropology* 16(2):269–278.

Slobin, D.I. (1992) Introduction. In Slobin, D.I. (ed.), *The Crosslinguistic Study of Language Acquisition*. Vol. 3. Hillsdale, NJ: Lawrence Erlbaum, pp. 1–13.

Smitherman, G. (1998) "It bees dat way sometime": sounds and structure of present-day Black English. In Clark, V., et al., (eds.), *Language: Readings in Language and Culture*. New York: St Martin's Press, pp. 328–343.

Smitherman, G. (2005) Black language and the education of black children: one mo once. In Ramirez, J.D., Wiley, T.G., de Klerk, G., et al. (eds.), *Ebonics: The Urban Education Debate*, 2nd edn. Clevedon, UK: Multilingual Matters, pp. 49–61.

Snow, C.E. (1995) Issues in the study of input: finetuning, universality, individual and developmental differences, and necessary causes. In Fletcher, P. and MacWhinney, B. (eds.), *The Handbook of Child Language*. Oxford: Blackwell, pp. 180–193.

Spitulnik, D. (2001) The social circulation of media discourse and the mediation of communities. In Duranti, A. (ed.), *Linguistic Anthropology: A Reader*. Oxford: Blackwell, pp. 95–118.

Spivak, G.C. (1980) Revolutions that as yet have no model: Derrida's *Limited Inc. Diacritics* 10(4):29–49.

Steinglass, M. (1998) International man of mystery: the battle over Mikhail Bakhtin. *Lingua Franca*, April, 33–41.

Stitt, G. (2002) Diverted to Delhi. Documentary film, 55 minutes. Greg Stitt Production, produced in association with the Australian Film Commission.

Strauss, A. (1987) *Qualitative Analysis for Social Scientists*. Cambridge: Cambridge University Press.

Strauss, C. (2007) Blaming for columbine: conceptions of agency in the contemporary United States. *Current Anthropology* 48(6):807–832.

Street, B. (1984) *Literacy in Theory and Practice*. Cambridge: Cambridge University Press.

Street, B. (ed.) (1993) *Cross-Cultural Approaches to Literacy*. Cambridge: Cambridge University Press.

Street, B. (2003) What's "new" in new literacy studies? Critical approaches to literacy in theory and practice. *Current Issues in Comparative Education* [Online] 5(2). At http://www.tc.columbia.edu/CICE/Archives/5.2/52street.pdf, accessed July 31, 2009, pp. 77–91.

Street, B.V. (2007) Foreword. In Lewis, C., Enciso, P., and Moje, E.B. (eds.), *Reframing Sociocultural Research on Literacy: Identity, Agency, and Power*. Mahwah, NJ: Lawrence Erlbaum, pp. vii–x.

Sztompka, P. (1991) *Society in Action: The Theory of Social Becoming*. Chicago: University of Chicago Press.

Tannen, D. (1990) *You Just Don't Understand: Women and Men in Conversation*. New York: Ballantine Books.

Taylor, C. (1985) *Human Agency and Language: Philosophical Papers*. Vol. 1. Cambridge: Cambridge University Press.

Thompson, E.C. (2006) The problem of "race as a social construct." *Anthropology News* 47(2):6–7. At http://www.understandingrace.org/resources/pdf/rethinking/thompson.pdf, accessed November 22, 2010.

Thompson, J.B. (1991) Editor's introduction. In Bourdieu, P., *Language and Symbolic Power*, ed. J.B. Thompson. Trans. G. Raymond and M. Adamson. Cambridge, MA: Harvard University Press, pp. 1–31.

Thompson, S.A., Park, J.S., and Li, C.N. (2006) *A Reference Grammar of Wappo*. University of California Publications in Linguistics. Vol. 138. Berkeley: University of California Press.

Tomasello, M. (2005) Comment on Daniel L. Everett's "Cultural constraints on grammar and cognition in Pirahã: another look at the design features of human language." *Current Anthropology* 46(4):640–641.

Tomasello, M. and Slobin, D.I. (2005) *Beyond Nature–Nurture: Essays in Honor of Elizabeth Bates*. Mahwah, NJ: Lawrence Erlbaum.

Trechter, S. and Bucholtz, M. (2001) White noise: bringing language into whiteness studies. *Journal of Linguistic Anthropology* 11(1):3–21.

Trudgill, P. (1996) Dialect typology: isolation, social network and phonological structure. In Guy, G.R., Feagin, C., Schiffrin, D., and Baugh, J. (eds.), *Towards a Social Science of Language*. Philadelphia: John Benjamins, pp. 3–22.

US Census Bureau (2000) *US Census 2000*. Chapter 8: Language. At http://www.census.gov/population/www/cen2000/censusatlas/pdf/8_Language.pdf, accessed August 25, 2009.

US Census Bureau (2006) America Speaks: A Demographic Profile of Foreign-Language Speakers for the United States: 2000. At http://www.census.gov/population/www/socdemo/hh-fam/AmSpks.html, accessed August 25, 2009.

Urban, G. (1991) *A Discourse-Centered Approach to Culture: Native South American Myths and Rituals*. Austin: University of Texas Press.

Urciuoli, B. (1991) The political topography of Spanish and English: the view from a New York Puerto Rican neighborhood. *American Ethnologist* 18(2):295–310.

Urciuoli, B. (1996) *Exposing Prejudice: Puerto Rican Experiences of Language, Race, and Class*. Boulder, CO: Westview.

Villiers, J.G. de and Villiers, P.A. de (2000) Linguistic determinism and the understanding of false beliefs. In Mitchell, P. and Riggs, K.J. (eds.), *Children's Reasoning and the Mind*. East Sussex, UK: Psychology Press, pp. 191–228.

Villiers, J.G. de and Villiers, P.A. de (2003) Language for thought: coming to understand false beliefs. In Gentner, D. and Goldin-Meadow, S. (eds.), *Language in Mind: Advances in the Study of Language and Thought*. Cambridge, MA: MIT Press, pp. 335–384.

Vygotsky, L.S. (1978) *Mind in Society: The Development of Higher Psychological Processes*, ed. M. Cole, V. John-Steiner, S. Scribner, and E. Souberman. Cambridge, MA: Harvard University Press.

Vygotsky, L.S. (1987) *Thinking and Speech*, ed. N. Minick. New York: Plenum.

Wardlow, H. (2006) *Wayward Women: Sexuality and Agency in a New Guinea Society*. Berkeley: University of California Press.

Waterston, A. (2006) Are Latinos becoming "white" folk? And what that still says about race in America. *Transforming Anthropology* 14(2):133–150.

Weinreich, M. (2008) *History of the Yiddish Language*. New York: YIVO Institute for Jewish Research.

Wenger, E. (1998) *Communities of Practice: Learning, Meaning, and Identity*. Cambridge: Cambridge University Press.

Wertsch, J.V., Tulviste, P., and Hagstrom, F. (1993) A sociocultural approach to agency. In Forman, E.A., Minick, N., and Stone, C.A. (eds.), *Contexts for Learning: Sociocultural Dynamics in Children's Development*. New York: Oxford University Press, pp. 336–356.

Whorf, B.L. (1956[1941]) The relation of habitual thought and behavior to language. In Carroll, J.B. (ed.), *Language, Thought, and Reality: Selected Writings of Benjamin Lee Whorf*. Cambridge, MA: MIT Press.

Wilce, J.M. (1998) *Eloquence in Trouble: The Poetics and Politics of Complaint in Rural Bangladesh*. Oxford: Oxford University Press.

Wilce, J.M. (2009) Medical discourse. *Annual Review of Anthropology* 38:199–215.

Williams, J.G. (1987) Proverbs and Ecclesiastes. In Alter, R. and Kermode, F. (eds.), *The Literary Guide to the Bible*. Cambridge, MA: Harvard University Press, pp. 263–282.

Williams, R. (1977) *Marxism and Literature*. Oxford: Oxford University Press.

Williams, R. (1983) *Keywords: A Vocabulary of Culture and Society*, rev. edn. New York: Oxford University Press.

Wilson, P.M. (1970) *Simplified Swahili*. Nairobi: Longman.

Winawer, J., Witthoft, N., Fran, M.C., et al. (2007) Russian blues reveal effects on color discrimination. *Proceedings of the National Academy of Sciences* 104(19):7780–7785.

Wittgenstein, L. (1958) *Philosophical Investigations*, 2nd edn. Trans. G.E.M. Anscombe. Oxford: Blackwell.

Woolard, K.A. (2004) Codeswitching. In Duranti, A. (ed.), *A Companion to Linguistic Anthropology*. Oxford: Blackwell, pp. 73–94.

Wortham, S. (2005) Socialization beyond the speech event. *Journal of Linguistic Anthropology* 15(1):95–112.

Zentella, A.C. (1996) The "chiquitification" of US Latinos and their languages; or, why we need an anthro*political* linguistics. In Ide, R., Parker, R., and Sunaoshi, Y. (eds.), *Proceedings of the Third Annual Symposium About Language and Society, Austin [SALSA]. Texas Linguistic Forum* 36:1–18. Austin: University of Texas Department of Linguistics.

Zuberbühler, K. (2000) Referential labeling in Diana monkeys. *Animal Behavior* 59:917–927.

Index

Page numbers in italics indicate illustrations.